# LITERACY PROFILES

## A Framework to Guide Assessment, Instructional Strategies and Intervention, K–4

**Sue Biggam**
*Consultant and Associate Director of Research and Development,*
*Vermont READS Institute at the University of Vermont*

**Kathleen Itterly**
*Westfield State College*

**Allyn & Bacon**
is an imprint of

Boston    New York    San Francisco
Mexico City    Montreal    Toronto    London    Madrid    Munich    Paris
Hong Kong    Singapore    Tokyo    Cape Town    Sydney

To our terrific husbands, Pat and Fred, and also to our families
and friends for their patient support and encouragement.
Thank you!

Vice President and Executive Publisher: Jeffery W. Johnston
Executive Editor: Linda Ashe Bishop
Editorial Assistant: Demetrius Hall
Senior Managing Editor: Pamela D. Bennett
Project Manager: Kerry J. Rubadue
Production Coordinator: Elm Street Publishing Services
Design Coordinator: Diane C. Lorenzo
Photo Coordinator: Sandy Schaefer
Cover Design: Jeff Vanik
Cover Image: Andrew McClure
Operations Specialist: Matt Ottenweller
Director of Marketing: Quinn Perkson
Marketing Coordinator: Brian Mounts

For related titles and support materials, visit our online catalog at www.pearsonhighered.com.

Between the time website information is gathered and then published, it is not unusual for some sites to have closed. Also, the transcription of URLs can result in typographical errors. The publisher would appreciate notification where these errors occur so that they may be corrected in subsequent editions.

**Library of Congress Cataloging-in-Publication Data**

Biggam, Sue.
   Literacy profiles: a framework for assessing, recording, and developing students' literary progress, K–4
Sue Biggam, Kathleen Itterly.—1st ed.
      p. cm.
Includes bibliographical references and index.
ISBN 978-0-13-238082-9
1. Language arts (Primary)  2. Language arts (Primary)—Ability testing.   I. Itterly, Kathleen.   II. Title.
LB1528.B54 2009
372.6—dc22

2008000396

Photo Credits: All interior photos by Kathleen Itterly.

Printed in the United States of America

10  9  8  7  6  5  4  3  2  1 STO 11 10 09 08

Allyn & Bacon
is an imprint of

# CONTENTS

## APPENDIX B
# FORMAL OR PUBLISHED ASSESSMENTS AND THEIR AREAS OF FOCUS   B-1

# PREFACE

## Why a Profile?

*Literacy Profiles: A Framework to Guide Assessment, Instructional Strategies and Intervention, K–4* is intended to assist teachers and teacher candidates as they assess and address the various aspects of literacy development. We know that beginning readers and writers are not the same, any more than all dancers or soccer players are the same. Each individual may have areas that are developing as expected, and some areas that are developing more slowly.

Central to this handbook is a *Literacy Profile,* a document for recording progress based on 10 key strands of early literacy development, including oral language, reading, and writing. Each of the 10 strands contains a guiding question and specific descriptors along a continuum ranging from pre-kindergarten to the end of Grade 4. These strands reflect current state and national standards and allow teachers and teacher-candidates to "see the big picture" of literacy development, while also noticing children's particular strengths and areas of need. Each strand also lists sample formal and informal assessment tools.

In the handbook itself, the initial chapter provides some essential key concepts; we call it our "foundations" chapter. The succeeding 10 chapters correspond to each strand on the *Literacy Profile.* Each chapter begins with a *Core Question* that we believe is central to the effective use of assessment in guiding and informing instruction. The *Core Question* frames assessment as a process of inquiry and sets the stage for linking assessment, standards, and instruction. Following the *Core Question* is a brief section that "sets the context" and provides a link to the reader's background knowledge. We then describe some core concepts and underlying research-based principles about that strand. Next, we describe some commonly used assessment tools, which are organized into two categories: formal, published assessments and informal assessments. Most chapters include a reference to ready-to-photocopy assessment tools, such as checklists, rubrics, and surveys, which are located in *Appendix A.* Finally, each chapter concludes with a close look at one child's literacy development, summarizing assessments that were administered and offering evaluative comments that lead to instructional "next steps." In the concluding chapter of the handbook, we address some final issues, lingering thoughts, and remaining questions.

There are a number of possible uses for the *Literacy Profile* and handbook:

- As a text in undergraduate or graduate courses, to structure case studies of selected K–4 students for the purpose of familiarizing course participants with the dimensions of literacy
- As a resource for practicing teachers to "see" the benchmarks of literacy development across the K–4 span
- As a "toolbox" from which practicing teachers can select a few specific strands to monitor the literacy development of an entire class of students in those areas
- As a progress-monitoring document for classroom teachers, literacy specialists, or special educators to closely monitor the development of individuals or small groups of striving readers or writers over time
- As a guide for literacy coaches to use in mentoring other teachers to familiarize them with the selected dimensions of literacy

## Acknowledgments

The *Literacy Profile* included in this handbook has many "roots." The concept of a literacy profile is certainly not new; we have been influenced by the fine work of Hill and Ruptic (1994) as well as resources from *First Steps*. The origin of this particular *Literacy Profile,* however, stems from some dedicated work in Vermont by teachers from the Orleans-Essex North Supervisory Union, the John F. Kennedy Elementary School in Winooski, Vermont, and teams of teachers across the state who piloted early versions of the *Literacy Profile*. Shayne Trubisz, Nancy Herman, and Sue Biggam were the primary developers of the *Literacy Profile* at that time, and later Kathleen Itterly and her colleagues at the Northampton School District and the Smith College Campus School in Northampton, Massachusetts, modified it. Special thanks go to the Vermont Department of Education, the Vermont READS Institute at the University of Vermont, and Westfield State College. In addition, we are very grateful to some key individuals: Dr. Marjorie Lipson, Dr. Marilou Hyson, and Jan Duncan, along with our families for their long-standing support.

We are also grateful to the following individuals who reviewed our work on this text: Kathleen Mohr, University of North Texas; Randal Donelson, The Ohio State University at Newark; Stephanie Grote, Texas A&M University–Corpus Christi; Diane Bottomley, Ball State University; and Valerie Helgren-Lempesis, California State University–East Bay. We would also like to offer a special thanks to our editor, Linda Ashe Bishop, for her patience, skillful support, and belief in the potential of this book.

Finally, we are particularly appreciative of one very special young person, Willa, who is featured in every chapter of this handbook as a real-life example of the use of the *Literacy Profile*. Meet Willa!

Meet Willa!

# INTRODUCTION

# Foundations for Using the Literacy Profile and Handbook

Most of us would agree that literacy acquisition is complex. Learning how to read and write involves many different components that often develop at different rates, sometimes in "fits and starts." Too often, though, teachers are asked to simply report whether students are at or below grade level in reading or writing, based on single or narrow measures. Profiles, on the other hand, offer a wider lens, permitting the teacher to notice and record students' development across different dimensions of literacy. The Profile in this Handbook is not an assessment tool; instead, it provides a *framework* for assessment by means of recording individual student's literacy progress observed through ongoing assessments. As one teacher commented, "The Profile lets us see the 'big picture,' not just piecemeal skills." Our intention is for the Profile in this Handbook to provide you with a framework for keeping the big picture in mind as you notice students' incremental steps toward becoming competent, confident readers and writers.

In this introductory chapter, we first explain some of our underlying assumptions and beliefs, and the theories that influenced the development of the Profile and this Handbook. Next we outline what the Profile and Handbook contain, and how the strands are related to key components of literacy. Finally, we discuss some different ways to get started using the Profile, along with a few caveats and cautions.

## BACKGROUND OF THE PROFILE AND HANDBOOK

Our assumptions and beliefs about teaching, learning, and assessment have strongly influenced our work on both the Profile and this Handbook. In turn, these assumptions and beliefs have been shaped by the work of important

FIGURE I.1 **Linking Standards, Instruction, and Assessment**

**Standards**

*What* students need to know and be able to do
- State Standards/Grade-level expectations
- District and local curriculum expectations
- Classroom-based expectations

**Instruction and Learning Opportunties**

*How* students achieve expectations of Standards
- Explicit instruction
- Scaffolded practice
- Authentic writing tasks
- Resources (books, etc.)
- Time

**Assessment**

Finding out *how well* students are achieving expectations of Standards
- Screening
- Diagnostic testing
- Progress monitoring
- Classroom-based
- Student self-assessment

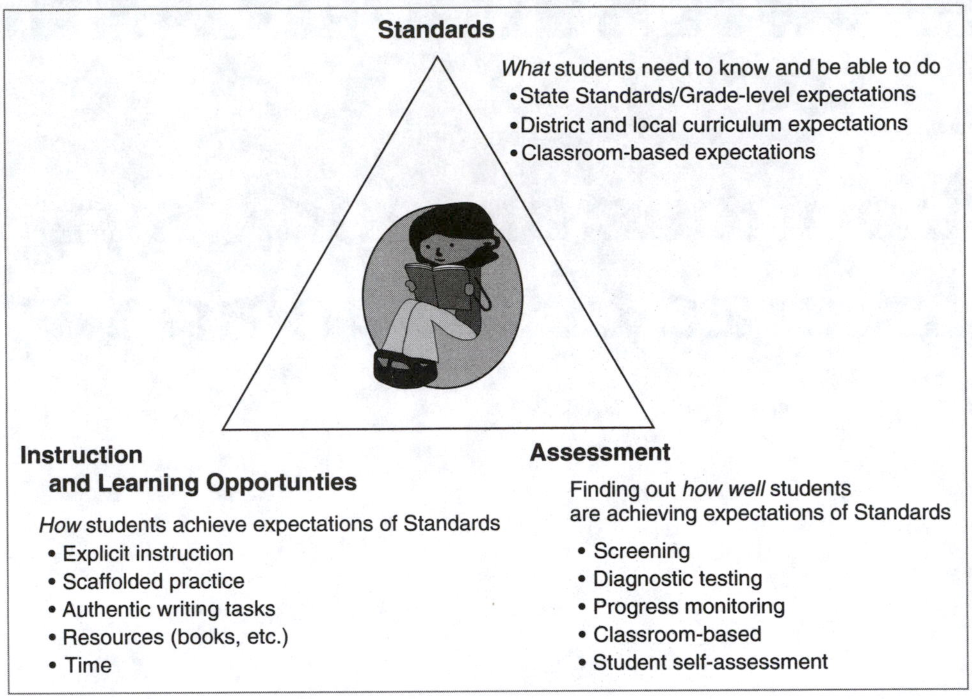

researchers and theorists in the field of literacy. We mention only a few; needless to say, many, many others have contributed to our current beliefs, understandings, and work.

One key assumption underlying the Profile and Handbook is the relationship among standards, instruction, and assessment. First of all, assessment should be closely linked with standards and instruction. Standards may be thought of as expectations for *what* students need to know and should be able to do at a given point in time. Instruction, of course, describes *how* teachers can help students achieve those standards. Assessments provide a means to determine *how well* students are meeting the standards. A helpful schematic for these three elements is provided in Figure I.1.

We realize that standards sometimes may seem vague or distant to teachers, so on the Profile we list observable descriptors that are linked to what we believe are commonly held standards. In developing the language of the Profile, we referred to many different state standards as well as to documents such as the New Standards Project's *Reading and Writing Grade by Grade* (Baker, 1999), and Hill and Ruptic's (1994) reading and writing continua. In addition, each strand of the Profile includes a list of sample assessments that are linked to the standards-based descriptors. Needless to say, the descriptors we chose to include on the Profile are not "the final word"; instead, they reflect a synthesis of a range of expectations. Also, the assessments and the instructional approaches that we suggest represent a sample of what you might use within and across each strand.

## Key Concepts Related to Assessment

In this section we first briefly explain several key concepts related to assessment, including:

- The different functions/purposes of assessment
- Vygotsky's "zone of proximal development"
- The teaching-learning cycle

***Different Functions/Purposes and Types of Assessment.*** One approach to thinking about the different kinds of assessment involves looking at the function of the assessment: summative or formative. Formative assessments are conducted on an ongoing basis in order to guide instruction and decision making regarding the next steps needed. Examples of formative assessments include anecdotal notes, records of oral reading, individual reading or writing conferences, and "every pupil response" activities. Summative assessments, on the other hand, are administered at a specific, selected point in time in order to systematically measure the impact of the instructional program. Some summative assessments include end-of-unit tests, state-level proficiency exams, and national norm-referenced tests.

Another way of thinking about different assessments involves looking at the design of the assessment tool: formal or informal. In general, formal assessments are standardized measures that have been field-tested, and they usually yield scores such as percentiles, stanines, or grade equivalents. Informal assessments are usually teacher-designed, criterion-referenced or performance-based, such as when teachers use rubrics to judge the quality of a student's retelling of a story, or when students self-assess their delivery of an oral presentation.

Recently the federal government, through the federal No Child Left Behind Act of 2001, outlined five types of assessment that serve different purposes:

1. *Outcome measures*—such as NAEP (National Assessment of Educational Progress), the Massachusetts state-level assessment (MCAS), and the Gates MacGinitie—are used to evaluate whether students have achieved grade-level performance or whether a particular program is effective.
2. *Screening measures*—such as Clay's Observation Survey of Early Literacy Achievement, the Gates MacGinitie Test, and the Peabody Picture Vocabulary Test—are used to identify students who are at risk in a particular area of learning. Often these students are then closely monitored or given diagnostic assessments.
3. *Diagnostic measures*—such as the Qualitative Reading Inventory (QRI IV) and the Comprehensive Test of Phonological Processing (CTOPP)—are administered to examine students' skills and instructional needs more closely, allowing teachers to then create specific instructional plans for individuals.
4. *Progress-monitoring assessments*—such as Dynamic Indicators of Basic Early Literacy Skills (DIBELS), running records using benchmark books, and on-demand writing assessments—are administered at least three times a year to check student progress and/or the effectiveness of instructional interventions.
5. *Classroom–based assessments*—such as work samples, unit tests, focused observations, running records, and checklists—provide systematic observations of student performance that can inform instruction and monitor whether students are making adequate progress.

As you look over the Profile, you might notice that some of the assessments appear in more than one strand. In fact, some assessments can serve more than one purpose, but it is important to consciously select an assessment tool with a particular purpose in mind. For example, a checklist would not be a useful outcome measure, but it could be an effective classroom-based assessment.

It is also important to distinguish between *assessment* and *evaluation*. Assessment is generally considered the collection of data about students' learning, whereas evaluation is the interpretation of that data (Harp & Brewer, 2005). Assessment without evaluation is incomplete because it stops short of really making use of the information collected. For example, simply collecting a student work sample or administering a spelling test is not the end point. It is essential to look at the student's product or performance through an investigative lens, in relation to some criterion, and to think about: what can the student actually do, or what does the student know? What can the student "almost" do, and what kinds of supports might the student need? Next we discuss an important theory that explains why careful evaluation is a critical link in the teaching and learning process.

***Vygotsky's "Zone of Proximal Development."*** Tharp and Gallimore (1988) provide a clear explanation of Vygotsky's (1978) concept of the "zone of proximal development" (ZPD). Vygotsky, after closely observing children in natural settings, documented the social nature of learning and identified four stages that facilitate the acquisition of new skills and concepts (see Figure I.2).

First, children engage in new learning with the support of a more capable "other," who often demonstrates or provides additional sources of assistance or "scaffolding." The next stage involves the learner's self-talk as she consciously assists herself in the learning task. These two stages (I and II) are referred to as the "zone of proximal development" because this is where the capacity for learning is greatest, primarily because of the social/interactive engagement that takes place. In Stage III the learning becomes even more automatic and internalized, and self–talk appears only when needed as the difficulty of the task calls for it. Finally, in the fourth stage, new learning that had appeared to be automatic and "fossilized" may regress and require new assistance. This assistance can come either from the self (if at all possible) or, if the need is greater, from a more capable "other." To illustrate, try to think about a geometry theorem that you may not have used in quite some time, yet had previously mastered during a math course. You may need to recall only your own mental steps, but others may need to recall the voice of a talented math teacher; still others may need an expert to "reteach" the concept from the start. The level of

FIGURE I.2 **Four Stages of the ZPD**

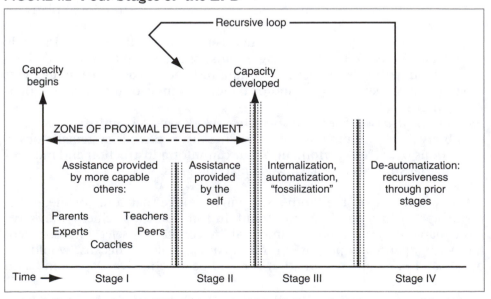

From R. G. Tharp and R. Gallimore (1988). *Rousing minds to life* (p. 35). Reprinted with the permission of Cambridge University Press.

need for restoring what may once have been learned is individualized and depends on many factors. Stage IV reminds us that learning is recursive, and may require maintenance.

This theory has some important implications for assessment, evaluation, and instruction. For example, classroom-based assessment will be most beneficial when it yields information about what is in the student's "zone of proximal development": what the student can do with some assistance from a skilled "other." Simply finding out that a student cannot read grade-level text is not very beneficial, but using a running record to determine the student's degree of accuracy and strategy use at his instructional level gives us much more useful information to be able to identify the next steps in instruction. This kind of assessment is key to the relationship between teaching and learning.

***The Teaching-Learning Cycle.*** The teaching-learning cycle helps to explain how Vygotsky's learning theory applies to classroom practice, particularly how we use assessment to inform instruction and support learners. One helpful diagram of this model, The Teaching and Learning Cycle (Owen, 1988), is shown in Figure I.3.

FIGURE I.3 **The Teaching and Learning Cycle**

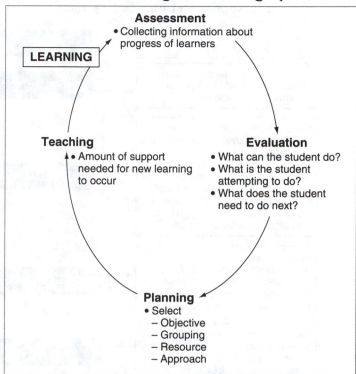

*Literacy Learning in the Classroom*, copyright (c) 2001. Richard C. Owen Publishers, Inc. Reprinted with permission of the publisher.

At the heart of this learner-centered model is a continuous assessment and evaluation process, asking the questions "What can the child do independently?" and "What can the child do with assistance?" Once this information is obtained, it can be used to plan instructional opportunities. Key to planning the next steps for instruction is professional decision making about focus, approaches, sources of assistance, and resources. After a plan has been formulated, instruction takes place. Then after sufficient opportunity for learning and internalization, assessment begins the cycle again.

## Key Concepts Related to Instruction

Two instructional models that have strongly influenced our work on the Profile and Handbook include Cambourne's conditions for literacy learning (1988) and Pearson and Gallagher's model of gradual release of responsibility (1983). Both models are widely used to design effective instructional practices and supportive environments. In addition, both models are consistent with a learner-centered approach that uses assessment to inform instruction.

***Cambourne's Conditions for Learning.*** Cambourne (1995) observed how learning takes place "in natural settings" to develop an "educationally relevant theory of learning" (p. 190). Specifically, he wondered why children who struggle to learn in school settings are able to successfully learn complex skills in other settings. Focusing primarily on the process of language learning, his research yielded a "set of indispensable circumstances that co-occur" (p. 184) and support each other. He identified seven conditions of learning that apply to literacy learning, which are shown in Figure I.4.

The first two conditions, immersion and demonstration, directly link to Stage I of Vygotsky's (1978) "zone of proximal development" model, and

**FIGURE I.4  A Schematic Representation of Brian Cambourne's Model of Learning as It Applies to Literacy Learning**

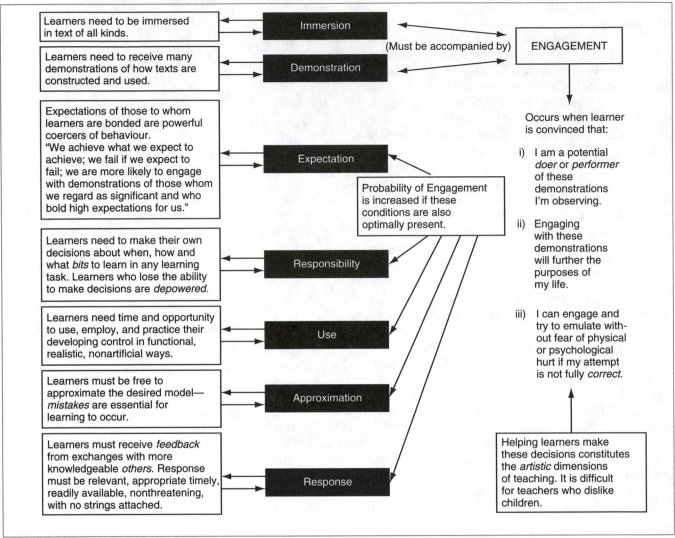

Cambourne, B. (1988). *The Whole Story.* Auckland, New Zealand: Ashton Scholastic. p. 33. Used with permission.

make it clear how essential it is for children to be actively engaged, not passively "receiving" information from a teacher. In order to maximize the likelihood of student learning, the other conditions are critical as well. These conditions will be referred to periodically within the Handbook, but take a few moments now to read them over, thinking about each one's link to the stages of Vygotsky's learning theory.

***The Gradual Release of Responsibility Model.*** Pearson and Gallagher (1983) describe a model of instruction that begins with teacher explanation and demonstration, moves on to guided practice, and then concludes with children's independent practice and use. Figure I.5 provides a graphic representation of this model.

Initially, the teacher has a high degree of responsibility for and control of instruction, but over time, the student gradually takes on more responsibility and control over learning a particular strategy or skill. This model, like Cambourne's conditions, emphasizes the importance of modeling and demonstrating, along with supporting children as they gain greater independence

FIGURE I.5 **The Gradual Release of Responsibility Model of Instruction**

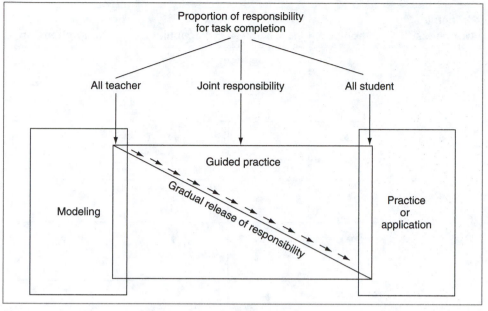

This article was published in *Contemporary Educational Psychology,* Volume 8, 1983, Pearson, P. D., & Gallagher, M. C. The instruction of reading comprehension, pages 317–345. Copyright Elsevier, 2007.

and control over what they are learning. Once again, the link to Vygotsky's theory is evident. We will refer to this model at different points in the Handbook. In the next section we discuss how the Profile and Handbook are organized, and how you might get started using them.

## STRUCTURE AND USE OF THE PROFILE

In this section we provide an overview of the Profile's structure, some suggestions for its use, some suggestions of how to get started, and finally some cautions, caveats, and tips. You may want to remove the Profile from the Handbook at this time and have it in front of you as you read this section.

### Strands of the Profile

The Profile itself outlines 10 strands of early literacy development, including the areas of oral language, reading, and writing development. They are:

1. Phonological Awareness and Oral Language Development
2. Concepts of Print, Knowledge of Letters, and Text Features
3. Decoding Skills and Word Analysis
4. Reading Strategies, Processes, and Dispositions
5. Reading Accuracy and Fluency at Increasing Text Levels
6. Comprehension and Reading Response
7. Writing Strategies, Processes, and Dispositions
8. Writing Effectiveness
9. Spelling
10. Writing Conventions and Handwriting

Descriptors that relate to oral language, the concepts of print, and reading are clustered in the first six strands, while writing and spelling are addressed in the last four strands. In Figure I.6 we have shown how the "five

FIGURE I.6  **Five Key Elements of Reading and the Literacy Profile**

| Profile Strands | Phonemic Awareness | Phonics | Fluency | Vocabulary | Comprehension |
|---|---|---|---|---|---|
| 1. Phonological Awareness and Oral Language Development | ◆ | ◆ | | | |
| 2. Concepts of Print, Knowledge of Letters, and Text Features | ◆ | ◆ | | ◆ | |
| 3. Decoding Skills and Word Analysis | ◆ | ◆ | | | |
| 4. Reading Strategies, Processes, and Dispositions | | ◆ | | ◆ | ◆ |
| 5. Reading Accuracy and Fluency at Increasing Text Levels | | ◆ | ◆ | | |
| 6. Comprehension and Reading Response | | | | ◆ | ◆ |
| 7. Writing Strategies, Processes, and Dispositions | | | | | |
| 8. Writing Effectiveness | | | | | |
| 9. Spelling | ◆ | ◆ | | ◆ | |
| 10. Writing Conventions and Handwriting | | | | | |

key elements of reading" (National Reading Panel, 2000) are included within the strands of the Profile.

The order in which the strands are listed does not intended to indicate the order in which learning occurs. In fact, each learner makes progress in a unique way, and the Profile helps to illustrate this point. The descriptors going *across* each strand delineate the progression from early to later development. Located in the far left column of the Profile, under the title of each strand, is a "core question," which is included to keep the assessment process purposeful. After all, the whole point of assessment is to *find out* something about the learner and to use that information in some way. Below the core question you will see a list of "Sample Assessment Tools." This is by no means a comprehensive list; in many cases we have referred to additional assessments within a chapter.

### Getting Started: Cautions, Caveats, and Tips

Before you begin chapter 1, a few tips may be helpful. We know from experience that it's more useful to "wade," rather than to "dive," into the process of using the Profiles and Handbook. This section will provide some scaffolding, or ideas for ways to get started, along with some cautions, caveats, and tips.

FIGURE I.7  **Some Ways to Get Started with the Profile**

| If . . . | Then . . . |
|---|---|
| You are preparing an individual case study as part of a literacy course or study group | • Begin with the "core questions" in each strand, selecting appropriate tools that are likely to yield useful information.<br>• Administer the assessments.<br>• Analyze the information obtained, and mark the Profile.<br>• Recommend next steps for instruction. |
| You are interested in exploring one or more strands of the Profile with all of the students in the classroom | • Select one or two strands that are a high priority for you at this time. Begin with the core questions, and select appropriate tools that are feasible to use and likely to yield useful information.<br>• Administer the assessments.<br>• Analyze the information obtained, and mark the Profiles.<br>• Plan appropriate next steps as needed for small groups of students. |
| You want to closely monitor the progress of an individual or small group of striving readers or writers | • Identify strands that are a high priority for the students you are concerned about at this time. Begin with the core questions, and select appropriate tools that are feasible to use and likely to yield useful information.<br>• Administer the assessments.<br>• Analyze the information obtained to identify particular gaps. Mark the Profiles, including specific assessment dates, and (possibly) annotate the Profiles.<br>• Plan appropriate interventions for individuals or the small group of students. Set targets for reassessment and follow up. |

*Getting Started.*  There are several ways to begin using the Profile, and how you begin depends on your purpose and situation. For example, some of you may be reading this as part of a course; others may be interested in trying out one or more dimensions of the Profile with all of the students in your class; and others may want to look closely at a particular student or small group of striving readers. Look over Figure I.7, which outlines some possible ways to get started. Next we will discuss some "nuts and bolts" topics such as efficiency of use, marking the Profile, and making decisions about sharing information in the Profile.

Efficiency is important to consider when using the Profile. Fortunately, a number of assessment tools can yield information that applies to several strands. For example, a running record can yield information about decoding, reading strategies, and reading accuracy and fluency. A writing sample can provide information about writing strategies and processes, writing effectiveness, spelling, and conventions.

Marking the Profile is another important topic to consider. You can mark the Profile in a number of ways, again depending on your purpose for using the Profile and your situation. In the final section of each chapter, you will see a sample Profile segment filled in for Willa, the student we assessed. In each sample segment of the Profile, we highlighted what Willa could do, based on the assessments administered. (*Note*: Descriptors on the Profile should be marked only if there is documented evidence that supports that specific item.) Sometimes you may find that you need to highlight only part of a descriptor; you may also find that you need to skip over some descriptors and mark one in the next column.

Some schools may decide to use the Profile as a summative recording document for a few agreed-upon strands, and select one highlighter color for each grade. For example, a school might decide to use the Reading Accuracy and Fluency strand along with the Writing Effectiveness strand because teachers and administrators want to use uniform assessments in these areas, and be able to see where students fall along a developmental continuum. In this case, it would not be necessary to date each descriptor, as everyone would complete those strands on the Profile during an agreed-upon month of the year, using the color assigned for that grade level.

Another set of decisions concerns what to do with the Profile information, beyond documenting progress and planning future steps. Ideally the Profile will be passed on to next year's classroom teacher or kept in a working file to be shared with other professionals working with the student. Some teachers use the Profile to communicate with parents during parent conferences, or as a resource to be shared during Open House, to explain how literacy development unfolds over time. In the concluding chapter, we will present more options for using the Profile as a tool for communication.

***Cautions, Caveats, and Tips.*** Needless to say, we are enthusiastic about the potential that the Profile can offer to both teachers and students. It is, however, important to point out that using the Profile may be a new learning experience for many teachers and teacher-candidates. Like most new learning experiences, becoming familiar with the Profile will take time and support. Our hope, of course, is that this Handbook will assist you. But it may also be useful for you to find a kindred spirit, someone who is willing to try this alongside you, to accompany you as you become familiar with the Profile and Handbook.

We'd like to close this introductory chapter by sharing a few cautions, caveats, and tips.

- *Cautions:*
  - Descriptors listed on the Profile may not be a perfect match with your state standards or state/district grade-level expectations. You may need to slightly modify the descriptors.
  - Prematurely marking the Profile without documented evidence does not benefit the child. If in doubt, use an additional assessment.
- *Caveats:*
  - Mandating the use of the Profile in a school without consensus decision making and sufficient professional development and support is unlikely to be successful.
  - Keep in mind that the Profile is not an assessment by itself; it is a framework for thinking about what is to be assessed, recording what is noticed, and thinking about next steps needed.
- *Tips:*
  - Start slowly, focusing on one strand at a time, if you are working with a whole class.
  - Find a partner to help you analyze and evaluate the results of your assessment, mark the Profile, and plan the next steps. Two heads are almost always better than one.

## REFERENCES

Baker, G. (1999). *Reading and writing grade by grade: Primary literacy standards for kindergarten through third grade.* Pittsburgh: University of Pittsburgh Learning Research and Development Center, New Standards Organization.

Cambourne, B. (1988). *The whole story.* Auckland, New Zealand: Ashton Scholastic.

Cambourne, B. (1995). Toward an educationally relevant theory of literacy learning: Twenty years of inquiry. *The Reading Teacher, 49*(3), 182–190.

Harp, B., & Brewer, J. A. (2005). *The informed reading teacher: Research-based practice.* Upper Saddle River, NJ: Pearson Education.

Hill, B. C., & Ruptic, C. (1994). *Practical aspects of authentic assessment: Putting the pieces together.* Norwood, MA: Christopher Gordon Publishers.

National Reading Panel. (2000). *Teaching children to read: An evidence-based assessment of the scientific research literature on reading and its implications for reading instruction.* Washington, DC: Author.

Owen, R. C. (1988). *Literacy learning in the classroom.* Katonah, NY: Richard C. Owen Publishers.

Pearson, P. D., & Gallagher, M. C. (1983). The instruction of reading comprehension. *Contemporary Educational Psychology, 8,* 317–345.

Tharp, R. G., & Gallimore, R. (1988). *Rousing minds to life.* Melbourne, Australia: Cambridge University Press.

Vygotsky, L. (1978). *Mind in society: The development of higher psychological processes.* Cambridge, MA: Harvard University Press.

# CHAPTER ONE

# Phonological Awareness and Oral Language Development

## CORE QUESTION

To what extent is the child developing phonological awareness and oral language skills?

"Remember to use your *1-foot voice* when you get into partnerships," adds Miss Allen just before she sends her first graders off to share their weekend stories with a partner. Miss Allen is referring to the *volume* of the conversation, reminding children to adjust their voices so that only their partners can hear what they are saying—hence a 1-foot voice, sound traveling approximately 12 inches. Although most children use oral language successfully by the time they enter school, teachers often need to guide them through the pragmatics of our language system, and the underlying social rules for communicating in various contexts. Pragmatics, however, is only one of several important considerations in oral language development. Let's take a closer look at the complexities of language.

Parker and Riley (2005) describe five language systems that operate simultaneously when we communicate: phonology, pragmatics, syntax, semantics, and morphology. The written system of language, known as *orthography,* adds yet another dimension to language use and will be addressed in subsequent chapters. How are these language systems embedded in our daily language use? In this chapter we will consider four broad areas of oral language and explain how each is related to a child's overall literacy development:

**LITERACY PROFILE** Consult your Literacy Profile as you read through this chapter. Refer to the question and indicators for Strand 1.

- Phonological awareness (a branch of phonology)
- Pragmatics (language use in a social context)
- Syntax (how words are put together in phrases, clauses, and sentences)
- Vocabulary development (which draws from semantics and morphology)

# UNDERLYING PRINCIPLES OF PHONOLOGICAL AWARENESS AND ORAL LANGUAGE DEVELOPMENT

If most children learn language even before they enter school (Pinker, 1994), you may wonder why there is such an emphasis on oral language and phonological awareness in the school setting. Language learning encompasses much more than speaking and listening; in fact, language is the very crux of literacy learning (Gunning, 2006). Reading, writing, and thinking are all processes that are built on language. Learning how to use language to communicate is critically important, but schools must have a larger focus.

Halliday (1982) describes three broad areas of language learning, all of which children manage simultaneously from birth on: learning language, learning about language, and learning through language. Briefly, these can be described as follows:

1. *Learning language* is the developing ability to use language effectively. As mentioned earlier, this usually occurs without formal instruction, as most children arrive at school with the basic ability to use language as a tool for communication. This is not to say that all children begin school with the same control over language use; rather, as Hart and Risley's study (1995) indicates, the experiential language backgrounds of children differ radically, most often favoring children of professional parents.

2. *Learning about language* refers to the underlying rules, components, and systems that comprise our language. In order to learn about language, we must put "meaning making" aside and look at language through a different lens, that of a linguist, someone who studies language (Yopp & Yopp, 2000). For instance, to identify the sounds in the word "cat," you do not need to think of the concept of a cat; instead, you must pay attention to the individual sounds that comprise the word. This chapter will focus primarily on learning *about* language as it applies to kindergarten through Grade 4 students.

3. *Learning through language* means that we learn about the world by using language—as we talk, listen, read, write, and reflect (Lee, 1986). For instance, by writing this Handbook, we use written language to convey information about literacy acquisition. Conversely, you are reading these words and thinking about the ideas and concepts they present, affirming things you already know, and adding new bits of information to your growing knowledge of literacy acquisition; that is, you are learning about language through language.

These three aspects of language learning are important to consider as we create authentic language opportunities for our students. Literacy learning develops parallel to oral language learning (Goodman, Smith, Meredith, & Goodman, 1987); even more specifically, the development of phonological awareness has been linked to success in reading and spelling for students through Grade 4 (Adams, 1990; Juel, 1988). In this chapter, we will first turn our attention to understanding some key concepts of phonological awareness and oral language development; then we will consider some assessment tools that are useful in obtaining information about these important foundational skills. We also will explore how language-rich classrooms help children build their oral language competence through pragmatics, syntax, and vocabulary, and consider some specific techniques to assist students who need more help.

## The Role of Phonological Awareness in Oral Language Development

Phonological awareness is the ability to think about, identify, and discuss the sounds of language (Adams, 1990; Yopp & Yopp, 2000). Teachers help children develop this awareness by temporarily drawing their attention away from the meaning of words and guiding them toward specific features of words and language (Yaden & Templeton, 1986; Yopp & Yopp, 2000). For instance, when a teacher says, "Listen carefully to the words *quick* and *stick*. They rhyme. How can we tell that they rhyme?", she draws attention to the sounds of language, building phonological awareness. Phonological awareness can be emphasized as a natural part of the oral language process, helping children learn about language as they use language (Opitz, 2000). Phonological awareness focuses on the sounds of language; in contrast, phonics involves matching sounds to print.

Researchers identify a general progression of phonological awareness skills, moving from whole units to parts:

- Rhyming
- Chunks of language, including words and syllables
- Onsets and rimes
- Phonemic awareness (Armbruster, Lehr, & Osborn, 2001; Cunningham, 2000; Gunning, 2006)

Although these four areas are listed from the easiest to the most difficult tasks, research has offered some interesting findings about the development of phonological awareness. And although some children enter school already proficient in manipulating sounds in all four areas of phonological awareness (Snow, Burns, & Griffin, 1998), most enter kindergarten without phonemic awareness, a skill that usually develops by the end of Grade 1 (Yopp, 1995). Also, even though most children move through the four levels of phonological awareness in developmental stages, we do not have convincing evidence that students must master each level before they can move on to the next level (Opitz, 2000). This indicates that we should not necessarily follow a lockstep process when we teach these skills. And of the four broad areas, rhyming and phonemic awareness have been found to be particularly critical in predicting children's successful development of reading and writing skills (Adams, 1990; Juel, 1988; Maclean, Bryant, & Bradley, 1987). Torgeson and Mathes (1998) explain that phonological awareness contributes to beginning word reading in three ways: helping children understand the alphabetic principle (the connection between letters and sounds), helping them notice the regular ways that letters represent sounds in words, and helping them generate possibilities for words that they can only partially sound out. Let's look more closely at each of the four skill areas.

***Rhyming.*** Language play for young children frequently involves nursery rhymes, short poems, and songs that contain rhyming words. Reciting poetry such as, "Hey diddle diddle, the cat and the fiddle" can be uplifting, even if the child has no idea what those first three words mean. The repetition, the rhyming, and the catchy rhythm create an unforgettable childhood fantasy in which magical things happen and, at the same time, they help children "develop an ear for rhyme" (Opitz, 2000, p. 21).

The words *fiddle* and *diddle* are rhymes because they end with the same ending sound unit, "iddle." Rhyming is not tied to the written spelling pattern of the word; rather, it refers to the oral structure of the word. For example, *chair* and *care* rhyme even though they do not have the same spelling at the end. Also, in poetry, multisyllabic words are frequently used as rhymes if the final syllables share the same ending sound, as in *fascinate* and *interrogate*.

As children learn to recognize rhyming words through language play, they can begin to create their own rhyming pairs. Although they may not be able to explain why words are considered rhymes, most children can manage the vocabulary and understand the concept of rhyming early in their oral language development if they have had repeated exposure to songs or rhyming language. This development is important, because the ability to distinguish rhymes has been correlated with early reading success (Maclean et al., 1987).

***Word Awareness and Syllabication.***    Another important discovery children make about the structure of our oral language is word boundaries (or word breaks). Oral language flows rather connectedly, often without even audible pauses between words. Young children frequently repeat long sequences of sounds without realizing where one word begins and another ends. Identification of word boundaries is associated more with written language than with oral language (Freeman & Freeman, 2004). For example, in a child's early writing, you may see the words, "Once upon a time" written as, "Wonsapponna time." As children begin to read more, they gradually develop a clearer understanding of word boundaries and transfer this understanding to their writing (Pinker, 1994).

Closely related to word breaks is syllabication, the notion that one word may contain multiple parts. A syllable is defined as a "chunk" or portion of a word that contains a separate vowel sound. For instance, "onomatopoeia" has six distinctive vowel sounds, on · o · mat · o · poe · ia (ŏn/ /ə/ /măt/ /ə/ /pē/ /ə/); each "break" corresponding with an unblocked flow of air that can be distinguished by a slight movement of the lower jaw (Freeman & Freeman, 2004). Children can hear the separate syllables in words more easily than they can hear the separate sounds or phonemes (Liberman, Shankweiler, Fischer, & Carter, 1974), and even young children delight in discovering and sharing multisyllabic words such as *onomatopoeia*.

Sentence structure is another organizing unit of oral language. Although young children are able to talk in complete sentences, their oral language is mostly casual, with conversations that reflect many inferred subjects and predicates (Clay, 1991). For instance, when they reply to one another, they often speak in phrases, and yet they communicate complete thoughts.

First child: "What'd you do last night?"

Reply of second child: "Watched TV."

With practice and supported discussion, children can be taught to recognize and use complete sentences in oral communication when the situation calls for more formal language. Terms such as words, syllables, and sentences can be introduced naturally as children engage in wordplay and other language activities (Gunning, 2006).

***Onsets and Rimes.***    The next level of phonological awareness addresses the ability to hear and isolate the initial sounds in words. The beginning consonant sounds up to the vowel in each syllable are collectively called the *onset* (Moustafa, 1997). In the word *man,* the onset is /m/, and in the word *bring,* the onset is /br/.

As children learn how to isolate initial sounds in words, they must also learn the difference between the letter name and the sound that it represents. Gunning (2006) suggests teaching the letters that represent the sounds as

Letters placed between forward slashes represent the sounds made by the letter. For instance, /t/ refers to the sound or phoneme represented by the letter *t*.

soon as children can perceive beginning sounds because when phonological awareness and phonics are taught in tandem, children learn to associate the sound and the symbolic representation (Bradley & Bryant, 1985). Children often link sounds and letters when they begin to recognize, spell, or write their own names. Here's an example of an interaction between a teacher and a child that begins with letter identification: "My name starts with 'T,'" Tonia announces proudly. The teacher replies, "What sound does the 'T' make?" And when Tonia answers, "/t/," this is an indication that she is beginning to isolate an initial sound in a word.

Eventually Tonia will notice that other words like *top* and *toy* also begin with the /t/ sound. The growing awareness that other words can also begin with this same /t/ sound is known as *phoneme identity* or *phoneme matching* (Armbruster et al., 2001). Many early books such as *The Berenstain's B Book* (Berenstain & Berenstain, 1971) use alliteration, the repetition of beginning sounds, to make language predictable and engaging. The use of alliteration isn't limited to early readers; people of all ages enjoy tongue twisters and sound repetitions in poetry.

In addition to onsets, another feature of this level of phonological awareness is the remainder of the syllable, the *rime*. The rime is defined as the blended *sounds* of the vowel plus the supporting consonant sounds that follow it (Moustafa, 1997). In the examples of "man" and "bring," the rimes are /an/ and /ing/, respectively. Keep in mind the following characteristics of rimes:

1. Every syllable must contain a rime, even though not all syllables contain an onset. An example is the word "and."
2. Each rime has one vowel sound that may or may not be associated with consonants. The rime for "me" is /ē/.

Two other terms that are often associated with rimes are *phonogram* and *word family*. The spelling pattern a rime shares with another word is known as a phonogram, such as the "at" in *cat* and *hat*. This term refers to both the sounds and the letters, as in the /at/ sound being consistently spelled as *a-t*. Rimes are important in early word work because they are the basis for rhyming activities, but one challenge children face when they begin to notice how words are spelled is that not all rhymes share the same phonogram.

A word family is simply a collection of words that share the same phonogram. Many teachers introduce the short vowel sounds through word families, since producing short vowel sounds in isolation can be challenging. The "at" word family is: *bat, cat, fat, hat, mat, pat, rat, sat, vat, chat,* and *that*. But it does not include "what." Do you hear the /u/ sound in "what" rather than the /a/ sound in "at"?

***Phonemic Awareness.*** Phonemic awareness is the ability to hear and manipulate the individual sounds in words (Yopp, 1995). Clay (1991) points out that in day-to-day speech, we generally do not articulate the individual sounds of words, which suggests that doing so is not a natural part of oral language development. For instance, the word *cat* is usually pronounced in a single flow, /kat/, rather than as /k/ /a/ /t/. Some children do learn to isolate these sounds through their early reading and writing experiences, but others will need explicit teaching and supported practice to learn to isolate the individual sounds of words. Researchers have identified a child's phonemic awareness by the end of first grade as an important predictor of early reading success (Adams, 1990; Ehri & Nunes, 2002; Juel, 1988; National Reading Panel, 2000); but we must be careful not to respond to this information by overemphasizing phonemic awareness. Cunningham (2003) reminds us that researchers recommend no more than 18 hours of phonemic awareness instruction a year. Mathematically, she breaks this down to approximately 10 minutes each day.

Let's review some of the nuances of phonology that make learning about phonemes so tricky for children. We'll begin with one simple word from the English language: *me*. As you say this word out loud, consider the physical movements of your mouth, including your lips, jaw, and tongue. Now say the word *me* out loud again, this time focusing on the airflow and your voice. Next, say the word *my*. Did you notice the changes in the shape of your mouth and in your voice? Linguists identify the speech sounds that differentiate one word from another as phonemes (Freeman & Freeman, 2004). "Me" and "my" each have two phonemes, a consonant sound and a vowel sound, but the production of each word varies based on the long *e* and the long *i* sounds.

A phoneme is defined as the smallest unit of sound that can distinguish one word from another (Fisher, 1993; Freeman & Freeman, 2004). Languages have different numbers of phonemes. The English language contains approximately 40 phonemes, while the Spanish language has only 22 (Freeman & Freeman, 2004). There are various ways to transcribe or record phonemes, but for the purpose of consistency, we will use the recording system found in Figure 1.1 for the remainder of this chapter.

*ENGLISH ELL LANGUAGE LEARNERS* If you are working with English Language Learners, it is important for you to identify the phonemes that they are familiar with from their first language. Start from what the child already knows.

FIGURE 1.1  **Pronunciation Guide Used with DIBELS Assessments**

| Phoneme | Phoneme Example | Phoneme | Phoneme Example |
|---|---|---|---|
| /ai/ | bait | /th/ | thin |
| /ea/ | bead | /TH/ | then |
| /ie/ | tie | /sh/ | shed |
| /oa/ | boat | /SH/ | measure *or* beige |
| /oo/ | food | /ch/ | chin |
| /a/ | bad | /j/ | jam *and* edge |
| /e/ | bed | /p/ | pen |
| /i/ | bid | /t/ | tap |
| /o/ | cod *or* law | /k/ | can |
| /u/ | bud *and* "a" *in* about | /b/ | bat |
| /uu/ | good | /d/ | dad |
| /ow/ | cow | /g/ | gun *or* frog |
| /oi/ | noise *or* point | /m/ | man *or* jam |
| /ar/ (1 phoneme) | car | /n/ | nap |
| /ir/ (1 phoneme) | bird | /ng/ | sing |
| /or/ (1 phoneme) | for | /f/ | fat |
| /ai/ /r/ (2 phonemes) | chair | /v/ | van |
| /ea/ /r/ (2 phonemes) | clear | /s/ | sit |
| /oo/ /r/ (2 phonemes) | tour | /z/ | zoo |
| | | /r/ | rat *or* frog |
| | | /l/ | lap |
| | | /w/ | wet |
| | | /h/ | hot |
| | | /y/ | yell |

Let's look again at the word "me." It has two phonemes, or individual sounds: /m/ and /ea/. Now say the word "meet," slowly stretching out the individual sounds. "Meet" has three phonemes, /m/ /ea/ /t/. As described in the onset/rime section, children usually first identify the initial sound in a word, and often this knowledge begins with the first sounds of a child's name. Generally, the next phoneme that children can isolate in short consonant-vowel-consonant (CVC) words is the final sound. (You will notice this sequence in sections 7, 8, and 9 of the assessment located in Appendix A-2, "Formative Assessment for Phonological Awareness.") This progression may seem illogical, but the isolation of a short vowel sound is often difficult for students because we generally do not separate consonants from vowels in rimes when we speak; also, in most cases, consonant sounds are more audible than vowel sounds (Freeman & Freeman, 2004).

Although isolating individual phonemes is not something we do in everyday communication (except, possibly, when we write), you can provide a model for manipulating individual phonemes through blending tasks. Blending occurs when the teacher articulates individual sounds of a word and then invites the child to bring them together to correctly pronounce the word. For instance, you might say, "Listen to these sounds and tell me the word: /m/ /a/ /t/." The child would then reply, "mat." Blending activities serve as a manageable starting point for this level of language analysis; you can begin even more gradually by teaching children to blend onsets with rimes before separating each individual sound of a CVC word, presenting /m/ /at/ before /m/ /a/ /t/ (Gunning, 2006). Be sure to practice accurately pronouncing the individual sounds because consonant sounds are sometimes difficult to separate from vowels, and you don't want to create distortions that could confuse children (Meyer, 2002). For instance, when segmenting the /b/ sound, be careful not to say, "Buh."

Opposite to blending phonemes is separating, or segmenting, them by stretching out the individual sounds in words. To teach segmentation, you could say, "Stretch out the sounds in *mat*." The child would respond, "/m/ /a/ /t/." With practice, blending and segmenting phonemes should become automatic and fluid, and both tasks can serve as useful tools for encoding and decoding language.

More advanced phoneme manipulation tasks include deleting, adding, and substituting phonemes. Deleting phonemes is the process of saying a word and then repeating it without a specific sound. A deletion prompt could sound like this: "Say *mat* without the /m/ sound." The child would reply, "At." Adding phonemes is the process of inserting a phoneme in front of other phonemes such as adding /m/ to *at*. Finally, substituting phonemes is the process of removing one phoneme, /m/, and changing it to another, /h/, as in changing *mat* to *hat*. Substituting phonemes can be a useful tool for learning to spell.

Phonemic awareness activities make the most sense to children if the activities are eventually incorporated into practical applications through phonics (Bus & van Ijzendoorn, 1999; Vandervelden & Siegel, 1997). Manipulation of phonemes then becomes a useful tool for reading and writing and furthers a child's knowledge of how our language works.

See Appendices A-1 and A-2 for sample prompts to support blending, segmenting, adding, deleting, and substitution skills.

### The Role of Pragmatics in Oral Language Development

Think about the differences between how you talk to your friends outside of a school setting and how you present yourself in your professional role as teacher. How did you learn these generally unspoken rules for communicating in diverse settings? Pragmatics is a branch of linguistics that studies how people receive and produce information through oral language (Liu, 2000). We vary our language style in many ways, including our choice of words, volume of speech, rate of speech, and level of formality, usually basing our decisions on a combination of context, purpose, and audience. School creates many opportunities to make this decision making transparent. For example, students must determine when they are permitted to talk and when they must be silent throughout the course of a school day. Various groupings within the same classroom setting require shifts in language use. For instance, whole-class, small-group, one-to-one interactions, and solitary desk work have different rules and demands for both listening and speaking.

Pragmatics also includes the skills we use when presenting information orally. When speaking to a whole class, children must learn to adjust their volume, make eye contact, and enunciate clearly. There is also the personal realm of communication. Independent periods such as lunch and recess can be stressful times for children who have poor skills in pragmatics. Often, teachers must intervene when a child uses words that are misunderstood or intentionally critical or mean-spirited. Pragmatics has many aspects, and one of our duties as teachers is to help children learn to use language appropriately and to adjust to socially acceptable language forms in various contexts.

## The Role of Syntax in Oral Language Development

Syntax, or grammar, can be described as the logical and meaningful way we structure our language using words, phrases, clauses, and sentences (Freeman & Freeman, 2004). Noam Chomsky's research in the 1950s and 60s challenged the traditional rule-based approach to teaching grammar and launched the current approaches, which are based on a generative theory. This theory is built around the idea that each sentence contains two structural levels, a deep-meaning level and a surface level that is used to communicate the deeper idea. Chomsky posited that children are able to derive meaning from complex yet novel language structures even though they have never been taught the underlying rules for these structures. He concluded that language use is based on an innate biological process that allows children to develop the underlying principles of language through use rather than through schooling (Chomsky, 1975). Because most children do acquire an awareness of deep language structures before they begin school, the role of schools then becomes building on the knowledge that children have already accumulated through their own experiences (Putnam, 1994–1995).

As children refine their logical use of surface language through observation, practice, and feedback, teachers should honor approximations as a natural part of the language acquisition process (Freeman & Freeman, 2004). For instance, children often overuse the "-ed" ending with irregular verbs in cases such as, "I goed to the football game." Teachers and adults are most helpful when they simply respond with the conventional form of the verb, "Oh, you went to the football game?" Eventually, with repeated exposure to correct syntax and an emphasis on meaning over "correct usage," children usually make the adjustments in oral language naturally. In fact, oral language development progresses more successfully if children are not corrected when they are attempting to make meaning through their conversations (Wells, 1986). Opportunities to explicitly teach standard English are plentiful when teaching *about* language during grammar studies that involve writing. See chapter 8 for examples of mini-lessons.

Since "book language" does not directly mirror oral language, children need to hear the language of texts from a variety of genres (Bertrand & Stice, 2002; Snow & Tabors, 1993). Consider two language structures often found in text: passive voice, "The cat was chased by the dog," and past participles, "The man had had enough of the cold, so he packed up his things and moved to Florida." When you choose your daily read-aloud materials, be sure to include texts that use a wide range of interesting language forms, including narrative and informational texts, that will broaden students' exposure to various syntactic structures

(Duke & Kays, 1998; Purcell-Gates, McIntyre, & Freppon, 1995). Language development is enhanced when students hear and analyze forms of language that occur in structures outside of typical oral language constructs. Reading aloud from a variety of genres also promotes vocabulary development.

### The Importance of Vocabulary in Oral Language and Literacy Development

Vocabulary is the primary vehicle for transmitting and receiving thoughts and ideas. In other words, the more words you can control, the more choices you have to precisely use and interpret language. Since word knowledge plays a key role in effective communication in all areas of language use (listening, speaking, reading, and writing), it is important to continually expand children's lexicons of words. But how can you do this? Let's review some key points.

It is important to remember that vocabulary development includes both the breadth of words a child knows and the depth to which the child understands them (Durkin, 2004). Measuring the number of words an individual "knows" can be difficult because of the different levels of word knowledge. For instance, you may understand a word that your sister uses in a specific context even though you don't use that word yourself. Another way to put this is the difference between your "active" vocabulary (i.e., words you use when you communicate) and your "passive" vocabulary (i.e., words you understand).

Word learning can be thought of as a continuum from not knowing a word to the active use of a word. Cunningham and Allington (2007) describe five levels of "knowing" a word:

- "I've never heard that word before."
- "I've heard that word but I'm not sure what it means."
- "I know what that word means."
- "I use that word in my writing."
- "I use that word in my everyday language."

If children learn how to assess their personal levels of word use, it will help them to self-monitor and further develop their active use of more "advanced" vocabulary.

***Broadening Vocabulary.*** Teachers cannot "teach" children every word they need to know; however, a systematic and active vocabulary program can ensure ever-expanding repertoires (National Institute of Child Health and Human Development, 2000; Snow et al., 1998). Such a program should involve creating an atmosphere of "word consciousness" by explicitly teaching words, teaching students strategies for expanding their own vocabularies, and exposing students to a range of words through reading, writing, speaking, and listening (Nagy, 1988). You can expose children to rich new words naturally through frequent read-alouds, discussions, and writing demonstrations, but you will also need to make important decisions about which words to teach directly. Because we can teach only a limited number of words each year, teachers must carefully and thoughtfully choose words for explicit instruction based on utility.

Beck, McKeon, and Kucan (2002) offer guidelines for choosing words to explicitly teach during vocabulary lessons. They describe three tiers of words:

- *Tier One:* the everyday words that are used in oral language (e.g., *run, love, mine*)
- *Tier Two:* the language used more frequently in books and the world of print (e.g., *ferocious, gleamed, insisted*)
- *Tier Three:* the words used within specific content-area studies (*continent, absorption, angle*)

**ELL** — ENGLISH LANGUAGE LEARNERS

Because English Language Learners frequently understand more language than they are able to produce, their speaking and writing may not accurately represent their level of comprehension (Krashen & Terrell, 1983). Visual representations and gestures allow them more opportunities to demonstrate their understanding and knowledge.

To support literacy learning, these researchers recommend choosing Tier Two words that are conceptually within a child's reach. For instance, because a child already understands the concept of happy, adding a new word that describes a more specific level of happiness, such as *ecstatic*, is more easily assimilated into the child's existing schema than a word that has no base. Also, context matters. For instance, if we teach this word during a read-aloud, the child will probably remember the word through the experience of the character who was apparently so happy that the author had to use a stronger word to describe this state than the simple and overused "happy."

Cunningham and Allington (2007) recommend teaching three words each time you read aloud to children. If you choose approximately three words to explicitly teach every time you read to children, and if you read to the children frequently and revisit those words frequently, you will assuredly broaden the children's vocabulary. Introducing Tier Two words from high-quality children's books will help learners access the world of printed language and build their comprehension of those texts. Remember, though, that these word introductions are only a beginning; children need to have "multiple encounters" (perhaps 10 to 40 in some cases) with new vocabulary words if permanence is the goal (Beck et al., 2002, p. 32).

Tier Three words might need a different approach. Many new words that are taught during content lessons require the development of conceptual understanding, not simply a new label. In this case, preteaching new words before students encounter them in content-level texts can support the comprehension process (Johnson, 2001; Nagy, 1988). To preteach words, Hoyt (2002) suggests a word-building strategy known as "frontloading," which bolsters the comprehension process using oral language and concrete experiences and deliberately builds background knowledge.

To frontload, choose a few words from an informational text and allow students to experience and discuss these terms before you assign the reading. For instance, in Grade 3, you might introduce students to the words *economy, producers,* and *consumers* in a social studies text. By connecting these terms to the more immediate geographic and cultural backgrounds of the children, you will better prepare them to read and understand the broader concepts being discussed in a generalized text. Increasing vocabulary knowledge favorably impacts reading comprehension (Beck, Perfetti, & McKeon, 1982; Nagy, 1988).

***Deepening Vocabulary.***    You can also build on foundation words that a child already knows and in so doing deepen a child's word awareness. For instance, "run" is a base word that is familiar to most children. It can be used in many different contexts to represent a variety of ideas, ranging from a noun naming the tear in a stocking or a term that refers to the score in baseball, to a verb that means moving rather quickly. Children will undoubtedly be familiar with many definitions of "run," and they will delight in discovering new ones. When children participate in class discussions of multiple-meaning words such as simple words like "run," they begin to fully realize the importance of context.

Next we will look at "run" from different angles, but before we do so, let's review some vocabulary from the area of morphology. *Run* is considered a morpheme; more specifically, it is known as a free morpheme since it holds meaning on its own (Freeman & Freeman, 2004). Recall that a morpheme is the smallest meaningful unit of language, so unlike phonemes, which describe the smallest units of sound, a morpheme has to do with meaning. New words can be made from a base word such as "run" by adding other morphemes called *affixes*. An affix is a meaningful unit of language that is added either to the beginning of a word (*prefix*) or to the end of a word (*suffix*). An affix is considered a bound morpheme because it cannot stand alone; it has meaning only when it is attached to another morpheme.

Adding the prefix "re-" to *run* creates an entirely new concept, "rerun." Cunningham and Allington (2007) have determined that the knowledge of four prefixes: *un* (not), *re* (back or again), *in* (the opposite), and *dis* (negation of, not exactly not) would help students unlock the meanings of more than 1,500 words. In the English language, suffixes can be inflectional or derivational. Derivational suffixes change the meaning or the part of speech of the base word and include *-less, -able,* and *-er.* On the other hand, inflectional suffixes do not change the meaning of the base word or the part of speech. There are eight inflectional morphemes, and they affect three parts of speech as follows:

* Nouns to plural or possessive through *-s, -es, -'s*
* Tenses of verbs through *-s, -ing, -ed,* and *-en*
* Degrees of comparison of adjectives through *-er* and *-est* (Freeman & Freeman, 2004)

How many affixes (both prefixes and suffixes) can you use with the base word *run?* Make a list, and try sorting them into columns of prefixes, derivational suffixes, or inflectional suffixes. Children naturally integrate the subtle rules for adding affixes to words through their everyday speech, and this, coupled with an increasing awareness of structural analysis, helps them to unlock new words in oral language and in print.

Compound words are also built from familiar, everyday words. Combining two Tier One words makes the word "runway," a paved road for an airplane. Children enjoy recognizing, collecting, and creating compound words from known words. Word study lessons can also reveal two-word compounds such as *home run* and hyphenated compounds such as *run-down.*

Another potentially confusing type of language is figurative language—such as puns, idioms, and metaphors—which requires interpretation beyond the literal meaning. Even though these phrases are usually comprised of familiar Tier One words, their underlying meanings can be confusing to someone who doesn't have the appropriate background knowledge and experience. Simple sentences such as "The girl's nose was running" or "My run today was like an escape" can be incomprehensible to a child who has never seen or heard this use of language. Many children's books help children become savvy users of figurative language and multiple meanings of words. English Language Learners especially benefit from explanations and discussions of the multiple meanings of words and phrases. For instance, children may collectively laugh at Amelia Bedelia's antics as she misinterprets the multiple meanings of words in the series of books that feature her silly actions, but does everyone really understand the humor? You might want to ask for a volunteer to explain what makes a particular line funny. Using language to compare the literal and nonliteral meanings can resolve confusions that some children might not want to admit they have.

***Promoting Word-Learning Strategies.*** Besides the tasks of broadening and deepening children's vocabularies, it is also important to teach children how to independently learn new words that they encounter outside of school (Armbruster et al., 2001). You can start by modeling a curiosity about words in both oral and written contexts and inviting children to see the world of words as a rich menu filled with many options. The more enthusiastic you are about word learning, the more likely children will also become word connoisseurs (Ray, 1999). Encourage children to listen for new words in their lives outside of school, and, if you notice a child using a newly introduced word, celebrate it publicly! Others will likely follow in using new words.

For older students, teachers can demonstrate ways to independently approach new word learning. One helpful strategy involves the discovery and appreciation of synonyms. Synonyms offer variety in word choice, such as using *furious* instead of *mad*. Students can explore the subtle distinctions between common synonyms, such as *thin, skinny, lean, lanky,* and *slender*, by placing each one on a gradient and considering why one word might be a better choice than another. Antonyms, homonyms, contractions, and slang are also important concepts related to word knowledge. Each should be explored and studied in ways that inspire students to broaden their word awareness.

To promote independent word study, you will want to have a collection of materials handy for student investigations. In language-rich classrooms, libraries often include a reference shelf with these types of resources:

- A range of dictionaries for various levels
- Thesauruses for various levels
- Rhyming dictionaries
- Homonym, idiom, and other word-puzzle books

Many computer programs and Web sites include links to word pronunciation, definitions, and synonyms, but be sure to carefully screen these sites because some provide only electronic worksheets or word searches under the heading of "vocabulary development." Well-selected resources combined with teacher modeling are key to building and sustaining student curiosity about words.

### Summary of Underlying Principles of Phonological Awareness and Oral Language Development

Although oral language is a complex process that involves five different systems operating simultaneously, children usually enter school rather proficient in everyday language use. Schools primarily support refinement and expansion of these language systems through the development of phonological awareness, pragmatics, syntax, and vocabulary. Because oral language and phonological awareness provide a foundation for reading and writing and are essential components of daily curriculum, they are important areas to asses.

## ASSESSING PHONOLOGICAL AWARENESS AND ORAL LANGUAGE DEVELOPMENT

Although children start school already having had years of listening and speaking experience, a variety of factors, including both the quality and the quantity of oral language opportunities, can affect the level of skill development in a child's early years. Through careful assessment procedures, you will be able to determine each child's strengths and entry level, thus ensuring continued growth in a child's oral language development.

### Formal or Published Measures for Assessing Phonological Awareness and Oral Language Development

Many formal assessments are available in the areas of phonological awareness skills and vocabulary development. Some tests are used as screening devices, and others are used to monitor growth. Syntax and pragmatics tend to be assessed more informally in the early grades unless concerns arise and specialists are asked to administer specialized tests.

***Formal Phonological and Phonemic Awareness Assessment Tests.*** Some commonly used formal tests for various aspects of phonological awareness skills are:

- The Test of Phonological Awareness (Torgensen & Bryant, 1994)
- The Yopp-Singer Test of Phoneme Segmentation (Yopp, 1995)
- Phoneme Segmentation Fluency (PSF) Test, a subtest of Dynamic Indicators of Basic Early Learning Skills (DIBELS, 2007)

The Test of Phonological Awareness is a norm-referenced test that measures children's abilities to segment phonemes in spoken words. It can be administered to individuals or to a group since it does not require spoken language. There are two versions, one for kindergarten and one for Grade 1. In the kindergarten-level assessment, children are instructed to draw a line through the picture that represents the same or a different sound from the picture clue. In the Grade 1 version, children must identify the ending sounds using picture clues.

The Yopp-Singer Test of Phoneme Segmentation is one of the most commonly administered tests (Freeman & Freeman, 2004). It measures a child's ability to segment 22 different words and is administered individually, requiring a child to orally repeat each word by segmenting the sounds. See Appendix A-1 for administration directions and a reproducible copy of this assessment.

The Phoneme Segmentation Fluency Test, a subtest of DIBELS, measures how many individual sounds in dictated words a child can segment correctly in 1 minute. Each accurate sound is credited, and the results can be compared to samples of children of the same age. This test is administered individually and is often used both for screening and for progress monitoring.

Careful analysis of the assessment results can help you identify specific areas for designing whole-class, small-group, and individual lessons, looking carefully for the "frontier of learning" (Clay, 1991, p. 65) or, as Vygotsky coined it, the "zone of proximal development" (1978, p. 86) for each child. If a more specialized test is required due to a child's lack of progress or other concerns about the general assessments, you may want to recommend a more complete diagnostic test such as the Comprehensive Test of Phonological Processing (CTOPP; Wagner, Torgesen, & Rashotte, 1999), which should be administered and interpreted by a specially trained professional.

***Formal Vocabulary Assessment Tests.*** Two commonly administered vocabulary tests are:

- The Peabody Picture Vocabulary Test (PPVT) (Dunn & Dunn, 2006)
- The Comprehensive Receptive and Expressive Vocabulary Test (CREVT) (Wallace & Hammill, 1994)

Each of these tests is individually administered, and both use pictures. Children are asked to point to a picture after a prompt, and, in the case of the CREVT, also use language to describe given words. Either test can be useful to determine whether a child needs more specialized instruction in vocabulary development or word retrieval. The PPVT is sometimes administered to all students during pre-kindergarten screening.

Vocabulary development is often included as a subtest in standardized reading tests such as the Iowa Tests of Basic Skills (Hoover, Dunbar, & Frisble, 2005). In the early levels of this group test, students are given a word and sometimes an accompanying sentence, and then they are asked to choose

---

Before you administer the Yopp-Singer Test of Phoneme Segmentation, you may want to transcribe the phonemes ahead of time so that you are comfortable recording the sounds a child says when responding to the prompts. Use the guide in Figure 1.1 (p. 17) to practice recording each individual sound in the 22 words.

which one of the three pictures shown represents the word. In later years, reading vocabulary is measured through written prompts. These tests are often used to monitor yearly progress.

## Informal Measures for Assessing Phonological Awareness and Oral Language Development

Careful listening and thoughtful, systematic recording are two of the most important tools a teacher can use for assessing oral language development (Clay, 1991). At any grade level, observing and recording, also known as "kidwatching" (Goodman, 1978, p. 41), can be used as informal, early screening devices to identify children who may need more in-depth assessment. These records also serve as formative data that can help you plan instruction. Predeveloped checklists, such as the Teacher Rating of Oral Language and Literacy (TROLL): A Research Based Tool (Dickinson, McCabe, & Sprague, 2001), can also be used to observe and record the development of oral language skills.

Teachers often create their own informal checklists based on the specific standards and expectations at the various grade levels. You can use the Literacy Profile in combination with your state's frameworks as a useful guide for creating such a checklist.

The TROLL rating scale is available at http://www.ciera.org/library/reports/inquiry-3/3–016/3–016.html

***Informal Measures for Assessing Phonological Awareness.*** In the past few years, many informal tools have been developed to measure each specific area of phonological awareness. For a reproducible sample tool, see Appendix A-2, "Formative Assessment for Phonological Awareness (FAPA)," which was adapted from Kathy Davis's "Phonemic Awareness Assessment" (n.d.). This informal tool is administered individually and can be broken down into a series of sessions based on the child's skill and attention levels. FAPA progressively moves from less complex to more complex tasks, allowing you to quickly and clearly identify a targeted learning objective within a child's "zone of proximal development" (Vygotsky, 1978).

Another useful resource is the text entitled *Phonemic Awareness in Young Children* (Adams, Foorman, Lundberg, & Beeler, 1998). This text includes a reproducible assessment section for phonological awareness. A benefit of these materials is that they can be administered in group settings and then used to determine instructional needs for the entire group or for individual children.

***Informal Measures for Assessing Pragmatics.*** Teachers begin on the first day of school teachers begin to observe children's awareness of socially acceptable language and behaviors. It is important to record behaviors and actions in a systematic fashion to ensure that a child's development is moving in a positive direction. In states such as Massachusetts, pragmatics is listed as a standard in the language arts curriculum framework. For example, under General Standard 1, Discussion, the learning standard for Grades preK–2 reads, "Follow agreed-upon rules for discussion (raising one's hand, waiting one's turn, speaking one at a time)" (Massachusetts English Language Arts Curriculum Frameworks, 2001, p. 13).

Oral presentations offer unique opportunities to focus on oral language development. Corresponding checklists can include concrete descriptions of skills that list age-appropriate goals for the delivery of oral information. When students help design the checklist, they have even more ownership of the targeted behaviors (Winograd, Paris, & Bridge, 1991). Following an oral presentation, some children may want to watch a videorecording to help them set personal goals or to determine whether they were successful at accomplishing a set goal. See Appendix A-3 for a reproducible checklist that was designed to support goal setting and self-reflection. Teacher/student conferences can also be held before and after presentations to provide guidance in developing these important skills.

Children who have difficulty adjusting to various language demands in a school setting may have other learning needs. Sometimes you might want to elicit support from language or counseling specialists to help identify whether a child's behaviors are language related or a result of some other factor. Consistent observations that are recorded during the various instructional settings might help reveal a child's strengths and needs more clearly.

***Informal Measures for Assessing Syntax.*** In general, systematically recording anecdotal notes can work well for assessing syntactical oral language development. When you put observations and directly quoted comments in writing, patterns and progress over time can be analyzed more objectively. See Figure 1.2 for a sample of kindergarten children's comments.

Comments can be kept in an individual's file to determine whether the overgeneralizations are lessening or continuing. One effective strategy for organizing notes is to write comments on self-adhesive address labels that are easy to separate and apply to the individual child's progress-monitoring sheet at day's end. Use the Literacy Profile as a general guide for oral language development, and if you have concerns about whether a child is making adequate progress, share your record keeping with the speech and language specialist in your school system.

***Informal Measures for Assessing Vocabulary.*** As a teacher, you have the unique opportunity to monitor children's vocabulary growth because you are a major contributor to classroom discourse. You know at which level the words have been introduced and supported. For instance, if you teach the Tier Two word (Beck et al., 2002) "fearless" while reading *Tough Boris* (Fox, 1994) and then extend the children's experiences with the word through supportive instructional strategies, you can expect the word to eventually become part of the children's active vocabulary. Quick oral check-ins, such as "Would you be fearless if you hid behind the door?" or "Can you tell about a time when you were fearless?", are one way to see whether the children understand the word; but you might also want to give the students opportunities to explain the word in writing. For younger children, you can ask them to draw and label a picture of someone or something that is fearless. They can then explain their drawings in partnerships.

Word knowledge can also be assessed through multiple-choice activities, but they do not really measure a student's active use of words. Beck et al. (2002)

FIGURE 1.2  **Oral Language Samples from Kindergarten Students**

Alex: "Oh yeah, my dad broughted in the drinks."

Sam: "I goed to bed at 7:30."

Marie: "When I got up, my leg, it was like, cracked."

Sarah: "I thought it was a poodle, you said a dog."
  (Teacher: "A poodle is a type of dog.")

John: "I shoveled in the snow."

Peter: "I throwed snowballs."

Fred: "I watched [watch tid] the football game."

recommend using some simple strategies, beginning with the obvious, "Ask students what words mean," and then use other strategies such as, "'Tell about a time you were____'" or "'Describe some things that make a person____'" (p. 97). In other words, ask students to use their own language to explain the meaning of a word so that you can assess whether or not they really understand the word. After all, the goal is helping children develop active and accurate uses of words.

### Summary of Procedures for Assessing Phonological Awareness and Oral Language Development

Both formal and informal testing procedures can be used to monitor and evaluate oral language development in the areas of phonological awareness and vocabulary; but it is primarily through informal assessments that teachers monitor pragmatics and syntax in oral language development during the elementary grades. Identifying learners' strengths and weaknesses in oral language is important to children's overall literacy development since research directly correlates rhyming abilities, phonemic awareness, and vocabulary acquisition with reading success. Each area of oral language development is linked to the others; by examining and monitoring a child's growing control over phonological awareness, pragmatics, syntax, and vocabulary, you will be better equipped to develop appropriate instructional approaches.

# INSTRUCTIONAL APPROACHES FOR TEACHING PHONOLOGICAL AWARENESS AND ORAL LANGUAGE SKILLS

Children learn language by using language (Halliday, 1982; Piaget, 1965; Vygotsky, 1962). Students need ample opportunities throughout the school day to talk so that they can practice their growing control over the multiple demands of our language system (Clay, 1991). Language learning requires time to talk, time to write, time to read, and time to ponder. Natural learning situations allow students to become collaborators within a learning community as they journey through their discoveries and investigations in all subjects and content areas, all the while using language as they learn about language and learn through language.

### Instructional Approaches for Building Phonological Awareness Skills and Oral Language Skills in All Students

Immersion and demonstration are the two conditions that most influence children's natural language development, providing you can actively engage them (Cambourne, 1995). How does this engagement translate into daily classroom experiences? First, at any grade level, you will want to incorporate speaking and listening opportunities into a wide variety of contexts. Think carefully about the balance of listening and speaking as you plan your school day. What instructional groupings provide the most opportunity for students to talk? When children use language to express their thoughts, they become active learners rather than passive receivers of language; in other words, they are producing language rather than simply receiving language.

***Classroom Practices That Support the Development of Phonological Awareness.*** Opitz (2000, p. 13) states that for most children, phonological awareness is "caught" rather than taught, which means that children must internally *feel* the playfulness and the underlying melodies of our language.

Because the rhymes, songs, and chants of childhood provide a foundation for language learning, it is imperative that children have numerous exposures to playful language. Many classrooms include singing, chanting, and reciting during each day's opening routines. Children love the familiarity of these daily routines, and repeated exposures to rhymes and familiar language provide children with shared experiences that create a common language. Musical accompaniments such as wooden sticks and shakers add sound effects to oral recitations. Gestures and sign language that accompany songs and rhymes also help children integrate the meaning and sequences of old favorites such as "The Itsy Bitsy Spider."

Although structured exposure may be enough for most children to successfully develop phonological awareness, some children will require a more explicit introduction to language patterns. It is thus important for you to be aware of the phonological awareness skills progression, as well as the sound-to-letter sequence (phonics) that your particular school has adopted, in order to integrate oral language objectives into the overall literacy program. Although phonological awareness in its purest form refers only to using sounds, adding the corresponding letters to these activities helps contribute to reading success (Armbruster et al., 2001; Gunning, 2006).

For an excellent resource filled with research-based instructional activities, see the book *Phonemic Awareness in Young Children* (Adams et al., 1998), mentioned earlier because of its useful group assessments.

*Rhyming Lessons.* Nursery rhymes are a time-honored method to introduce or reinforce rhyming. Nursery rhymes can be used to create word games with a deleted rhyming word or syllable that the group must fill in: "Hickety, pickety, my black hen, she lays eggs for gentle_____." Children love to supply the rhyme, and in doing so they gain confidence to produce rhyme pairs on their own. Many children's books that use rhyming patterns lend themselves to interactive read-alouds that engage children as they practice active listening through stories. Cunningham (2003) recommends books such as *The Hungry Thing* and *There's a Wocket in My Pocket* to support the production of rhymes through shared reading. She also describes an activity known as "Rounding Up Rhymes" (2000), which should follow a read-aloud that contains rhyming pairs. Encourage children to listen for rhyming words as you *reread* several pages at a time. Cunningham (2000) also recommends listing the identified pairs on separate index cards, keeping only those that have pairs with similar spelling patterns. In this way, the children will be able to connect sounds of language to printed language; you can also use the rhyming pairs later for matching games. Older children enjoy reading through rhyming dictionaries and discovering unusual rhymes when they are brainstorming or drafting poems, jingles, songs, or stories. Teachers, too, can model this process during writing demonstrations and word investigations.

*Syllable Lessons.* When children first arrive at school, they are interested in knowing the names of their classmates. As children are introduced, you might want to have them clap syllables as they recite each other's names. Each child then has an opportunity to hear his or her name chanted; the class also gets a chance to break each name into chunks and count the syllables. One technique for "feeling" each syllable is to place the back of one hand under your jaw. When saying a multisyllabic name such as "Anthony," you can identify each syllable by how many times your jaw drops. Have the children try this procedure with a few multisyllabic words.

You can also demonstrate a practical application of syllabication when you are reading aloud to the children and modeling the process of chunking unfamiliar words and names during decoding. As you introduce and examine new vocabulary words, break them into their syllabic units to help children practice the pronunciation of the new words; add visuals to reinforce correct articulation. For instance, when introducing the word "frequently," write it on chart paper as: fre-quent-ly.

Poetry is also a useful medium for teaching syllables. The cadence of poetry is often based on the number of syllables; thus a study of poetry lends itself to identifying syllables. Think of haiku; the five, seven, five lines are about the syllables, not the words. Oral recitations such as "choral speaking" (children reciting in a shared voice) and "read and response" (in which the teacher reads a line and the children immediately repeat it) are two techniques that offer children a chance to not only hear the cadence but also practice the varied syllabic stress within words and sentences.

*Onset and Rime Instruction.* Children can develop the ability to blend onsets and rimes through guided wordplay. A teacher might say, "If you add /m/ to *at*, what word do you get?" The child would respond, "Mat." Onsets become more complex when they are made up of several consonant sounds known as *blends*, as in the word *street*: /s/ /t/ /r/. When you first introduce this blending task, you will want to guide children carefully through the progressing levels of difficulty, beginning with single consonant onsets, adding digraphs (two letters that represent one phoneme) such as /sh/, and then adding blends such as the "str" in "street" (Gunning, 2006). Once children have learned how to isolate the initial sounds in words, their attention can be turned to an even more precise level of phonological awareness: the individual phonemes within simple words or syllables.

At emergent and early levels, onsets and rimes can also be taught through a shared reading of big books by the whole class or in a small-group setting. You can mask (i.e., cover with a small piece of paper or Post-it note) the endings of words and ask children to supply the rime based on the clue. Also during shared writing and morning messages, you might leave off parts of words and later ask children to help supply the missing sounds, as in "Good morning, b____and g____."

Another way to help children develop knowledge of onsets and rimes is through whole-class scavenger hunts. For instance, you can ask, "How many words can we make using the word family 'at'?" Through the use of an ABC chart, children can systematically explore the possible onsets that make words when combined with the rime "at." For instance, you can begin with the letter *b*: "b-at, *bat*. Is this a word?" Next move to *c*: "c–at. Is this a word?" "d-at. Is this a word?" Some students will include consonant digraphs and various blends. As they explore the possibilities, be sure to record and post their findings on a chart.

ABC books also promote the identification of beginning sounds in words, many using alliteration and other wordplay. See Figure 1.3 for a list of recommended ABC books; keep in mind, however, that many more equally delightful books are available, including those on a range of topics and with a range of readability levels. Consider dedicating a shelf in your classroom library to ABC books for easy access.

Tongue twisters are appropriate for all ages. Children enjoy identifying, pronouncing, and creating tongue twisters such as the classic, "Sue sells seashells down by the seashore." Another related activity for older children is the creation of acrostic poems using the first letter of their names or some other important topic to begin each line of poetry.

*Phonemic Awareness.* Children can be taught to use their fingers to "stretch out" the sounds of words when working in whole-class settings. One way to do this is to use a rubber band analogy to help students think about the

FIGURE 1.3 **A Sampling of Recommended ABC Books**

Bayer, J. (1984). *A My Name Is Alice*. New York: Dial.

Cohen, I. (1997). *ABC Discovery: An Alphabet Book of Picture Puzzles*. New York: Mulberry Books.

Elting, M., & Folsom, M. (1980). *Q Is for Duck*. New York: Clarion Books.

Feelings, M., & Feelings, T. (1985). *Jambo Means Hello: Swahili Alphabet Book*. New York: Dial.

Hepworth, C. (1992). ***Antics! An Alphabet Anthology***. New York: Putnam Books.

Isadora, R. (1999). *ABC Pop!* New York: Viking Press.

Lobel, A. (1981). *On Market Street*. New York: Greenwillow Books.

Martin, B., Jr., & Archambault, J. (1991) *Chicka Chicka Boom Boom*. New York: Scholastic.

Musgrove, M. (1977). *Ashanti to Zulu: African Traditions*. New York: Dell.

Pallotta, J. (many titles encompassing a wide range of topics). Watertown, MA: Charlesbridge Publishing.

Suess, Dr. (1963). *Dr. Suess's ABC Book*. New York: Random House.

individual sounds in a word. If you consistently use your whole hand to "clap syllables" and your fingers to "stretch out sounds," children will more easily be able to distinguish the difference between bigger "chunks" of words and the individual sounds within each syllable. Initially, phonemic awareness is best taught and practiced using two-sound words such as "me" or three-sound words such as "mat" (Gunning, 2006).

When kindergarten and Grade 1 students are first learning how to identify each sound (or phoneme) in a word, you can use counters from manipulative math tools, modeling on an overhead projector as students push one counter each time they articulate a sound. This is a modified version of "Elkonin Boxes." Elkonin Boxes are little squares that are drawn on a piece of paper to represent the number of sounds in a word. For instance, in the word *cat,* three squares would be drawn in a row, each large enough to hold a token or counter. Children are then asked to say a word slowly, pushing a token into each box as a new sound is identified. This technique can be used to support the identification of individual phonemes in words (Elkonin, 1973). (See the photo on page 31.)

Students can move to letter cards or magnetic letters once they can identify the names of letters. Eventually, phoneme tasks such as deletion, addition, and substitution can be added. As students learn to write letters, you can move this activity to individual whiteboards or spelling notebooks. Older children can learn to hear the sounds in each syllable as they stretch out words to encode them in their writing. By modeling the practical uses of phonemic awareness during writing demonstrations, you can help children identify the value and purpose of phoneme segmentation, deletion, and substitution.

***Classroom Practices That Support the Development of Pragmatics.*** Children learn the underlying rules of pragmatics best when teachers explicitly demonstrate and describe the behaviors associated within various contexts. Let's revisit the opening vignette of Miss Allen reminding her first graders to use a "1-foot voice." As you already know, we cannot assume that "telling" a child to do something is sufficient for learning.

Successful imitation is more likely to occur if children are supported through a task analysis of both the obvious and the subtle actions involved (Denton & Kriete, 2000). "This is what it looks like when you are talking in a partnership," states Miss Allen as she physically models how to sit in close proximity to another person. "And this is what it sounds like," continues the teacher as she demonstrates the voicing of a sentence that is intended for her partner only. Naming and demonstrating the actions of using a "1-foot voice" make this classroom routine crystal clear to children and prevents confusions in the future. Figure 1.4 shows how a chart can be useful.

Following the explicit instructional period, children must be given multiple opportunities to practice the specific skills until they can regulate their own volume controls and physical behaviors. Many classroom routines such as "turn to a neighbor and talk" can be established using this process, enabling talk to be used effectively and frequently in the classroom and school setting.

To support the development of oral presentation skills, it is useful to analyze the process through a task analysis. You might ask children to pay close attention to all of your observable behaviors during a presentation you give as a demonstration. Collectively, the class can prepare a checklist or rubric that identifies the desired behaviors. Students can also prepare a written outline for an upcoming presentation by listing three main points—an opening, a middle, and an end—thus freeing up their concentration on delivery rather than content. Oral rehearsals in smaller group settings might also help students gain confidence and set appropriate goals before presenting to a larger group.

Willa is using manipulatives to segment the sounds in the word "mat."

***Classroom Practices That Support the Development of Syntax.*** As stated earlier in this chapter, children should not be corrected when they are trying to communicate through oral language; rather, the focus should be on the message itself. The most effective way to support a child who speaks with immature syntactical structures is to rephrase the sentence using correct grammar. Modeling standard English also works well during

FIGURE 1.4  "One-Foot Voice": A Classroom Chart Describing
            Specific Behaviors for Partnership Communication

| Sounds Like: | Looks Like: |
|---|---|
| • *a murmur of voices in the classroom* | • *each partner sitting eye to eye* |
| • *quiet, low-level sounds* | • *each partner sitting knee to knee* |
| • *occasional but controlled laughter* | • *one partner talking, one listening* |
| • *almost like humming* | • *conversational, taking turns* |

interactions with English Language Learners (Echevarria, Vogt, & Short, 2004). When a child states, "My grandma eated the cookies I baked," the teacher could reply, "Oh, your grandma ate the cookies you baked? Did she like them?"

Although the emphasis should be on the intended communication, you will want to note the syntactical errors. These issues could later be incorporated into explicit lessons during writing or language study. For instance, after children share weekend stories orally in cooperative groups, you might demonstrate how to retell a weekend story in writing. This could include telling an anecdote about a food you ate, thus reinforcing the use of the verb "ate." You could also create a shared writing activity that uses a sentence frame such as, "Today for breakfast I ate ____." The quick publication and shared reading of a structured sentence activity can naturally reinforce the use of an irregular verb form such as "ate." This method requires thoughtful and deliberate integration of skills based on the formative assessments you collect throughout the day.

In the upper grades children can begin "grammar" lessons by investigating a particular concept in texts. To teach past tense forms of verbs, you can have the class list all of the verbs from a page in a story. Through an analysis of the collected words, students can generate questions, rules, and discussion around various forms of past tense verbs. Figure 1.5 shows a chart that second graders created when identifying the various pronunciations for the past tense form *-ed*. When the teacher fosters a sense of curiosity about the syntactical structure of our language, a child's awareness and control of language choice can become more personalized.

***Classroom Practices That Support Vocabulary Development.*** Children should be exposed to rich language every day through speech, books, and other printed materials. If you demonstrate an interest in words, your students are more likely to also appreciate words. Teach new words in a meaningful context to help children attach the words to their existing mental structures or schemata (Beck et al., 2002). For instance, if a child learns about the word *giant* while reading and imagining the giant in the story "Jack and the Beanstalk," it isn't necessary to "preteach" this concept, since the meaning of "giant" becomes very clear through the context and illustrations provided by the story. Children are more likely to remember a new word or concept if it is grounded in something meaningful or memorable and if the word is revisited and repeated often.

If it is unlikely that a child will be able to unlock the meaning of a word through the context of the story when you are reading aloud, one effective instructional strategy is to briefly pause and identify the meaning as you are

FIGURE 1.5  **Second-Grade Collection of "-ed" words**

**Different Sounds of "-ed "**

| /d/ | /ed/ | /t/ |
|---|---|---|
| played | painted | walked |
| leveled | forwarded | talked |
| married | | hoped |
| opened | | |

reading aloud. For instance, in Mem Fox's book *Tough Boris* (1994), she describes the pirate as such: "He was scruffy. All pirates are scruffy." The illustration does show a disheveled-looking pirate, but that does not really ensure that a young child will understand the word. You might simply add an aside during the read-aloud: "That means he doesn't shave or comb his hair" and then keep right on reading. At the end of the book, as children discuss the story and reread it, they will become more familiar with the new word "scruffy" in the context of the story.

But even this doesn't guarantee that children will remember the word; thus you will also need to provide an opportunity to do further word study. Besides offering a student-friendly definition, Beck et al. (2002) suggest that children should learn how to say a new word phonetically, repeating it several times as it becomes comfortable to pronounce. Next, help them broaden their understanding of the word by having them think of other examples of how the word can be used in the world. For example, you could ask children to describe times when they or someone they know looked scruffy. The word can be extended to the description of a pet or to another meaningful context identified by the children. After analyzing the word more thoroughly, the teacher can put the titles of read-aloud books on a chart (or make a copy of the book covers using a copy machine) and attach up to three new words that the class discovered during their read-aloud of each book (Cunningham & Allington, 2007).

Children can also make personal dictionaries to "record" new words that they select from their reading (Rudell, 2001). Each new word can be added to pages labeled in alphabetical order along with some meaningful format for remembering the word. You can model various ways to define and record word meanings using a grade-appropriate variation of a definition map, which is a graphic representation of a word (often designed to look like a web) that includes prompts to help students think deeply about the meaning of the word. For example, with the word "scruffy," you can model a representation such as this:

"What is it?" [a word that means messy or unclean]

"What's it like?" [when you wake up and rush off to school without brushing your hair]

"What are some examples?" [wearing torn or wrinkled clothes; a man who doesn't shave for several days; the pirate in *Tough Boris*] (Buell, 2001; Schwartz & Raphael, 1985)

Adaptations can include other grade-appropriate prompts such as "Add a synonym," "Draw a picture," "Write a definition in your own words," "Add an antonym," or "Use the word in a sentence." Personalized dictionaries are useful tools when children are empowered to control the content.

Also, word sorts, which are often used to support spelling and decoding, can be used in a variety of creative ways to expand children's vocabulary (Bear, Invernizzi, Templeton, & Johnston, 2000). To do word sorts with a whole class, prepare a collection of word cards for each partnership. Guide the children in placing the words into groups, using specific categories that match your teaching objective. For example, you might ask students to "place all the action words in one pile and all the describing words in another pile." Following each word sort, be sure to ask children to explain why they placed words where they did. Word sorts can be used in all curricular areas.

### Instructional Approaches for Building Phonological Awareness Skills and Oral Language Skills for Students with Specific Needs

Children who start school without a language-rich background or who have specific language disabilities often need more specifically designed language explorations that are based on identified needs rather than on age-related curriculum standards (Seifert, 2004). In this case, small-group (or sometimes individual/specialized) instructional settings allow teachers to tailor the instruction to the specific learning needs of the child (Gunning, 2006).

***Explicit and Individualized Phonological Awareness Activities.*** Screening materials and diagnostic assessments can help you identify whether a child has specific areas of difficulty in phonological awareness. As you examine the results of an assessment, choose the least complex area of phonological awareness in which the child first begins to show confusion. For instance, if a child cannot determine whether two words such as *cat* and *sat* are the same or different, you may want to start with simple sounds from the environment (such as tapping on a desk or snapping your fingers) to focus the child's auditory awareness and to help the child begin to understand the concepts of same and different (Adams et al., 1998). Plan instruction carefully, building skills by adding incremental complexities. As children move on to words, keep instructional activities interactive and geared to the children's developmental level, and provide opportunities for children to "feel" the sounds with their mouths as they produce them (Seifert, 2004). Listed below are a few ways to build supportive and successful sequences for children who struggle with developing phonological awareness.

If a child has difficulty with rhyming, begin with pictures and interactive, instructional conversations (Gunning, 2006). You can use picture cards that have rhyming counterparts to support instruction without the use of print. The child should *first* practice naming each picture and afterward try to find pairs that rhyme, such as *sheep* and *jeep*, since not knowing a word will interfere with the child's ability to learn about the word (Adams et al., 1998).

For children who have syllabication difficulties, begin with two-syllable words and gradually move toward having children learn how to discern the multiple syllables in longer words. You can use gestures such as clapping, foot tapping, or the jaw dropping described earlier. Some teachers use Elkonin's (1973) technique when they have children listen for sounds in words in order to identify larger word parts such as syllables and sentences. In this process, children use tokens to identify each word in a sentence, pushing one token for each word. For example, in the sentence, "I went to school," a child would push one token for each word, four in all. Eventually, you can cut up sentence strips and help a child push one word at a time, using the student's own language in simple sentence structures to bring the sounds of language to print in a meaningful way.

To help children who are struggling to hear the individual sounds in words, Gunning (2006) offers several suggestions. Start with onset-rime instruction by helping children develop phoneme identity at the beginning of words, slowly emphasizing sounds in words that begin with the same consonant sounds such as *man* and *mop*. As you move into segmenting whole words, begin with two-sound words such as "me." Use the Elkonin technique and have the child push a token into each box as he articulates the phoneme. Move to three-sound words when the child is ready. Be sure to use a similar pattern until the child's identification of sounds becomes automatic. Begin with tokens but gradually move to letter tiles or magnetic letters as the child progresses. Later you can help children move toward learning the spelling of the words by supplying three letters in a mixed-up fashion and asking the children to put the letters into the correct order as they say and hear each sound, as in /h/ /a/ /t/.

***Explicit and Individualized Pragmatics and Syntax Lessons.***  Children who need extra support in oral language development can be homogenously grouped for skill development in pragmatics or syntax. For instance, a pragmatics lesson can be designed with taking turns as the learning objective. A small group of children can be brought together to identify what taking turns looks like and sounds like and then practice the skill with an oral language topic such as weekend stories. Sometimes role-playing can help children practice appropriate language behaviors. To role-play, bring together a small group of children and describe a hypothetical scenario that illustrates the topic being explored. For instance, you can take on the role of a person who dominates a conversation while the children try to take their turns telling a weekend story. Decide together how the group could function more smoothly and then practice taking turns.

Sometimes visual reminders are helpful when a child is having difficulty monitoring the level of her voice. For example, you might try using a personalized visual reminder such as a number system corresponding to volume levels, with 0 representing no volume, 1 representing a personal conversation, 2 representing a voice projected to the whole class, and 3 representing a loud "outside" voice.

For children who have immature syntactical language constructions or who have difficulty articulating words clearly and distinctly, it is important to schedule time to listen carefully and respond in private interactive conversations throughout the day, focusing primarily on meaning, but modeling standard language usage as you do so. Conversational language between teachers and students is key in a classroom setting (Allington, 2006) because it indicates to students that the teacher values and respects their thoughts and ideas. Conversational language also helps children develop "range and flexibility" in their sentence patterns (Clay, 1991, p. 37). Some teachers try to schedule themselves to eat snacks or lunch with a "chat group" of students who need particular support in language development a few times a week.

Listening centers also support oral language development and, if you include text, they help connect printed language to the stories, songs, and poems that children hear. Audiobooks allow children to hear the cadence, vocabulary, and syntax of book language; they also provide access to texts that are beyond a student's independent reading level.

You can also use small-group interactive read-alouds to foster listening comprehension and oral language development. These supported and structured group discussions give children the opportunity to express themselves as they receive appropriate responses from adults and classmates, which reinforces standard grammar and discussion practice. Shared reading and writing activities also help children develop oral language skills in pragmatics and grammar; each will be described in more detail in subsequent chapters.

***Explicit Vocabulary Instruction.***  Children who have deficits in vocabulary development need intensive intervention. Because vocabulary is closely linked to reading success, these children will have a difficult time catching up unless their needs are addressed, especially since fluent readers are continuously exposed to more and more words as their reading skills flourish (Stanovich, 1986). For low-achieving students, vocabulary instruction must be deliberate, frequent, and, most importantly, linked to meaningful contexts.

Gunning (2006) recommends a four-part program: (1) Choose words to teach students as they are needed; (2) specifically plan to introduce between 5 and 10 words each week; (3) have students select five words each week on their own; (4) include daily small-group instruction in word identification skills such as morphemic analysis, and include conversation as well. Gunning also suggests that students keep personal vocabulary notebooks to record their new words. Striving learners need abundant opportunities to actively use the language they are hearing and reading.

## LOOKING CLOSELY AT ONE CHILD'S ASSESSMENTS FROM STRAND 1 OF THE LITERACY PROFILE

Willa's assessments for phonological awareness and oral language were administered in late February of her first-grade year. See Figure 1.6 for a sample of how we recorded Willa's phonological awareness and oral language development on Strand 1 of the Literacy Profile.

### Results of Oral Language and Phonological Awareness Assessments

Willa's teacher used the "Formative Assessment of Phonological Awareness" tool in Appendix A-2 to identify Willa's awareness of the various phonological tasks and then developed a focused instructional plan using that information. She also assessed Willa's overall oral language primarily using the interactions and conversations that took place during the informal assessment periods.

***Willa's Phonological Awareness Development.*** The results from each of the four general areas of phonological awareness are briefly described below.

*Rhymes.* Willa is able to recognize and produce rhymes. She even used nonsense words in two cases when she was unable to think of a word from her oral vocabulary, as in *fun-lun* and *feet-leet.*

*Syllables.* Willa does not completely understand the concept of syllables, but she did score 3 out of 6 words correctly. She seemed to confuse phonemes and syllables, as in *farm* "3" and *shovel* "4." For *remember,* Willa replied that it has two syllables. She was able to blend all six of the words in the syllable-blending portion of the assessment, which indicates that she can synthesize the parts of language into a whole.

*Onsets and Rimes.* In the onset-rime blending, Willa had only one confusion, stating *fog* for *frog.* This follows with the general sequence of a child's first recognizing beginning consonants and then recognizing digraphs and blends.

*Phonemic Awareness.* In phonemic awareness assessments, Willa scored 6 out of 6 in the blending tasks. When asked to blend /s/ /u/ /n/, she replied, "Which kind of sun, the sun in the sky or a son like a boy?" This question, although not significant for phoneme blending, indicates that Willa is aware of multiple uses of words that sound the same. Willa was able to accurately segment three out of six words in the phoneme segmentation task. Specifically, she was able to accurately identify the phonemes in words with

EMERGENT

EARLY

| Strand *Question & Sample Assessment Tools* | Pre-K – Early K | Late K | Early–Mid Grade 1 |
|---|---|---|---|
| **6. Comprehension and Reading Response**<br>*How is the child developing an ability to understand text and demonstrate thoughtful responses to text?*<br><br>**Sample Assessment Tools**<br>· Gates MacGinitie Test<br>· Developmental Reading Assessment<br>· Discussions<br>· Retellings<br>· Journals<br>· Drawings<br>· Observation notes<br>· Performances<br>· Conferences<br>· Constructed Responses | Actively listens to a story being read aloud<br><br>Offers basic emotional response (likes/dislikes) to what is read | Connects what is read to background knowledge<br><br>Begins to retell parts of stories | Communicates basic "gist" of story line through drawings, story maps, or other representations<br><br>Identifies main characters of narrative text<br><br>Retells the beginning, middle, and end of story<br><br>Tells what was learned from informational text |
| **7. Writing Strategies, Processes, and Dispositions**<br>*To what extent does the child use the processes of writing? How engaged is the child with writing?*<br><br>**Sample Assessment Tools**<br>· Elementary Writing Attitude Survey<br>· Portfolios<br>· Writing samples<br>· Interviews<br>· Self-evaluation | With prompting, generates ideas for drawing or dictates ideas to an adult | Draws, labels, and writes to express ideas<br><br>Often generates original ideas and responds to others' prompts<br><br>Participates in shared writing activities | Writes with increasing independence<br><br>Uses resources such as word walls and letter-sound visuals for support<br><br>With support, will reread what has been written |
| **8. Writing Effectiveness**<br>*How is the child's independent writing developing with regard to purpose, organization, details, and voice/tone?*<br><br>**Sample Assessment Tools**<br>· Writing samples (prompted and/or independent writing) with checklists, scales, rubrics, or portfolios | Draws pictures to express ideas; describes content of drawing<br><br>Writes at least part of first name | Writes labels that describe drawings<br><br>Written messages consist of a phrase or short sentence | Writes one to two understandable sentences to tell information or tell a story (often a personal narrative) |
| **9. Spelling**<br>*How is the child's spelling developing in independent writing?*<br><br>**Sample Assessment Tools**<br>· Writing samples (prompted and independent writing) with scales, rubrics, or checklists<br>· Elementary Spelling Inventory<br>· Developmental Spelling Analysis | May use lines and letter-like forms to accompany drawings | Uses beginning and ending consonants to spell some words, demonstrating some sound-symbol correspondence (*KT* for *CAT*) | Represents each phoneme in a word with a grapheme (*LUV* for *love*); beginning to use some short vowels |
| **10. Writing Conventions and Handwriting**<br>*To what degree does the child use acceptable conventions of grammar, usage, and mechanics in written language? How is handwriting developing?*<br><br>**Sample Assessment Tools**<br>· Writing samples and writing prompts, with scoring guides | Orients the page to start drawing or writing<br><br>Uses a variety of tools for writing or drawing (pencils, crayons, etc.) | Uses preferred hand consistently for writing<br><br>Writes from left to right, top to bottom<br><br>Writes most uppercase letters legibly | Usually leaves spaces between words<br><br>Includes lowercase letters in writing<br><br>Attempts to use end punctuation |

Name: _____

| Late Grade 1–Early Grade 2 | Late Grade 2–Early Grade 3 | Late Grade 3–Early Grade 4 | Late Grade 4 |
|---|---|---|---|
| Manipulates phonemes by deleting and substituting | Uses basic subject-verb agreement correctly | Shows a developing awareness of slang, jargon, and different language styles | Flexibly uses expressive language and gestures in a variety of language contexts |
| Develops appropriate audience behaviors | Recognizes that language can be used figuratively | Paraphrases to explain or describe information learned | Uses knowledge of word structure (common roots, bases, and affixes) to expand vocabulary |
| Uses more descriptive language and more complex sentences | Develops a range of delivery skills and organizational skills for presentations | Understands multiple meanings of common homonyms | Expands vocabulary |
| Seeks clarification of unfamiliar vocabulary | Shows awareness of audience by varying tone, volume, pace, word choice | Demonstrates understanding of common prefixes | |
| Expands vocabulary | Demonstrates understanding of concepts of synonym and antonym | Expands vocabulary | |
| | Expands vocabulary | | |
| Identifies and utilizes various parts of a book: title page; table of contents | Identifies and utilizes index, glossary in informational text | Identifies and utilizes text features, such as tables, diagrams, headings, boldface, and timelines | Identifies and utilizes increasingly sophisticated text features, such as subheadings and captions during reading |
| Controls voice-print matching including words with multiple syllables | Identifies and attends to commas and quotation marks during reading | Identifies and attends to more sophisticated print conventions, such as italics, colons, and parentheses during reading | |
| Shows full understanding of the alphabetic principle | Uses knowledge of common syllable types (closed, vowel teams, *r* controlled) and patterns to decode one-syllable "regular" words, such as *shade* and *crown* and some multisyllabic words, such as *uncurled* and *protecting* | Uses knowledge of syllable types, patterns, and affixes to decode multisyllabic words, such as *freckled, pilot,* and *predicting* and applies this in reading multisyllabic words | Flexibly uses knowledge of all six syllable types, patterns, affixes, and common roots to decode multisyllabic words, such as *respectable* and *portion* |
| Reads one-syllable short-vowel words and words with silent *e* | | | |
| Reads words with blends and inflected endings | | | |
| Uses familiar word patterns to decode common two-syllable words, such as *happen* and *sticky* | | | |
| Reads basic contractions and compound words | | | |
| Uses multiple cues and self-corrects with increasing frequency when meaning is altered | Predicts and confirms during reading | Flexibly uses a variety of comprehension strategies, such as predicting, rereading, and making connections | Flexibly uses a variety of comprehension strategies, including analyzing text structure and utilizing text features |
| | Begins to self-monitor comprehension; often rereads as a fix-up strategy | Uses simple context clues to determine the meaning of unfamiliar vocabulary | Uses context clues to determine the meaning of unfamiliar vocabulary |
| Reads four or more little books, short text selections, or two to three short chapters each day | Makes connections during reading | Reads the equivalent of at least two books a month | Reads the equivalent of at least two books a month |
| | Reads approximately two books a month or two chapters a day | | |
| Can sustain reading for at least 10 minutes (independently or with a partner) | Can sustain silent reading independently for at least 15 minutes a day | Can sustain silent, independent reading for at least 20 minutes | Can sustain silent, independent reading for at least 30 minutes |
| Independently reads books, such as *Little Bear* and *Frog and Toad Are Friends* with acceptable accuracy and developing fluency | Independently reads books, such as *Freckle Juice* and *Cam Jansen* with acceptable accuracy and fluency | Independently reads books, such as *The Stories Julian Tells* and *Ramona the Brave* with acceptable accuracy and fluency | Independently reads books, such as *The Story of Harriet Tubman* and *Bunnicula* with acceptable accuracy and fluency |
| Text Level Target: _____ | Text Level Target: _____ | Text Level Target: _____ | Text Level Target: _____ |

# LITERACY PROFILE

**TEACHER TIP:** Date, initial, and color code each of your entries.

EMERGENT

EARLY

| Strand *Question & Sample Assessment Tools* | Pre-K – Early K | Late K | Early–Mid Grade 1 |
|---|---|---|---|
| **1. Phonological Awareness and Oral Language Development**<br>*To what extent is the child developing phonological awareness and oral language skills?*<br>**Sample Assessment Tools**<br>• Yopp-Singer<br>• Phoneme Segmentation Fluency (DIBELS)<br>• Comprehensive Test of Phonological Processing (CTOPP)<br>• Peabody Picture Vocabulary Test (PPVT)<br>• Comprehensive Receptive and Expressive Vocabulary Test (CREVT)<br>• Observation Notes<br>• Checklists<br>• Vocabulary Probes<br>• Oral presentations with rubrics<br>• Language samples | With support, recites nursery rhymes<br><br>With support, recognizes, predicts, and completes rhymes<br><br>Expresses thoughts and needs with phrases and simple sentences<br><br>Participates in two-way communications, mostly staying on topic<br><br>Expands vocabulary | Produces rhymes<br><br>Claps parts of multisyllabic words<br><br>Blends syllables into words<br><br>Isolates beginning sounds of words<br><br>Isolates the final sounds of words<br><br>Blends onsets and rimes<br><br>Follows two-step directions<br><br>Self-corrects some language inconsistencies<br><br>Expands vocabulary | Blends phonemes<br><br>Segments phonemes in simple words<br><br>Uses correct sentence structure most of the time<br><br>Asks for clarification when needed<br><br>Expands vocabulary |
| **2. Concepts of Print, Letter Identification, and Text Features**<br>*How familiar is the child with concepts of print, letter identification, and text features?*<br>**Sample Assessment Tools**<br>• Concepts About Print<br>• Letter ID test<br>• Letter Naming Fluency<br>• Observation notes<br>• Concepts of Print checklist<br>• Untimed Letter Naming Test | Recognizes own first name<br><br>Notices difference between print and pictures<br><br>Turns pages of a book from beginning to end<br><br>Identifies the book cover and where the story starts | Follows print from left to right; knows to sweep back left<br><br>Can identify difference between words and letters<br><br>Recognizes and names most letters of the alphabet | Recognizes and names all uppercase and lowercase letters<br><br>Controls voice-print matching with one- to two-syllable words<br><br>Identifies and attends to periods when used at the end of sentences during reading<br><br>Identifies and attends to question marks and exclamation points during reading |
| **3. Decoding Skills and Word Analysis**<br>*To what extent is the child learning the decoding and word-identification skills needed for reading?*<br>**Sample Assessment Tools**<br>• Names Test<br>• Sound-symbol correspondence tasks<br>• Initial Sound Fluency (DIBELS)<br>• Sight word lists<br>• Running records<br>• Records of oral reading<br>• Quick Text Level Check-In<br>• Informal Phonics Surveys | Recognizes some sound–symbol correspondences | Produces sounds for most consonants<br><br>Knows 10–12 sight words | Produces sounds for all consonants and common consonant digraphs (*ch, sh, th, wh*)<br><br>Knows 20–50 sight words |
| **4. Reading Strategies, Processes, and Dispositions**<br>*To what extent does the child use early processing strategies and comprehension strategies during reading? How engaged is the child with reading?*<br>**Sample Assessment Tools**<br>• Running Records<br>• Records of oral reading<br>• Think-Alouds<br>• Interviews<br>• Observations and anecdotal notes<br>• Book logs<br>• Elementary Reading Attitude Survey | Uses pictures or pattern/repetition to read a story or environmental print "emergently"<br><br>Listens to books read aloud each day | Begins to use more than one cueing system to read, such as some finger pointing for visual information plus picture cues<br><br>Reads at least one or two little books, short text selections, or alphabet books each day | Uses more than one cueing system (meaning, visual, and language cues) and begins to cross-check independently<br><br>Reads two or three little books or short text selections each day |
| **5. Reading Accuracy and Fluency at Increasing Text Levels**<br>*To what degree is the child reading books of increasing complexity with accuracy and fluency?*<br>**Sample Assessment Tools**<br>• Running records<br>• Records of oral reading using benchmark books<br>• Quick Text Level Check-In<br>• Oral Reading Fluency (DIBELS)<br>• Three-Way Fluency Rubric<br><br>**Text Leveling approach used:** _____ | Reads some names and environmental print, such as family names, signs, labels, symbols | Reads simple, predictable, or decodable books (previously introduced), such as *Have You Seen My Cat* and *Monster Sandwich*<br><br><br>Text Level Target: _____ | Independently reads books, such as *Five Little Monkeys* and *All by Myself* (previously introduced) with acceptable accuracy<br><br>Text Level Target: _____ |

| Late Grade 1–Early Grade 2 | Late Grade 2–Early Grade 3 | Late Grade 3–Early Grade 4 | Late Grade 4 |
| --- | --- | --- | --- |
| Retelling and responses show developing understanding of story elements: character, problem, and solution<br><br>Identifies some key ideas and details after reading informational text<br><br>Answers both literal and basic inferential questions in response to text read | Retellings include: initiating event, setting, character, key events, and solution (reflecting appropriate inferences)<br><br>Uses some evidence from text to support responses to reading<br><br>Answers both literal and basic inferential questions, including questions that call for searching across parts of text, in response to text read<br><br>Identifies character traits | Identifies main ideas and supporting details from informational text<br><br>Identifies and describes story elements in narrative text<br><br>Makes inferences from what is read, including possible themes<br><br>Produces simple summaries of narrative and informational text read, paraphrasing as appropriate<br><br>Identifies character traits and provides supporting evidence<br><br>Recognizes author's craft: simile, descriptive language, and dialogue | Draws inferences, using examples and evidence from text, to support opinions and responses<br><br>Distinguishes fact from opinion, produces short summaries of informational text, and identifies author's purpose or message<br><br>Summarizes narrative text, identifies characters' changes over time, and identifies theme<br><br>Recognizes a variety of expository text structures used by authors: description, compare–contrast, problem–solution, time sequence, cause and effect<br><br>Describes author's craft by referring to literary devices, such as suspense, exaggeration, personification, and metaphor) |
| With support, uses prewriting strategies, such as making a plan, sketch, or map.<br><br>Writes independently<br><br>Adds on to what is written when prompted | Independently brainstorms and makes a written plan before writing<br><br>With support, revises by adding details<br><br>With some support, edits own work | Selects prewriting strategies to match the form of writing<br><br>Writing shows a broader range of topics and forms, reflecting a developing understanding of purpose and audience<br><br>Rereads own writing to see if it makes sense and to add details<br><br>Edits own work | Independently and flexibly uses steps of the writing process, including prewriting, drafting, revising, and editing<br><br>Writing shows a broader range of topics and forms, and reflects an understanding of purpose and audience<br><br>Revises for clarity of meaning and to enhance word choice<br><br>Reflects on growth as a writer and sets goals |
| Writes three to four understandable sentences on a single topic — to communicate information or tell a story | Writes a narrative with a beginning, middle, and end<br><br>Writes a simple procedure<br><br>When provided with a structure, writes short informational pieces including details relevant to the topic<br><br>With some support, writes poetry as a form of expression, using simple poetic forms | Writes narratives that include more than one character, details, and some dialogue<br><br>Writes procedures with steps, materials, and relevant vocabulary<br><br>Writes informational pieces with appropriate organization and relevant details<br><br>Writes poetry as a form of expression, using simple poetic forms | Writes narratives that include a clear problem and solution, as well as relevant and descriptive details<br><br>Writes procedures with clear directions and explanations<br><br>Writes informational pieces with clear organization, elaborated and relevant details, and appropriate citing of sources<br><br>Writes poetry as a form of expression, with a clear topic and use of sensory details |
| Represents most beginning and ending consonants, most consonant digraphs, and regular short vowels<br><br>Begins to spell silent *e* words<br><br>Spells grade-appropriate high-frequency words | Spells most words with blends, silent *e* and common vowel teams (*oa, ee, ai, ou*)<br><br>Spells many *r* controlled words correctly<br><br>Spells grade-appropriate high-frequency words | Spells past tense (*ed*) and most plural endings<br><br>Spells words with *r* controlled vowels and less common vowel teams (*oi, oy, igh*)<br><br>Spells most high-frequency words<br><br>Spells common homophones (*their/there; to/too*) | Applies spelling rules for inflected endings and affixes: doubling rule, changing *y* to *i*, dropping silent *e*<br><br>Uses a variety of strategies to correct own spelling |
| Uses capitals at beginning of sentences, lowercase within words<br><br>Uses periods appropriately at the end of sentences<br><br>Writes in complete sentences<br><br>Uses a consistent handwriting style, with spaces between words | Uses uppercase letters for proper nouns<br><br>Uses some expanded sentences in writing, such as compound sentences<br><br>Uses a variety of end punctuation | Uses commas for lists<br><br>Uses a variety of sentences, including compound or complex sentences<br><br>Uses commas in a list<br><br>Writes contractions with apostrophes<br><br>Uses accurate end punctuation (. ? !)<br><br>Can write in cursive with some support | Paragraph structure is evident in writing<br><br>Uses correct subject-verb agreement most of the time<br><br>Uses correct verb forms most of the time<br><br>Accurate use of common irregular verbs<br><br>Increasingly correct use of commas and quotation marks<br><br>Can write in cursive |

| Late Grade 1–Early Grade 2 | Late Grade 2–Early Grade 3 | Late Grade 3–Early Grade 4 | Late Grade 4 |
|---|---|---|---|
| Retelling and responses show developing understanding of story elements: character, problem, and solution<br><br>Identifies some key ideas and details after reading informational text<br><br>Answers both literal and basic inferential questions in response to text read | Retellings include: initiating event, setting, character, key events, and solution (reflecting appropriate inferences)<br><br>Uses some evidence from text to support responses to reading<br><br>Answers both literal and basic inferential questions, including questions that call for searching across parts of text, in response to text read<br><br>Identifies character traits | Identifies main ideas and supporting details from informational text<br><br>Identifies and describes story elements in narrative text<br><br>Makes inferences from what is read, including possible themes<br><br>Produces simple summaries of narrative and informational text read, paraphrasing as appropriate<br><br>Identifies character traits and provides supporting evidence<br><br>Recognizes author's craft: simile, descriptive language, and dialogue | Draws inferences, using examples and evidence from text, to support opinions and responses<br><br>Distinguishes fact from opinion, produces short summaries of informational text, and identifies author's purpose or message<br><br>Summarizes narrative text, identifies characters' changes over time, and identifies theme<br><br>Recognizes a variety of expository text structures used by authors: description, compare–contrast, problem–solution, time sequence, cause and effect<br><br>Describes author's craft by referring to literary devices, such as suspense, exaggeration, personification, and metaphor) |
| With support, uses prewriting strategies, such as making a plan, sketch, or map.<br><br>Writes independently<br><br>Adds on to what is written when prompted | Independently brainstorms and makes a written plan before writing<br><br>With support, revises by adding details<br><br>With some support, edits own work | Selects prewriting strategies to match the form of writing<br><br>Writing shows a broader range of topics and forms, reflecting a developing understanding of purpose and audience<br><br>Rereads own writing to see if it makes sense and to add details<br><br>Edits own work | Independently and flexibly uses steps of the writing process, including prewriting, drafting, revising, and editing<br><br>Writing shows a broader range of topics and forms, and reflects an understanding of purpose and audience<br><br>Revises for clarity of meaning and to enhance word choice<br><br>Reflects on growth as a writer and sets goals |
| Writes three to four understandable sentences on a single topic — to communicate information or tell a story | Writes a narrative with a beginning, middle, and end<br><br>Writes a simple procedure<br><br>When provided with a structure, writes short informational pieces including details relevant to the topic<br><br>With some support, writes poetry as a form of expression, using simple poetic forms | Writes narratives that include more than one character, details, and some dialogue<br><br>Writes procedures with steps, materials, and relevant vocabulary<br><br>Writes informational pieces with appropriate organization and relevant details<br><br>Writes poetry as a form of expression, using simple poetic forms | Writes narratives that include a clear problem and solution, as well as relevant and descriptive details<br><br>Writes procedures with clear directions and explanations<br><br>Writes informational pieces with clear organization, elaborated and relevant details, and appropriate citing of sources<br><br>Writes poetry as a form of expression, with a clear topic and use of sensory details |
| Represents most beginning and ending consonants, most consonant digraphs, and regular short vowels<br><br>Begins to spell silent *e* words<br><br>Spells grade-appropriate high-frequency words | Spells most words with blends, silent *e* and common vowel teams (*oa, ee, ai, ou*)<br><br>Spells many *r* controlled words correctly<br><br>Spells grade-appropriate high-frequency words | Spells past tense (*ed*) and most plural endings<br><br>Spells words with *r* controlled vowels and less common vowel teams (*oi, oy, igh*)<br><br>Spells most high-frequency words<br><br>Spells common homophones (*their/there; to/too*) | Applies spelling rules for inflected endings and affixes: doubling rule, changing *y* to *i*, dropping silent *e*<br><br>Uses a variety of strategies to correct own spelling |
| Uses capitals at beginning of sentences, lowercase within words<br><br>Uses periods appropriately at the end of sentences<br><br>Writes in complete sentences<br><br>Uses a consistent handwriting style, with spaces between words | Uses uppercase letters for proper nouns<br><br>Uses some expanded sentences in writing, such as compound sentences<br><br>Uses a variety of end punctuation | Uses commas for lists<br><br>Uses a variety of sentences, including compound or complex sentences<br><br>Uses commas in a list<br><br>Writes contractions with apostrophes<br><br>Uses accurate end punctuation (. ? !)<br><br>Can write in cursive with some support | Paragraph structure is evident in writing<br><br>Uses correct subject-verb agreement most of the time<br><br>Uses correct verb forms most of the time<br><br>Accurate use of common irregular verbs<br><br>Increasingly correct use of commas and quotation marks<br><br>Can write in cursive |

# LITERACY PROFILE

**TEACHER TIP:** Date, initial, and color code each of your entries.

EMERGENT

EARLY

| Strand *Question & Sample Assessment Tools* | Pre-K – Early K | Late K | Early–Mid Grade 1 |
|---|---|---|---|
| **1. Phonological Awareness and Oral Language Development**<br>*To what extent is the child developing phonological awareness and oral language skills?*<br>**Sample Assessment Tools**<br>• Yopp-Singer<br>• Phoneme Segmentation Fluency (DIBELS)<br>• Comprehensive Test of Phonological Processing (CTOPP)<br>• Peabody Picture Vocabulary Test (PPVT)<br>• Comprehensive Receptive and Expressive Vocabulary Test (CREVT)<br>• Observation Notes<br>• Checklists<br>• Vocabulary Probes<br>• Oral presentations with rubrics<br>• Language samples | With support, recites nursery rhymes<br><br>With support, recognizes, predicts, and completes rhymes<br><br>Expresses thoughts and needs with phrases and simple sentences<br><br>Participates in two-way communications, mostly staying on topic<br><br>Expands vocabulary | Produces rhymes<br><br>Claps parts of multisyllabic words<br><br>Blends syllables into words<br><br>Isolates beginning sounds of words<br><br>Isolates the final sounds of words<br><br>Blends onsets and rimes<br><br>Follows two-step directions<br><br>Self-corrects some language inconsistencies<br><br>Expands vocabulary | Blends phonemes<br><br>Segments phonemes in simple words<br><br>Uses correct sentence structure most of the time<br><br>Asks for clarification when needed<br><br>Expands vocabulary |
| **2. Concepts of Print, Letter Identification, and Text Features**<br>*How familiar is the child with concepts of print, letter identification, and text features?*<br>**Sample Assessment Tools**<br>• Concepts About Print<br>• Letter ID test<br>• Letter Naming Fluency<br>• Observation notes<br>• Concepts of Print checklist<br>• Untimed Letter Naming Test | Recognizes own first name<br><br>Notices difference between print and pictures<br><br>Turns pages of a book from beginning to end<br><br>Identifies the book cover and where the story starts | Follows print from left to right; knows to sweep back left<br><br>Can identify difference between words and letters<br><br>Recognizes and names most letters of the alphabet | Recognizes and names all uppercase and lowercase letters<br><br>Controls voice-print matching with one- to two-syllable words<br><br>Identifies and attends to periods when used at the end of sentences during reading<br><br>Identifies and attends to question marks and exclamation points during reading |
| **3. Decoding Skills and Word Analysis**<br>*To what extent is the child learning the decoding and word-identification skills needed for reading?*<br>**Sample Assessment Tools**<br>• Names Test<br>• Sound-symbol correspondence tasks<br>• Initial Sound Fluency (DIBELS)<br>• Sight word lists<br>• Running records<br>• Records of oral reading<br>• Quick Text Level Check-In<br>• Informal Phonics Surveys | Recognizes some sound–symbol correspondences | Produces sounds for most consonants<br><br>Knows 10–12 sight words | Produces sounds for all consonants and common consonant digraphs (*ch, sh, th, wh*)<br><br>Knows 20–50 sight words |
| **4. Reading Strategies, Processes, and Dispositions**<br>*To what extent does the child use early processing strategies and comprehension strategies during reading? How engaged is the child with reading?*<br>**Sample Assessment Tools**<br>• Running Records<br>• Records of oral reading<br>• Think-Alouds<br>• Interviews<br>• Observations and anecdotal notes<br>• Book logs<br>• Elementary Reading Attitude Survey | Uses pictures or pattern/repetition to read a story or environmental print "emergently"<br><br>Listens to books read aloud each day | Begins to use more than one cueing system to read, such as some finger pointing for visual information plus picture cues<br><br>Reads at least one or two little books, short text selections, or alphabet books each day | Uses more than one cueing system (meaning, visual, and language cues) and begins to cross-check independently<br><br>Reads two or three little books or short text selections each day |
| **5. Reading Accuracy and Fluency at Increasing Text Levels**<br>*To what degree is the child reading books of increasing complexity with accuracy and fluency?*<br>**Sample Assessment Tools**<br>• Running records<br>• Records of oral reading using benchmark books<br>• Quick Text Level Check-In<br>• Oral Reading Fluency (DIBELS)<br>• Three-Way Fluency Rubric<br><br>**Text Leveling approach used:** _____ | Reads some names and environmental print, such as family names, signs, labels, symbols | Reads simple, predictable, or decodable books (previously introduced), such as *Have You Seen My Cat* and *Monster Sandwich*<br><br><br>Text Level Target: _____ | Independently reads books, such as *Five Little Monkeys* and *All by Myself* (previously introduced) with acceptable accuracy<br><br>Text Level Target: _____ |

| Strand *Question & Sample Assessment Tools* | Pre-K – Early K | Late K | Early–Mid Grade 1 |
|---|---|---|---|
| **6. Comprehension and Reading Response** *How is the child developing an ability to understand text and demonstrate thoughtful responses to text?* Sample Assessment Tools · Gates MacGinitie Test · Developmental Reading Assessment · Discussions · Retellings · Journals · Drawings · Observation notes · Performances · Conferences · Constructed Responses | Actively listens to a story being read aloud  Offers basic emotional response (likes/dislikes) to what is read | Connects what is read to background knowledge  Begins to retell parts of stories | Communicates basic "gist" of story line through drawings, story maps, or other representations  Identifies main characters of narrative text  Retells the beginning, middle, and end of story  Tells what was learned from informational text |
| **7. Writing Strategies, Processes, and Dispositions** *To what extent does the child use the processes of writing? How engaged is the child with writing?* Sample Assessment Tools · Elementary Writing Attitude Survey · Portfolios · Writing samples · Interviews · Self-evaluation | With prompting, generates ideas for drawing or dictates ideas to an adult | Draws, labels, and writes to express ideas  Often generates original ideas and responds to others' prompts  Participates in shared writing activities | Writes with increasing independence  Uses resources such as word walls and letter-sound visuals for support  With support, will reread what has been written |
| **8. Writing Effectiveness** *How is the child's independent writing developing with regard to purpose, organization, details, and voice/tone?* Sample Assessment Tools · Writing samples (prompted and/or independent writing) with checklists, scales, rubrics, or portfolios | Draws pictures to express ideas; describes content of drawing  Writes at least part of first name | Writes labels that describe drawings  Written messages consist of a phrase or short sentence | Writes one to two understandable sentences to tell information or tell a story (often a personal narrative) |
| **9. Spelling** *How is the child's spelling developing in independent writing?* Sample Assessment Tools · Writing samples (prompted and independent writing) with scales, rubrics, or checklists · Elementary Spelling Inventory · Developmental Spelling Analysis | May use lines and letter-like forms to accompany drawings | Uses beginning and ending consonants to spell some words, demonstrating some sound-symbol correspondence (*KT* for *CAT*) | Represents each phoneme in a word with a grapheme (*LUV* for *love*); beginning to use some short vowels |
| **10. Writing Conventions and Handwriting** *To what degree does the child use acceptable conventions of grammar, usage, and mechanics in written language? How is handwriting developing?* Sample Assessment Tools · Writing samples and writing prompts, with scoring guides | Orients the page to start drawing or writing  Uses a variety of tools for writing or drawing (pencils, crayons, etc.) | Uses preferred hand consistently for writing  Writes from left to right, top to bottom  Writes most uppercase letters legibly | Usually leaves spaces between words  Includes lowercase letters in writing  Attempts to use end punctuation |

# Name: _____

| Late Grade 1–Early Grade 2 | Late Grade 2–Early Grade 3 | Late Grade 3–Early Grade 4 | Late Grade 4 |
|---|---|---|---|
| Manipulates phonemes by deleting and substituting<br><br>Develops appropriate audience behaviors<br><br>Uses more descriptive language and more complex sentences<br><br>Seeks clarification of unfamiliar vocabulary<br><br>Expands vocabulary | Uses basic subject-verb agreement correctly<br><br>Recognizes that language can be used figuratively<br><br>Develops a range of delivery skills and organizational skills for presentations<br><br>Shows awareness of audience by varying tone, volume, pace, word choice<br><br>Demonstrates understanding of concepts of synonym and antonym<br><br>Expands vocabulary | Shows a developing awareness of slang, jargon, and different language styles<br><br>Paraphrases to explain or describe information learned<br><br>Understands multiple meanings of common homonyms<br><br>Demonstrates understanding of common prefixes<br><br>Expands vocabulary | Flexibly uses expressive language and gestures in a variety of language contexts<br><br>Uses knowledge of word structure (common roots, bases, and affixes) to expand vocabulary<br><br>Expands vocabulary |
| Identifies and utilizes various parts of a book: title page; table of contents<br><br>Controls voice-print matching including words with multiple syllables | Identifies and utilizes index, glossary in informational text<br><br>Identifies and attends to commas and quotation marks during reading | Identifies and utilizes text features, such as tables, diagrams, headings, boldface, and timelines<br><br>Identifies and attends to more sophisticated print conventions, such as italics, colons, and parentheses during reading | Identifies and utilizes increasingly sophisticated text features, such as subheadings and captions during reading |
| Shows full understanding of the alphabetic principle<br><br>Reads one-syllable short-vowel words and words with silent *e*<br><br>Reads words with blends and inflected endings<br><br>Uses familiar word patterns to decode common two-syllable words, such as *happen* and *sticky*<br><br>Reads basic contractions and compound words | Uses knowledge of common syllable types (closed, vowel teams, *r* controlled) and patterns to decode one-syllable "regular" words, such as *shade* and *crown* and some multisyllabic words, such as *uncurled* and *protecting* | Uses knowledge of syllable types, patterns, and affixes to decode multisyllabic words, such as *freckled, pilot,* and *predicting* and applies this in reading multisyllabic words | Flexibly uses knowledge of all six syllable types, patterns, affixes, and common roots to decode multisyllabic words, such as *respectable* and *portion* |
| Uses multiple cues and self-corrects with increasing frequency when meaning is altered<br><br>Reads four or more little books, short text selections, or two to three short chapters each day<br><br>Can sustain reading for at least 10 minutes (independently or with a partner) | Predicts and confirms during reading<br><br>Begins to self-monitor comprehension; often rereads as a fix-up strategy<br><br>Makes connections during reading<br><br>Reads approximately two books a month or two chapters a day<br><br>Can sustain silent reading independently for at least 15 minutes a day | Flexibly uses a variety of comprehension strategies, such as predicting, rereading, and making connections<br><br>Uses simple context clues to determine the meaning of unfamiliar vocabulary<br><br>Reads the equivalent of at least two books a month<br><br>Can sustain silent, independent reading for at least 20 minutes | Flexibly uses a variety of comprehension strategies, including analyzing text structure and utilizing text features<br><br>Uses context clues to determine the meaning of unfamiliar vocabulary<br><br>Reads the equivalent of at least two books a month<br><br>Can sustain silent, independent reading for at least 30 minutes |
| Independently reads books, such as *Little Bear* and *Frog and Toad Are Friends* with acceptable accuracy and developing fluency<br><br><br>Text Level Target: _____ | Independently reads books, such as *Freckle Juice* and *Cam Jansen* with acceptable accuracy and fluency<br><br><br>Text Level Target: _____ | Independently reads books, such as *The Stories Julian Tells* and *Ramona the Brave* with acceptable accuracy and fluency<br><br><br>Text Level Target: _____ | Independently reads books, such as *The Story of Harriet Tubman* and *Bunnicula* with acceptable accuracy and fluency<br><br><br>Text Level Target: _____ |

**FIGURE 1.6  Willa's Profile for Phonological Awareness and Oral Language Development**

Note: This figure has been excerpted from the full Literacy Profile chart for illustrative purposes.

## LITERACY PROFILE    Name: *Willa*

TEACHER TIP: Date, initial, and color code each of your entries.

| Strand *Question & Sample Assessment Tools* | EMERGENT — Late K | EARLY — Early–Mid Grade 1 | Late Grade 1–Early Grade 2 |
|---|---|---|---|
| **1. Phonological Awareness and Oral Language Development**<br>*To what extent is the child developing phonological awareness and oral language skills?*<br>**Sample Assessment Tools**<br>• Yopp-Singer<br>• Phoneme Segmentation Fluency (DIBELS)<br>• Comprehensive Test of Phonological Processing (CTOPP)<br>• Peabody Picture Vocabulary Test (PPVT)<br>• Comprehensive Receptive and Expressive Vocabulary Test (CREVT)<br>• Observation Notes<br>• Checklists<br>• Vocabulary Probes<br>• Oral presentations with rubrics<br>• Language samples | Produces rhymes<br><br>Claps parts of multisyllabic words<br><br>Blends syllables into words<br><br>Isolates beginning sounds of words *[some, still working on blends (fr)] KI*<br>Isolates the final sounds of words<br><br>Blends onsets and rimes<br><br>Follows two-step directions<br><br>Self-corrects some language inconsistencies<br><br>Expands vocabulary | Blends phonemes<br><br><br>Segments phonemes in simple words<br><br><br>Uses correct sentence structure most of the time<br><br><br>Asks for clarification when needed<br><br><br>Expands vocabulary | Manipulates phonemes by deleting and substituting<br><br>Develops appropriate audience behaviors *[eye contact good] KI*<br><br>Uses more descriptive language and more complex sentences<br><br><br>Seeks clarification of unfamiliar vocabulary *["What kind of well, like wishing well?"] KI*<br><br>Expands vocabulary *[Classifying evident, mentioned sad/mad as feeling words; identified gravel when reading text] KI* |

Developed by Sue Biggam and Kathy Itterly. Copyright ©2009 Pearson Education, Inc. May be reproduced for classroom use only.

Gray areas represent highlighting added by the teacher, preferably using a different color for each year (e.g., yellow highlights for Late K, orange highlights for Early–Mid Grade 1, etc.).
Bracketed material represents teacher/examiner comments from February, Grade 1.

three phonemes, but not those with four phonemes. She identified three phonemes in the word "went"—/w/ /e/ /t/—and three in "jump"—/j/ /u/ /p/—again supporting the general developmental pattern of Grade 1 students. Finally, she was able to identify only three phonemes in the word *box*, but this is not surprising since the individual /k/ and /s/ sounds that link to the letter *x* sound like a blended sound to many young children.

Willa was able to correctly identify the first and last consonant sounds in the six words; however, she had some difficulty identifying the vowel sounds in *pet* and *rock* (a practice word). Willa was able to successfully delete phonemes from both the beginning position and the final position of words; however, she was able to substitute only beginning sounds, not the ending sounds of words. In the practice round, when asked to replace the first sound in *sad* with an /m/, she said, "Mad, they're both feelings." Willa's comment indicated that she was also thinking about the word meanings and that she was able to classify *sad* and *mad* as feeling words.

***Willa's Pragmatics and Syntax Development.*** Willa engages in two-way communication and employs eye contact and clarifications when she is explaining her thinking. Her Grade 1 teacher reports that Willa is able to function successfully in classroom settings. Willa corrects language inconsistencies, which was noted when she interrupted her own sentence by saying, "No, I mean. . . ." Willa uses correct syntax when communicating even when discussing past tense events.

***Willa's Vocabulary Development.*** Willa seems to have a strong vocabulary for a Grade 1 student. She asked for clarification of *well*: "Which well, the wishing well or to get well?" This question again demonstrates her awareness that there are multiple meanings for common words. Willa's ability to classify words as feeling words and her recognition of homophones such as *sun* and *son* provide further evidence that her vocabulary is developing breadth and depth.

### Overall Evaluation of Willa's Phonological Awareness and Oral Language Development

Willa is making steady progress in her phonological awareness development. She could benefit from some instruction in identification of syllabic units and simple phoneme segmentation, both skills that should further support her encoding and decoding development. For example, the teacher might show Willa how to place the back of her hand below her jaw as she says a two-syllable word so that she can feel the various syllabic units. Once she matches the word "syllable" to the concept of the separate word parts in two-syllable words, then three- and four-syllable words can be added. A word-sorting game using the names of her classmates and friends could be then used to reinforce syllabication.

To improve Willa's phonemic awareness, the teacher can work with Willa in a one-to-one setting to explain and model the stretching-out process, using tokens to represent each sound and physically pushing a token every time a sound is heard. The teacher can gradually increase the number of phonemes in words to four-phoneme words, then five-phoneme words, adding blends and digraphs such as *through* and *sleep*. These lessons can be short, fast-paced, and presented in a game-like manner.

Overall, Willa's oral language skills are effective, and she is demonstrating a natural curiosity about words.

## REFERENCES

Adams, M. J. (1990). *Beginning to read: Thinking and learning about print*. Cambridge, MA: MIT Press.

Adams, M. J., Foorman, B. R., Lundberg, I., & Beeler, T. (1998). *Phonemic awareness in young children*. Baltimore: Paul Brookes Publishing Co.

Allington, R. L. (2006). *What really matters for struggling readers*. Boston: Pearson/Allyn & Bacon.

Armbruster, B., Lehr, F., & Osborn, J. (2001). *Put reading first: The building blocks for teaching children to read*. Washington, DC: National Institute for Literacy.

Bear, D. R., Invernizzi, M., Templeton, S., & Johnston, F. (2000). *Words their way: Word study for phonics, vocabulary, and spelling development* (2nd ed.). Upper Saddle River, NJ: Merrill-Prentice-Hall.

Beck, I. L., McKeon, M. G., & Kucan, L. (2002). *Bringing words to life*. New York: Guilford.

Beck, I., Perfetti, C., & McKeon, M. G. (1982). The effects of long term vocabulary development on lexical access and reading comprehension. *Journal of Educational Psychology, 74*, 506–521.

Berenstain, S., & Berenstain, J. (1971). *The Berenstain's b book*. New York: Random House Books for Young Readers.

Bertrand, N. P., & Stice, C. F. (2002). *Good teaching*. Portsmouth, NH: Heinemann.

Bradley, L., & Bryant, P. E. (1985). *Rhyme and reason in reading and spelling*. Ann Arbor: University of Michigan Press.

Buehl, D. (2001). *Classroom strategies for interactive learning* (2nd ed.). Newark, NJ: International Reading Association.

Bus, A. G., & van Ijzendoorn, M. H. (1999). Phonological awareness and early reading: A meta-analysis of experiential training studies. *Journal of Educational Psychology, 91*, 403–414.

Cambourne, B. (1995). Toward an educationally relevant theory of literacy learning: Twenty years of inquiry. *The Reading Teacher, 49*(3), 182–190.

Chomsky, N. (1975). *Reflections on language.* New York: Pantheon Books.

Clay, M. M. (1991) *Becoming literate: The construction of inner control.* Portsmouth, NH: Heinemann.

Cunningham, P. (2000). *Phonics they use* (3rd ed.). New York: HarperCollins.

Cunningham, P. (2003). What research says about teaching phonics. In L. M. Morrow, L. B. Gambrell, & M. Pressley (Eds.), *Best practices in literacy instruction* (2nd ed.). New York: Guilford Press.

Cunningham, P. M., & Allington, R. L. (2007). *Classrooms that work: They can all read and write.* Boston Pearson.

Davis, K. (n.d.). *Phonemic awareness assessment: Grades K–3.* Crandall, TX: Frog Street Press.

Denton, P., & Kriete, R. (2000). *The first six weeks of school.* Greenfield, MA: Northeast Foundation for Children.

DIBELS—Dynamic Indicator of Early Literacy Skills. (2007). Retrieved from http://www.dibels.uoregon.edu

Dickinson, D. K., McCabe, A., & Sprague, K. (2001). *Teacher rating of oral language and literary (TROLL): A research based tool* (CIERA Report #3–016). Ann Arbor, MI: Center for the Improvement of Early Reading.

Duke, N. K., & Kays, J. (1998). "Can I say 'once upon a time?'": Kindergarten children developing knowledge of information book language. *Early Childhood Research Quarterly, 13*, 295–318.

Dunn, L., & Dunn, M. (1997). *Peabody picture vocabulary test* (4th ed.). Circle Pines, MN: American Guidance Services.

Durkin, D. (2004). *Teaching them to read* (6th ed.). Boston: Pearson.

Echevarria, J., Vogt, M., & Short, D. (2004). *Making content comprehensible for English Language Learners: The SIOP model.* Boston: Allyn & Bacon.

Ehri, L. C., & Numes, S. R. (2002). The role of phonemic awareness in learning to read. In A. E. Farstrup & S. J. Samuels (Eds.), *What research has to say about reading instruction* (pp. 110–139). Newark, DE: International Reading Association.

Elkonin, D. B. (1973). Reading in the USSR. In J. Downing (Ed.), *Comparative reading* (pp. 551–579). New York: Macmillan.

Fisher, P. (1993). *The sounds and spelling patterns of English.* Farmington, ME: Oxton House.

Fox, M. (1994). *Tough Boris.* San Diego, CA: Voyager Books.

Freeman, D. E., & Freeman, Y. S. (2004). *Essential linguistics: What you need to know to teach reading, ESL, spelling, phonics, and grammar.* Portsmouth, NH: Heinemann.

Goodman, K., Smith, E., Meredith, R., & Goodman, Y. (1987). *Language and thinking in schools: A whole language curriculum* (3rd ed.). Katonah, NY: R. C. Owen.

Goodman, Y. M. (1978). Kidwatching: An alternative to testing. *National Elementary Principal, 57*(4), 41–45.

Gunning, T. (2006). *Closing the literacy gap.* Boston: Pearson.

Halliday, M. A. K. (1982). Three aspects of children's language development: Learning language, learning through language, learning about language. In Y. Goodman, M. Hausler, & D. Strickland (Eds.), *Oral and written language development research: Impact on schools.* Urbana, IL: National Council of Teachers of English.

Hart, B., & Risley, T. (1995). *Meaningful differences in the everyday experiences of young American children.* Baltimore: Brookes.

Hoover, H. B., Dunbar, S. B., & Frisble, D. A. (2005). *Iowa tests of basic skills*. Rolling Hills, IL: Riverside Publishing.

Hoyt, L. (2002). *Strategies for success with informational texts*. Portsmouth, NH: Heinemann.

Johnson, D. D. (2001). *Vocabulary in the elementary and middle school*. Boston: Allyn & Bacon.

Juel, C. (1988). Learning to read and write: A longitudinal study of 54 children from first to fourth grades. *Journal of Educational Psychology, 80*(4), 437–447.

Krashen, S. D., & Terrell, T. D. (1983). *The natural approach: Language acquisition in the classroom*. New York: Pergamon/Alemany.

Lee, D. (1986). *Language, children, and society*. New York: NYU Press.

Liberman, I. Y., Shankweiler, S., Fischer, F. W., & Carter, B. (1974). Explicit syllable and phoneme segmentation in the young child. *Journal of Experimental Psychology, 18*, 201–212.

Liu, S. (2000). *Pragmatics*. In M. Byram (Ed.), *Encyclopedia for language teaching and learning [A]* (pp. 382–384). London: Routledge.

Maclean, M., Bryant, P., & Bradley, L. (1987). Rhymes, nursery rhymes, and reading in early education. *Merrill-Palmer Quarterly, (33)* 3, 255–282.

Massachusetts Language Arts Curriculum Frameworks. (2001). Retrieved from http://www.doe.mass.edu/frameworks/ela/0601.doc

Meyer, R. (2002). *Phonics exposed: Understanding and resisting systematic direct intense phonics instruction*. Mahwah, NJ: Erlbaum.

Moustafa, M. (1997). *Beyond traditional phonics: Research discoveries and reading instruction*. Portsmouth, NH: Heinemann.

Nagy, W. E. (1988). *Teaching vocabulary to improve vocabulary instruction*. Urbana, IL: National Council of Teachers of English.

National Institute of Child Health and Human Development. (2000). *Report of the National Reading Panel. Teaching children to read: Reports of the subgroups*. Washington, DC: NICHD.

National Reading Panel. (2000). *Teaching children to read: An evidence-based assessment of the scientific research literature on reading and its implications for reading instruction: Reports of the subgroups* (National Institute of Health Publication No. 00–4754). Washington, DC: National Institute of Child Health and Human Development.

Opitz, M. (2000). *Rhymes and reasons: literature and language play for phonological awareness*. Portsmouth, NH: Heinemann.

Parker, F., & Riley, K. (2005). *Essential linguistics for the non-linguist*. Boston: Pearson.

Piaget, J. (1965). *The language and thought of the child*. New York: Meridian Books.

Pinker, S. (1994). *The language instinct*. New York: William Morrow.

Purcell-Gates, V., McIntyre, E., & Freppon, P. (1995). Learning written storybook language in school: A comparison of low-SES children in skills based and whole language classrooms. *American Educational Research Journal, 32*, 659–685.

Putnam, L. R. (1994–1995). An interview with Noam Chomsky. *The Reading Teacher, 48*, 328–333.

Ray, K. W. (1999). *Wondrous words: Writers and writing in the elementary classroom*. Urbana, IL: National Council of Teachers of English.

Rudell, M. R. (2001). *Teaching content reading and writing* (4th ed.). New York: John Wiley.

Schwartz, R., & Raphael, T. (1985). Concept of definition: A key to improving students' vocabulary. *The Reading Teacher, 39*, 198–205.

Seifert, K. L. (2004). Cognitive development and the education of young children. In B. Spodek & O. Saracho (Eds.), *Handbook of research on the education of young children* (2nd ed.). Mahwah, NJ: Erlbaum.

Snow, C. E., Burns, S., & Griffin, P. (Eds.). (1998). *Preventing reading difficulties in young children*. Washington, DC: National Academy Press.

Snow, C. E., & Tabors, P. O. (1993). Language skills that relate to literacy instruction. In B. Spodek & O. Saracho (Eds.), *Yearbook in early childhood education*. New York: Teacher's College Press.

Stanovich, K. E. (1986). Matthew effects in reading: Some consequences of individual differences in the acquisition of literacy. *Reading Research Quarterly, 21,* 360–407.

Torgesen, J. K., & Bryant, B. R. (1994). *The test of phonological awareness*. Austin, TX: Pro-Ed.

Torgesen, J. K., & Mathes, P. G. (1998). *What every teacher should know about phonological awareness*. Tallahassee, FL: Department of Education, Division of Public Schools and Community Education, Bureau of Instructional Support and Community Services.

Vandervelden, M. C., & Siegel, L. S. (1997). Teaching phonological processing skills in early literacy: A developmental approach. *Learning Disabilities Quarterly, 20,* 68–81.

Vygotsky, L. S. (1978). *Mind in society*. Cambridge: MA: Harvard University Press.

Wagner, R. K., Torgesen, J. K., & Rashotte, C. A. (1999). *Comprehensive test of phonological processing*. Austin, TX: Pro-Ed.

Wallace, G., & Hammill, D. (1994). *Comprehensive receptive and expressive vocabulary test*. Examiner's manual. Austin, TX: Pro-Ed.

Wells, G. (1986). *The meaning makers: Children learning language and using language to learn*. Portsmouth, NH: Heinemann.

Winograd, P., Paris, S., & Bridge, C. (1991). Improving the assessment of literacy. *The Reading Teacher, 45,* 108–116.

Yaden, D. B., Jr., & Templeton, S. (Eds.). (1986). *Metalinguistic awareness and beginning literacy: Conceptualizing what it means to read and write*. Portsmouth, NH: Heinemann.

Yopp, H. (1995). A test for assessing phonemic awareness in young children. *The Reading Teacher, 49,* 20–28.

Yopp, H. K., & Yopp, R. H. (2000). Supporting phonemic awareness development in the classroom. *The Reading Teacher, 54,* 130–143.

# CHAPTER TWO

# Concepts of Print, Letter Identification, and Text Features

CORE QUESTION

How familiar is the child with concepts of print, letter identification, and text features?

A child often sings the ABCs to the tune of "Twinkle, Twinkle, Little Star" and only later discovers that the letters are actually *l, m, n, o, p* and not "*l and n and p.*" Print awareness begins when a child connects oral language to printed symbols, but this awareness does not develop all at once; rather, it is a gradual process that includes many approximations. For example, when a child sees her name written again and again, she makes the link between the visual representation and her name. She may be attending to only the first letter, but that link is a milestone in her emerging literacy development. On a broader level, a child may recite a much-loved story from memory while using only the illustrations as a guide as he pages through a familiar book. The child has discovered that the story remains within the covers of the book, but it may be some time before he realizes that the *text* is what holds the language constant.

In this chapter we will identify some of the benchmarks that indicate children's growing awareness about our written language. Three overarching aspects of print awareness include:

**LITERACY PROFILE**
Consult your Literacy Profile as you read through this chapter. Refer to Strand 2 and follow its indicators.

- Understanding concepts of print
- Identifying and naming letters
- Recognizing and attending to text features

## UNDERLYING PRINCIPLES OF PRINT CONCEPTS, LETTER IDENTIFICATION, AND TEXT FEATURES

Just as children are immersed in oral language from the time they are born, so, too, are they exposed to print of all kinds. Beginning with visual and auditory discrimination skills, infants eventually learn to identify similarities and differences in both sounds and objects. Children continue to refine these foundational skills through their many encounters with language and other stimuli, including interactions with people and with objects such as toys and books.

The term *emergent literacy* describes the underlying developmental understandings that humans gain through their early childhood years in regard to written language (Morrow & Sulzby, 1995; Teale & Sulzby, 1986). Young children often display these understandings through their behaviors as they interact with books and other written materials. Written language development is similar to oral language development in that children gain control over written language through the same conditions identified in Cambourne's framework for natural language learning: immersion, demonstration, expectation, responsibility, use, approximation, and response (1995). In other words, children learn to read and write in much the same way they learn to speak and listen (Barron, 1990).

Like oral language, written language has receptive and expressive modes—that is, we receive ideas by reading and we express ideas by writing. In this chapter, we will explore the receptive mode as it relates to print awareness while keeping in mind that reading and writing development occurs in a parallel manner with all language systems (Snow, Burns, & Griffin, 1998).

Print awareness begins at a very early age, with each new discovery building upon previous ones. Through repeated encounters with familiar text, often starting with environmental print, children begin to recognize printed messages, frequently relying on the visual cues associated with the words (Clay, 1991; Ehri, 1991). For instance, children can often identify the names of favorite cereals and restaurants through logos, fonts, and letter shapes long before they can name all the individual letters that make up those words. Children develop a progression of understandings about print in order to make the leap from recognizing a logo to reading unfamiliar text.

Print awareness also continues beyond emergent reading development. As students are exposed to more and more varieties of text, they continue to identify, define, and use many features of our printed language such as captions, punctuation marks, diagrams, and subheadings (Moline, 1995; Mooney, 2001). We will first look closely at the underlying concepts children need to develop about print. Next we will describe alphabet knowledge, and then we will provide an overview of various text features and forms.

## Understanding Concepts of Print

Marie Clay (1975, 1991), through her research in emergent literacy acquisition, highlights the importance of a child's early book and pencil explorations. Her careful analyses of children's early literacy behaviors have been instrumental in identifying the underlying progression of skills and concepts that help create a sturdy foundation for literacy learning. Pressley's review of emergent literacy research (2002, p. 91) finds that literacy researchers now widely believe ". . . the environment the preschool child experiences is a critical determinant of reading and writing abilities once formal school begins."

As we review foundational skills that children often develop before they attend kindergarten, keep in mind that children start school with a wide array of experiences. Some children begin school with a stark disadvantage because they weren't immersed in positive early literacy experiences (Morrow, 1997; Snow, Burns, & Griffin, 1998). By familiarizing ourselves with emergent literacy skills, we can identify each learner's strengths and specific learning needs, thereby enabling us to create supportive instructional settings to help all learners achieve success. Consider your own early experiences as we explore the development of the early concepts of print across the following four topics:

- Book-handling skills
- Control over directionality of print
- Awareness of words and sentences
- Knowledge of print conventions

***Book-Handling Skills.*** During a child's early years, interacting with adults during what Clay calls "book sharing" (1991, p. 29) demonstrates not only the way the world of print works, but also the "feelings, understandings, and language patterns" of the reader. These shared experiences lead to independent book handling, often with cloth books and board books. Initially, toddlers may use books as toys (or for teething), but eventually they will page through the books, interacting and retelling portions of a much-loved story. Some early book-handling skills that a teacher might observe include gross motor skills and notable milestones such as:

- Holding a book "right side up" so that it faces the reader
- Opening the book from left to right
- Turning pages one at a time
- Noticing that illustrations help tell the story (Clay, 1991)

Personal encounters with books are necessary to help children develop the confidence to handle books naturally and skillfully. Can you recall some of your earliest experiences with books?

***Control Over Directionality of Print.*** As a child begins to attend to the text on each page, he will often identify various features of the text layout before he attends to the finer features such as the words and letters (Clay, 1991). For instance, an early discovery might be that text is presented from top to bottom on a page. If there is a double-spread layout, the child must decide whether the text runs across the double pages from top to bottom or from left to right, or whether the story is contained on the left page first and then on the right page. In other words, a child needs to figure out where to start attending to the text and how to proceed from that point. These decisions are text-specific and are necessary to access the story sequentially.

Clay (1991) reminds us that the directional movements written text requires are essentially motor movements that children must acquire. These early movements include coordination of the head, hand, and eyes. Adults often model directionality in a natural way by first orienting a book properly and then by using a finger to point to the words while reading aloud. As time goes on, a child frequently begins to mimic this procedure, moving his finger as well.

If there are multiple lines of text on a single page, children must learn to move to the second line of text with a full return to the left and then again proceed in a left-to-right fashion. Correctly moving through multiple lines of text is described as a "return sweep." Interestingly, a child may show understanding of directionality before she has full control of text reading. Once a child begins word-by-word reading, she may use a finger to point to each word as she speaks it aloud. Teachers sometimes describe this process as "finger-voice-print matching."

***Awareness of Words and Sentences.*** Children learn to identify many words through environmental print and frequent exposures to words. From a very young age, a child might identify the symbol of McDonald's restaurants by the large yellow *M* and other common sight words by the logo or constancy of the message, as in "STOP" on neighborhood stop signs. Erhi describes this early phase of sight reading as "prealphabetic," because the child relies primarily on visual clues rather than on using letters as sound representations (1992). Later, children learn to recognize words by noticing a familiar beginning letter or the combination of first and last letters. In this second phase of sight-word identification, "partial alphabetic," you may find children identifying their own names or the names of their family members based on partially recognized letters (Erhi, 1992). Although they might make inaccurate connections such as confusing *kitten* and *kitchen*, this stage represents another milestone in children's language development, indicating a beginning awareness of some sound-to-letter correspondences (Erhi, 1992; Gaskins et al., 1996).

As children are learning to identify words, early print awareness also requires them to develop a new vocabulary, the terms we use to talk *about* our language (Durkin, 2004; Halliday, 1982). For instance, children may learn to read a word such as *stop* before they know that when those four letters appear together in that order, they represent a word. Talking about language as we use language is known as "metalanguage." Some early terms we use to discuss language structures include *letter, line, word,* and *sentence.* Children usually learn the concept of "letter" first, with written language being key to their development of other concepts such as "words" and "sentences" (Francis, 1977). Children can learn that words are made up of a collection of letters, but issues such as one-letter words and multisyllabic words may confuse them (Clay, 1991). Written language is helpful because the white spaces between words plainly show the word boundaries and signal where each word begins and ends. Sentences, too, have concrete identifiers, including the beginning uppercase letter and the ending punctuation mark.

As you use terminology to discuss text, be aware of other words that can cause confusion, such as *line* when it is used to represent a line of text. Initially, students may not fully understand the concepts of words, lines, and sentences, but learning to identify the boundaries between individual words, the top-to-bottom layering of text in rows, and the clues that show where one sentence begins and ends is a good starting point. This vocabulary will help children gain increasing control over the organizational aspects of our language structures.

> Development of word-identification skills will be discussed further in chapter 3, "Decoding and Word Recognition."

***Knowledge of Print Conventions.*** Print conventions are the agreed-upon rules that we use to record oral language (Cunningham & Allington, 2007). Rules range in complexity from the white spaces between words (described in the previous section) to the more complex use of conventions such as footnotes, which we will discuss under the topic of text features. In kindergarten and Grade 1, children learn to discriminate between upper- and lowercase letters, a necessary skill for using capital letters intentionally.

Think about the complex set of rules we employ for deciding when to use capital letters: the start of a sentence, proper nouns, titles, headings, and sometimes for emphasis, such as in exclamatory phrases. And this is not even an exhaustive list! Children cannot appreciate the varied uses of capital letters until they can discriminate between upper- and lowercase letters. Children must be able to distinguish between upper- and lowercase letters *and* recognize the terminology associated with the differences (*capital letter, upper-* or *lowercase*) in order to gain control over when and how to use this print convention.

Punctuation marks, another written language convention, allow a writer to suggest intonation, reveal implied meanings, and signal completion of messages. Emerging readers learn punctuation marks as another symbol for representing our oral language, similar to alphabetic symbols (Clay, 1975). In her 1975 text (p. 42), Marie Clay counted the number of punctuation marks on her typewriter to be 11 different symbols; on a modern computer keyboard, the number increases to 30, in addition to the alphabet. By encouraging children to notice various punctuation marks while they're reading, and modeling their effects as you read aloud, you might find students experimenting with these symbols in their own writing.

The important connection between reading (receptive) and writing (expressive) cannot be overstated. Brown and Cambourne (1987) describe a *linguistic spillover effect,* noting that when children are asked to retell what they have read, they frequently use vocabulary and print conventions similar to those in the original piece, often trying out new words and punctuation marks that they had not used before. For instance, imagine a third-grade child reading a story filled with rich, descriptive words and, sprinkled throughout the story, commas separating serial phrases. If the child is asked to produce a written retelling of the story, there is a good chance that her retelling will include some of the same stylistic language and some attempts to use commas in a series.

See chapter 10, "Writing Conventions and Handwriting," for more information about using punctuation and text features in writing.

### Identifying and Naming Letters

In English, our alphabet shapes our writing. Key to this connection is the alphabetic principle, which identifies the systematic relationship between the sounds of our speech and words in print (Adams, 1990). At first glance the alphabetic principle may seem straightforward, but its underlying concepts are complex. To fully grasp the principle, kindergarteners and first graders need to learn to distinguish each letter from the others using their physical representations; they need to learn the name for each of those shapes; and they need to be able to associate sounds corresponding with each letter (Adams, 1990; Gibson, Gibson, Pick, & Osser, 1962).

The 26 letters of our alphabet may not seem like many. However, with upper- and lowercases of each letter and various shapes of some letters such as lowercase *a* and *g*, there are actually over 54 symbols to be recognized as letters (Clay, 1975). Fortunately, many children arrive in kindergarten with quite a bit of letter knowledge; our job as teachers is to determine what each child knows and then plan how to continue building on that existing knowledge.

### Knowledge of Text Features

Earlier we explained that conventions of print, such as white space, uppercase letters, and punctuation, are the rules we use to record language. Some written conventions are also known as "text features," which authors use to present information in various forms, sometimes for efficiency, sometimes to enhance comprehension, and sometimes for effect (Mooney, 2001). Text features can include:

- Graphic representations (diagrams, graphs, charts, labels)
- Language forms (abbreviations, acronyms, contractions)
- Aids to structure content (headings, subheadings, glossaries, indexes)

The use of a specific text feature must match the goals of the writing, satisfy the intended audience, and be consistent with the writer's style. For instance, an author might choose to use an abbreviation for "doctor" when the term is used with a surname, such as "Dr. Adams." In the children's story *Doctor DeSoto* (1990), the author, William Steig, uses the full word, *Doctor*, throughout the text, rather than the abbreviation. Yet when referring to the doctor's wife, Steig uses "Mrs.," a common abbreviation for a married woman.

Text features can provide a supportive structure for a reader, but they can also become a challenge if a reader is not familiar with the format (Mooney, 2001). The term *visual literacy* is often used to describe the dual processes of accessing and presenting information through the combined modes of images, graphics, and print (Hyerle, 1996; Moline, 1995). Visual literacy begins with the awareness of text features, but it also includes interpreting and creating the features. All forms of written communication—including narrative texts, nonfiction, media, and other electronic sources—have distinctive features that require interpretation. Let's briefly examine some text features that you might find in narrative text and informational text.

Refer to chapter 6, "Comprehension and Reading Response," for further discussion about narrative and informational text structures and the use of graphic organizers.

**Narrative Text.** Narrative texts are books that tell a story (Galda & Cullinan, 2006) and span the genres of contemporary realistic fiction, science fiction, fantasy, and historical fiction. Children seem to almost effortlessly learn the special features used in narrative texts when adults and teachers read interactively with them. Children love to identify the title, author, and illustrator as they reread favorite books and discover new ones by a favorite author or a familiar illustrator. Kindergarteners often squeal with delight as they spread open the cover of a book to reveal a continuous illustration expanding the front cover over to the back, announcing it as an "extended" cover.

Besides the information provided on the cover and title page, a narrative text may include other interesting features such as a labeled map of the story's setting, a timeline, or a dedication. Other features such as scripts, speech bubbles, a table of contents, and chapter headings can become common language when children and adults explore a wide range of texts and the accompanying features through interactive read-alouds.

**Informational Text.** Informational text is filled with opportunities to help children develop visual literacy through text features. Organizational structures such as the table of contents, index, and glossary allow the reader to access the information she needs to understand the text. Children can naturally learn the specific vocabulary of these text features as they discover the usefulness of each. For instance, if a second-grade child is investigating the diet of vampire bats, the index of a book about bats becomes a valuable resource when the appropriate page is listed.

Children also learn the various names of text features such as tables, diagrams, labels, captions, photographs, graphs, maps, and charts as they discover each feature's value and unique purpose. For example, when an adult reads and interprets an important diagram about the life cycle of a butterfly, children realize how much additional information can be gleaned from the various features that often accompany an article or story. Learning how to "read" this information also brings children's attention to the *typography,* which refers to the presentation of ideas including:

- The specific font that is used such as Times New Roman, Courier New, or Comic Sans MS
- The style of the fonts such as italics, boldfaced, underlining, and outlining
- Signposts such as bullets, arrows, asterisks, and numbering (Moline, 1995)

Print is all around us and with encouragement, children begin to notice and recognize the variety of ways text is presented in their day-to-day world. Some examples of text forms include newspapers, magazines, computer programs, e-mail, Web sites, mail containing envelopes filled with a variety of brochures and other printed material, recipe cards, labels on food products, television menus, and more. Each form uses a wide variety of text features, often in combination with images, and some even include three-dimensional representations.

Our world of print continues to change and evolve as technology broadens our methods of communication. Text messaging on cell phones and instant messages using computers have introduced a form of shorthand that children often use well before adults venture into that world. Teachers and children can support each other's growing awareness and access to the new literacies that are emerging through technology by staying current and connected to the ever-changing world of communication that's well beyond the traditional world of printed text (Leu, 2002).

### Summary of Print Concepts, Letter Identification, and Text Features

In our modern world, children are surrounded by print of all kinds; however, their awareness of how print works is an evolving process, beginning with meaningful environmental print and continuing through complex text features and print conventions. To ensure continued growth, teachers can track a child's developing awareness of print concepts such as book handling, control over directionality of print, and the ability to identify words, sentences, and print conventions. Other important aspects of print awareness are accurate and automatic identification of letter names and attention to various text features. In the next section we will consider how to assess this growing control of the concepts of print, letter identification, and text features.

## ASSESSING CONCEPTS OF PRINT, LETTER RECOGNITION, AND AWARENESS OF TEXT FEATURES

Children begin school with a wide array of literacy experiences. By the time some children start kindergarten, they may have had over a thousand interactions with books and the world of print. On the other hand, some children have little exposure to books, book language, or print before they enter school. These children have a great disadvantage compared to their classmates who have been saturated with stories and language since birth (Morrow, 1997; Snow et al., 1998). Careful assessment allows teachers to identify what a child can already do, what a child is attempting to do but needs support in order to do successfully, and what a child is not yet attempting (Clay, 1991). This section will describe some assessment tools that provide useful evidence to support instructional planning tailored to your students' needs in the area of print and letter recognition.

### Formal or Published Assessment Tools for Evaluating Concepts of Print and Letter Recognition

A variety of standardized assessment tools are available to help teachers identify children's print awareness and letter recognition skills. "An Observation Survey of Early Literacy Achievement," developed by Marie Clay (1993), can be used to determine the range of skills and concepts that an individual child has acquired from early reading and writing experiences. This tool, sometimes referred to as "the Observation Survey," contains six subtests: Letter Identification, Concepts About Print, Hearing and Recording Sounds in Words, Word Reading, Writing Vocabulary, and Text Reading. This comprehensive assessment can be used to identify a child's beginning skill level when he or she first enters kindergarten, and it can also be used to monitor a child's literacy growth. A teacher can give the test in its entirety or only its relevant subtests. In this section we will describe two of these subtests, Concepts About Print and Letter Identification. As the name of the overall survey indicates, this test is designed to help teachers carefully observe and record a child's behaviors as she engages in literacy tasks.

Another series of tests known as the Dynamic Indicators of Basic Early Literacy Skills (DIBELS) (2007) is also designed to identify and monitor a child's growing skills in early literacy development. DIBELS is comprised of five subtests: Initial Sound Fluency, Letter Naming Fluency, Phoneme Segmentation Fluency, Nonsense Word Fluency, and Oral Reading Fluency. The subtests are designed to be administered at different points in a child's literacy development, ranging from preschool to Grade 3. As the names imply, the subtests stress fluency, meaning the speed at which children respond to prompts factors into each of these subtests. In this section, we will describe the subtest that relates most specifically to print awareness—Letter Naming Fluency.

***Concepts About Print: A Subtest of An Observation Survey of Early Literacy Achievement.*** The Concepts About Print subtest includes a recording sheet that contains 24 items and an accompanying story booklet such as *Sands and Stones* (Clay, 1991). This subtest takes approximately 5 to 10 minutes to administer. The teacher (or test administrator) reads each page of the booklet aloud and asks the child to respond to prompts such as, "Show me where to start reading" or "Show me one letter." On some of the pages in the booklets, Clay has deliberately included inaccurate print features and text placements, and during the reading, the test administrator carefully records the child's behaviors and responses. For instance, one page has two words transposed, while another has the text upside down but the illustrations right side up. Once the assessment is completed and scored, a child's progress can be compared to that of other children of the same age group through the stanine tables listed in the administration guide.

***Letter Identification Test: A Subtest of An Observation Survey of Early Literacy Achievement.*** The Letter Identification subtest of the Observation Survey consists of two documents: one sheet containing all of the letters of the alphabet randomly listed in rows, uppercase preceding lowercase; and a recording sheet for the administrator. The lowercase letters have two fonts for *a* and *g*. The Letter Identification subtest allows the student to respond to the letters by naming the letter, by saying the sound the letter represents, or by stating a word that begins with that letter. Similar to the Concepts About Print subtest, a child's score can be compared to the scores of others in the same age group using stanine tables.

***Letter Naming Fluency: A Subtest of the Dynamic Indicators of Basic Early Literacy Skills.*** Some schools use the Letter Naming Fluency subtest of DIBELS to assess a child's skill at naming letters within a 1-minute time period. In this test, the printed letters are a mix of upper- and lowercase and appear in a left-to-right, row-by-row setup. Benchmark goals are established for each grade level and time of year that the test is administered. Children are categorized as "at risk, some risk, or low risk" in the area of letter naming fluency based on the number of accurately named letters (DIBELS, 2007).

If a child cannot finish within the 1-minute testing time limit, you might want to consider using another assessment, such as an informal letter-identification test, to identify which particular letters the child can name independently and which letters you will need to teach explicitly.

Go to www.dibels.uoregon.edu for a complete description and free copy of the DIBELS Letter Naming Fluency Test.

### Informal Assessment Tools for Assessing Concepts of Print, Letter Identification, and Awareness of Text Features

For informal assessments, teachers frequently use checklists to guide their "kidwatching." Checklists provide a structure for systematically recording a child's literacy behaviors based on an identified list of standards or expected behaviors. The same checklist can be used several times during a school year to monitor a child's progress. Other teachers may choose to take anecdotal notes, jotting down relevant, notable behaviors as the children engage in literacy activities.

***Informally Assessing Concepts About Print.*** Many informal checklists have been adapted from the Concepts About Print and other subtests of the Observation Survey. One benefit of a predeveloped checklist is that you can use it during independent reading periods to closely observe and systematically record an individual child's natural book-handling behaviors while holding an interactive conversation. See Appendix A-4 for an example of one informal assessment, the Concepts of Print Checklist.

To use such a checklist, sit side by side with a child and ask questions as he reads a self-selected text. For instance, you might read aloud a page with three words on it, "The bird sings," and then ask the child, "How many words are on this page?" You can also incorporate a masking technique to have the child indicate his knowledge of various concepts (Clay, 1991; Holdaway, 1979). Index cards can be used to help children isolate various portions of text. For instance, you might first show a child how to use two small pieces of an index card to "bookend" or "frame" a specific part of the text, such as a letter. Next, ask the child to use the same technique to identify a word or a specific punctuation mark. In the accompanying photograph, Willa is using pieces of an index card to demonstrate her understanding of the concept of a "word" in connected text.

***Informally Assessing Letter Identification.*** There are also many informal versions of letter naming tests. Appendix A-5 provides an untimed assessment tool that will help you identify a child's ability to name randomly placed

Willa demonstrates her understanding of the concept of a "word."

uppercase and lowercase letters. If a child has difficulty following the letters in a left-to-right finger pointing manner, you can allow her to use an index card or bookmark to isolate each line. Be sure to record in the comment section this additional need for "tracking support."

Informal letter-identification tools include magnetic alphabet letters and other physical representations of the alphabet such as flash cards. To use flash cards, print each letter of the alphabet on a separate card, and as you randomly turn each one over, ask the child to name the letter. Keep the incorrectly guessed letters in a separate pile so that you can record them afterward.

***Informally Assessing Awareness of Text Features.***  To assess a child's ability to identify and utilize text features, you can create a simple checklist that identifies the text features that are appropriate for your age level of students. You can generate the list by combining the Literacy Profile and your district's and state's curriculum standards. Also, look around your classroom and examine the materials through the lens of visual literacy. What visual literacy skills does a child need in order to fully comprehend the various genres in your classroom library, on your classroom bulletin boards, in the computer software, and in your regular textbooks?

Another way to identify what text features a child already knows is through a "scavenger hunt" format, which can be presented orally in small reading groups or through a written worksheet. Simply provide a variety of informational texts and ask children to locate various text features such as a table of contents, labels, and subheadings. See Figure 2.1 for an example.

## Summary of Assessing Concepts of Print, Letter Identification, and Awareness of Text Features

Formal tools are available for assessing concepts of print and letter identification; however, many teachers informally collect and record data on an ongoing basis. This investigative work is useful for identifying and tracking each child's knowledge and growing awareness of the world of print. Checklists also serve as guides that help sharpen observation skills, which in turn supports the development of specific instructional objectives.

**FIGURE 2.1  Scavenger Hunt for Text Features: Sample Format**

**Find an example of each of the following text features by looking in our Nonfiction Book Buckets and Bookshelves. One sample line is filled in.**

| Nonfiction Text Feature | Where I found It (List Book or Magazine) | Page |
|---|---|---|
| Photograph | *National Geographic Explorer,* April 2003 | 8 |
| Table of contents | | |
| Boldfaced print | | |
| Subheading | | |
| Caption or label | | |
| Tables or graphs | | |

## INSTRUCTIONAL APPROACHES FOR TEACHING PRINT CONCEPTS, LETTER IDENTIFICATION, AND TEXT FEATURES

Children often learn print concepts, letter identification, and text features from authentic reading, writing, and language experiences before they begin attending school. Continued exposure to printed language will reinforce these skills and support the development of new ones. Through formal and informal measures, we can identify and monitor this development. Careful interpretation of diagnostic assessments may also reveal some gaps in knowledge or confusions about specific concepts or information.

In this section we will describe a few instructional approaches that support the development of print awareness, letter identification, and awareness of text features using whole-class strategies. Later we will identify some lessons designed specifically for students who need explicit skill development through individualized or small-group approaches.

### Approaches for Building Print Concepts, Letter Identification, and Awareness of Text Features in All Students

Daily engagement in learning experiences that are built on authentic language interactions and a wide range of written materials promotes children's natural development of print concepts, letter recognition, and knowledge of text features. Print awareness is a gradual process that expands through multiple exposures to written language of all kinds. Children can be immersed in print through a variety of routines and structures including interactive read-alouds, shared reading, and shared or interactive writing activities, all of which connect spoken language, written language, and higher-order thinking skills.

***Classroom Practices That Support the Development of Print Concepts.*** The physical environment of the classroom is a good place to begin thinking about how to immerse children in print. When a child arrives on the first day of school and discovers her name in print, it is a signal that she belongs there, in that classroom. Some kindergarten or Grade 1 children may be able to identify only the first letter of their first name; others will be able to read first, middle, and last names; but just knowing that their names are recorded is important. Eventually they will be able to identify not only their own names but also the names of their classmates, and in doing so, they will be learning important information about written language.

Many early childhood and kindergarten teachers label materials around the classroom to help students associate the label with the object or place, essentially re-creating inside the classroom the world of environmental print. These practices support the development of sight-word recognition, first through visual cues, later through partial-letter recognition, and eventually to the full alphabetic phrases when children can decode by using letter-to-sound associations (Ehri, 1992).

In all grades, daily schedules can be posted and discussed for children to see and use. Visual postings remind children to use these practical tools to identify the days of the week and segments of their day. You can expedite this process by referring to these charts frequently, reading aloud as you track the printed text. Charts and lists can serve as navigational guides for classroom routines and procedures while also encouraging children to rely on printed material. For instance, charts can list morning arrival routines in a step-by-step fashion such as: "1. Hang up your coat. 2. Empty your backpack. 3. Sign your name." Construct the list with the children as a shared writing experience, which will give them a sense of ownership and shared responsibility. When you use printed language to help students become more self-sufficient, you also reinforce the importance of print.

Your classroom library is also an important consideration. Fill your library with print of all kinds, enticing children to enter and sample the many forms. It may be helpful to organize your books so that children can easily browse, perhaps placing similar books in small manageable bins, such as an ABC book collection, an informational animal book collection, word puzzle books, and so on. If children have ready access to colorful, exciting, high-interest books, they are more likely to choose to read when they have extra time.

Book-handling skills can develop naturally when they are modeled through read-alouds and shared reading experiences. When choosing books for read-alouds, be sure to select a wide variety of books and other printed materials that are at the children's listening comprehension level. High-quality read-alouds continually expose students to new genres and text features that they cannot yet access by themselves, and at the same time, they help children realize the emotional power of the written word. As you read aloud, interact with the children and draw them into your comprehension processes by sharing the meaningful responses you have to the written language, reinforcing both your *efferent* responses, which include new information and ideas, and your *aesthetic* responses, which include emotions (Rosenblatt, 1982).

Shared reading with big books, overhead transparencies, or large poetry posters can give the entire group of children access to text and provide a powerful way to build print concepts. Shared reading occurs when the teacher's voice leads the reading and the students are invited to add their voices. One important feature of shared reading is that all children can see the text as it is being read. Sometimes teachers use an enlarged text known as a "big book." Holdaway (1982) likens the use of big books to holding the entire class of children on your lap, emulating the personalized bedtime-story setting. Shared reading demonstrates how skillful readers handle books and the world of print. Shared reading also allows teachers to demonstrate how to match voice to print, how to follow text from left to right, and how to make the return sweep when dealing with multiple lines of text. Following an initial reading during which the teacher emphasizes enjoyment and the creation of meaning, the teacher frequently rereads the text to discuss the various language and text features with the children. You can use a small pointer to help track the movement of the shared reading and to keep everyone's voice and focus together. Children love to reread familiar text both as a group and with varied speaking roles, and these multiple readings provide valuable practice time. (You will learn more about shared reading in subsequent chapters.)

Keep in mind that children also need time to practice book-handling skills on their own, even before they can manage the decoding process independently; thus they will need many opportunities to read independently throughout the day. By incorporating independent reading and partner reading into your schedule, students have the opportunity to try out their newly developing skills.

Another excellent way to demonstrate concepts of print is through morning messages or other shared writing opportunities. These daily routines include reading and writing practices and also reinforce the conventions of print. For instance, if you write morning messages to the children in the form of a letter, children should begin to identify the conventions of friendly letters such as the greeting and the closing. After reading the message together, teachers can include some analysis of the text. A first-grade child might be asked to circle an uppercase letter or a period. During shared reading and writing experiences, teachers naturally incorporate the vocabulary of language structures into the analysis portion of the text, including such terms as *word, letter, sentence,* and *line.*

You can also add printed text to routine auditory experiences. For instance, if your school has morning announcements that include the Pledge of Allegiance, prepare a printed chart of the words. Also, as children sing songs and recite poems, large charts or overhead projections can help students see the printed form of the lyrics and stanzas. In addition, consider making individual copies of songs and poems for children to use during independent or partner-reading activities and adding headphones to the listening center so that children can listen to familiar stories or songs as they follow along with the text (Miller, 2002).

***Classroom Practices That Support the Development of Letter Identification.*** Letter knowledge is best learned through engaging activities that integrate phonological awareness, high-interest books, and socially interactive language use rather than through isolated skill work (Adams, 1990). High-interest activities include engaging children with songs, charts, visual discrimination games, manipulatives, and alphabet books (Cunningham & Allington, 2007). Of course, learning how to write each letter of the alphabet also supports letter identification. Clay (1975) points out that when children are encouraged to write, their attention moves toward the finer features of each letter, which in turn supports letter identification.

You can provide a link between letter names and oral recitations by displaying a printed alphabet strip and pointing to the printed forms of the letters as the children recite or sing the names of the letters. Because many children already know the names of the letters, this activity may not be necessary for all of the children in your classes, but most kindergarteners enjoy singing familiar songs such as the alphabet song. Some teachers create a mnemonic alphabet that reinforces the name of each letter, the sound that each letter makes, and a sample word containing each letter as an onset. (Mnemonic devices are stories or pictures that connect an idea to memory.) The first three letter rehearsals might sound something like this: "A, /a/, apple; b, /b/, boy; c, /k/, cat," with the pictures of the letters resembling the word they represent (Pressley, 2002).

Repeated readings of alphabet books also reinforce the names of letters and the sounds associated with them. For instance, *Dr. Seuss's ABC* book uses silly alliterations and repeated letter naming for each letter. "Big C, little c, what begins with C? Camel on the ceiling, C. . .c. . .C!" (Seuss, 1996). Incorporated into each of the 26 letters are upper- and lowercase formations, repeated naming of the letters to fit into the rhythm of the jingles, and creative sound representations of letters such as the "c" in *camel,* /k/, and *ceiling,* /s/.

You might also encourage children to gather items from their own lives to create a personal ABC book. The first word in a child's individual book could be his first name accompanied by a photograph. Many teachers also create a word wall that is organized alphabetically. In the beginning of the school year, the word wall can include each child's name and photograph in the corresponding alphabetical section. Even older students enjoy creating themed alphabet books for content-area research projects, and you can find many examples to use as models. Author Jerry Pallotta designs entire books around a single topic, such as *The Airplane Alphabet Book* (Pallotta & Stillwell, 1999), which alphabetically lists and describes interesting aircraft and aviation terms from A to Z.

Refer to Figure 1.3 in chapter 1 for a list of recommended ABC books.

***Classroom Practices That Support Awareness of Text Features.***   Children can discover the usefulness of text features during read-alouds when you demonstrate how you use text features to find or clarify information and share some of your own thinking process as you use or interpret the various features. In other words, try to make your own thinking "visible" (Collins, Brown, & Holum, 1991). For instance, if you are demonstrating how to research a topic such as the size of the moon, model this procedure by gathering several informational books. Next, search through the books looking for features that might help you, thinking out loud as you do so. "Let's see if this book has an index so that I can find out which pages talk about the moon's size. Mmm, s, size, s, yes, here it is, page 22, let's turn there to see just how big the moon is!" Encourage the children to use these features when they do their own research.

In smaller groups you can reinforce new terminology by using guided practice (Pearson & Gallagher, 1983). In a lesson that incorporates guided practice, you usually sit with the children, offering instructional support as they begin to use a new skill. Read through the following example of introducing the term *index* to third graders.

First, you might gather multiple copies of a book about foxes, one for each group member, and in a supported session, begin by brainstorming questions about a fox. Next, choose one question to research together. Encourage the children to think about how to categorize this idea so that they can locate it in an index. For instance, if they ask the question, "How long do foxes live?", they will need to identify words that might be used in the index to represent this idea. In the case of a fox's life span, children might guess the words *age* or *life*. Through a combination of trial and error and some supported "detective work," students will be able to use the book's index to locate the information they are seeking. Plus, they will be better prepared for future research projects.

Through interactive class discussions and activities, most children naturally and seamlessly absorb the vocabulary associated with the concepts of print and the features of text. Some children, however, may need more directed and explicit instruction to fully grasp some of the print concepts, letter names, and vocabulary about text features.

## Approaches for Building Print Concepts, Letter Identification, and Knowledge of Text Features for Students with Specific Needs

Although many children develop concepts about print through natural exposure, whole-class discussions, and small-group teaching sessions, some may need more explicit instruction in individualized or small-group settings. Early intervention is important because research has shown that children who are poor readers by the end of Grade 1 often continue to be poor readers through Grade 4 and beyond (Strickland, 2002). Careful identification of a child's specific needs can lead to appropriate, focused instructional lessons.

***Explicit and Individualized Instruction for Concepts of Print.***   If a child is having difficulty understanding that print holds meaning or is challenged by the physical management of book handling, plan individualized ways to provide supported interactions with texts. Try to schedule additional small-group teacher read-alouds to simulate "lap reading" experiences, deliberately sitting side by side with the identified child to model how a book is held and how pages are turned one by one. You might also enlist the support of an instructional assistant, an older student, or a school volunteer to sit side by side, reading *to* the child, naturally guiding him to notice language and print connections. These read-aloud sessions should be interactive and casual, naturally incorporating conversational responses and book language. Give the child a chance to read independently, too, because striving learners need ample time to practice handling books by themselves so that they can develop increasing independence as readers.

Clay (1991) offers some recommendations for assisting children who are still developing the habit of left-to-right directionality of print and return sweep. First, you will need to carefully select the resources to use in your individualized instructional settings. For instance, some early texts have more white spaces between words and only one or two words per page. Some texts add more spacing between lines when multiple lines of text are included on a page. Look for early books that have consistent placement of the text until a struggling child has developed the habit of left-to-right and return sweep behaviors during reading. If a child continues to have difficulty with directionality, Clay advises a temporary visual support such as a sticker or colored dot at the top left side of a page. Some teachers use a green sticker to indicate "go" at the left side of a line of text or, in writing, to indicate where to begin writing the next line. As children move to multiple lines of text, they may or may not use their hands to guide them. The use of a paper strip (often a bookmark) supports the movement of eyes across a line of text.

Some software programs also reinforce the left-to-right directionality of text by highlighting words as the text is read through audio channels. Although computer programs can enhance literacy development, they should not be used as a substitute for explicit instruction. Cowen and Cowen (2008) suggest that you limit the amount of time young children use a computer, have an adult or older child present to support the experience, and carefully select the learning opportunities based on the specific needs of the learner.

As children gradually move toward text reading, you can encourage voice-print matching through a technique known as "assisted reading" (Bertrand & Stice, 2002). A child should practice assisted reading with a text that she has already heard. After an initial reading, the adult, sitting side by side with the child, encourages her to read along, using word-by-word finger pointing if she is able (or the adult can point to the words). As the adult and child read together fluently and with expression, the adult varies the volume of her voice, sometimes even whispering as the child's voice gains confidence. The word–by-word pointing should move to a sweeping motion as the child gains fluency. Any challenging words should be discussed after the reading rather than during it, in order to keep the emphasis on meaning making. The teacher can share this technique with the child's parents so that they can reinforce the supported rereading of books that are introduced at school. A similar technique, called Paired Reading (Topping, 1987), is described in chapter 5.

For children who are having difficulty gaining control over print concepts and understanding the "vocabulary" of reading such as letter, word, line, and sentence, the masking technique described earlier can be an effective teaching tool (Clay, 1991). Start with one concept at a time, and limit the number of items you teach. For instance, if you are trying to teach the child to identify the idea of a letter, use one word and ask the child to move the paper sliders to show you the first letter. Next ask the child to show you the last letter. Gradually increase the task, asking for two letters and so forth. If you are teaching the concept of "word," use a simple two-word-per-page book with the physical spacing exaggerated as you encourage the child to mask the word. You can also do these activities in small groups with the shared reading of a simple story.

FIGURE 2.2  **Willa's Profile for Concepts of Print, Knowledge of Letters, and Text Features**

Note: This figure has been excerpted from the full Literacy Profile chart for illustrative purposes. Please consult the full pull-out chart to identify the column headings and development phases.

| Strand *Question & Sample Assessment Tools* | Early–Mid Grade 1 | Late Grade 1–Early Grade 2 | Late Grade 2–Early Grade 3 |
|---|---|---|---|
| **2. Concepts of Print, Letter Identification, and Text Features**<br>*How familiar is the child with concepts of print, letter identification, and text features?*<br>**Sample Assessment Tools**<br>• Concepts About Print<br>• Letter ID test<br>• Letter Naming Fluency<br>• Observation notes<br>• Concepts of Print checklist<br>• Untimed Letter Naming Test | Recognizes and names all uppercase and lowercase letters<br><br>Controls voice-print matching with one- to two-syllable words<br><br>Identifies and attends to periods when used at the end of sentences during reading<br><br>Identifies and attends to question marks and exclamation points during reading | Identifies and utilizes various parts of a book: title page; table of contents<br><br>Controls voice-print matching including words with multiple syllables | Identifies and utilizes index, glossary in informational text<br><br>Identifies and attends to commas and quotation marks during reading<br><br>*[Willa's oral reading reflects her attention to punctuation; and she knows the label, "comma"] KI* |

Gray areas represent highlighting added by the teacher, preferably using a different color for each year (e.g., yellow highlights for Late K, orange highlights for Early–Mid Grade I, etc.).
Bracketed material represents teacher/examiner comments from February, Grade I.

***Explicit and Individualized Instruction for Letter Identification.*** Some children may need extra support in learning the names of the alphabet letters. Recall that in order to identify letter names, children must be able to visually discriminate the physical features of the letters. Use three-dimensional letters such as magnetic letters to reinforce letter identification. The following sequence is adapted from ideas developed by the Neuhaus Education Center in a 1992 publication. Refer to Figure 2.2 to see how Willa's developing knowledge of print concepts is recorded and annotated on Strand 2 of the Literacy Profile.

To begin your instruction, schedule multiple practice sessions with a limited number of letters. You will need to decide how many letters to use based on the learner's needs, but let's suppose you can begin with the first 10 letters of the alphabet. Show the child the letter *A* and then ask him to find one in his collection. Have the child find the letter and then place it on a small magnetic board (a cookie sheet covered with contact paper works well) as he says the name of the letter. Next show the letter *B* and say its name. Have the child find his B and place it next to the A. Review the two letters as you point and say, "A, B." Continue this process until all 10 letters are named and reviewed, keeping the activity lively and paced according to the child's ability level. Each day, the child can practice these letters and you can introduce new ones, until the child can name the entire alphabet automatically, letter by letter.

Sometimes a child might have only a few confusions with letter names. If a child becomes confused by a single letter name such as "w," you can work together on that specific letter. You can ask the child to find a "w" in a small group of letter tiles, naming the letter each time. One technique Cunningham and Allington (2007) suggest is using a printed group of words such as children's names to help children discriminate letters within words. For example, in a small-group setting, have children stand up if they see a *w* in their name.

If a child continues to confuse two letters, try to help him learn the specific distinctions of the letters by adding little stories about the letters or other mnemonic devices such as pictures. For instance, some children have a hard time distinguishing the lowercase *b* and *d* letters. You could help the child make a visual image by drawing a little bed, reviewing the letter order, *a, b, c, d,* and prompting the child to think about the *b* as the pillow for the bed because it comes before *d* in the alphabet, and to think about the *d* as the foot of the bed because it comes after the *b* in the alphabet. You can reinforce this distinction through a word sort, asking the child to put the words that begin with a *b* in one column and the words that begin with *d* in another. It is also useful to have the child draw the shapes of the letters. See chapter 10 for specific instructional practices to reinforce the writing of letters, a reciprocal act that reinforces the visual discrimination of letters.

***Explicit and Individualized Instruction for Text Features.***  For children who are having difficulty recognizing or remembering various text features, you can reinforce these concepts through small, interactive reading groups. For instance, you can create flash cards and then gather books or articles that contain the features you are reviewing. If you want to reinforce the terms *glossary, index,* and *title page,* write the words on cards. Have the children read the name of the feature when a card is turned over and help them review what the feature looks like and does; then, together with the children, locate examples in a variety of books. Be sure also to talk about the usefulness of these tools as you practice using them and reading the information you discover.

## LOOKING CLOSELY AT ONE CHILD'S ASSESSMENTS FROM STRAND 2 OF THE LITERACY PROFILE

Willa's assessments for Concepts of Print, Letter Identification, and Knowledge About Text Features were administered in late February of her first-grade year. The testing was done in a relaxed, informal, one-to-one setting.

### Assessment Results of Concepts of Print, Letter Identification, and Knowledge About Text Features

Willa's teacher administered the informal Concepts of Print Checklist and Untimed Letter-Naming Test listed in Appendices A-4 and A-5, respectively, to observe Willa's developing control over concepts of print, letter identification, and awareness of text features. Willa was invited to choose one narrative text from a group of three to use for this assessment. She chose *Where's Spot?* by Eric Hill. Additionally, a simple nonfiction book was chosen to assess text features using an oral adaptation of the scavenger hunt format described in Figure 2.1. Willa was asked to identify the following text features listed on the Literacy Profile under Strand 2: title page, table of contents, index, and glossary.

***Willa's Concepts of Print Development.***  Willa demonstrated expert book-handling skills as her teacher read aloud *Where's Spot?* Willa independently turned the pages and carefully attended to all of the illustrations, including the little cardboard "flip windows" on each page. She was able to follow the directionality of text including multiple lines on a page. Willa had awareness of letters and words within connected text. She was able to identify one word and then two words when prompted. She had some confusion over the terminology of capital letters. When Willa was asked to identify various print conventions, she was able to show the teacher a period, question mark, exclamation mark, and comma. Even though she was unable to name quotation marks, her oral reading certainly indicated that she understands their function.

***Willa's Letter-Recognition Development.***  Willa named every upper- and lowercase letter accurately and fluently, including the various fonts for *a* and *g.* She did not need to use a bookmark to track her recitation; in fact, she rarely even used her finger to point.

***Willa's Awareness of Text Features.***  Willa was able to identify the title page and the table of contents in a teacher-selected sample of nonfiction text. Further, when she was asked to locate the index and glossary, she showed an interest in the contents of the book, although she was unable to find these text features. She then explained that she was not familiar with these terms.

## Overall Evaluation of Willa's Concepts of Print, Letter Recognition, and Knowledge About Text Features

Willa has successfully mastered the emergent and early concepts about print with the exception of the terminology "capital letter." Her behaviors indicated that she has expert book-handling skills as well as control over directionality of print even when it is not in a consistent format on the page. Willa can name each of the upper- and lowercase letters, but she needs some direct instruction to supply the *label* for this concept. Although quotation marks are not generally taught at this point of Grade 1, they seemed to be within Willa's grasp, as she used different voices when she discussed the text *Where's Spot?* Again, teaching Willa the label "quotation marks" would be a sensible next step.

Another possible instructional focus could include an explicit small-group session that directly addresses the vocabulary of uppercase and capital letters. These letters can then be located both in isolation and within a context. After instruction, Willa's control over the new vocabulary can be reinforced and later reassessed to determine whether she has successfully learned these terms. This same process can be applied to quotation marks.

Willa has fluent and accurate letter-recognition skills. No further attention is needed in this area. Finally, her knowledge about text features is coming along well, and her knowledge of nonfiction text features might be expanded through teacher read-alouds, small instructional reading groups, and additional independent-reading opportunities.

## REFERENCES

Adams, M. J. (1990). *Beginning to read: Thinking and learning about print.* Cambridge, MA: MIT Press.

Barron, M. (1990). *I laen to raed and wrt the wa I laen to tak.* Katonah, NY: Richard C. Owen Publishers, Inc.

Bertrand, N. P., & Stice, C. F. (2002). Good teaching: An integrated approach to language, literacy, and learning. Portsmouth, NH: Heinemann.

Brown, H., & Cambourne, B. (1987). *Read and retell.* Portsmouth, NH: Heinemann.

Cambourne, B. (1995). Toward an educationally relevant theory of literacy learning: Twenty years of inquiry. *The Reading Teacher, 49*(3) 182–190.

Clay, M. M. (1975). *What did I write?: Beginning writing behavior.* Portsmouth, NH: Heinemann.

Clay, M. M. (1991). *Becoming literate: The construction of inner control.* Portsmouth, NH: Heinemann.

Clay, M. M. (1993). *An observation survey of early literacy achievement.* Portsmouth, NH: Heinemann.

Collins, A., Brown, J. S., & Holum, A. (1991). Cognitive apprenticeship: Making thinking visible. *American Educator,* Winter Issue.

Cowen, V. L., & Cowen, J. E. (2008). *Literacy for children in an information age: Teaching reading, writing, and thinking.* Belmont, CA: Thompson/Wadsworth.

Cunningham, P. M., & Allington, R. L. (2007). *Classrooms that work: They can all read and write.* Boston: Pearson.

Durkin, D. (2004). *Teaching them to read* (6th ed.). Boston: Pearson.

Dynamic Indicator of Basic Early Literacy Skills (DIBELS). (2007). http://dibels.uoregon.edu/benchmarkgoals.pdf

Ehri, L. C. (1991). Development of the ability to read words. In R. Barr, M. Kamil, P. Mosenthal, & P. D. Pearson (Eds.), *Handbook of reading research: Vol. II* (pp. 383–417). White Plains, NY: Longman.

Ehri, L. C. (1992). Reconceptualizing the development of sight word reading and its relation to recoding. In P. Gough, L. Ehri, & R. Treiman (Eds.), *Reading acquisition* (pp. 107–143). Hillsdale, NJ: Erlbaum.

Francis, H. (1977). *Language in teaching and learning.* London: George Allen & Unwin.

Galda, L., & Cullinan, B. E. (2006). *Literature and the child* (6th ed.). Belmont, CA: Wadsworth/Thomson Learning.

Gaskins, I. W., Ehri, L. C., Cress, C., O'Hara, C., & Donnelly, K. (1996/1997, December/January). Procedures for word learning: making discoveries about words. *The Reading Teacher, 50*(4), pp. 312–327.

Gibson, E. J., Gibson, J. J., Pick, A. D., & Osser, H. A. (1962). A developmental study of the discrimination of letter-like forms. *Journal of Comparative and Physiological Psychology, 55,* 897–906.

Halliday, M. A. K. (1982). Three aspects of children's language development: Learning language, learning through language, learning about language. In Y. Goodman, M. Hausler, & D. Strickland (Eds.), *Oral and written language development research: Impact on schools.* Urbana, IL: National Council of Teachers of English.

Hyerle, D. (1996). *Visual tools for constructing knowledge.* Alexandria, VA: American Society for Curriculum Development.

Holdaway, D. (1979). *The foundations of literacy.* Sydney: Ashton Scholastic.

Holdaway, D. (1982, November/December). The big book—A discussion with Don Holdaway. *Language Arts, 59,* 815–821.

Leu, D. (2002). The new literacies: Research on reading instruction with the Internet. In A. Farstrup & S. J. Samuels (Eds.), *What research has to say about reading instruction* (pp. 310–336). Newark, DE: International Reading Association.

Miller, D. (2002). *Reading with meaning: Teaching comprehension in the primary grades.* Portland, ME: Stenhouse.

Moline, S. (1995). *I see what you mean: Children at work with visual information.* Portland, ME: Stenhouse.

Mooney, M. E. (2001). *Text forms and features: A resource for intentional teaching.* Katonah, NY: Richard C. Owens Publishers, Inc.

Morrow, L. M. (1997). *Literacy development in the early years: Helping children read and write* (3rd ed.). Englewood Cliffs, NJ: Prentice-Hall.

Morrow, L., & Sulzby, E. (1995). *Teacher's workshop: An instructional handbook for kindergarten teachers.* Glenview, IL: Scott Foresman.

Neuhaus Education Center. (1992). *Reading readiness.* Bellaire, TX: Texas Center for Reading and Language Arts.

Pallotta, J., & Stillwell, F. (1999). *The airplane alphabet book.* New York: Scholastic.

Pearson, P. D., & Gallagher, M. C. (1983). The instruction of reading comprehension. *Contemporary Educational Psychology, 8,* pp. 317–345.

Pressley, M. (2002). *Reading instruction that works: The case for balanced teaching* (2nd ed.). New York: Guiford Press.

Rosenblatt, L. M. (1982). The literacy transaction: Evocation and response. *Theory into Practice, 21*(4), pp. 268–278.

Seuss, Dr. (1996). *Dr. Seuss's ABC: An amazing alphabet book.* New York: Random House Books for Young Readers.

Snow, C. E., Burns, S. M., & Griffin, P. (1998). *Preventing reading difficulties in young children.* Washington, DC: National Academy Press.

Steig, W. (1990). *Doctor DeSoto*. New York: Farrar, Straus and Giroux.

Strickland, D. S. (2002). The importance of early intervention. In A. Farstrup & S. J. Samuels (Eds.), *What research has to say about reading instruction* (pp. 69–86). Newark, DE: International Reading Association.

Teale, W., & Sulzby, E. (1986). *Emergent literacy: Writing and reading*. Norwood, NJ: Ablex.

Topping, K. (1987). Paired reading: A powerful technique for parent use. *The Reading Teacher, 40,* 608–614.

# CHAPTER THREE

# Decoding and Word Recognition

## CORE QUESTION

To what degree is the child learning the decoding and word recognition skills needed for reading?

"Try sounding it out" is a refrain heard frequently in classrooms and homes, in response to a child who does not immediately recognize a word. In many cases "sounding it out" (or decoding "regular" words such as *log, strike,* or *kidnap* from left to right) does work well, but in other cases (such as when trying to sound out the words *two, enough,* or *friend*), it does not, because the word is irregular, or not easily "decoded." The process of figuring out how to read particular words is called *word identification,* and it involves a number of skills and strategies including decoding, automatic word recognition, and structural analysis. According to the report of the National Reading Panel (2000), there is substantial evidence of a strong relationship between systematic instruction in phonics and children's later success in learning to read.

As we explore the concepts of decoding and word recognition, it's important to keep in mind that professionals and researchers often have a particular "stance" regarding decoding, phonics in particular. Some professionals have a "structured language" perspective, others take a more "holistic" approach, and still others (such as the authors of this book) might describe themselves as "balanced." We will, however, try to include the perspectives of others when it seems important to do so.

In this chapter we will particularly focus on the development of decoding skills (using phonics and structural analysis) and word recognition, or the automatic reading of sight words. The "line" between these skills and strategies and those listed in chapter 9, on spelling, and in chapter, 4 on reading strategies, is a fine one; as a result, you will find that we will sometimes refer ahead to those chapters. Spelling and decoding definitely support each other, as do decoding and the use of reading strategies. However, *too much* emphasis on decoding, without attention given to the use of other strategies such as using context, will cause problems for students, as will *too little* emphasis on decoding and word recognition.

**LITERACY PROFILE**
Have your Literacy Profile available as you read through this chapter, referring to the question and indicators for Strand 3.

## UNDERLYING PRINCIPLES OF DECODING AND WORD RECOGNITION

Decoding and word recognition are definitely key components of the reading process, and instruction in these areas is critical for children's success (Chall, 1967; Pressley, 2002). However, we also know that it is important to keep decoding and word recognition in perspective, because they are necessary, but not sufficient, abilities for the developing reader. We sometimes hear a child proudly announce, "I learned how to read today!", but, while that certainly is cause for celebration, it's most likely that the child made a breakthrough in "cracking the code." With instructional support in areas such as vocabulary, comprehension, fluency, and lots of opportunities to build stamina in reading, the child should thrive and grow into a thoughtful and competent reader.

Recent research offers useful insights into best practices regarding decoding and word recognition (Adams, 1995; Gentry, 2006; Moats, 2004, Pressley, 2002). We know now that having children memorize rules of phonics that are well beyond their stage of development simply does not work. Neither is there evidence that having children read heavily decodable text ("Dan can tap the fan") is more effective than other approaches (Pressley, 2002). At the same time, opinions still vary as to the proper degree of emphasis on decoding and the role of decodable text during early reading instruction. In this section we will first consider the nature of decoding and word recognition, and then we will turn to a few key points and principles that have implications for assessment and instruction.

### Understanding the Nature of Decoding and Word Recognition

A good place to start is to distinguish among the terms involved in this area of literacy. Harp and Brewer (2005) differentiate between two primary ways of dealing with print: word recognition and word identification, explaining that "if we recognize a word, it is one that we have already learned" (p. 154). *Word recognition*, then, is "instantaneous" and automatic. When we encounter words that we do *not* immediately recognize, we must make some use of strategies and skills. This process is called *word identification*.

Word identification can include a range of strategies and skills. In chapter 4 we will discuss the multiple cueing systems (graphophonic, syntactic, and semantic) that readers use to strategically identify a word.

Refer to chapter 4 to learn more about these three cueing systems.

The *graphophonic* cueing system is where phonics and decoding come in. The term *phonics* often refers to the method of instruction that focuses on sound-symbol correspondences and patterns (e.g., that the /f/ sound can be represented by the letter *f* or the combination *ph* or sometimes even *gh*). It can also refer to the set of strategies that children use to bring attention to parts of a word. The term *decoding*, which refers to a method that uses knowledge of phonics, involves starting with written symbols to get to the intended pronunciation of a word.

According to Ehri (1998), the process of decoding involves three components: acquiring the alphabetic principle (i.e., recognizing that letters represent sounds), blending letters into sounds, and using phonograms (also known as word patterns) and analogies. The phrase *word attack* is often used interchangeably with *decoding* to describe the process of figuring out how to pronounce a word, or how to "unlock the code" of a word. We will look first at what is involved in learning to decode a word, starting with sound-symbol correspondence, and then we will discuss additional kinds of knowledge and skills that children need to be able to identify words, including structural analysis and syllable types and patterns.

**Decoding and Phonics.**  Ehri's (1998) components of decoding provide a helpful organizer for thinking about what children need to learn in order to unlock the code. We'll first address the three areas she identified, and then we'll turn to syllable types and patterns that can be helpful tools for children in Grades 3, 4, and above. It's important to keep in mind, though, that other aspects of knowledge and skills—such as phonological awareness (i.e., noticing and manipulating the sounds of language) and concepts of print (e.g., knowing the difference between letters and words, tracking print from left to right)—provide a critical foundation for this area of reading development.

*Acquiring the Alphabetic Principle.*  The alphabetic principle refers to understanding that letters and spoken sounds have systematic and predictable relationships. This may seem to be something that children learn automatically, but actually it is a hallmark of a child's beginning to read (Adams, 1990). Acquisition of this principle is highly influenced by the kinds of print experiences a youngster has had, as well as the child's development of phonological awareness (Snow, Burns, & Griffin, 1998).

Learning the sounds that letters represent is known as "sound-symbol correspondence." Again, this sounds like a straightforward kind of learning, but because English is a relatively complex language, it's not a simple task. English has 44 phonemes (sounds) but over a thousand graphemes, or letters and letter combinations that can represent those sounds. That's not exactly a one-to-one correspondence! Children need to learn the different ways these letters and letter combinations can work together. This involves learning the sounds of consonants, short and long vowels, consonant blends and digraphs, and other vowel patterns. Fortunately, the English language has many predictable patterns regarding how letters and sounds are related that children can learn.

*Blending Sounds into Words.*  Knowing what sounds might be made by a letter or a combination of letters in a word is a good start, but children also need to be able to work from left to right to blend those sounds into a real word, which involves "mapping," or matching, the sounds represented by the letters in the word and stringing them together. Some students can do this quite easily; others need a good deal of modeling and support to overcome this stumbling block. One common challenge children face occurs when they add a vowel sound to a consonant sound like /b/ or /g/ so that it ends up sounding like "buh" and "guh." When a child tries to blend the sounds of the word *big* together, it sometimes comes out sounding like "buh-i-guh." Blending "successively" by linking the first sound with the second and then linking the sounds that follow (/bi/, then "big"), is especially helpful to students; eventually they need to learn to blend the sounds together silently.

*Using Phonograms and Decoding by Analogy.*  Phonograms are simply clusters of letters, word parts, or spelling patterns, such as words that end with "at" or "ock." Learning to recognize these patterns or clusters of letters greatly helps a child gain efficiency and move toward automaticity and independence (Cunningham & Allington, 2007). The terms *onset* and *rime* refer to the parts of single-syllable words; these terms are highly useful to

As you read this section, you may want to refer to the part of chapter 9 that describes stages of spelling. Stages of spelling and the levels of acquiring decoding skills are closely aligned.

teach students how to see similarities among words as they learn to decode by analogy.

Being able to recognize familiar rimes (also called *phonograms*) is very helpful for young readers and allows them to decode by analogy. For example, a first grader might see the unfamiliar word "stuck" in a story about a cat caught in a tree. If the child looks closely at "stuck" and notices that the rime part looks a lot like the rime at the end of "truck" (which is a word he knows well), he can use that knowledge to help him figure out "stuck." That is a case of decoding by analogy.

The concepts of *onset* and *rime* were discussed in chapter 1.

*Syllable Types and Patterns.* Knowing how syllables work in words is also highly useful, for both reading and spelling (Moats, 2004). English has six types of syllables, some of which can stand alone as words and some of which are present only in multisyllabic words. Brief descriptions, labels, and examples of each syllable type are shown in Figure 3.1.

Children in first and second grade almost always learn about closed syllables, syllables with "silent *e*," and "*r*-controlled" syllables, although schools and programs vary in how directly they teach the other types of syllables. Teachers who use a developmental approach to spelling tend to address syllable types while having children explore words with different spelling patterns.

In addition, syllable patterns, or rules for syllable division, are often taught in third and fourth grades; gaining this knowledge can be quite helpful for both decoding and spelling (Moats, 2004). For example, children learn that when a multisyllabic word has two consonants in the middle, they can usually divide the syllables between the consonants (unless the consonants are a digraph such as /sh/ or /ch/). The words "pumpkin" and "banner" are examples of this kind of pattern. Another pattern is vowel-consonant-vowel, seen in words like "lady" and "migrate." It's helpful for third and fourth graders to know that in words with this type of arrangement of vowels and consonants, 75% of the time the first vowel will be long because the syllables divide before the consonant (Time Online, 2000). Again, you will find that schools and teachers differ in terms of the amount of time they spend on teaching these patterns.

*Structural Analysis.* To help children decode multisyllabic words, which are encountered much more frequently in second, third, and fourth grades, concepts of *structural analysis* are taught. These concepts include learning to decode compound words (*doghouse*), contractions (*couldn't*), words with inflectional endings (*swimming*), and words with bases, roots, prefixes, and suffixes (*unbelievable*). Lipson (2007) emphasizes that children in Grades 3 and beyond "often need to engage in structural analysis *before* they can apply their phonics knowledge" (p. 172).

Needless to say, the elements noted above need to be taught gradually, from late first grade onward, and are most effectively addressed in

FIGURE 3.1 **Syllable Types**

| Syllable Type | Description | Example(s) |
|---|---|---|
| Closed | Syllable that ends in a consonant (or consonants) and has one vowel, which is short | cap<br>itch |
| Open | Syllable that ends in a vowel, and has only one vowel, which is long | no<br><u>cra</u>zy |
| Silent *e* | Syllable where *e* makes the vowel sound long | hope<br>flame |
| *r*-controlled | Syllable that includes a vowel sound influenced by *r* | art<br><u>curv</u>ing |
| Vowel teams | Syllable that includes two or more vowels that work together to make one sound | couch<br><u>crowd</u>ed |
| Consonant -*le* | Syllable that includes "-le" and has the "schwa" sound | purple<br>marble |

conjunction with spelling instruction. In addition, work on common bases, roots, prefixes, and suffixes will also help expand students' knowledge of vocabulary. You probably agree that it's a good thing these aspects of literacy support each other.

***Word Recognition.***    As we explained at the beginning of this chapter, word recognition involves the automatic or instantaneous reading of a word, as opposed to analyzing or decoding the word sound by sound or part by part. Automaticity in word recognition is an important skill, one that usually develops as a result of wide and frequent reading. A number of different terms are used to describe words that are recognized automatically. *Sight words* are those that a child pronounces automatically, which tend to differ from child to child, depending on reading instruction and experiences. For one child, "to" might be an early sight word, whereas for another, "love" will be an early sight word. Sometimes sight words are simply learned visually, "by sight," but at other times they become "represented in memory as a unit" (Pressley, 2002) after initial exposure by sounding out that's followed by repeated readings of the word.

*High-frequency words* are those that researchers have identified as appearing in print very often, and therefore worth learning. Schumm (2006) notes that the "100 most common words actually make up about 50% of the text that we read" (p. 164). These include some "decodable" words such as *did* and *name* as well as some "irregular" words such as *through* and *again*. Fry, Kress, and Fountoukidis (2000) have a very helpful listing of high-frequency words broken down by grade level.

Gaining skill in word recognition is critical because our brains have limited "working memory." Pressley (2002) explains that because we have only five to nine "slots" in our short-term memory, we need to make sure that it is not overloaded. When observing some beginning readers, you can almost see the overload on their working memory as they labor to decode every word. Once they develop some automaticity, their reading process is much less labored, allowing them to concentrate on the meaning of what they are reading.

## Understanding Key Principles of Decoding and Word Recognition

Knowing what needs to be taught in the area of decoding and word recognition is important, but it is also good to reflect on some key principles and recommendations from research and best practice. Again, keep in mind that educators still vary quite a bit in their views concerning the area of phonics. The "reading wars" have ebbed and flowed over the past decades, but differences in perspective persist. By the "reading wars" we are referring to the tensions between educators with different views regarding the proper focus of reading instruction. Usually this breaks down to educators who emphasize phonics on one side and those who favor a literature-based approach on the other side.

***Recommendations from the National Reading Panel.***    In 2000, the Report of the National Reading Panel, *Teaching Children to Read: An Evidence-Based Assessment of the Scientific Research Literature on Reading and Its Implications for Reading Instruction*, was released. This research review had very specific criteria for the kinds of research that it considered and has been lauded by some and criticized by others because of topics it did not address and research it did not include. Focusing primarily on the five key components of reading that we discussed in the introductory chapter, the report particularly focused on recommendations in the areas of phonemic awareness, phonics, and comprehension. Regarding phonics, the report emphasized systematic instruction in phonics and stressed the importance of teaching phonics sequentially and explicitly, but stopped short of recommending any particular program or specific technique as "the answer." The report did recommend that systematic phonics instruction include:

- The direct teaching of letter-sound relationships in a clearly defined sequence
- Materials that provide children with a large number of words that they can decode using learned letter-sound relationships
- Many opportunities for learning to spell words and write stories (Armbruster, Lehr, & Osborn, 2001)

***Other Key Principles and Recommendations.*** Some very helpful guidance concerning how to address phonics, decoding, and word recognition comes from Harp and Brewer (2005) as well as from Cooper, Chard, and Kiger (2006). The following are some key points to keep in mind:

- Children develop the ability to use phonics/decoding strategies in stages, and instruction should always be based on what children know.
- Phonics is a means, not an end in and of itself. As much as possible, the teacher should connect phonics instruction to real-text reading, using appropriate material.
- Phonics instruction should be systematic and explicit, but also active and engaging.
- Instruction in word identification should also address irregular words, teaching the most useful words first, and monitoring children's progress.

### Summary of Understanding the Nature of Word Recognition and Phonics

In this section we discussed the differences between decoding (word attack, using phonics strategies) and word recognition (automatic reading of words), and we also clarified some key terms used in this area. We outlined some key topics for instruction, including sound-symbol correspondences, phonograms, structural analysis, and syllable types, and reviewed the kinds of words that students need to learn to recognize with automaticity. Finally, we discussed some key recommendations from the National Reading Panel concerning phonics instruction, along with some key points raised by others in the field. Summing up, we suggest that teachers address phonics and word recognition through a systematic approach, making sure that they link instruction to students' assessed needs and connect it to real reading and writing.

## ASSESSING DECODING AND WORD RECOGNITION

Because learning to decode and recognize words automatically is so critical for the early stages of learning to read, having access to effective and informative assessment to guide instruction is also vital. As noted earlier, it isn't effective to teach a child phonics rules and patterns that are beyond his or her current stage of development. Thus, the most successful assessment practices will be tailored to the level of the child's development and provide information that the teacher can directly translate into appropriate next steps for instruction. First we will review some formal and commercial measures, and then we will consider some informal tools and assessment approaches that can be used on an ongoing basis.

## Formal or Published Measures for Assessing Word Recognition and Phonics

A variety of formal assessment tools are available for assessing children's progress in decoding and word recognition. Some assessment tools may be administered to a group; others should be administered individually. In general, assessments that are individually administered will provide more information that can be used to inform instruction. Some of the tools mentioned will provide information in the area of spelling as well, which can be advantageous for the teacher who is trying to be both strategic and efficient in selecting and scheduling assessments and using the results of assessment to inform teaching.

***Group-Administered Tools.*** A number of standardized tests administered at the primary level include a section on word identification. For example, the Stanford Diagnostic Reading Test (Karlsen & Gardner, 2005) and the GRADE assessment (Williams, 2005) both include subtests at the early levels to help identify children's needs in the area of phonics. Some state-level assessments, such as the New England Common Assessment program used in Vermont, Rhode Island, and New Hampshire, include a word-identification subtest (at Grades 3 and 4), but this assessment is not intended to provide information about individual needs as much as program-level information concerning a school or district. For example, a school might see that in the area of word identification, their third graders are doing less well than third graders at other schools in the district or state, and then take measures to strengthen the curriculum or the professional development of its teachers. In general, teachers should be cautious when interpreting the results of these state- or program-level assessments regarding individual students, partly because of the limitations of the group-administered format, but also because the purpose of these assessments is to provide program-level evaluation, not diagnostic or progress-monitoring information.

***Individually Administered Tools.*** A variety of individually administered, commercially published assessment tools are available in the areas of decoding and word recognition. Some are formal diagnostic assessments, such as the Roswell-Chall Diagnostic Reading Test (Roswell & Chall, 1997) and the Woodcock-Johnson Diagnostic Reading Battery (Woodcock, Mather, & Schrank, 2004). Both of these tests include subtests that specifically assess phonics knowledge along with other areas.

Other tests that measure phonics and decoding abilities include the Initial Letter Sound Fluency Test of DIBELS (Dynamic Indicators of Basic Early Literacy Skills; University of Oregon, 2005), the PALS assessment (Phonological Awareness Literacy Screening; Invernizzi, Meier, & Juel, 2005), Scholastic's CORE Phonics survey, developmental spelling assessments such as the Elementary Spelling Inventory (Bear, Invernizzi, Templeton, & Johnston, 2008), and the Developmental Spelling Analysis (Ganske, 2000).

The DIBELS Nonsense-Word Fluency subtest, as the name suggests, includes only nonwords (*kov, luj, feg*) and takes 1 minute to administer. Scores that are obtained let the teacher know whether the student demonstrates low risk, moderate risk, or high risk, or whether the student's score indicates that he or she is above average in this skill. Because some children respond differently to tests using nonsense words than they do to tests using real words, if you use the DIBELS nonsense-word fluency test, we believe you should supplement it with measures of decoding that use real words. Another reason to use additional assessment tools is that the DIBELS Nonsense-Word Fluency subtest assesses only words that have the CVC pattern. DIBELS tests are available online at http://dibels.uoregon.edu

To locate the CORE Phonics survey, which is available online from Scholastic, go to http://www.scholastic.com/dodea/Module_2/resources/dodea_m2_tr_core.pdf

Two tools from McKenna and Stahl (2003) are particularly valuable for isolating areas of word identification that are "in place" and those that need more work. Their Informal Phonics Survey provides a flexible and straightforward way to monitor children's skill acquisition, including subtests of consonant sounds, digraphs, short vowels, blends, long vowels, vowel digraphs (*oa, ea, ay, ai*), vowel diphthongs (*oy, oi, ou*), etc. By using the scoring guide, teachers can identify which areas students have mastered, which need a bit of review, and which need systematic instruction.

The Developmental Test of Word Recognition has an even broader range of items (from the concept of a word to polysyllabic words) and involves having the child point to one target word out of a set of words. For example, for one item the choices are *propose, purpose,* and *papoose,* and the child is asked to point to "purpose" and say why she or he selected that word. This "explanation" component can be particularly helpful to teachers who need to uncover possible misunderstandings children have about how words work.

One additional assessment worth mentioning, because it is particularly appropriate for older students (from late second grade on), is the Names Test, which was originally developed by Cunningham (1990) and later revised/enhanced by Duffelmeyer, Kruse, Merkley, and Fyfe (1994). These tests yield information about children's decoding skills but do so in a unique format that uses made-up names. See Figure 3.2 for a sample of the items on this assessment. More recently, Mather, Sammons, and Schwartz (2006) developed an adaptation of the original Names Test, called the Early Names Test, that is appropriate for most second graders and targets children's grapheme-phoneme knowledge. An added benefit of these assessments is that they have children read *real* words as opposed to nonsense words, which makes the assessments seem relatively authentic to children.

Several other published assessment tools evaluate students' *word-recognition* skills and are particularly useful for identifying strengths and weaknesses in this area. Most informal reading inventories, such as the Ekwall-Shanker Inventory (Shanker & Ekwall, 2000), and Jerry Johns's Basic Reading Inventory (2001), include graded word lists. These inventories use the word lists as a way to determine at which level of text a child might be able to start during an informal reading inventory. They may also provide some information about a child's ability to read words in isolation. Other assessments commonly used are the Fry Instant Word List (mentioned earlier in this chapter), the San Diego Quick Assessment (LaPray & Ross, 1969), and the Dolch Basic Sight Vocabulary list.

To obtain copies of the enhanced version of the Names Test (which is appropriate for students in Grade 3 and up) and the Early Names Test (which is appropriate for students in Grade 2), go to the Web site of the International Reading Association, www.reading.org, and search for the articles (by the authors listed) that contain these helpful assessment tools.

You can download copies of both the Dolch and the Fry lists from the Web site of the National Institute for Literacy. The link for the Dolch list is http://www.nifl.gov/readingprofiles/Dolch_Basic.pdf and the link for the Fry list is http://www.nifl.gov/readingprofiles/Instant_Words.pdf

## FIGURE 3.2  Sample items from the Names Test

| Directions: Tell the student that he/she is to pretend to be a teacher, reading a list of student names to take attendance. Explain that you cannot help at all, but to make a guess if he/she comes to a name he/she is not sure about. Have the student read the list orally. |
| --- |
| Kimberly Blake |
| Chester Wright |
| Wendy Swain |
| Ned Westmoreland |
| Troy Whitlock |

Cunningham, P. M. (1990, October). The names test: A quick assessment of decoding ability. *The Reading Teacher 44*(2) 124–129.

## Informal Measures for Assessing Word Recognition and Phonics

Many of the assessments noted in the previous section involve children decoding or identifying words in isolation. While valuable (and quite specific) information can be obtained from such tools, it is important to find out the degree to which children use decoding and word recognition skills when they are reading "connected" text, not words in insolation. There are a number of ways to check children's knowledge and use of decoding skills and word recognition on an ongoing, everyday basis. Reviewing running records and records of oral reading, and using checklists and anecdotal records are all very flexible and can be highly informative, because these strategies help uncover to what degree a child is applying decoding and word recognition skills in real reading situations.

***Review of Running Records and Records of Oral Reading.*** In chapter 4 we will describe running records and records of oral reading in some detail. Basically they provide a way for teachers to record what children actually say during oral reading. By looking closely at children's behaviors during oral reading, you can see real evidence of their use of decoding skills and sight-word recognition. Most forms for taking running records and records of oral reading do not prompt the teacher to specifically analyze a child's use of decoding skills and understanding of graphophonic cues, but with the information so close at hand, the teacher can certainly analyze that information when needed. In such cases we suggest looking at students' substitution errors (i.e., errors in which students say a different word than the one in the text) and asking the questions included in the Decoding Application Scale presented in Appendix A-6.

***Checklists.*** Many teachers use checklists to evaluate children's use of decoding and word recognition skills during oral reading. For successful evaluation, keep the checklist simple and geared to each child's stage of development. If a child is just getting started with reading, you might use a checklist like the one in Figure 3.3 (in addition to other assessments of print concepts and phonological awareness), but for a child who is reading more complex words and text, a checklist like the one in Figure 3.4 might be more appropriate.

FIGURE 3.3  **Checklist for an Emergent Reader: Focus on Decoding and Word Recognition**

| Name: | Date: | Text Read: | |
|---|---|---|---|
| **Behavior** | | **Observed?** | **Notes:** |
| Recognizes some high-frequency words (e.g., *I, me, said*) | | | |
| Recognizes own name and its individual letters | | | |
| Tracks print accurately with hand or finger | | | |
| Notices similarities in words | | | |
| Uses knowledge of initial and final consonants during reading | | | |
| Uses knowledge of familiar rimes/phonograms | | | |
| Attempts to sound out word | | | |
| Overall Comments: | | | |

FIGURE 3.4  **Checklist for an Intermediate Reader: Focus on Decoding and Word Recognition**

| Name: | Date: | Text Read: | |
|---|---|---|---|
| **Behavior** | | **Observed?** | **Notes:** |
| Shows automatic recognition of high-frequency words (e.g., *although, through, against*) | | | |
| Uses word roots, prefixes, suffixes, and inflected endings to read words | | | |
| Reads contractions and compound words | | | |
| Notices similarities in words; uses analogy strategy to decode unfamiliar words | | | |
| Understands that vowel sounds may be represented in a variety of ways in words | | | |
| Overall Comments: | | | |

***Anecdotal Notes.***  Anecdotal notes can also provide a flexible way to record your observations of students' developing skills. You can take these notes any time a student is reading orally (or even whisper-reading) as long as you have some Post-its, note cards, or a form for taking notes. To make the most of anecdotal notes, make sure that you know in advance what you are looking for. For example, if you just finished teaching a lesson on inflected endings (*-s, -ed, -ing*) and you want to investigate whether students are applying that skill, you might record an anecdotal note such as the one displayed in Figure 3.5.

## Summary of Assessing Decoding and Word Recognition

Finding out what children can control in the area of decoding and word recognition is critical, and a variety of tools are available to help you evaluate children's progress. While group-administered assessments can provide some useful information, primarily for program planning, individually administered assessments are preferable in terms of guiding instruction because of the

FIGURE 3.5  **Sample Anecdotal Note**

| | |
|---|---|
| **Student:** | *Kris, Gr 1* |
| **Date:** | *May 6* |
| **Setting:** | *Buddy Reading time* |
| **Focus:** | *inflected endings* |

*K reading* Fox at School *with a buddy.*

*K read "playing" instead of "played"—but then said, "That doesn't make sense!"*

*We wrote* played *and* playing *on the whiteboard, and he made a box around the -ing and -ed parts.*

*Then K read the next pg—and read "played" a-ok.*

specific information they can provide. In order to get a balanced picture of children's skills, we recommend that you use assessments that include word lists in conjunction with ongoing, informal assessments of children's actual use of decoding and word recognition skills during reading. In the next section we turn to how you can use this assessment information to inform your instruction.

## INSTRUCTIONAL APPROACHES FOR DECODING AND WORD RECOGNITION

The early years of schooling are the best time to teach decoding and word recognition. We know that learning to crack the code of reading is essential for a child to become a competent and confident reader, and we also know that children learn best when instruction matches their stage of development. In this section we will first consider some common approaches for addressing decoding and word recognition with all students, and then we will discuss how assessment information might help teachers make decisions about what approaches or techniques to use, and when to use them. Finally, we will review some approaches and techniques that are often useful for students who demonstrate particular difficulty with decoding and word recognition.

### Instructional Approaches for Supporting Decoding and Word Recognition in All Students

A wide range of approaches exist to help children make progress in this important area of reading, and a good deal of research has been conducted on determining which approaches are most effective. It's important to note that there are still some persistent differences regarding some key issues, such as the use of decodable text, the integrated word-study approach, or the implicit/embedded approach to phonics instruction. There are also several different labels for different approaches to phonics instruction; see Figure 3.6 for a list of commonly referred-to approaches and descriptions of each.

FIGURE 3.6  **Common Approaches to Phonics**

---

*Synthetic phonics* Children learn how to convert letters or letter combinations into sounds, and then how to blend the sounds together to form recognizable words.

*Analytic phonics* Children learn to analyze letter-sound relationships in previously learned words. They do not pronounce sounds in isolation.

*Analogy-based phonics* Children learn to use parts of word families they know to identify words they don't know that have similar parts.

*Phonics through spelling* Children learn to segment words into phonemes and to make words by writing letters for phonemes.

*Embedded phonics* Children are taught letter-sound relationships during the reading of connected text. (Since children encounter different letter-sound relationships as they read, this approach is not systematic or explicit.)

*Onset-rime phonics instruction* Children learn to identify the sound of the letter or letters before the first vowel (the onset) in a one-syllable word and the sound of the remaining part of the word (the rime).

---

From Armbruster, B., Lehr, F., & Osborn, J. (2001). *Put reading first: The building blocks for teaching children to read.* Washington, DC: National Institute for Literacy.

As noted previously, though, perspectives still vary as to what kind of research "counts," and which approach (or approaches) work best. For example, Louisa Cook Moats (2007) is critical of what she terms *whole-language derivative* styles of reading instruction. These approaches, she argues, include no systematic presentation of sound-symbol correspondence, have teacher-made mini-lessons that address student errors, and avoid phonics readers, instead using leveled books with no phonetically controlled vocabulary.

A similar view is expressed in the National Institute for Literacy's *Put Reading First* (Armbruster et al., 2000) document, which reports that "systematic and explicit phonics instruction makes a bigger contribution to children's growth in reading than instruction that provides non-systematic or no phonics instruction" (p. 13). This document, which is a summary of the NRP report, defines systematic phonics instruction as the direct teaching of a set of letter-sound relationships in a clearly defined sequence.

An earlier report from the National Research Council, titled *Preventing Early Reading Difficulties in Young Children* (Snow et al., 1998), was less emphatic and recommended that beginning readers have explicit instruction in the "mechanics" of reading. It also emphasized that "those who have grasped the alphabetic principle and can apply it productively should move on to more advanced learning opportunities" (p. 321).

An often-cited study of first-grade classrooms by Juel and Minden-Cupp (2000) found that poor readers benefit from early and heavy exposure to phonics, but that as soon as they are able to read independently, they benefit from a more balanced program that's focused on vocabulary, text discussion, and wide reading. A resource from the International Reading Association (Braunger & Lewis, 2006) includes 13 "core understandings," one of which states that "children develop phonemic awareness and knowledge of phonics through a variety of literacy opportunities, models and demonstrations" (p. 77). Finally, Meyer (2003), in his article "Captives of the Script: Killing Us Softly with Phonics," is clearly critical of the emphasis on explicit phonics and argues that scripted phonics programs are holding teachers and students as *curriculum hostages*.

Given the diversity of views regarding instruction in phonics and decoding, it can sometimes be hard for a teacher to know how to proceed. But the key points referred to earlier in this chapter can serve as helpful guidance for assessment and instruction. In this section we first review some approaches commonly used in kindergarten through fourth-grade classrooms, including commercial, comprehensive, and skill-focused programs as well as specific techniques that are useful for most children, as indicated by assessment.

***Whole-Class Approaches.*** Phonics is often addressed through systematic instruction with the whole class in a large-group setting, either as part of a comprehensive "core" (basal) program or as a stand-alone program. One stand-alone program is Fundations (Wilson Language Training, 2005), a whole-class adaptation of the Wilson Structured Language program, which was originally developed for older, struggling readers. This approach, following a carefully constructed sequence, involves highly explicit and active teaching and learning techniques and combines phonics and spelling instruction.

Another "stand-alone" whole-class approach is Month-by-Month Phonics (Cunningham & Hall, 2003). As the title indicates, this approach offers a sequence of activities for each month and for each grade level. While activities differ as the year continues, most of the monthly outlines include word wall routines, techniques for spelling, making words, sorting words, and "guess the covered word" techniques. This approach is less structured and explicit than those mentioned previously. Several of these activities will be described in more detail below.

Other whole-class approaches include Phonics Lessons by Fountas and Pinnell (2003), which provides a grade-specific curriculum for kindergarten through second grade and active learning techniques. Topics addressed include early print concepts, letter knowledge, spelling patterns, high-frequency words, and word structure, depending upon the grade level.

Although the approaches described above do include some recommendations for differentiating according to the assessed needs of children, they basically are designed for whole-group instruction. Therefore, when using these approaches teachers need to be mindful of the needs of children at either end of the spectrum: those who already know the skills and concepts you are teaching and those for whom the skills and concepts are too advanced.

***Small-Group Approaches.***   Because students vary in how they develop skills in decoding and word recognition, small-group approaches are often needed to more closely match instruction to learners' assessed needs. A number of such approaches are available, some addressing phonics and word identification along with areas such as reading fluency and comprehension. In chapter 9, which focuses on spelling, we will describe developmental word-study groups, which are formed based on children's assessed stages of spelling development. Usually teachers have no more than three of these groups operating in a classroom, and they use this instructional opportunity to teach both spelling and decoding. When using this approach, it's very important to build in opportunities for children to apply this knowledge and skill through actual reading practice.

Tyner's (2004) model of differentiated small-group reading instruction includes a carefully sequenced component on phonics and decoding. Each lesson includes activities that are appropriate to children's assessed needs and build on previous patterns studied. In addition, word patterns and other resources for each stage are included. For example, children at the emergent stage review simple high-frequency words in their "word bank," match letters of the alphabet, play a "concentration" game with letters, and engage in a quick "spell-check" activity of writing letters that are dictated. Benefits of this model include the built-in match between assessment and instruction and the connection between word study and reading, but it may be a challenge for teachers to find sufficient time to fit in all groups each day.

***Specific Techniques for Decoding and Word Recognition.***   A wide range of routines and techniques can be used to support children as they learn to decode and build their automaticity with sight words. We'll note a few techniques in this section that are often used with all students; later we will consider some techniques that are specialized for children with particular or intensive needs.

Techniques for building early letter-sound correspondences take many forms, and some are more explicit than others. Teachers in a particular school or district often use a shared set of key pictures with a corresponding letter (such as Aa apple) and review combinations learned daily. Many use sound-symbol cards, alphabet puzzles, alphabet books, flip books, and games such as concentration or dominoes.

To build recognition of high-frequency words, teachers often have children locate on a chart a word that was introduced during shared reading (e.g., "want"). The teacher might call on individual children to point to that word using a yardstick, wand, or pointer. The students who were not called up to the front are asked to "frame" the word in their heads and share (in a quiet voice) its location on the chart with someone sitting near them.

Teachers can use additional decoding activities with students at later stages of development as well. Word hunts, in which children search through books, wall charts, and other resources for words with particular sounds and patterns (such as /er/, /ar/, /or/), are especially effective because they help children notice graphophonic features in actual texts, not just in isolation. Word sorts, such as those described in *Words Their Way* (Bear et al., 2003) and *Word Journeys* (Ganske, 2000), provide a hands-on way to help students notice features that words have in common. In addition, word games such as Scattergories (Bear et al., 2008) are quite engaging and effective with children who are beyond the emergent stage of development.

*Cut-Up Sentences*. This technique, sometimes called "sentence strips," is widely used with kindergartners and first graders to help them look closely at words and letters. Key to this approach is the teacher's decision of *where* to cut apart the sentence or the words within the sentence. For example, with a group of emergent readers, the teacher might write on oak-tag paper a short sentence such as, "I like to play soccer" and then cut it into five parts: "I," "like," "to," "play," and "soccer"—because these children are just starting to attend to beginning consonants. The teacher might place the "I like" part of the sentence in the middle of the table and ask the children to locate the remaining words "to," "play," and "soccer," place them in sequence, and then reread the sentence to double check.

With a group of students who are closer to a transitional stage, the teacher might use the same sentence but cut apart the word "like" into "l" and "ike" and the word "play" into "pl" and "ay." This will provide an opportunity for more advanced children to look closely at the structure of the words displayed.

*Word Walls*. These visual displays of large-print words on a wall are usually arranged alphabetically, but there are all kinds of word walls: walls for vocabulary building, for content-area words, for high-frequency words, and for different word patterns. Cunningham and Allington (2007) offer the following guidance regarding word walls used for high-frequency words and different word patterns. They suggest that teachers be selective in choosing words, and add words gradually, perhaps five or six each week. Posted words should be large, easily visible, and easily accessible by children. Easily confused words (e.g., *what* and *went*) might be written in different colors. Cunningham and Allington also recommend that teachers and children spend approximately 10 minutes a day chanting the words, noticing similarities, and writing them from dictation.

As an added bonus, Cunningham and Allington suggest having students turn their papers over and do what they call "on the back activities." For example, the teacher might ask the class to listen to five words (*jump, eat, look, work,* and *play*) pronounced orally. Then the teacher says five sentences that use the same words but with the "-ing" inflected ending (e.g., "She is jumping rope"). Students locate the original word on the word wall and then write the word with the "-ing" ending (or perhaps the whole sentence) on the back of their paper. "On the back activities" can be adjusted to any level of development.

*Making Words*. This activity combines spelling with decoding, and involves having children think about the letters in words by manipulating letters in response to teacher prompts. Initially developed by Cunningham (1990), the technique is highly flexible and has many variations. Children can respond either by manipulating tiles or letter cards, or by writing letters

For more information about "making words" activities, consult Cunningham and Allington's *Classrooms That Work* (2007), or *Making Words: Multilevel, Hands-On, Developmentally Appropriate Spelling and Phonics Activities* (2001)—or the resource for children in Grade 3 and up, *Making Big Words* (by the same authors).

FIGURE 3.7  **Sample Making Words Activity**
            **(for Students at a Transitional Stage of Development)**

---

**Materials:** sets of index cards or tiles with the following letters:

a  m  c  a  i  n  i  g

(Also make one set of large cards for the front of the classroom.)

---

**Procedures:**

Hand out letter cards or tiles to children. Have one student use the large cards at the front of the room. Students might work individually or in pairs.

Say:

   I want you to make a two-letter word: "in."
   Now, change one letter to make the word "an."
   Now, add one letter to make the word "can."
   Then, change one letter to make the word "man."
   Now, add one letter to make the word "main."
   Then, take one letter away and add two letters to make the word "magic."
   Can anyone see what our mystery word could be if we added the
      letters that are left?

---

on paper. Figure 3.7 provides a sample set of instructions for a Making Words activity. In the next section we turn to approaches that have been helpful for children with specific difficulties in the areas of decoding and word recognition.

## Instructional Approaches for Supporting Decoding and Word Recognition for Students with Specific Needs

Critical to making a difference with children who struggle in this area is noticing the particular areas of need a student shows and then carefully planning instruction and monitoring progress. Using multiple sources of information to identify these areas of need is key. For example, a third-grade student, Joe, was a concern to his third-grade classroom teacher because of his poor oral reading skills, and the teacher may have asked for help from the reading specialist at the school. Joe was eventually administered the Woodcock-Johnson III Diagnostic Reading Battery (Woodcock et al., 2004), and test results showed a significant gap in decoding, as seen through the Word Attack subtest, which uses nonsense words. When presented with third-grade-level text, Joe read with 89% accuracy (frustration level) and made some substitution errors but also many omissions, in which he would simply skip over a word that looked challenging. Joe showed the following patterns on the Informal Phonics Survey (McKenna & Stahl, 2003): mastery of consonant sounds, digraphs, and short vowels in CVC words, but 50% accuracy on silent *e* words, and 30% accuracy on vowel digraphs and vowel diphthongs.

Clearly, using multiple assessments gave the teacher more information concerning Joe's knowledge and use of phonics. The teacher now can see some particular areas that need work, notably long vowel patterns as well as building Joe's confidence in trying out his skills on decoding words during reading. Now Joe's teacher and the reading specialist can make a plan for addressing these needs.

*Remedial Approaches and Techniques.*     Children who struggle with decoding and word recognition need support given in a timely and sensitive manner so that they do not see themselves as "nonreaders" or "poor readers" and give up on reading. Supplemental or supportive instruction for these children should have sufficient intensity, focus, and duration to make a difference. Support should be provided early because there is good evidence that beyond second grade, phonics intervention has less of an effect on the achievement of students who struggle. Key to effective intervention is making sure that children who struggle with decoding and word identification are provided both scaffolding/coaching and ample opportunity to read easy material—not just flash cards and isolated word drills, but also connected text (Allington, 2006; Pressley, 2002). We'll mention some frequently used approaches and techniques and describe a few of them in more detail.

Some children should receive specialized instruction and support in the form of a formal "program." For example, in many schools, first graders who show evidence that they are lagging behind their peers are provided daily tutoring (usually for 10 to 12 weeks) through the Reading Recovery program. (This will be described more in chapter 4.) Other children receive individual or small-group tutoring through structured-language programs such as Orton-Gillingham (Orton, 1966), the Wilson Reading System (Wilson, 1988), or reading approaches that stress a synthetic (part-to-whole) focus and use direct instruction techniques. The Benchmark Word Identification Program, which has been used successfully with a variety of children who struggle with reading, including learning-disabled students, stresses decoding by analogy, or "using what you know to figure out what you don't know" (Gaskins, Gaskins, & Gaskins, 1992). In addition, the small-group model developed by Beverly Tyner (2004), briefly described in the previous section, may be used as a remedial or supplementary program.

When teachers use such programs regularly with students, it is critical for the classroom teacher and the specialist to communicate regarding the child's progress and the approach being used in each setting. Sometimes children become confused when different language is used in pull-out programs (i.e., support services such as individual or small-group tutoring, provided *outside of* the classroom), and close communication can help avoid that. In addition, frequent communication can help plan ways to support the child in generalizing newly learned skills and strategies.

Cunningham and Allington (2007) describe another small-group format called *coaching groups* in which children meet with the teacher to practice their word-solving and comprehension strategies. In coaching groups the teacher selects a passage that is appropriate for all children in the group, and then children read parts of the selection on their own. The teacher then asks one student to read a section aloud and demonstrate problem solving of challenging words by using the steps of a "word coach," which is shown in Figure 3.8.

Having appropriate materials available and accessible is also important in addressing children's decoding difficulties. For example, letter cubes, magnetic letters, sand trays, whiteboards, erasers, and markers are very useful to have close by. A number of resources for work on decoding and word recognition can either be downloaded from the Internet or directly accessed by teachers and children. An easy-to-access Web site for teacher resources, sponsored by the International Reading Association, may be found at www.readwritethink.org; a Web site that is particularly engaging for children is the School Bell (www.theschoolbell.com). Many computer software programs are available now as well, including "talking books" and complete programs for beginning readers. It is wise, however, to locate research reviews about such programs'

FIGURE 3.8  **Coaching Steps: How to Figure Out a Hard Word**

*How to Figure Out a Hard Word*

1. *Put your finger on the word and say all the letters.*

2. *Use the letters and the picture clues.*

3. *Look for a rhyme you know.*

4. *Keep your finger on the word and finish the sentence; then pretend it's the covered word.*

From Cunningham, Patricia M., & Richard L. Allington. *Classrooms That Work: They Can All Read and Write*, 4e. Published by Allyn and Bakon, Boston, MA. © by Pearson Education. Adapted by permission of the publisher.

effectiveness before investing heavily in them, as they definitely vary in their quality as well as their appeal to children.

In addition, using effective practices that reflect the gradual release of responsibility model—such as clear explanation, modeling, and providing guided practice with feedback—is essential (Pearson & Gallagher, 1983). For example, when trying to provide support for Joe (whose assessment results were described earlier), the classroom teacher might meet with Joe and some other children to provide some additional, explicit instruction in reading words with and without silent *e*. After clearly explaining what she will be teaching, the teacher might display some word pairs (*cap/cape; mad/made; kit/kite*) and model noticing the silent *e* and its effect on the vowel that precedes it. Using magnetic letters or a whiteboard, the teacher would then guide the children in first noticing the silent *e*, then verbalizing why it's important, and then reading the word pairs or engaging in a word sort.

Coaching or scaffolding effective decoding skills during reading is particularly important for children who have difficulty in this area (Taylor, Pearson, Clark, & Walpole, 2000). The general rule of thumb should be: provide "just enough" scaffolding to support the child on her road to independence. When listening to a child read and observing the skills and strategies she uses, think about the degree of support the child needs. If we provide too much support, we often end up teaching students "learned helplessness"; if we provide too little support, students will not be successful.

There is no recipe, however, for just how much support a child needs, and when it should be provided. It depends upon, among other things, the child's skills, the challenge of the task, and the degree of confidence the child has. Some examples of providing *minimal* support while a child is trying to decode a word are giving prompts such as,

- "What could you try?"
- "What are you going to do to help yourself?"

A *moderate* degree of support might be seen through teacher prompts such as, "Do you know a word like that?"; and *maximal* or *intensive* support might be evident when the teacher makes a word out of magnetic letters and guides the student in blending the sounds to make the word.

Peter Johnston (2004), in his book *Choice Words*, encourages teachers to use their own language to help children become problem solvers as they develop into readers and writers. Asking, "How did you figure that out?" is an example of this kind of intentional coaching that builds, rather than erodes, students' sense of "agency."

Lipson and Wixson (2003) recommend the following four steps to help children who have some skill in word identification but need to gain a degree of independence in using their decoding skills.

1. Look at all the letters from left to right.
2. As you look for letters, look for word parts you know.
3. Use the sound-plus-sense strategy (thinking about what sounds right and makes sense).
4. If the word is important and you're still not sure, ask someone for help.

A few specific techniques for children who struggle with decoding and word recognition follow.

*"Three Strikes and You're Out."*  This routine from McKenna and Stahl (2003) is a simple, low-key, but motivating routine for students who need work on word recognition. Teachers (or possibly students) identify words missed during oral reading and put them on 3 × 5 index cards. Students practice reading these words with a partner, and when they correctly read a word (these are called "strikes") on three different occasions, the word is declared "out" and put into a separate container of "retired" words. Students enjoy seeing their stack of "retired" words grow.

*"Folding in" Flash Cards.*  For children who have a very difficult time learning to recognize words and build automaticity, the "folding in" technique (Daly, Chafouleas, & Skinner, 2005) might be needed. This intensive approach involves having the child respond to both known and unknown words on flash cards. Most of the words presented to the child should be ones that he or she knows well; new or challenging words are "folded in" systematically. The teacher selects three unknown words and seven known words. After modeling how to read the three unknown words, the teacher:

1. Presents the first unknown word, followed by the first known word
2. Presents the first unknown word again, followed by the first and second known words
3. Presents the first unknown word again, followed by the first, second, and third known words
4. Repeats the process until all seven of the known words are folded in
5. Repeats the procedure using the first two unknown words, and then finally with the third unknown word
6. Assesses all the words at the end of the session, and when a previously unknown word is read correctly on two consecutive days, counts it as a "known" word

Most children definitely don't need this procedure, but for those children who have significant challenges in sight-word recognition, the procedure will be rewarding, will build fluency, and will avoid the laborious task of working on only unknown words. If this technique is used, though, it will be important to build in practice of the newly learned words in "connected text" in order to promote generalization.

*Phoneme–Grapheme Mapping.*  For students who have acquired the alphabetic principle (i.e., they know that letters match sounds) but need more work in application, the phoneme-grapheme mapping technique can be very useful. This approach is described in chapter 9 because it is particularly supportive of spelling development.

A helpful resource that outlines the full sequence of steps for phoneme-grapheme mapping is Kathryn Grace's *Phonics and Spelling Through Phoneme-Grapheme Mapping* (2006).

### Summary of Instructional Approaches for Supporting Decoding and Word Recognition

In this section we stressed that decoding and word recognition need to be taught systematically but also with attention to matching instruction to children's stages of development and application to "real reading" of connected text. Whole-group instruction has its place in addressing some key grade-level concepts of decoding, but for the most part, teachers will want to use some form of small-group (or sometimes individualized) instruction to best address the assessed needs of children.

For students with particular needs in decoding and word recognition, a range of programs and techniques are available. What is critical is carefully planning or selecting such interventions, regularly monitoring the progress children make in response to the interventions, and making adjustments as needed. In the next section we look at Willa's development in the areas of decoding and word recognition, see how it has been recorded on the Literacy Profile, and think about what next steps will be useful for her.

## LOOKING CLOSELY AT ONE CHILD'S ASSESSMENTS FROM STRAND 3 OF THE LITERACY PROFILE

In order to evaluate Willa's progress in decoding and word recognition, we administered the Informal Phonics Survey (McKenna & Stahl, 2003) and also reviewed her performance on the Primary Spelling Inventory (Bear et al., 2008). The Primary Spelling Inventory will be described in chapter 9. In addition, we asked Willa to read the Dolch (1936) lists of sight words at the first- and second-grade levels. Finally, we used the Decoding Application Scale (see Appendix A-6) to analyze the substitution errors Willa made while reading orally. Refer to Figure 3.9 to see how Willa's developing skills in decoding and word recognition are recorded and annotated on Strand 3 of the Literacy Profile. On the Informal Phonics Survey, Willa demonstrated strong "mastery" in decoding words with the following elements: consonant sounds, short vowel words, and consonant blends in short vowel words. Her skills in reading words with consonant digraphs, and words with "silent *e*" showed that she could "use review." Regarding vowel digraphs, vowel diphthongs, and *r*-controlled vowels, Willa needs "systematic instruction." However, it should be noted that those areas of decoding are the logical next stage of development for Willa at this point in time, so it makes sense that she would need instruction in those areas.

These patterns are generally consistent with Willa's performance on the Primary Spelling Inventory as well, where her stage of development appeared to be at the late Letter-Name stage. That assessment, along with analysis of her spelling during independent writing, revealed a need for some (probably brief) review in the areas of digraphs and blends, along with instruction in long vowel patterns and vowel combinations. For example, on the Primary Spelling Inventory, Willa spelled "stick" as "sick" and "wait" as "waot." In her independent writing sample, Willa spelled "rope" as "rop" and "boat" as "boot"—but also correctly spelled long vowel pattern words such as "fire," "name," and "time." Willa is definitely ready to work on more closely analyzing words with vowel patterns.

Regarding recognition of sight words, Willa's performance was interesting. She read the Dolch first-grade word list with 90% accuracy but the Grade 2 list

**FIGURE 3.9** **Willa's Profile for Decoding and Word Recognition.**

Note: This figure has been excerpted from the full Literacy Profile chart for illustrative purposes. Please consult the full pull-out chart to identify the column headings and development phases.

| Strand *Question & Sample Assessment Tools* | Early–Mid Grade 1 | Late Grade 1–Early Grade 2 | Late Grade 2–Early Grade 3 |
|---|---|---|---|
| **3. Decoding Skills and Word Analysis** *To what extent is the child learning the decoding and word-identification skills needed for reading?* **Sample Assessment Tools** • Names Test • Sound-symbol correspondence tasks • Initial Sound Fluency (DIBELS) • Sight word lists • Running records • Records of oral reading • Quick Text Level Check-In • Informal Phonics Surveys | Produces sounds for all consonants and common consonant digraphs (*ch, sh, th, wh*) Knows 20–50 sight words *[Occasionlly shows some confusion with diagrams, but mostly fine. Strong sight word recognition—well beyond what is expected] KI* | Shows full understanding of the alphabetic principle Reads one-syllable short-vowel words and words with silent *e* Reads words with blends and inflected endings Uses familiar word patterns to decode common two-syllable words, such as *happen* and *sticky* Reads basic contractions and compound words *[Reads many "silent e" words but not firm yet...] KI* *[Tends to add or delete inflected endings while reading—but most blends are ok] KI* | Uses knowledge of common syllable types (closed, vowel teams, *r* controlled) and patterns to decode one-syllable "regular" words, such as *shade* and *crown* and some multisyllabic words, such as *uncurled* and *protecting* |

Gray areas represent highlighting added by the teacher, preferably using a different color for each year (e.g., yellow highlights for Late K, orange highlights for Early–Mid Grade 1, etc.). Bracketed material represents teacher/examiner comments from June, Grade 1.

with 96% accuracy. At first her lower performance on the first-grade list seemed odd. But Willa's errors (e.g., *lets* for *let*, *then* for *when*, *thanks* for *thank*) seemed mostly due to her tendency to respond quickly, without looking carefully at words.

Looking at Willa's substitutions as she orally read a story confirmed what was observed on the decoding and word recognition tests that used words in isolation. Using the Decoding Application Scale (see Appendix A-6), we saw evidence of many decoding skills, but also judged that she could use some continued support and encouragement in trying different vowel patterns and in using a decoding-by-analogy strategy. In addition, during story reading we saw evidence of Willa's tendency to skip over or inaccurately read "little" words ("the" for "a," "they" for "there") and also to misread some contractions and words with inflected endings (*wheels* for *wheel*, *like* for *liked*).

In considering specific next steps for Willa, some review of digraphs and blends seems appropriate, along with some reminders to pay attention to "little" words and inflected endings on words. In addition, Willa will soon be ready for some focused instruction on long vowel patterns, including silent *e*, followed by instruction in vowel teams and digraphs.

To review blends and digraphs, one approach that might be used is "making words." Also, during individual reading conferences, it might be helpful for her teacher to help Willa reflect on her miscues after she reads orally, and talk about ways for her to self-monitor her accuracy. The instructional "next steps" that were suggested at the end of chapter 1 (phoneme segmentation and identification of syllables) will also support Willa's development in decoding. Another possibility could be including Willa in the kind of "coaching" groups described by Cunningham and Allington (2007), which were mentioned earlier in a previous section of this chapter.

Overall, Willa's decoding and word recognition skills are coming along well, with only a few areas that need review. She is ready to learn more about different vowel patterns and syllable types in the coming year.

## REFERENCES

Adams, M. J. (1990). *Beginning to read: Thinking and learning about print.* Cambridge, MA: MIT Press.

Allington, R. (2006). *What really matters for struggling readers.* Boston: Pearson Education.

Armbruster, B. B., Lehr, F., & Osborn, J. (2001). *Put reading first.* Washington, DC: National Institute for Literacy.

Bear, D. R., Invernizzi, M., Templeton, S., & Johnston, F. (2008). *Words their way.* Upper Saddle River, NJ: Pearson Education.

Braunger, J., & Lewis, J. P. (2006). *Building a knowledge base in reading.* Newark, DE: International Reading Association.

Chall, J. S. (1967). *Learning to read: The great debate.* New York: McGraw-Hill.

Cooper, J. D., Chard, D. J., & Kiger N. D. (2006). *The struggling reader: Interventions that work.* New York: Scholastic.

Cunningham, P. (1990). The names test: A quick assessment of decoding ability. *The Reading Teacher, 44,* 124–129.

Cunningham, P. M., & Hall, D. (2001). *Making words: Multilevel, hands-on developmentally appropriate spelling and phonics activities.* Lancaster, CA: Frank Schaffer.

Cunningham, P. M., & Hall, D. (2001). *Making BIG words: Multilevel, hands-on developmentally appropriate spelling and phonics activities.* Lancaster, CA: Frank Schaffer.

Cunningham, P. M., & Allington, R. (2007). *Classrooms that work: They can all read and write.* Boston: Pearson Education.

Cunningham, P. M., & Hall, D. (2003). *Month by month phonics: Systematic, multi-level instruction for second grade.* Greensboro, NC: Carson Dellosa.

Daly, E. J., Chafouleas, S., & Skinner, C. H. (2005). *Interventions for reading problems.* New York: Guilford Press.

Dolch, E. W. (1936). A basic sight vocabulary. *Elementary School Journal, 36,* 456–460.

Duffelmeyer, F. A., Kruse, A. E., Merkley, D. J., & Fyfe, S. A. (1994). Further validation and enhancement of the names test. *The Reading Teacher, 48,* 118–128.

Dynamic Indicators of Basic Early Literacy Skills DIBELS. (2007). http://dibels.uoregon.edu/benchmarkgoals.pdf

Ehri, L. C. (1998). Grapheme-phoneme knowledge is essential for learning to read words in English. In J. L. Metsala & L. C. Ehri (Eds.), *Word recognition in beginning literacy* (pp. 3–40). Mahwah, NJ: Erlbaum.

Fountas, I., & Pinnell, G. S. (2003). *Phonics lessons: Letters, words and how they work.* Portsmouth, NH: Heinemann.

Fry, E., Kress, J., & Fountoukidis, D. (2000). *The reading teacher's book of lists.* Paramus, NJ: Prentice Hall.

Ganske, K. (2000). *Word journeys.* New York: The Guilford Press.

Gaskins, R. W., Gaskins, J. C., & Gaskins, I. (1992). Using what you know to figure out what you don't know. *Reading and Writing Quarterly, 8,* 197–221.

Gentry, R. (2006). *Breaking the code: The new science of beginning reading and writing.* Portsmouth, NH: Heinemann.

Grace, K. (2006). *Phonics and spelling through phoneme-grapheme mapping.* Natick, MA: Cambium Learning.

Harp, B., & Brewer, J. (2005). *The informed reading teacher: Research-based practices.* Upper Saddle River, NJ: Pearson Education.

Invernizzi, M., Meier, J., and Juel, C. (2005). *PALS 1–3: Phonological awareness literacy screening 2002–2003.* Charlottesville: Curry School of Education, University of Virginia Press.

Johns, J. L. (2001). *Basic reading inventory* (8th ed.). Dubuque, IA: Kendall-Hunt Publishing Co.

Johnston, P. (2004). *Choice words: How our language affects children's learning.* Portland, ME: Stenhouse.

Juel, C., & Minden-Cupp, C. (2000). Learning to read words: Linguistic units and instructional strategies. *Reading Research Quarterly, 35,* 458–492.

Karlsen, B., & Gardner, E. (2005). *Stanford diagnostic reading test* (4th ed.). San Antonio, TX: Harcourt.

LaPray, M. H., & Ross, R. R. (1969). The graded word list: Quick gauge of reading ability. *Journal of Reading, 12,* pp. 305–307.

Lipson, M. Y. (2007). *Teaching reading beyond the primary grades.* New York: Scholastic.

Lipson, M. Y., & Wixson, K. K. (2003). *Assessment and instruction of reading and writing difficulty.* Boston: Pearson Education.

Mather, N., Sammons, J., & Schwartz, J. (2006, October). Adaptations of the names test: Easy-to-use phonics assessments. *The Reading Teacher, 60*(2), 114–122.

McKenna M., & Stahl, S. (2003). *Assessment for reading instruction.* New York: Guilford Press.

Meyer, R. J. (2003). Captives of the script: Killing us softly with phonics. Language Arts. Retrieved from http://www.edexcellence.net/foundation/global

Moats, L. C. (2004). *LETRS: Language essentials for teachers of reading and spelling.* Longmont, CO: Sopris West Educational Services.

Moats, L. C. (2007). *Whole language high-jinks.* Washington, DC: Thomas B. Fordham Institute.

National Reading Panel. (2000). *Teaching children to read: An evidence-based assessment of the scientific research literature on reading and its implications for reading instruction—Reports of the subgroups.* Washington, DC: National Institute of Child Health and Development.

Orton, J. L. (1966). The Orton-Gillingham approach. In J. Money (Ed.), *The disabled reader* (pp. 19–146). Baltimore: Johns Hopkins University Press.

Pearson, P. D., & Gallagher, M. (1983). The instruction of reading comprehension. *Contemporary Educational Psychology, 8,* 317–344.

Pressley, M. (2002). *Reading instruction that works: The case for balanced teaching.* New York: The Guilford Press.

Roswell, F., & Chall, J. (1997). *Roswell-Chall screening tests: Auditory blending and diagnostic test of word analysis skills.* Cambridge, MA: Educators Publishing Service.

Schumm, J. S. (2006). *Reading instruction and assessment for all learners.* New York: The Guilford Press.

Shanker, J., & Ekwall, E. (2000). Reading Inventory (4th ed.). Boston: Allyn and Bacon.

Snow, C. E., Burns, M. S., & Griffin, P. (Eds.). (1998). *Preventing Early reading difficulties in young children.* Washington, DC: National Academy Press.

Taylor, B. M., Pearson, P. D., Clark, K., & Walpole, S. (2000). Effective schools and accomplished teachers: Lessons from primary grade instruction in low-income schools. *Elementary School Journal, 101,* 121–165.

Time Online. (2000). Stern Center for Language and Learning. Williston, VT.

Tyner, B. (2004). *Small group reading instruction: A differentiated teaching model for beginning and struggling readers.* Newark, DE: International Reading Association.

University of Oregon. (2005). *DIBELS: Dynamic indicators of basic early literacy skills.*

Williams, K. T. (2005). *Group reading assessment and diagnostic evaluation.* Circle Pines, MN: American Guidance Service.

Wilson, B. (1988). *Wilson reading system.* Oxford, MA: Wilson Language Training.

Woodcock, R. W., Mather, N., & Schrank, K. (2004). Woodcock-Johnson III Diagnostic Reading Battery. Itasca, IL: Riverside.

# CHAPTER FOUR

# Reading Strategies and Dispositions

**CORE QUESTION**

To what extent does the child use early processing strategies and comprehension strategies during reading? How engaged is the child with reading?

**LITERACY PROFILE**
Have your Literacy Profile on hand as you read through this chapter, and refer to the question in the left-hand column and the indicators across the columns for Strand 4.

"I figured out how to read that all by myself!" is a comment that signals both a milestone on the way to success as a reader and a sense of control and competence in the reading process. This kind of remark indicates that the child is being *strategic,* or using cognitive processes to solve a problem during reading. Such processes (or strategies), which allow a reader to figure out a word, phrase, or the meaning of what she or he is reading, are vital to the development of competent readers (Clay, 1991; Taberski, 2000).

Other hallmarks of reading growth that are related to the development of strategies include reading a lot, reading longer books, and exploring a range of different genres. We sometimes call these behaviors reading "dispositions" or "habits."

## UNDERLYING PRINCIPLES OF READING STRATEGIES AND DISPOSITIONS

One important distinction that is helpful for understanding reading strategies is the difference between skills and strategies. Although the distinction between the two is not always clear, it may be helpful to think of *skills* as automatic, routine, and associated primarily with lower levels of thinking and learning. In contrast, Schumm (2006) describes *strategies* as processes that "are controlled by the reader, are metacognitive, are intentional, are flexible, and emphasize reasoning" (p. 229). Afflerbach, Pearson, and Paris (2008) argue that there is a real need to clarify the differences between skills and strategies; they explain that "reading strategies are deliberate, goal-directed attempts to control and modify the reader's attempts to decode text, understand words and construct meanings

of text. Reading skills are automatic actions that result in decoding and comprehension, with speed, efficiency and fluency and usually occur without awareness
of the components of control involved" (p. 368). One of the important implications of this distinction is that skills (for example, recognizing letters of the
alphabet or recognizing sight words such as "would" and "should") can be
"mastered," but strategies (such as asking questions or visualizing during reading),
because of their nature, should be viewed more flexibly. One individual might
use one strategy in one situation, while another individual might use a different
strategy entirely, perhaps because of his or her purpose for reading, background
knowledge, or level of skill or because of the nature of the text being read.

Habits and dispositions of reading are not something that can be
"mastered," either. Instead, individuals develop and grow as readers often as
a result of the literacy environment that surrounds them. Because of this, it is
important for teachers to distinguish between loving to read and reading. As
teachers, we cannot expect mastery of "loving to read" (although we might
wish that we could!). We can, however, expect children to develop a habit of
reading or at least some degree of "breadth" and "depth" of reading. And we
can certainly *lead* students toward a love of reading.

In this chapter we will first consider what is involved in the development of
reading strategies, from early reading processing strategies through comprehension strategies, and then we will discuss reading dispositions or habits. Finally,
we will address assessment options and instructional considerations for each.

## Early Reading Processing Strategies

Marie Clay (1991) defined reading as a "message-getting, problem-solving
activity, which increases in power and flexibility the more it is practiced" (p. 6).
A key part of such practice involves the use of *strategies*, which she described as
"mental activities, initiated by the child, to get meaning from text" (1993, p. 18).

***Use of Three Cueing Systems During Reading.*** Processing strategies focus
on figuring out unknown words encountered during reading, and good readers need to use a variety of cues, or sources of information (Goodman, 1996):

- *Phonological and visual/orthographic information:* the sound system of
  language (phonemes/sounds in words) and the orthographic system of
  language (letters, letter clusters, and patterns)—and how they work
  together to form words
- *Language structure:* patterns or rules by which words are put together into
  meaningful phrases and sentences
- *Meaning:* background knowledge, and understandings of word meanings
  and how stories and other texts work

Noticing how beginning readers start to use these early strategies is fascinating.
Each child is different, and while one child might begin by relying almost
entirely on pictures and other meaning cues, another child may rely primarily
on visual cues, trying to "sound out" every word, even sight words as irregular
and tricky as "through." On the Literacy Profile, this variability in the use of
strategies is reflected in the descriptors for late kindergarten: "Begins to use more
than one cuing system to read." See Figure 4.1 for a list of sample early reading
processing strategies that beginning readers use. Soon, though, most children
learn that they need to use these sources of information in combination.

This leads to what is called "cross-checking," which simply means checking one source of information against another source (Goodman, Watson, &
Burke, 1987; Smith, 1978). For example, a child who is learning to read might
read the sentence, "I can run up the hill" as "I can *read* up the hill" but then

FIGURE 4.1  **Sample Processing Strategies**

- Tracking print from left to right
- Noticing patterns in text (e.g., "said the bear")
- Using pictures to predict the story and subsequent words
- Attending to orthographic and phonemic information (letters and letter clusters at the beginning, middle, and end of words)
- Noticing similarities between a known word and an unknown word
- Looking through a word to its end
- Monitoring and self-correcting
- Using meaning, structure, and print cues simultaneously
- Rereading to clarify meaning
- Skipping a word and returning to it
- Using context clues to figure out the meaning of an unfamiliar word

cross-check his use of visual information (i.e., the beginning sound of "run") with another source of information (e.g., meaning) by asking himself, "Does that make sense?" In other words, in order to cross-check, students need to monitor how well their reading strategies are working together (e.g., whether what *looks right* also *makes sense or sounds right*). Eventually they will learn to self-correct when cross-checking alerts them to a mismatch.

*Use of Self-Correction During Reading.*  When beginning readers self-correct, they sometimes (but not always) tell us why they did so. For example, Andrew, a first-grade reader who was initially overrelying on meaning and not paying much attention to visual and phonics information, misread by saying, "I'll fix your *house*" instead of the *actual* text, "I'll fix your *walls*," and then commented, "Uh-oh—that can't be *house*—there's no 'h.'" Clearly Andrew's cross-checking resulted in a self-correction.

The use of self-correction often follows a predictable route. Self-correction is rarely evident with *very* beginning readers (Clay, 1978). Then, usually some time early in first grade (for typically developing children), self-correction begins to appear. Later, however, self-correction is not as evident because as children develop competence, they begin to self-correct silently, "inside their heads," before they utter the mistake. You will notice on the Literacy Profile that self-correction is not listed until late first grade/early second grade.

Marie Clay (1978) found that high-progress readers self-correct more than twice as frequently as low-progress readers, but, as mentioned previously, she also noticed that self-correction tends to become "invisible" after a point. In other words, processing strategies eventually become largely unconscious, at which point children use them silently and as needed during reading. You should keep this in mind when observing developing readers.

How do these strategies get under way? Children usually acquire these strategies as a result of lots of modeling and guided practice by a teacher, parent, or other more skilled reader. Vygotsky (1978) termed this sort of assistance "scaffolding," a critical concept in terms of teaching and learning in a variety of domains. The authors of this book have often thought of literacy scaffolding as being similar to the scaffolding that surrounds buildings as they are being constructed; you may find this a useful comparison, too. For example, think about the kinds of support (or scaffolding) children need before they can begin to use an index to locate information. A source of assistance or scaffolding might be a teacher or a parent first modeling how to find the index and use it and then, with a bit of coaching, giving the child a chance to try it on his or her own.

Some of the earliest strategies children need to get started include tracking print from left to right, using a picture to figure out a word, predicting what an upcoming unfamiliar word might be, and using their familiarity with one word to decode a word that is similar to the familiar one. Later, students need to learn how to use context clues to figure out the *meaning* of unfamiliar words. If teachers provide children with the key conditions needed for learning (e.g., Cambourne's conditions), the likelihood that children will develop effective processing strategies is much greater.

This stage of beginning to read—learning to flexibly use processing strategies—often includes both excitement and hard work. Some describe this stage of reading as a juggling act; others compare it to conducting an orchestra, since children must simultaneously use several processes and strategies to figure out a text's message.

Next we turn our attention to comprehension strategies. It is important to recognize that even though we discussed early reading strategies first, in your classroom you should focus on both sets of strategies. Emphasis will shift from one grade to the next, however, because teachers need to pay less attention to processing strategies when students enter the intermediate grades.

Cambourne's conditions were outlined in the introductory chapter (pp. 5–6); now might be a good time to review them.

## Comprehension Strategies

While it seems obvious to adults that thinking while reading is essential to understand what we read, it is often not obvious to children who are just beginning to learn to read. The National Reading Panel (2000) strongly recommends teaching reading comprehension strategies in order to strengthen children's reading abilities and identified six key strategies:

- Monitoring comprehension (i.e., noticing when a child's understanding is disrupted), and teaching rereading or "chunking" strategies to help the child remedy the situation
- Using graphic organizers (e.g., maps, webs, charts)
- Generating questions (when *children* ask questions before, during, and after reading)
- Answering questions
- Recognizing story structure
- Summarizing

Others (for example, Harvey & Goudvis, 2007; Keene & Zimmerman, 1997; Pearson & Duke, 2002) include other strategies such as predicting, inferring, making connections, and using text-structure clues to identify organizational patterns in text—all of which should be used flexibly to increase comprehension. See Figure 4.2 for a list of commonly used comprehension strategies.

## FIGURE 4.2  Sample Comprehension Strategies

- Stopping to think
- Predicting during reading
- Visualizing during reading
- Thinking about what the author is trying to say
- Making connections
- Asking questions during reading (e.g., to enhance understanding, solve problems, etc.)
- Making inferences (e.g., to connect ideas, fill in information to make sense of unstated ideas)
- Self-monitoring/regulating to correct comprehension difficulties
- Summarizing during or after reading
- Evaluating (making judgments about the text, forming opinions, or determining author's purpose)

You can find another list of reading comprehension strategies, with helpful descriptions of strategies and guidelines for comprehension strategy instruction, in *Teaching Reading Beyond the Primary Grades*, by Marjorie Lipson (2007).

By "text-structure" clues, we mean the words or phrases that authors use to organize their thoughts in expository text. For example, when an author is writing a paragraph that compares one thing to another, he or she often uses "signal" words and phrases such as "however," "different," and "on the other hand"; but when an author is using a sequential text pattern, he or she uses words and phrases such as "to begin with," "next," and "finally." Snow (2002) urges teachers to introduce as early as kindergarten strategies for understanding expository text. We will present more information about using "signal" words for different text patterns later in this chapter and also in chapter 6.

How do readers use comprehension strategies? Most of us tend to use a combination of comprehension strategies, usually when the text presents enough challenges that we truly *need* to think as we read. Because of this, many researchers (Duke & Pearson, 2002; Lipson, 2007; Pressley, 2002) encourage teachers initially to present an entire set of comprehension strategies. Then, as needed, teachers may focus on and explicitly teach individual strategies one by one.

Children often need extensive support in using strategies flexibly and in developing a "repertoire" of tools that they can use across a variety of texts and genres. If we spend 4 months teaching students how to use a particular strategy such as making connections, and then spend another 4 months teaching them how to use predicting, they may very well forget about making connections, thinking we have *moved on* to predicting and eliminated the need to use the making connection strategy!

You may want to refer back to the introductory chapter for a more complete description of the gradual release of responsibility (pp. 6–7), a key principle of instruction.

It is particularly important when teaching comprehension strategies to use the "gradual release of responsibility" model (Pearson & Gallagher, 1983), which includes teacher modeling and explanation, guided practice, and independent practice with feedback. Too often commercial (basal) reading programs include minimal or only intermittent opportunities for modeling and guided practice; a teacher thus needs to look carefully at the program's teacher's manual to discover when to supplement the provided modeling and demonstration as well as when to supply guided practice (Dewitz, 2006). Unless teachers provide sufficient modeling and include ample opportunities for guided practice strategies, children will have difficulties internalizing the strategies.

## Reading Dispositions

If children have learned the necessary skills and strategies to be good readers but don't read much, what is the point of teaching the skills and strategies? Because not all children are active or eager readers, it is important for teachers to think about the dispositions or habits of developing readers as they grow. Several different aspects of reading dispositions or habits are useful to consider. First, keep in mind that children need to read a lot and build their *stamina*, by which we mean the ability to sustain their reading and concentrate as they read for increasingly longer periods of time. A great deal of research shows that children who read more also achieve more (Allington, 2006; Anderson, Wilson, & Fielding, 1988).

In addition to increasing the amount they read, we also know that children need to feel comfortable reading a range of genres. It is perfectly normal (and also desirable!) for students to get "hooked" on a particular topic, author, or series (for example, the Magic Tree House books), but we also want to make sure that children read books with some degree of diversity, particularly when they enter the intermediate grades.

You should also consider children's attitude toward reading. As Paris, Lipson, and Wixson (1983) assert, in order for children to become effective readers and writers, they must demonstrate both *skill* and *will*. The "will" part, involving personal perceptions, interests, and attitudes, is clearly influenced by family and cultural factors. What others (i.e., family, classmates, teacher, members of the community) think about reading and how a child perceives her effectiveness as a reader will significantly impact both her attitude toward reading and her reading behaviors.

### Summary of Reading Strategies and Dispositions

This section provided some background information concerning reading strategies and dispositions. We distinguished between early reading strategies and comprehension strategies as well as discussed several aspects of reading dispositions. Two important points to keep in mind while assessing children's reading strategies are the developmental nature of early processing strategies and the flexible nature of comprehension strategies. Afflerbach et al. (2008) offer some concise, helpful advice: "The general rule is, teach children many strategies, teach them early, reteach them often, and connect assessment with reteaching" (p. 371). Reading habits and dispositions include a variety of factors such as stamina and breadth and depth of reading. In the next section we discuss methods of assessing reading strategies and dispositions to guide instruction and classroom practice.

## ASSESSING READING STRATEGIES AND DISPOSITIONS

Compared to the other strands listed in the Literacy Profile, reading strategies and dispositions may be one of the more "elusive" strands to assess because reading strategies and dispositions are not quite as "visible" as some other aspects of reading and writing. Nevertheless, a number of ways to assess these dimensions of reading are available, and it is important to assess this key dimension of reading.

### Formal or Published Measures for Assessing Reading Strategies and Reading Dispositions

Most resources for assessing reading strategies and dispositions are informal, but several published tools are available for practitioners to use. Many of these assessments are multidimensional and help teachers gather information about other aspects of reading such as decoding and comprehension as well as children's use of strategies during reading.

***Tools That Include Assessment of Reading Strategies.*** A number of informal reading inventories and other published assessments provide procedures to evaluate children's use of reading strategies. Most of these tools prompt teachers to *analyze* students' use of strategies after recording oral reading and students' behaviors while reading. Most assessment tools provide some sort of scoring guide such as a checklist to help teachers know what to look for as they analyze the children's oral reading. For example, both the Rigby PM Benchmark Kit (Rigby Education, 2001) and the Developmental Reading Assessment (Beaver, 2003) provide short books and passages at increasing levels of difficulty for children to read. A checklist of student behaviors prompts teachers to notice student behaviors such as using picture cues or adjusting intonation in response to ending punctuation.

At upper levels (Grades 4 and up), the DRA2 (Beaver & Carter, 2006) includes a section that evaluates the degree to which children use comprehension strategies. This component, called "metacognitive awareness," refers to an individual's ability to think about, or reflect on, his or her own thinking and how well it is working. On the DRA, students are prompted to check off the comprehension strategy they used while they read and give an example of how they used that strategy to help them understand the text selection. The DRA provides a scoring guide (or rubric) ranging from "vague explanation of the use of one strategy" to "effective explanations of the use of more than one strategy; explicit examples from the text" to facilitate teachers' evaluation of children's responses.

***Tools That Assess Reading Dispositions.*** A few published tools are available to help teachers evaluate students' reading dispositions. One frequently used measure is the Elementary Reading Attitude Survey (McKenna & Kear, 1990), which uses *Garfield* cartoon figures to find out children's attitudes toward reading at home and at school. Items may be read aloud to primary-level children, who then indicate the Garfield figure (shown as excited, okay, not so okay, not happy) that best matches their own feelings. For example, in one item the teacher asks a child: "How do you feel when you read out loud in class?" The child then circles one of the four choices. The teacher can calculate two subscores (recreational and academic) and a total "reading attitude" score using this measure.

Another resource that gauges students' perceptions of reading is the Motivation to Read Profile (Gambrell, Palmer, Codling, & Mazzoni, 1996), which includes a written survey and a conversational interview. This assessment, which is appropriate for children in second through sixth grade, provides separate scores for "self-concept as a reader" and "value of reading." This breakdown of scores can be particularly useful when planning interventions for students who demonstrate low motivation for reading. For example, if you find out that a third- or fourth-grade child has a low "value of reading" score but a high "self-concept" score, you might decide to set up partner-reading sessions and match that child with an older child or an adult whom the child regards highly. You might also locate reading materials of high interest and utility, such as sports magazines or video game directions, to attempt to increase the value the child places on reading.

An assessment tool that provides information about students' exposure to print is the Title Recognition Test—Primary Level (McDowell, Schumm, & Vaughn, 1993). The format of this assessment task involves giving children a list of book titles, some of which are the titles of real, well-known books (e.g., *Amelia Bedelia*) and some of which are the titles of books that aren't real (e.g., *The Haunted Hallway*). Children are asked to check off which titles belong to *real* books, which indicates the students' breadth of reading experience. Because several of the real books on the list are those that many kindergarteners and first graders may not yet have been exposed to, we consider this assessment to be more appropriate for students at the second-, third-, and fourth-grade levels. The results of this assessment might help guide interventions such as "book immersion" (e.g., setting up daily opportunities for extra read-alouds or partner reading) for children whose results indicate that they have had little previous exposure to books and reading.

## Informal Measures for Assessing Reading Strategies and Reading Dispositions

Running records, records of oral reading, miscue analyses, vocabulary probes, and anecdotal notes are effective and valuable ways to gain insight into children's use of processing strategies during reading. By analyzing what the student is and is not doing during oral reading, the teacher gains insights that he can then use to tailor instruction in effectively using reading strategies.

***Running Records, Records of Oral Reading, and Miscue Analysis.*** Running records, developed by Marie Clay (1985), involve recording and analyzing a child's reading behaviors and strategies during oral reading. When taking a running record, the teacher listens carefully to the child as he or she reads aloud, makes a check mark on a sheet of paper for each word read accurately, and uses other symbols to note other reading behaviors and strategies used or not used. See Figure 4.3 for Fountas and Pinnell's (1996) chart depicting the common conventions used in taking running records. Some teachers add additional notation to indicate when a child is sounding out a word ("th-i-ck") or pausing (//). Neither of these behaviors is counted as an error because they indicate the child's problem solving.

Willa reads orally while a teacher takes a running record.

Running records can help determine the student's reading accuracy and whether or not the text is at the appropriate level for the child. Guidelines of what percent of accuracy is appropriate for independent reading and instructional-level reading vary across sources, but nearly all sources agree that when a student's oral reading accuracy is below 90%, that text is frustrating for that particular student. (*Note:* The nature of independent, instructional, and frustration levels during oral reading will be discussed more in chapter 5.) Running records also provide highly useful and timely information concerning children's use of processing strategies, and we will provide examples later in this section.

Records of oral reading, although similar to running records, involve the use of a printed script of text. For ease of use, several commercial assessment companies provide printed "records of oral reading" scripts of passages to be used during assessment. Although you may find records of oral reading easier to use at first, it is good practice to learn how to take a running record without a script, since that will allow you to closely observe children's oral reading behaviors and strategies at *any* point in time.

An excellent resource to learn more about taking running records is Peter Johnston's *Running Records: A Self-Tutoring Guide* (2000).

As noted earlier, besides recording the accuracy of oral reading, running records provide an ideal opportunity to make qualitative observations of how effectively children are using reading strategies. Looking carefully at the positive reading behaviors that children display as well as their miscues (or errors) allows teachers to notice how the process of reading is developing. Even more important, this kind of *miscue analysis* allows teachers to decide what kind of instruction is needed to support particular students *at that point in time.*

To analyze running records, teachers should do two things: They need to note the *positive behaviors* that facilitated accurate, fluent, and meaningful reading, and they also need to analyze children's *errors or miscues.*

*Analyzing Running Records: Positive Behaviors to Be Observed.* When we first learn to do something (such as drive a car or ride a bike), it is important for the person who is helping us learn to notice, or call attention to, what we are doing *right* so that we can keep on doing those correct things. When children are learning to read, the same principle holds true. Positive behaviors

FIGURE 4.3 Running Records Conventions

| Coding a Running Record | | |
|---|---|---|
| **Behavior** | **Code** | **Description** |
| Accurate Reading | √ √ √ √ √ | Record a check for each word read accurately. The line of checks matches the layout of print. |
| Substitution | attempt / text<br><br>attempt \| attempt \| attempt / text \| | The reader's attempt is placed over the accurate word on a line. When the child makes multiple attempts, each is recorded above the line with a vertical line in between. |
| Told | — / text \| T | When the reader makes no attempt, he is instructed to try it. If there is no attempt, the word is told and a T is written below the line. |
| Appeal and Told | — \| A \| √ / text \| — \|<br><br>√ √ √ √<br><br>√    — \| A \| / text \| — \| T | The reader's appeal, either verbal or nonverbal, is recorded with an A above the line. If the child reads correctly, a check is made. If the child makes an attempt it is recorded above the line; if he doesn't or it is incorrect a "told" is recorded. |
| Omission | — / text | A dash is placed on a line above the word in the text. |
| Insertion | word / — | The word inserted by the reader is placed above the line and a dash is placed below. |
| Repetition | √ √ √ √ R √ √<br>√ R<br>√ √ √ √ R2 | Place an R after a single word repeated; for a phrase or more of text repeated draw a line to the point to which the child returned. The number indicates number of repetitions. |
| Self-Correction | √ √ attempt \| SC √ √ R / text \| | The symbol SC following the child's corrected attempt indicates SC at point of error. A small arrow can be used to indicate that the SC was made on the repetition. |

to look for when observing very early readers (usually those at the kindergarten or first-grade level) include:

- Tracking print with his/her finger
- Going back to reread
- Getting a running start (i.e., returning to the beginning of a line or sentence)
- Noticing that something is not quite right
- Trying different sounds for a letter or combination of letters
- Taking off the beginning or ending of an unfamiliar word to see whether the remaining word is familiar
- Thinking about a word that is similar to an unknown word

*Errors or Miscues.* It is equally important to look closely at what happens when children are *not* reading accurately. When analyzing errors (which are called *miscues*), teachers compare what the student said (e.g., "house") with the actual text (e.g., "home") and write "M" (for "meaning"), "S" (for "structure"), and "V" (for "visual," which includes the use of both orthographic and phonological information) near the miscue (what the child said). Then teachers ask themselves, "What sources of information did the child use when he/she said the miscue?" and circle one or more of the letters (M, S, or V) to indicate which sources of information the child used.

To decide whether the student used meaning cues, the teacher asks herself, "Did the student pay attention to the meaning of the text? Did what the student read make sense?" If so, she circles the M. To decide whether the student used structure or language cues, the teacher asks, "Is what the child read syntactically/grammatically acceptable? Did it sound like language?" If so, she circles the S. Finally, to decide whether the student used visual information, the teacher asks whether the student used the visual information in the printed text—more than just minimally. If so, the teacher circles the V.

Let's consider a few examples using the sample record of oral reading displayed in Figure 4.4. The child (Maria) who read this text made quite a few errors (her oral reading accuracy was 89%), but she did self-correct about a third of her errors, which was encouraging. Looking more closely at her errors, we can see some patterns. For example, in the first sentence, Maria read, "a few house later" instead of "a few hours later" but then, at the end of the sentence, she realized her error and made a self-correction. To analyze her errors and self-corrections, we asked ourselves: what information did she use when she first said, "house"? We decided that she was primarily using visual information. We did not circle M because "a few house later" does not make sense. We did not circle S because Maria's sentence does not sound like language, either. In the next column, we thought about what information Maria probably used as she self-corrected. We circled both M and S because it appeared that she'd gone back to correct her error after she recognized that "a few house later" does not make sense or sound right.

Next, let's look at the last error on that page—where Maria came to the word "harbor" and appealed to the teacher for help. The teacher then told her the word. Because it was not possible to observe any sources of information that Maria used—i.e., she didn't say anything—we couldn't circle M, S, or V. Finally, let's consider the last error that Maria made, when she substituted "wanted" for "worried." She did not self-correct this error, and it appears that Maria was primarily using visual and syntactic information; but her error doesn't make much sense given the context of the story. Thus, we circled S and V, but not M.

FIGURE 4.4 **Analysis of Record of Oral Reading**

RECORD OF ORAL READING

STUDENT Maria TEXT: Storm Warning

DATE: Nov. 9

| Page | Text | Count E | Count SC | Analysis of errors and self-corrections: E (MSV information used) | Analysis of errors and self-corrections: SC (MSV information used) |
|---|---|---|---|---|---|
| 6 | A few hours later (house → SC) | | 1 | MSV | MSV |
| | dark clouds began to form. (begin; from) | 1<br>1 | | MSV<br>MSV | |
| | The wind picked up | | | | |
| | and Julie could see (called; to) | 1<br>1 | | MSV<br>MSV | |
| | lots of fishing boats | | | | |
| | coming back to the harbor. (in; A/T) | 1 | | MSV | |
| 7 | But not one of the boats | | | | |
| | looked like her dad's. | | | | |
| | Julie watched the sky, (watched → SC) | | 1 | MSV | MSV |
| | and then the sea, | | | | |
| | back to the sky, | | | | |
| | and back to the sea. | | | | |
| | With every look (even → SC) | | 1 | MSV | MSV |
| | Julie worried more. (wanted) | 1 | | MSV | |
| | | 6 | 3 | | |

## FIGURE 4.5  Practice Exercise: Analyzing Oral Reading Miscues

| Text | What the Student Read | Cues Used |
|---|---|---|
| 1. Joe heard the owl hoot. | Joe had the owl hoot. | M S V |
| 2. The decaying leaves give off a little heat and keep the eggs warm. | The dying leaves give off a little heat and keep the eggs warm. | M S V |
| 3. Until night fell, it was unsafe to wander outside. | Until night fell, it was unsafe to go outside. | M S V |
| 4. Rabbit saw the fox and ran away quickly. | Rabbit was the fox and ran away quickly. | M S V |

*Note:* Answers and explanations for this practice task can be found in Appendix A-7.

When we look over the patterns observed by analyzing Maria's record of oral reading, we see that Maria used visual information a good deal but meaning and structure to a lesser extent. Although she is beginning to self-correct nicely, she still makes quite a few errors and does not seem to cross-check to see whether what she reads makes sense. If, over time, there are multiple instances of this pattern (i.e., underutilizing meaning and structure cues), the teacher might decide to provide some additional focused, explicit instruction as well as guided practice and coaching to help Maria (perhaps along with other children who need the same support) do more cross-checking. The teacher could encourage Maria to think about the meaning and what makes sense—*and also* use visual information and structure—to make sure that what she attempts looks right, sounds like language, *and* makes sense.

See whether you can evaluate the cues, or sources of information the child used, when saying each error in the sample sentences displayed in Figure 4.5. Remember to think about what cues the child actually *used*, and circle those letters. Answers are provided in Appendix A-7. Children's use of cues during reading can and should change over time. McKenna and Stahl (2003) reviewed research on students' miscues and noticed some interesting patterns. They found that about half of first graders' miscues are omissions and that as children mature, substitutions become more common. This certainly makes sense, since it mirrors the development of students' use of strategies. Children use no strategies when they make omissions, but they use at least some strategies when they make substitutions. Reliance on context (i.e., meaning and structural cues) is strongest among first graders and older, poorer readers. Also, children's substitutions often begin as mere guesses (e.g., "ant" instead of "bug") but gradually become more sophisticated and bear greater graphophonic resemblance to the actual word in the text (e.g., "beside" instead of "behind").

This kind of information is important to keep in mind as you analyze children's miscues. For example, if a first-grade beginning reader is using meaning and structure cues a great deal, you should probably not be surprised. But if a child at the second-grade level is doing the same thing, you should probably see it as an indication that the child's strategy use isn't as balanced as it should be; thus, you'll need to provide further instruction to increase the child's attention to print. Later in this chapter we will again refer to the patterns that teachers can detect on records of oral reading and discuss how the patterns were noted on Willa's profile.

***Vocabulary Strategy Probes.***   As children read more complex texts, they begin to encounter words that are unfamiliar to them in meaning—not just words that are unfamiliar to them in terms of decoding. Children need to use vocabulary-solving strategies to figure out the meaning of words. To find out how children use strategies to figure out unfamiliar vocabulary, you can administer informal assessments (Johnson, 2001). At the primary level, it is usually during read-alouds or guided reading lessons that teachers pose questions about solving vocabulary "puzzles" to help determine the degree to which students can use context to figure out unfamiliar words.

To informally assess vocabulary strategy use, a teacher first needs to make sure that it is *possible* to figure out the meaning of the unfamiliar word from context, because in some situations, context doesn't provide clues to a word's meaning. For example, it might be possible for a third grader to figure out the approximate meaning of the word *snare* in the first sentence below, but it is unlikely that he could figure out the meaning of *baffling* in the second sentence.

- The fox was tangled in the *snare* and could not get out, no matter how hard he tried.
- "This is baffling," thought Julia as she stared at the message scribbled in the notebook.

After reading the first sentence, a teacher might say to a group of children, "Hmm, *snare* is an interesting word; what do you think it means? What might help you figure it out? Turn to a partner and share your ideas." To assess students' use of strategies to figure out unfamiliar vocabulary, the teacher might listen in on a few pairs of students and make notes about what he observed. Some teachers might try to more efficiently gather information about *all* of the children in the class or group by having children respond in writing on a slip of paper, folded in half, with two headings: "What I Think It Means" and "Clues I Used to Predict What I Think It Means." This kind of quick, "every pupil response" technique can provide on-the-spot information to guide instruction. For example, if several students wrote that they thought "snare" means "sneaky" because the sentence was about a fox and the word sounded a bit like "sneaky," that group might benefit from some lessons in using context clues—especially language cues—to predict the meaning of unfamiliar words.

***Think-Alouds, Surveys, and Interviews of Comprehension Strategy Use and Reading Dispositions.***   Like a number of other techniques, think-alouds, which involve children verbalizing their comprehension strategies or thought processes during reading, can be used for both assessment and instruction. Talking with students about what they are thinking as they read also reinforces the notion that reading *is* thinking (Lipson & Wixson, 2003).

Interviews and surveys can also help teachers learn about children's use of processing or comprehension strategies, especially in Grades 3, 4, and beyond. Two surveys that involve student self-assessment are provided in Appendices A-8 and A-9. The first is more appropriate for students at an early stage of reading; the second is more appropriate for students who have most early reading processing strategies already under control. You may want to keep in mind, however, that children sometimes respond by checking off what they *think* the teacher wants, so it is best to supplement the use of surveys with think-alouds, running records, or other means of more directly observing children's use of strategies. Interviews of reading strategy use and dispositions can be conducted with individual students; a

You can find more information concerning the use of think–alouds in chapter 6, on comprehension.

ready-to-photocopy reading strategies and dispositions interview can be found in Appendix A-10.

***Book Logs and Individual Conferences.***   To find out how students are developing reading habits and dispositions, book logs and individual conferences can be very useful. Even with kindergarteners and first graders, the use of these tools not only yields important information for the teacher but also signals *to the child* that reading is important and that teachers (and others) care about the child's opinion of what he or she has read.

*Book Logs.*   A book log is basically a list or record of what has been read. For very young children it can be as simple as having them write down the titles of the books they finish reading. As children become more proficient at recording information, book logs can include the date, the author, and the genre of the book. Some book logs also include a place for students to record whether they thought the book was Easy (E), Just Right (JR), or Challenging (Ch), and also a place to rate their opinion of what they read. See Appendix A-11 for a book log that might be appropriate in a second-, third-, or fourth-grade classroom.

Keep in mind, though, that a book log by itself does not necessarily provide a teacher (or a student) with a way to evaluate the degree to which a student is gaining breadth and depth of reading. Some sort of "lens" or set of criteria is needed to evaluate what has been listed and compare it to desired outcomes. The Literacy Profile provides some guidelines for evaluating book logs. For example, at the third-grade level, the descriptors related to reading dispositions indicate that children at this stage should be able to read "the equivalent of at least two books a month" and "sustain silent, independent reading for at least 20 minutes." These expectations mirror those in a number of state frameworks and also in the resource *Reading and Writing Grade by Grade: Primary Literacy Standards for Kindergarten Through Third Grade* from the New Standards Organization (Baker, 1999). Naturally, teachers should use their own judgment in determining what "counts" as a book. For example, most of the *Harry Potter* books should "count" as multiple books (perhaps two or three if they are read independently) because they are so long. And the magazines and online resources children read should certainly also "count." Actually, the "counting" of books read is not the real goal; children's building stamina as readers is what really matters, and the number of books they read is simply one indication of this reading disposition.

Also consider the rubric/scoring guide in Figure 4.6 as another way to evaluate the reading habits and dispositions of third or fourth graders, using their book logs.

An excellent practice that many teachers use involves enlarging a rubric such as the one displayed in this figure and posting it on the wall so that the shared goals and expectations displayed within the rubric are visible to everyone in the classroom. In some situations, teachers and students draft rubrics collaboratively so that the rubrics include student-friendly language. In this way, assessment is not a "secret" owned by the teacher, but rather a set of shared practices that allow everyone to judge how close they are to achieving a shared goal. Raphael, Highfield, and Au (2006) describe a wonderful process of having students develop what they call "I Can" statements by helping students understand the ideas behind some important benchmarks and then, with the students, drafting phrases that are in the students' own language. Over time, children will be able to use and internalize these statements to take responsibility for their own learning.

FIGURE 4.6  **Reading Habits Scoring Guide (for Students in Grades 3 or 4)**

| Reading Habits | Getting started . . . | On your way . . . | On target! | Wow! |
|---|---|---|---|---|
| Reading a LOT | Reading part of one book or its equivalent, each month | Reading one book or its equivalent, each month | Evidence of reading enough to meet goal (2 books or their equivalent a month) | Evidence of reading *more than enough* to meet goal! |
| Reading Widely and in Depth | Reading one genre only, **OR** Reading one book or its equivalent—on one subject, from one author, or in one genre | Reading 2 different genres, **OR** Reading 2–3 books or their equivalent—in one subject, from one author, or in one genre | Evidence of reading enough different genres to meet goal for the year! (Goal = at least 3 different genres/kinds of text) **AND** Evidence of reading enough in-depth books to meet goal (at least 4 books or equivalent from one author, subject, or genre) | Evidence of very wide or in-depth reading—*More than enough* to meet goal! |

© Sue Biggam, VT READS Institute at the University of VT; 2005.

*Individual Conferences.* Individual student conferences can provide a valuable opportunity to find out various things about a developing reader (and writer). Like many other assessment tools, individual conferences often seem somewhere between instruction and assessment—but that is actually a good thing! Despite their benefits, though, teachers sometimes find individual conferences challenging for a variety of reasons: it can be tricky to stay focused and know what to talk about during a conference; conferences can be hard to schedule and manage within a literacy block; and they can be challenging to keep track of.

To stay focused during an individual conference and to know what to talk about, a prepared conference form can be helpful. The individual student conference form provided in Appendix A-12 is adapted from a form developed by Routman (2003). It includes questions concerning reading dispositions as well as questions that involve other areas of literacy, such as reading accuracy and fluency, as well as comprehension/reader response. Many teachers simply circle (ahead of time) the questions that they plan to ask during a particular conference, since it is rare that a teacher will have time to ask all of the questions. It is often particularly helpful to tell children ahead of time what the focus of the conference will be so that they can also be prepared.

Scheduling, managing, and keeping track of individual student conferences can be challenging, too. Some teachers use a monthlong grid to schedule conferences and adjust the frequency according to student need. Other teachers hold individual conferences only one day of the week, and schedule them *instead of* that day's teacher-guided reading groups. To help keep track of what takes place during conferences, some teachers set up individual "student conference notebooks" that each student keeps at his/her desk or "cubbie." That way, when the teacher confers with the child, all of the conference notes about the child's reading are in one place. This also signals to the child that when "next steps" are decided upon, there *will* be follow up. See Figure 4.7 for a sample page of a student conference notebook for Leo, a first grader.

## Summary of Assessing Reading Strategies and Dispositions

Many informal tools and approaches, along with more formal tools, are available for teachers to determine how well children are progressing in their reading strategies and dispositions. These include assessment tools and approaches such as running records, conferences, think-alouds, interviews, surveys, and book logs. When assessing children's development of reading strategies, it is particularly important to keep in mind that, although strategies are a critical contributing factor to the development of competence and confidence in reading, children do not master them, individuals use strategies flexibly and in relationship to the text and context. Interestingly, Afflerbach et al. (2008) contend that "the main reason for assessing strategies is to find clues about what

**FIGURE 4.7  Student Conference Notebook for Leo, Grade 1 Student (Who Is Reading at a Mid-First Grade Level)**

### April 10, '08

*Leo read from "Greedy Cat"*

*said it was "easy"—chose it because I had read it to the class.*

*but < 90% oral reading acc. (was/went; asked for many words) Said he used pictures to help figure out hard words.*

*Next step: Look closely at hard words, think about what sounds the letters make*

### April 21, '08

*Leo brought "I'm the King of the Mountain"—chose it because of the cover and Ben had just read it.*

*said it was OK/just right and said he had tried to look harder at the hard words*

*read with 92% acc and DID look more closely at words like "shook" "voice" "cried"*

*retold story with a real sense of pride—and also attention to beginning/middle/end*

*Next step: read some less patterned books, or informational books?*

the student is not doing or what is being done incorrectly so that teachers can reteach better strategies" (p. 371). At this point we will turn our attention to how all this information can be applied to instruction to increase student growth in reading strategies and dispositions.

## INSTRUCTIONAL CONSIDERATIONS FOR READING STRATEGIES AND DISPOSITIONS

Reading strategies and dispositions need careful cultivation in order for them to develop and thrive in children. To support the development of reading strategies, both explicit instruction and supported practice are essential, along with time for application and feedback (Dole, Duffy, Roehler, & Pearson, 1991). Reading dispositions and habits should flourish, in most children, when they are engaged in a literate community, surrounded by high-quality and appropriately challenging books, and provided with challenging tasks, encouragement for effort, and motivating reasons to read (Baker, 1999; Pressley, 2002).

In thinking about how to use the results of assessment to support student growth in the development of strategies, it will be important to keep in mind two points made earlier: that strategies are flexible tools for processing text and thinking during reading, and that strategies are mostly used as needed, depending upon a variety of factors such as the text being read, the reader, and the context. For example, Jasmine, a second grader, might need to use both rereading and questioning strategies when reading one of the Magic Tree House books because the text is slightly challenging for her and because she has limited background knowledge about the book's topic, the solar system. Another reader, Toby, might use a visualization strategy when reading a poem by Shel Silverstein about a messy room because the poem invites the use of visualization, and also because Toby very likely has extensive background knowledge and previous experience with messy rooms!

Similarly, when thinking about how to influence children's reading habits and dispositions, remember that we cannot *make* children "love to read" (any more than someone can make us love to watch football or listen to opera), but we can certainly use our observations of students' current reading dispositions and habits to provide, as needed, increased opportunities in reading and discussion across a variety of genres. And, fortunately, we can *lead* children toward loving to read.

Results of assessment in reading strategies and dispositions can reveal both general and particular patterns of need. In this section we will briefly describe some commonly used approaches for developing reading strategies and dispositions; in the next section we will turn our attention to approaches that might be used with those children whose assessments reveal that they have particular needs in reading strategies and dispositions.

### Instructional Approaches for Building Reading Strategies and Dispositions in All Students

Two critical opportunities that *all* students need to have in order to develop strategies include explicit instruction through a gradual release of responsibility model and supported practice in flexible strategy application using "real" or authentic text (Dole et al., 1991). When teachers don't use the "gradual release" model, children are often "assigned" to complete a task—and thus do not receive sufficient modeling and scaffolding to be successful.

To develop productive dispositions and habits toward reading, all children need support and encouragement from "skilled others"; a rich literate environment; and authentic motivating reasons to read. Having access to high-quality, engaging books and other text materials, including those from the Internet and other digital resources, also promotes motivation for reading. First we'll discuss opportunities for strategy development, and then we'll turn to reading dispositions.

***Instructional Opportunities for Development of Early Reading Processing Strategies.*** Many of the key components of a balanced literacy block (i.e., shared reading, teacher-guided reading, explicit teaching through mini-lessons, etc.) are critical to the development of early reading processing strategies, and include opportunities for both explicit instruction and supported practice with feedback. Some of these instructional opportunities are more conducive to explicit teaching; others are designed to provide supported practice, often using prompts. Interestingly, Fountas and Pinnell (1996) caution that "just as strategies cannot be directly observed, neither can they be directly taught. We teach *for* strategies" (p. 149). In other words, it is important to recognize that strategy use takes place inside the child's head and that we cannot *make* it happen; we can, however, provide intentional modeling and scaffolding to lead the way and support the development of strategy use.

*Shared or Interactive Reading.* One key opportunity for supported practice is shared or interactive reading, in which the teacher is the primary reader and children follow along by reading aloud together with enlarged text displayed on chart paper, a "big book," or an overhead projector. Shared reading can also provide an opportunity for explicit instruction *if* the teacher intentionally models and explains the use of a strategy. Simply reading together is excellent for developing fluency, but explicit demonstration and explanation are needed in order to make the use of early processing strategies "transparent" to young students.

As an example, if a teacher is reading a poem with kindergarten children, an excellent way for her to model cross-checking as a strategy would be for her to use a pointer while reading a line of the poem and intentionally skip a word. Then she might say, "Huh? That didn't sound right. I'd better go back and read that again and make sure I look closely at all the words." By doing this sort of think-aloud, she provides a valuable bit of explicit instruction in cross-checking.

*Guided Reading for Early Strategies.* Similarly, guided reading provides another key opportunity for explicit instruction and supported practice. Fountas and Pinnell (2001) describe guided reading as "a teaching approach designed to help individual students learn how to process a variety of increasingly challenging texts with understanding and fluency" (p. 193). A guided-reading lesson in the early stages of reading usually takes place with a small group of children who have been grouped together because the teacher has, through ongoing assessment, determined that they read approximately the same level of text and have similar needs. The teacher provides the text materials, introduces the story, and then guides the children through the reading process. The goal is for the children to eventually read the text independently and silently, with understanding.

Central to the guided-reading approach at the early stages of reading is the use of teacher-provided prompts to support students' development of strategies. Some sample prompts (adapted from Fountas & Pinnell, 1996) are shown in Figure 4.8.

When a teacher selects a particular prompt to use with a student, he usually does so based on what he has already observed about the student's use of strategies, frequently from a running record but sometimes from informal observation.

Two excellent resources for prompts that can support children's use of strategies are *Guided Reading: Good First Teaching for All Learners* (1996) by Fountas and Pinnell and Sharon Taberski's (2000) *On Solid Ground*.

**FIGURE 4.8  Strategy Prompts for Early Readers**

| Strategies Needed by the Student | Sample Prompts by the Teacher |
| --- | --- |
| Beginning reading behaviors | • Read it with your finger.<br>• Did you have enough (or too many) words?<br>• Try ____: would that make sense? Sound right? Read that again and start the word. |
| Self-monitoring | • Were you right?<br>• Why did you stop? (after hesitation or stop)<br>• It could be ____, but look at ____.<br>• Check it—does it look right and sound right to you?<br>• Try that again. |
| Use of multiple sources of information | • Does that make sense?<br>• Does that look right?<br>• Does that sound right?<br>• Try that again and think what would make sense/sound right.<br>• Look at all the letters in the word. |
| Fluency | • Can you read this quickly?<br>• Put your words together so it sounds like talking. |
| Self-correction | • I like the way you worked that out<br>• You're nearly right. Try that again. |

It is also important to keep in mind that the kind of reading material children encounter during guided-reading lessons should be only *one* part of a balanced literacy program. For a number of students, the material they read during guided reading will be grade-level text or perhaps even more challenging, but for other children, the text they encounter during guided reading will need to be below grade level, at their instructional level. It is important that all children have access, by reading or listening, to grade-level (or higher) text to ensure that they are exposed to and engaged with age-appropriate background knowledge, rich language, advanced vocabulary, and high-quality literature. All students also need ample opportunities to read easy, independent-level text so that they become confident and fluent readers.

*Mini-Lessons and Other Activities.* Other opportunities for explicit instruction include mini-lessons and teacher-led whole group lessons from a comprehensive program. In addition, supported practice and semi-independent activities can also be useful if the teacher has previously modeled and/or explained to children. Mini-lessons are short, focused lessons that are often conducted with children sitting on the rug so that everyone can be "up close" and engaged. Mini-lessons will be described in more detail in the next section, which focuses on supporting the development of comprehension strategies.

Semi-independent activities, sometimes referred to as "center" or "station" activities, often take place while the teacher is working with another small group or a guided-reading group during the literacy block. They can be very useful in the early primary grades to provide supported practice for children as they develop early reading processing strategies and other skills. One possibility for "center" or "station" activities is a partner-reading station, where pairs of children read together, one child using a bookmark to support the other child's use of reading strategies. An example of a bookmark that might be used for this purpose can be found in Appendix A-13.

Other center or station activities that could take place in a primary-level classroom include students in small (usually heterogeneous/mixed-ability) groups reading short poems or other pieces of text on an overhead projector that's placed on the floor, or students "reading around the room" (i.e., pointing to and reading charts, labels, directions, and posters with a pointer, dowel, or set of chopsticks). Buddy reading, listening to books on tape, using the writing center, or contributing to a class book or poster are other examples of literacy-based center or station activities. In later grades, activities usually include independent reading, research or "investigation" work, and a variety of responses to reading. These independent and semi-independent activities are valuable opportunities for practicing strategies. Later in the day, providing an opportunity to discuss with children the strategies they used and how well the strategies worked will greatly enhance the impact of this sort of activity. It is important to make sure that while children are involved in center or station activities, they are actually reading or writing connected text most of the time, as opposed to completing worksheets or isolated skill work.

### Instructional Opportunities for the Development of Reading Comprehension Strategies.
All children need explicit instruction in reading comprehension strategies (including modeling, guided practice, and independent practice with feedback) along with supported practice. Pearson and Duke (2002) stress that, at the primary level, teachers need to provide explicit instruction in comprehension strategies and also carefully plan activities such as discussion, prediction, and shared reading to support children's understanding of what is read in class.

*Comprehension-Focused Teacher Read-Alouds.* A good deal of comprehension strategy instruction in kindergarten and Grade 1 (but often in Grades 2 and up as well) takes place through teacher read-alouds, which are intentionally planned with a focus on comprehension and carefully selected text. Comprehension is also a key focus of guided reading, of course, but this is true primarily from the middle of Grade 1 onward. One benefit of teachers using read-alouds to teach comprehension strategies is that the text material is challenging enough to warrant the use of such strategies. During guided reading at the earliest levels, the text is often straightforward and limited so that comprehension strategies are not needed. This is not always the case, however. Sometimes you will find ambiguity in pre-primers and emergent reading books because of the limited language in the text, lack of background, or other factors.

The first step in planning a comprehension-focused teacher read-aloud involves selecting a text that is a good match to the particular comprehension strategy that the teacher wants to model. Selecting and using the *best* of children's literature to read aloud is, as Lucy Calkins (2001) stresses, absolutely essential.

When the teacher reads aloud for the purpose of building comprehension, it often sounds like a "think-aloud." For example, while reading *The Very Busy Spider* (Carle, 1984), a kindergarten teacher might demonstrate the strategy of "making connections" in the following way: "Oh, I get it! They keep saying the spider is busy; I know that when I am really busy, I sometimes don't answer because I want to get something done!" Students might then be asked to turn and talk with a partner to share a connection they made (that helped them understand the story) when listening to the rest of the story.

Two excellent resources for books to read aloud for demonstrating or guiding comprehension strategies are *Reading for Meaning* (2002) by Debbie Miller and *Strategies That Work* (2007) by Harvey and Goudvis.

*Comprehension-Focused Mini-Lessons.* Mini-lessons are short (10–20 minutes), tightly organized lessons that generally involve four parts: a connection to what children have previously learned or already know, a few teaching points that often include a demonstration, active engagement by the children, and a link to independent application (Fountas & Pinnell, 2001; Harvey & Goudvis, 2007; Miller, 2002). Students often sit on the rug during the mini-lesson and later apply the teaching points during their own independent reading. When conducting comprehension mini-lessons, teachers frequently use either a picture book or a very short piece of text that they have photocopied or retyped from its original source and made into an overhead transparency. Some excellent sources for short text include books of poems as well as periodicals such as *Kids Discover, WR News* (formerly *Weekly Reader*), *Click, National Geographic Explorer, Ask,* and *Appleseeds,* to name just a few.

Mini-lessons provide an excellent opportunity for demonstrating the use as well as the usefulness of comprehension strategies. Teachers often use an overhead transparency, chart paper, or other means of displaying enlarged text to model the use of a particular strategy or set of strategies. Suppose you wanted to show a classroom of second-grade students how to use the strategy of thinking about text structure to understand a compare-contrast passage about frogs and toads. You might decide to conduct a mini-lesson using a Venn diagram (i.e., two interlocking circles) graphic organizer as scaffolding to help the children visualize the pattern you are using.

Graphic organizers are particularly useful for teaching children about organizational patterns such as classification, compare-contrast, sequence, problem-solution, explanation, and others. Appendix A-14 includes a ready-to-photocopy poster (designed for fourth-grade students) of graphic organizers for these common expository text structures as well as some "signal" or "transition" words that authors frequently use as they write in

Many professional resources for teachers of literacy provide examples of graphic organizers. Several Web sites contain graphic organizers as well. You might try www.ncrel.org, http://www.readwritethink.org, http://freeology.com/graphics.org, or http://www.region15.org/curriculum/graphicorg.html

one or another pattern. You may want to simplify the chart and list of transition words if you decide to use it with younger children. To foster more active engagement and ownership, you may want to encourage students to create their own graphic organizers as well.

The sample mini-lesson outline in Figure 4.9 is similar to others and has been adapted from a variety of sources (Fountas & Pinnell, 2001; Harvey & Goudvis, 2007; Miller, 2002). The outline in this figure provides an example of how you might go about helping children use the strategy of noticing text-structure clues or signal words to support their understanding of a compare-contrast passage about frogs and toads. Notice how the mini-lesson format includes elements that reflect the "gradual release of responsibility" model: modeling, guided practice (with pairs of children), and (for some children) independent practice. A number of different formats for mini-lessons are presented in this Handbook; you will want to choose the style that feels most comfortable to you.

*Guided-Reading Lessons Focused on Comprehension Strategies.* Comprehension strategies are also a key area of focus for guided-reading lessons, usually from mid to late first grade onward. They provide an ideal opportunity

> Two excellent resources for comprehension mini-lessons include Harvey and Goudvis's (2007) *Strategies That Work* and their *Comprehension Tool Kit,* which provides fully developed mini-lessons that are appropriate for children in Grades 3–8.

FIGURE 4.9 **Sample Mini-Lesson for Teaching a Comprehension Strategy (Noticing Text-Structure Cues in a Compare–Contrast Passage)**

---

**Connection:**

- Last week we talked about different ways authors use patterns to organize their thoughts, right?
- Today we're going to read a piece about frogs and toads that uses one of those patterns . . . who remembers what we call it when we say some things are alike and different (comparing or contrasting)? Right—so you (Joey) and you (Marco) are alike because you are both _____ (boys). And how are you different?

**Teaching Points:**

- Authors sometimes use special words that we call "signal words" to let the reader know how they are organizing their thinking. I like to think of these words as signal lights or traffic lights—they let us know what is going on!
- Let's look at this list of words that writers sometimes use when they want to compare two things (show list, as in Appendix A-14)
- Now, watch me as I read the first paragraph (on the overhead), and notice some of these signal words.
- (Read aloud and think aloud, noticing signal words like "both" and "similar"—explaining how they help the reader understand the text.)

**Active Engagement/Application:**

- Now let's read the next paragraph together. As we're reading, see if you notice any of our signal words for compare-contrast. But—don't call out, OK?
- Let's list the ones we found. How did these help us?
- Now I'd like you to work with a partner sitting beside you to read the rest of this page and see if you can find some more signal words that the author used to help us learn about how frogs and toads are alike and different.
- (Call on a few pairs to respond.)
- Today, as you are doing your independent reading, some of you will probably be reading informational text. If you are, see if you notice any signal words that the author used to help show comparison.

**Reflection/Debriefing:**

- Did anyone read something where the author was comparing two things? Great! Can you share what you found with us? Were there any signal words or clues that helped you notice that the author was comparing those things? Do you think noticing those words helped you to understand what the author was trying to say? How?
- Nice job reading today!

for children to learn to apply strategies with selected text, including literature, informational text, or other text sources such as social studies, science, magazines, or material downloaded from the Internet.

For example, a teacher might use a short poem to teach a guided-reading lesson to a group of students who had displayed a need for more work on inferring. The sample guided-reading lesson provided in Figure 4.10 shows how this short lesson might work for a group of third graders. It is important to keep in mind that guided-reading lessons should focus on teaching particular children particular skills, strategies, or concepts using appropriate text.

FIGURE 4.10  **Sample Guided-Reading Lesson Focused
on Using Comprehension Strategies**

---

**Guided Reading Planning Sheet**

Date: _____

Teacher:  *M. Bates*

Students:  *Jared, Kayla, Anton, Assad, Juanita*

---

Notes about students:  *Three of the five students were in ELL class last yr; all need work in inferring.*

**Planning:**
- Focus of the lesson (what strategy, concept, and/or skill is being taught?):
  *inferring during reading*
- Text materials: Poem:  *"The Sky Zoo"—on chart paper and indiv. copies*
- Why selected?  *Short, accessible, yet calls for inference. Approximately OK for reading level of these students (Grade 2+)*
- Necessary background information:  *animals that might be in a zoo? Preteach: pelican, jaw, other? (briefly explain drooping?)*
- Key vocabulary:  *grumpy, fuzzy*

**Lesson Plan:**

Before reading (introduction, key points I will teach):
- *Remember how we have talked about inferring—how it is like connecting the dots? That we need to use what is in the text and what we already know to come up with our own ideas? The author doesn't always tell us what to think, right? Let's think about the title, "The Sky Zoo"—kind of interesting, yes?*

Read to:  *find out what you think the poet is really saying.*

Reading (how will reading take place: shared reading, silent, partners? When? Where?):
*1st time—all together/shared reading*
*2nd time—silently*
*make T chart (together) of clues/what we think*

Return to reading for discussing and revisiting selected parts
of the text:  *Discussion—what clues helped most?*

Optional:  Word work, extension, or application:
*Vocabulary work with fuzzy and grumpy: Would you be grumpy if you got an ice cream cone? Which is fuzzy: a bunny or a snake? I would be grumpy if . . . Something else that might be fuzzy could be a . . .*

This contrasts with what takes place in some classrooms, where teachers simply read a chapter or book with students and guide them in completing follow-up activities or assignments. Guided-reading lessons should involve actual teaching of skills, strategies, or concepts because the designated students need the skills to understand the selected text. The goal, again, is for students to learn how to apply what they have learned when they read silently and independently.

*Routines That Foster Integrated Use of Comprehension Strategies.* Supportive practice in the flexible use of comprehension strategies has been shown to be essential for building comprehension (Pearson & Duke, 2002). Two specific techniques that support children's development in using flexible comprehension strategies include the Reciprocal Teaching approach (originally developed by Palinscar & Brown, 1985) and My Turn, Your Turn (Biggam, 2009). Both techniques may be used in a variety of settings: during a teacher read-aloud, shared/whole-group reading, or small–group teacher-led guided reading.

Reciprocal teaching is a technique that the National Reading Panel (2000) has identified as highly effective and very useful in providing supportive practice for children in using multiple comprehension strategies. Even students in kindergarten can use this engaging and interactive technique. It is highly flexible and can be used in large and small groups, with both narrative and informational text. Here's what is involved: after introducing and explicitly teaching four key strategies of

- Predicting
- Asking questions
- Clarifying
- Summarizing,

the teacher gradually "releases responsibility" to the children so that they take turns "being the teacher" and leading discussion of what was just read, using the four strategies as tools for thinking and discussion.

For example, when using the Reciprocal Teaching technique to read a potentially confusing informational selection about mollusks, a third- or fourth-grade teacher might begin to model using the strategy of prediction by referring to the title ("Mansion for a Mollusk"): "Hmm, I think the author is going to tell us about the mollusk's home, because of that word 'mansion'—I think it means a pretty fancy house." Next the teacher might have the children silently read several paragraphs of the text. Then she would model the remaining reciprocal teaching strategies (clarifying, asking questions, and summarizing) at appropriate points.

To model clarifying, the teacher might say, "I'm not sure what they mean here by 'you grow yourself a house'; I think maybe it means the mollusk can make its own home, but they don't explain how . . . ; is that what you think?" Then, to model asking questions, she might continue, "Here's a tough question: 'do all mollusks have hard shells?'" and call on a student to respond. Finally, she might summarize by saying, "Okay, this section was chock-full of information. I think the most important points the author made were that mollusks' homes come in all shapes and sizes and that mollusks often carry their houses with them, but not always. Does anyone have something I should add to my summary? . . . Now, who will be our next teacher? Okay—Jules!"

Jules then acts as the teacher, directing students to read the next section, then using the four strategies as described above and inviting discussion. (The teacher often acts as a facilitator, to clarify as needed, and to keep the pace going.) Then, when Jules's turn is completed, he will select another student to act as teacher. There is a good amount of flexibility in using reciprocal teaching; all strategies do not necessarily need to be employed at every stopping point. Key to the reciprocal teaching technique is the discussion involved so that all children are actively engaged and the focus is on understanding the meaning of what is read (Oczkus, 2003).

Another routine, called My Turn, Your Turn (Biggam, 2008), is adapted from and similar in many ways to Reciprocal Teaching, but utilizes more frequent teacher modeling. In a nutshell, after introducing the comprehension strategies involved (predicting, clarifying, making connections, inferring, and paraphrasing/summarizing), the teacher and students take turns (first the teacher, then the students) selecting one strategy to use and using that strategy to talk about their thinking as they were reading a section of a text. Both the teacher and the students use a bookmark with strategy prompts each time they stop to reflect on what they read. Two different versions of My Turn, Your Turn bookmarks that may be photocopied and used for this purpose can be found in Appendix A-15. The version with icons is intended for early primary-level children; the other is more appropriate for second, third, or fourth graders.

A few tips for successful implementation of My Turn, Your Turn include the following: First, when it is the teacher's turn ("my turn"), make sure that you actually *model* using the strategy. (It's tempting to instead *ask students to use* the strategy, but modeling by the teacher is essential!) Secondly, if using the technique with a whole class or small group of children, vary the format during the "your turn" segments to maximize student engagement. You might decide to have students "turn and talk," and then call on one or two pairs to share what they talked about, or you might use some form of "every pupil response" technique, such as picking a child's name out of a box or a set of Popsicle sticks. (Such "every pupil response" techniques provide an efficient way to informally assess students' skills and knowledge as well.) Finally, make sure that you use the technique with a selection that has enough content or ambiguity to warrant the use of comprehension strategies. For most kindergarteners and first graders, My Turn, Your Turn will make the most sense when used during a teacher read-aloud; with second to fourth graders, you can use the routine with many different kinds of reading, including stories, informational text, and content-area selections.

### Opportunities for Development of Reading Dispositions and Habits.
Overall, the best ways to increase students' positive dispositions toward reading include providing a rich literacy environment and a high-quality, balanced literacy program. Some educators talk about aiming to have children "immersed" or "marinated" in books and talk *about* books; we think that provides a nice visual image and makes a lot of sense!

*Increasing Time for Reading.* We know that both in-school and out-of-school reading are strongly correlated with stronger reading performance (Foertsch, 1992). We also know that it is easy to become discouraged when we attempt to increase out-of-school reading but have limited success. Teachers have some degree of influence over the amount of reading that takes place within the classroom, however; and school administrators often specify guidelines for the length of time to be spent in a literacy block. For example, in Grades 1 and 2 literacy blocks are often $2\frac{1}{2}$ hours long, since they include word study, reading, and writing instruction. In Grades 3 and 4, a reading block is often 90 minutes, with an additional 30- to 60-minute writing block. Within the literacy block it is important to strategically plan schedules and resources in order to maximize the amount of time children spend actually reading. This often requires careful planning and collaboration with other teachers and staff to allow for extended literacy blocks that have few interruptions.

Equally important is making sure that within those blocks (as well as during other times of the day), children have access to high-quality and appropriate books and spend substantial amounts of time reading connected, meaningful text. Often, classroom teachers and specialists collaborate to construct "shared book centers" where multiple copies of books are kept (often arranged by level, author, or topic) and where teachers can borrow books for use in the classroom.

An important goal during the primary and lower intermediate grades is building reading "stamina," or children's capacity to sustain reading for an extended period of time. Like stamina in running or bicycling, reading stamina takes time and practice to build. Notice on the Literacy Profile that the indicators for Strand 4 at the second-, third-, and fourth-grade levels include expectations for students to be able to read independently and silently for increasing amounts of time. Additional forms of reading (partner reading, guided reading, shared reading, etc.) during the day are essential as well, of course. Allington (2006) calls for schools to allocate at least 90 minutes a day to *actually reading*. Needless to say, we also want to strongly encourage out-of-school reading in a variety of ways.

*Book Talks.* Book talks provide a quick and motivating way to increase students' interest in reading. A book talk, which Fountas and Pinnell (2001) describe as a "brief commercial for a book," simply involves:

- Talking about the title and author
- Showing the cover and a few illustrations
- Giving a brief synopsis of the book
- Reading a short selection aloud
- Some of the following: connecting the book to students' lives or to other books students have read, posing questions, or sharing your own response

Initially, book talks are led by the teacher, but children can also learn to give book talks; some teachers schedule a time for these each week. "Book Recommendations" posters or "Class Picks" baskets or bins provide additional ways to have children let others in the class know about a book worth reading. Think back to our earlier discussion of reading motivation and how much the perceived "value of reading" contributes to that motivation.

*"Check It Out!" Circles.* Sometimes children get "stuck in a rut" of reading and are hesitant to explore new genres or authors. To address this issue, consider the "Check It Out!" circle approach (Sibberson & Szymusiak, 2003); directions for using this approach are outlined in Figure 4.11.

This activity encourages the exploration of new genres and conversation about books, and also reminds children that book choice is unique to each reader. When teachers use this technique, children learn new ways to preview and choose books (another important reading strategy), and most come away with a book they want to explore during independent reading.

Just about all students will benefit from the approaches listed above, which are designed to increase children's use of reading strategies and their dispositions toward reading. However, some children will need more tailored instruction or intensive approaches. Some sample ideas for addressing a few specific needs are described in the next section, where we talk about a few techniques and approaches in more detail.

FIGURE 4.11  **Check It Out! Circle: A Technique to Support Wide Reading by Children**

## Check It Out!  Circle

- The teacher selects enough books for the number of students in the circle. The selections may be the same genre or topic, or a random collection of titles.

- All of the students sit in a circle on the floor. (or you may decide to have two smaller circles that take place simultaneously)

- Explain the kinds of books you have collected and the purposes for the "Check it out" circle. ( to practice previewing books and to find book they might be interested in reading independently.) Give each child a book and explain that they should  preview their book, and  then, after a signal is given, pass the book to the  next child .

- Ring a bell or give a signal after one minute (or thirty seconds) and ask students to pass the book to the child on their right. (Limit the time so students have just enough time to preview the book  . )

- Continue doing this until every child has had a chance to briefly preview each book.

Once everyone has  has had a chance to look at each book, pose  questions such as:
1.  Which books did you see that you want to go back
        to at independent reading time?  Why?
2.  How did you go about previewing the books in
      such a short time?

You might want to have students talk about these questions in pairs, or as a whole-class debriefing.

From *Still Learning to Read: Teaching Students in Grades 3–6* by Franki Sibberson and Karen Szymusiak, © 2003, with permission of Stenhouse Publishers (www.stenhouse.com).

## Instructional Approaches for Building Reading Strategies and Dispositions for Students with Specific Needs

When particular areas of need have been identified through assessments such as records of oral reading, reading conferences, interviews, think-alouds, or book logs, the next steps involve deciding when and how to intervene. First we will discuss approaches that have been successful with children who have specific needs related to early reading processing strategies and comprehension strategies. Then we will address ways to enhance the reading habits and dispositions of children who tend to read very little. Often children who read very little do so because of their skill level, while others may read quite well but choose not to.

***Reading Processing Strategies.***    Some students have a difficult time getting started using effective reading processing strategies. Because strategy use varies from child to child and situation to situation, there is a real need to closely link what is learned through assessment with appropriate plans for intervention. For example, some students overrely on meaning cues and do not pay sufficient attention to letters and sounds, while others use several cueing systems but do not cross-check or self-correct when what they read does not make sense. To address such needs, some teachers and schools design their own individual tutoring or small-group lessons; others use programs based on research done with striving or struggling children. Three successful research-based approaches for helping students develop strategies are described in this section.

*Reading Recovery.*    This short-term, one-to-one intervention seeks to reduce the number of first-grade students who have significant difficulty in learning to read and write. Developed by Marie Clay in New Zealand, the approach involves daily, 30-minute lessons, which should supplement good classroom instruction. This individually tailored assistance is provided to the lowest achieving first graders by teachers who have received a full year of specialized training. Lessons include several predictable components, such as rereading for fluency, writing a sentence, and introducing a new book; but each lesson is carefully crafted to meet the individual child's needs, based on continuing assessment information obtained the previous day.

Although some educators and policymakers have been concerned about the cost of the intensive professional development needed for implementation of Reading Recovery, the program has received very high marks from the federal "What Works" educational clearinghouse. Schwartz, Askew, and Gomez-Bellengé (2007), in an analysis of that report, explain that since 1984, 75% of children who received the full series of Reading Recovery lessons reached grade-level expectations.

*Other Approaches.*    Teaching students to use metacognitive strategies has been shown to be an effective way to strengthen their comprehension (Pressley, 2002). A recent study by Boulware-Gooden, Carreker, Thornhill, and Joshi (2007) demonstrated the effectiveness of this approach. The project involved teaching third-grade students to "think-aloud" as they read, whispering "yes" if they were right about something, "oops" if they needed to correct something, and "wow" or "aha!" if they learned something new. Children in the "intervention" school made significant gains in both reading comprehension and vocabulary within only 5 weeks' time. Several other programs have been developed for individuals or small groups of students who need more intensive support in developing reading strategies.

Book Buddies (Morris, 2006) uses volunteers or college students trained and supervised by reading teachers to provide lessons to individual first or second graders twice a week. Lessons focus on guided reading, word study, and fluency, and reading teachers administer assessments three times a year and maintain communication with the classroom teacher.

Reading Intervention for Early Success (Houghton Mifflin, 2003) is another research-based program designed for children in Grades 1 and 2.

Lessons are provided to groups of five to seven students and include three components: Rereading for Fluency, Reading the Books of the Week, and Working with Words/Writing Sentences. Periodic assessment is built into the program to monitor children's progress.

***Reading Comprehension Strategies.*** By the time students reach third or fourth grade, assuming that assessments of reading comprehension have been used to screen and then diagnose the children's needs, teachers should have an idea of which children need particular work on developing reading comprehension strategies. In some cases, this need may be evident as early as first or second grade—if teachers have paid close attention to students' comprehension during teacher read-alouds and guided reading. Many of the approaches listed above (and in other chapters as well) will support the development of reading comprehension strategies—particularly if utilized in a small group setting where it is more likely that children at risk will take part and respond. For example, with a small group of English Language Learners who may be reluctant to speak in a larger group, you might do an "up close and personal" version of a reading comprehension mini-lesson that you had previously done with the whole class. One specialized commercial program called Visualizing and Verbalizing (Bell, 2007) is sometimes used with children who particularly need work on strengthening their concept imagery. The goal of this program is to improve language comprehension, critical thinking, and expressive language. Two additional techniques and programs will be described in this section.

*Individual Think-Alouds.* Think-alouds were discussed earlier in this chapter as an assessment tool, but they also can be used as an instructional intervention. To make strategy use more evident and "transparent" to students, Lipson and Wickizer (1989) demonstrated that think-alouds can be used with students who struggle with comprehension. They found think-alouds to be effective in "slowing down" the reading process, and helping children more readily stop to think as they read. One "generic" think-aloud prompt that a teacher might use during an individual student think-aloud conference is, "What were you doing and thinking as you read that part?" Providing the child with a list of think-aloud prompts so that he begins to internalize the process of thinking during reading makes sense, too. Some prompts to use might include:

- "I am thinking that . . ."
- "This part must mean . . ."
- "I don't understand . . ."
- "I am picturing . . ."

Sometimes students need to be convinced that this kind of "slowing down" is worth the effort, so you might consider having them do a quick comprehension check or summary—once after reading with no think-aloud, and then again after reading *with* a think-aloud.

*Soar to Success.* Designed for children from Grade 3 on, Soar to Success (2000) is a small-group intervention designed to accelerate students' reading abilities and help them apply comprehension and decoding strategies to a range of texts across content areas. Key to the approach is the use of reciprocal teaching techniques, which foster the use of the cognitive strategies of predicting, clarifying, questioning, and summarizing. Soar to Success is implemented daily in groups of five to seven students for 30- to 40-minute periods over an 18-week time frame. In addition to the program's effectiveness in contributing to children's reading achievement (Cooper, Boschken, McWilliams, & Pistochini, 1997), other benefits include the lively pace and high-quality, varied text materials included.

**_Reading Dispositions._** When children are not experiencing success as readers, it is perfectly understandable for them to avoid reading. However, that is precisely the opposite of what they need to do! Dealing with the challenge of helping striving or reluctant readers read _more_ takes both creativity and persistence. In general, keys to success involve keeping the risk level low, making reading pleasurable, and finding materials that have relevance or a connection to the child. Using the results from assessments such as reading interviews and surveys can also help plan the kind of intervention needed.

Some teachers and schools have had success with reading incentive programs. Some incentive programs are commercial, such as Pizza Hut's; others are more homegrown such as setting goals for reading a certain number of minutes (when the children reach the goal, the principal dyes her hair green!). The eventual goal, of course, is to have incentives become _internalized_ for the student. Three additional approaches for influencing the reading dispositions of students who avoid reading or who read very little are described below.

_Interest-Based Book Clubs._ Some teachers have found success with setting up interest-based book clubs. Based on children's expressed interests (identified through surveys, interviews, or questionnaires), interest-based book clubs are scheduled for a period of time, and involve children either reading the same material or reading different sources on the same topic and discussing what they have learned. Topics sometimes end up including areas that are not usually a focus of the school curriculum (video games, paintball, movie reviews, etc.).

Series books and specific genres such as mysteries and adventures are likely to be of high interest to students in Grades 3 and 4, too. The school librarian can be valuable in locating sources, which may include Internet sites and magazines as well as books. For children whose reading ability is especially limited, some accommodations may be needed, such as having someone audiotape the reading so that the child can read along.

_Goal Setting._ The idea of reading a whole book is simply daunting to some students. Setting achievable goals, such as reading a particular number of pages, might be much more accessible and increase the chances of success. You might consider adapting the rubric provided in Figure 4.6 so that it is tailored to a particular child's goals and needs. For example, for a reader who is really struggling, the "Wow!" column might read "Read 10 pages in 1 day!" Gradually, the descriptors can be increased to "raise the bar" of the amount of reading the child needs to accomplish.

In addition, you might use the questions regarding "reading dispositions and habits" from the Reading Strategies and Dispositions Interview in Appendix A-10 to help plan goals and next steps with the child. Setting goals can be tricky, however, if children set "out-of-reach" goals. For example, if a second grader who is reading at an early first-grade level wants to set a goal of reading the _Harry Potter_ books, it's clear that that may take the child a while to achieve. You might consider making a "staircase" with the child, listing titles of benchmark books (perhaps using some of those listed on the Literacy Profile) that will be indications of getting closer to the goal. At the same time, you might obtain a copy of one of the _Harry Potter_ books on tape (or CD), even if you suspect that the child can read only about 20% of the words, and encourage him to follow along as he listens. Remember that listening comprehension is an important contributor to overall comprehension and reading achievement.

*Literary Lunches.* An excellent idea for generating interest in books and reading comes from Michael Sullivan (2007), who describes setting up "literary lunches." The initial setup involves doing brief book talks with children regarding 5 to 10 books that an adult reader either from the school or the community will read aloud. (Excellent candidates might be a local firefighter, soccer coach, the school librarian, or a favorite retired teacher.) Students list their top two or three choices (or they can decline to participate, of course), and during the week that the "literary lunch reader" comes to the school to read the book aloud, those children go to the head of the lunch line and then proceed to a classroom set aside for this activity. All children need to do is listen to the story, although there may be some discussion afterward. This is a simple, low-cost approach that can reap many benefits, particularly for reluctant readers who *really* need extra opportunities to be "immersed" in books. Michael Sullivan particularly recommends including authors such as Jon Scieszka, David Martin, and Dav Pilkey and genres such as humor, adventure, and fantasy, which have special appeal to boys.

Michael Sullivan's Web site www.talestoldtall.com has many ideas for engaging children (especially boys) in reading, along with some excellent lists of books.

## LOOKING CLOSELY AT ONE CHILD'S ASSESSMENTS FROM STRAND 4 OF THE LITERACY PROFILE

### Results of Reading Strategy and Dispositions Assessments

To find out Willa's development of reading strategies and dispositions toward reading, several assessment tools were used. These included a record of oral reading, a reading strategies and disposition interview, and the Elementary Reading Attitude Survey. As is often the case, several of these assessments provided information about other areas of reading as well.

***Willa's Reading Strategy Development.*** From the record of oral reading, it is clear that Willa has most early reading processing strategies well under way. An analysis of the miscues that Willa made during her oral reading of instructional-level text showed that in 10 out of the 11 miscues, she used meaning and structure cues. In other words, most of the times when Willa incorrectly substituted one word for another, the word that was substituted made sense and sounded right.

This indicates that Willa reads for meaning, and the fluency of her reading provides additional evidence for this, since she reads with a good deal of appropriate phrasing and expression. Willa's inattention to the visual features of many "small words" was interesting, though. Several of her errors involved substitutions of words such as "he" instead of "it" and "they" for "there." Her strong focus on reading for meaning seems to override her attention to print at times, and while it did not interfere with her comprehension at this time, it might be wise to monitor this tendency as she begins to read more complex texts or unfamiliar genres in succeeding grades.

Concerning the development of reading comprehension strategies, during the reading strategies and dispositions interview, Willa was asked what she does when she comes to a word she is not sure of. Her reply was that she sometimes asks the teacher, sometimes sounds it out, but sometimes skips it if it gets really hard and she gets annoyed. She added that she might then go back to the word when she is done reading. When asked what strategies she uses to help her understand what she reads, Willa commented that she often rereads, and added that if she reads something too fast, she goes back to "make it a good sentence." These responses show impressive self-awareness on her part, and recognition of her tendency to sometimes read too fast. Based on this evidence from her records of oral reading and responses to the interview questions, we marked the descriptors related to strategy use on her Literacy Profile (see Figure 4.12) accordingly.

## FIGURE 4.12  Willa's Profile for Reading Strategies and Dispositions

Note: This figure has been excerpted from the full Literacy Profile chart for illustrative purposes. Please consult the full pull-out chart to identify the column headings and development phases.

| Strand *Question & Sample Assessment Tools* | Early–Mid Grade 1 | Late Grade 1–Early Grade 2 | Late Grade 2–Early Grade 3 |
|---|---|---|---|
| **4. Reading Strategies, Processes, and Dispositions** *To what extent does the child use early processing strategies and comprehension strategies during reading? How engaged is the child with reading?* **Sample Assessment Tools** • Running Records • Records of oral reading • Think-Alouds • Interviews • Observations and anecdotal notes • Book logs • Elementary Reading Attitude Survey | Uses more than one cueing system (meaning, visual, and language cues) and begins to cross-check independently  Reads two or three little books or short text selections each day | Uses multiple cues and self-corrects with increasing frequency when meaning is altered*  Reads four or more little books, short text selections, or two to three short chapters each day  Can sustain reading for at least 10 minutes (independently or with a partner)  *[Meaning is the "driver" of Willa's reading, and she sometimes does not self-correct—even when meaning is slightly altered, if she feels meaning is acceptable enough] KI | Predicts and confirms during reading  Begins to self-monitor comprehension; often rereads as a fix-up strategy  Makes connections during reading  Reads approximately two books a month or two chapters a day  Can sustain silent reading independently for at least 15 minutes a day  [Willa is proud of being able to read hard chapter books like Junie B. Jones!] KI |

Gray areas represent highlighting added by the teacher, preferably using a different color for each year (e.g., yellow highlights for Late K, orange highlights for Early–Mid Grade 1, etc.).
Bracketed material represents teacher/examiner comments from June, Grade 1.

***Reading Dispositions Development.*** We know from talking with her mother that on most days, Willa spends at least 15 minutes independently reading three or four short books or several chapters from books. From the "reading strategies and dispositions" interview, we learned that Willa believes herself to be a "really good reader" and is proud that she can read "really hard chapter books like Junie B. Jones."

In addition, we administered the Elementary Reading Strategies Survey to Willa, and learned some interesting information. Overall, the results of *this* survey showed Willa's level of interest in reading to be somewhat lower than that of others at her grade level: her responses placed her at the 43rd percentile in terms of overall attitude toward reading. Her responses to the recreational items yielded a recreational subscale score at the 32nd percentile; her academic subscale was at the 44th percentile. Willa's comments as she completed the survey, though, were interesting and informative. For example, as she filled out an item that asked, "How do you feel when you read a book in school during free time?", she remarked, "I feel grumpy—I have to do two book logs!" Willa's responses showed that she prefers playing to reading, although she also indicated that she does like to spend time reading, enjoys getting books as presents, and likes to learn from books.

Reviewing this survey provides an interesting example of how important it is to have *several* sources of assessment information. Willa's responses to the Elementary Reading Attitude Survey *might* make one think that Willa's attitude toward reading is an area of concern. But in fact, Willa reads widely and talks about herself as a really good reader. In marking the descriptors concerning reading habits and dispositions on the Literacy Profile, we took into account all of the information obtained.

## Overall Evaluation of Willa's Reading Strategies and Dispositions

Willa has a solid foundation in early reading strategies and clearly reads for meaning. She self-corrects when meaning is disrupted, and her substitutions almost always make sense. The assessments of her decoding skills (discussed previously at the end of chapter 3) confirm that, although Willa has a good foundation in phonics and decoding, she does need further instruction in areas such as vowel digraphs, long vowels, and other areas normally taught at the end of first grade and the beginning of Grade 2. Willa does have a tendency to let meaning "override" print at times, though, when she reads quickly. She is aware of this tendency, and it may be useful for teachers to help her monitor this, particularly as she begins to read text material in which such substitutions might make a difference in terms of comprehension. Willa's comprehension strategies are beginning to develop as well. Most indications are that Willa is already a confident reader who likes reading and spends time enjoying books. Keeping reading time pleasurable for Willa will be crucial.

## REFERENCES

Afflerbach, P., Pearson, P. D., & Paris, S. G. (2008). Clarifying differences between reading skills and reading strategies. *The Reading Teacher, 61*(5), 364–373.

Allington, R. L. (2006). *What really matters for struggling readers*. Boston: Pearson.

Anderson, R. C., Wilson, P., & Fielding, L. (1988). Growth in reading and how children spend their time out of school. *Reading Research Quarterly, 23*(3), 285–303.

Baker, G. (1999). *Reading & writing grade by grade: Primary literacy standards for kindergarten through third grade.* University of Pittsburgh, New Standards Organization, University of Pittsburgh Learning Research and Development Center.

Beaver, J. (2003). *Developmental reading assessment K–3.* New York: Pearson Education.

Beaver J. M., & Carter, M. A. (2006). *Developmental reading assessment 4–8.* New York: Pearson Education.

Bell, N. (2007). *Visualizing and verbalizing for language comprehension and thinking.* Retrieved from http://www.lindamoodbell.com

Biggam, S. C. (2009). My turn, your turn: Promoting generalized use of comprehension strategies. *VT Council on Reading Journal.*

Boulware-Gooden, R., Carreker, S., Thornhill, A., & Joshi, R. M. (2007). Instruction of metacognitive strategies enhances reading comprehension and vocabulary of third-grade students. *The Reading Teacher, 61*(1), 70–77.

Calkins, L. M. (2001). *The art of teaching reading.* Boston: Allyn and Bacon.

Carle, E. (1984). *The very busy spider.* New York: Philomel.

Clay, M. (1978). *Reading: The patterning of complex behavior.* London: Heinemann.

Clay, M. M. (1985). *The early detection of reading difficulties.* Aukland, New Zealand: Heinemann.

Clay, M. (1991). *Becoming literate: The construction of inner control.* Portsmouth, NH: Heinemann.

Clay, M. (1993). *An observation survey of early literacy achievement.* Portsmouth, NH: Heinemann.

Cooper, J. D., Boschken, I., McWilliams, J., & Pistochini, L. (1997). *Project success: A study of the effectiveness of an intervention program designed to accelerate reading in the upper grades.* Unpublished manuscript.

Dewitz, P. (2006). Reading comprehension in five basal reading programs. Paper presented at the annual meeting of the National Reading Conference, Los Angeles, CA.

Dole, J. A., Duffy, G. G., Roehler, L. R., & Pearson, P. D. (1991). Moving from the old to the new; Research on reading comprehension instruction. *Review of Educational Research, 61*(2), 239–264.

Duke, N. K., & Pearson, P. D. (2002). Effective practices for developing reading comprehension. In A. E. Farstrup & S. J. Samuels (Eds.), *What research has to say about reading instruction.* Newark, DE: International Reading Association.

Foertsch, M. A. (1992). *Reading in and out of school: Achievement of American students in grades 4, 8 and 12 in 1989–90*. Washington, DC: U.S. Government Printing Office.

Fountas, I., & Pinnell, G. S. (1996). *Guided reading; Good first teaching for all learners*. Portsmouth, NH: Heinemann.

Fountas, I., & Pinnell, G. S. (2001). *Guiding readers and writers, Gr. 3–6*. Portsmouth, NH: Heinemann.

Gambrell, L. B., Palmer, B. M., Codling, R. M., & Mazzoni, S. A. (1996). Assessing motivation to read. *The Reading Teacher, 49*, 518–533.

Goodman, K. (1996). *On reading*. Portsmouth, NH: Heinemann.

Goodman, Y. M., Watson, D. J., & Burke, C. L. (1987). *Reading miscue inventory: Alternative procedures*. Katonah, NY: Richard C. Owen.

Harvey, S., and Goudvis, A. (2005). *Comprehension ToolKit*. Portsmouth, NH: Firsthand, Heinemann.

Harvey, S., & Goudvis, A. (2007). *Strategies that work*. York, ME: Stenhouse.

Johnson, D. (2001). *Vocabulary in the elementary and middle school*. Boston: Allyn and Bacon.

Johnston, P. (2000) *Running records: A self-tutoring guide*. York, ME: Stenhouse.

Keene, E. O., & Zimmerman, S. (1997). *Mosaic of thought: Reading comprehension in a readers workshop*. Portsmouth, NH: Heinemann.

Lipson, M. Y. (2007). *Teaching reading beyond the primary grades*. New York: Scholastic.

Lipson, M. Y., & Wickizer, E. A. (1989). Promoting self-control and active reading through dialogues. *Exceptional Children, 21*(2), 28–32.

Lipson, M. Y., & Wixson, K. K. (2003). *Assessment and instruction of reading and writing difficulty*. Boston: Pearson Education.

McDowell, J. A., Schumm, J. S., & Vaughn, S. (1993). Assessing exposure to print: Development of a measure for primary children. In D. J. Leu & C. Kinzer (Eds.), *Examining central issues in literacy research, theory and practice* (pp. 101–107). Chicago: National Reading Conference.

McKenna, M. C., & Kear, D. J. (1990). Measuring attitude toward reading: A new tool for teachers. *The Reading Teacher, 43*, 626–639.

McKenna, M. C., & Stahl, S. A. (2003). *Assessment for reading instruction*. New York: The Guilford Press.

Miller, D. (2002). *Reading for meaning*. York, ME: Stenhouse.

Morris, D. (2006). Using non-certified tutors to work with at-risk readers: An evidence-based approach. *The Elementary School Journal, 106*(6), 351–362.

National Reading Panel. (2000). *Teaching children to read: An evidence-based assessment of the scientific research literature on reading and its implications for reading instruction*. Washington, DC: National Reading Panel.

Oczkus, L. (2003). *Reciprocal teaching at work*. Newark, DE: International Reading Association.

Palinscar, A. S., & Brown, A. L. (1985). Reciprocal teaching: Activities to promote read(ing) with your mind. In T. L. Harris & E. J. Cooper (Eds.), *Reading, thinking and concept development: Strategies for the classroom*. New York: The College Board.

Paris, S. G., Lipson, M. Y., & Wixson, K. K. (1983). Informed strategies for learning: A program to improve children's reading awareness and comprehension. *Journal of Educational Psychology, 76*, 1239–1252.

Pearson, P. D., & Duke, N. K. (2002). Comprehension instruction in the primary grades. In C. C. Block & M. Pressley (Eds.), *Comprehension instruction: Research-based best practices*. New York: The Guilford Press.

Pearson, P. D., & Gallagher, M. (1983). The instruction of reading comprehension. *Contemporary Educational Psychology, 8*, 317–344.

Pressley, M. (2002). *Reading instruction that works: The case for balanced teaching.* New York: The Guilford Press.

Raphael, T. E., Highfield, K., & Au, K. H. (2006). *QAR NOW.* New York: Scholastic.

*Reading intervention for early success.* (2003). Boston: Houghton Mifflin.

Rigby Education. (2001). *Rigby PM benchmark kit.* Barrington, IL: Author.

Routman, R. (2003). *Reading essentials.* Portsmouth, NH: Heinemann.

Schumm, J. S. (2006). *Reading assessment and instruction for all learners.* New York: Guilford Press.

Schwartz, R. M., Askew, B. J., & Gomez-Bellengé, F. X. (2007). What works? Reading recovery: An analysis of the What Works Clearinghouse Intervention Report, March 19, 2007. Worthington, OH: Reading Recovery Council of North America.

Sibberson, F., & Szymusiak, K. (2003). *Still learning to read: Teaching students in grades 3–6.* York, ME: Stenhouse.

Smith, F. (1978). *Understanding reading: A psycholinguistic analysis of reading and learning to read.* New York: Holt, Rinehart and Winston.

Smith, F. (1979). *Reading without nonsense.* New York: Teacher's College Press.

Snow, C. E., Burns, M. S., & Griffin, P. (Eds.). (1998). *Preventing reading difficulties in young children.* Washington, DC: National Academy Press.

*Soar to success.* (2000). Geneva, IL: Houghton Mifflin.

Sullivan, M. Retrieved from: http://www.talestoldtall.com

Taberski, S. (2000). *On solid ground: Strategies for teaching reading in K–3.* Portsmouth, NH: Heinemann.

Vygotsky, L. (1978). *Mind in society: The development of higher psychological processes.* Cambridge, MA: Harvard University Press.

# CHAPTER FIVE

# Reading Accuracy and Fluency at Increasing Text Levels

CORE QUESTION

To what degree is the child able to read books of increasing complexity with accuracy and fluency?

We often hear a 7- or 8-year-old proudly proclaim, "I can read chapter books now!" This statement reflects a child's awareness that he has reached a milestone (like losing a tooth, or riding a bike with only two wheels). Certainly, this accomplishment is worthy of pride, since reading "harder" books is what makes a child feel as though he or she is becoming a "good" reader. Gradually increasing a child's ability to read more complex and challenging texts *is* certainly a central outcome of reading instruction.

But becoming a good reader is not just a matter of being able to "say the words" in a particular book. Reading increasingly complex texts requires a child to decode text with increasing *accuracy* as well as *fluency*. These two characteristics of skilled reading further depend upon a number of other factors of the child's development (which are listed on the Literacy Profile), such as concepts of print, phonological awareness, and the use of reading strategies.

The strong connection between reading fluency and overall reading achievement is well supported by research (Dowhower, 1994; National Reading Panel, 2000; Samuels, 1979). We also know that teachers have a critical role in developing children's accuracy and fluency by using several important teaching practices:

- Engaging children in reading texts at their appropriate instructional levels so that they can use what they know in texts that provide "just enough" challenge (Allington, 2003, 2006; Fountas & Pinnell, 1996, 2001)

- Closely monitoring the accuracy that children demonstrate during reading (Adams, 1995; Clay, 1985)
- Noticing various aspects of fluency that children demonstrate as they read (Rasinski, 2003; Zutell & Rasinski, 1991)

## UNDERLYING PRINCIPLES OF READING ACCURACY AND FLUENCY AT INCREASING TEXT LEVELS

Allington's (2003) research suggests that many children are frequently given texts that are too difficult for them to read, in both independent and instructional settings. The impact of this practice is often dramatic: Beginning readers who are presented with texts that are too difficult for them often feel unsuccessful, and many, as a result, then avoid reading, which is understandable, since few of us like to do what we don't do well. Clearly, then, teachers need to carefully choose texts for students to read. Selecting a "just right" text takes some judgment, though. Several factors affect the difficulty levels of text written for young readers.

### Understanding Text Levels

Books and other text materials that children read during the early years of schooling vary in difficulty because of a wide range of factors. Commonly noted factors (Clay, 1991; Fountas & Pinnell, 1996) include:

- Word difficulty
- Prior knowledge required for understanding
- Syntax
- Features of the printed text

***Word Difficulty.*** In general, texts for very beginning readers include simple words that are both familiar in meaning and easy to decode, but texts with increased difficulty use words that are more complex in both their structure and their meaning. For example, in texts written for young children, the word "hot" might be used to describe a desert. In texts written for more advanced readers, the word "torrid" might be used because it is both an unfamiliar word for a familiar concept (hot) and also because it has a more complex word structure.

***Prior Knowledge.*** In general, text materials that are about unfamiliar topics will be more difficult for children to read independently. Anderson and Pearson (1984) contend that what children already know about the topic of a text they are reading strongly influences their understanding of that text. Keep in mind, though, that books about new or unusual topics are excellent to read aloud to children at any level. Along with discussion and experiential learning, read-alouds are key to building childrens' background knowledge.

***Syntax.*** Syntax is a language system that includes rules for how to combine words into phrases and sentences to create clear communication. Syntax can be simple or complex. For example, the sentence, "I see a frog" is simpler than "Along the road he met a frog" and much simpler than "Although frogs are amphibians, while in water their movements can often be mistaken for those of fish." Particularly for children who are just beginning to learn English, more complex syntactical (i.e., sentence) structures, such as the third sentence

**LITERACY PROFILE** Be sure you have your Literacy Profile available as you read through this chapter so that you can refer to the question in the left-hand column and the indicators across the columns for Strand 5.

above, can be very tricky to understand. Even relatively "easy" books, though, can have syntactical challenges. For example, even an "easy-to-read" book such as *Green Eggs and Ham* (Seuss, 1960) has parts that are likely to pose some reading difficulty. "That Sam I am" is hardly a familiar–sounding use of language when children first hear it! And the language structure of "would you, could you . . . in a boat?" is equally unusual. Fortunately, in this book the patterned language and wonderful illustrations provide additional supports that make the difficulty of the syntax not as challenging as it might be otherwise.

***Features of the Printed Text.*** It is important to understand the supports and challenges that printed text itself presents, and how they impact the level of the text's difficulty. This is especially important to keep in mind when selecting reading material for beginning readers.

Think about some of the earliest books you read as a child. Most likely, the pictures gave you lots of clues (supports) as to what might be coming on the next page. The factors listed below are typically present in the earliest books that children read:

- Pictures connected to text
- Few words on a page
- Words placed on the page in a predictable way
- Repetition of words or phrases

On the other hand, any given book may also have challenging text features. For example, some books have print arranged in unique ways, while others use an unusual font or have illustrations that are complex or ambiguous.

Right about now, you might be wondering, "How is it possible to put all of these factors together to determine how easy or hard a given text is?" That's a very good question. It's also a question that, unfortunately, does not have an easy answer. Nevertheless, professionals in the field have attempted in a variety of ways to determine and categorize text difficulty and text levels. But most professionals agree that each system has some benefits as well as some drawbacks.

***Systems for Determining Text Difficulty of Books.*** Books have been categorized in several ways to reflect their increasing degrees of complexity. One system is called "leveling"; another involves determining readability; and others involve combinations of approaches. Understanding the degree of difficulty of a particular book helps the teacher decide how to use the book: whether to read it aloud to children (if it is challenging); whether to present it to all children, along with varying degrees of assistance (if it is somewhat challenging); or whether to use it in a small-group format with some children (if it is "just right").

*Leveling Books.* "Leveling" refers to categorizing books according to the supports and challenges they present to the reader. Many schools currently use text materials that are already leveled so that teachers can select books for instructional reading groups and make appropriate books accessible for children to choose from during independent reading time. Leveled books, which are used today in many primary classrooms, provide a "ladder of support so students can take on more difficult texts with teacher support, and in the process, expand their strategies for thinking within, beyond and about texts" (Scharer, Pinnell, Lyons, & Fountas, 2005, p. 27). One commonly used system for leveling, developed by Fountas and Pinnell (2005), uses a gradient or scale of increasing difficulty from A to Z.

FIGURE 5.1  **Characteristics of Leveled Books for Beginning Readers**

| Characteristics of Books at Levels C, D: Typically Used Early in Grade 1 | Sample "Benchmark" Titles |
| --- | --- |
| • Repetition of 1–2 sentence patterns<br>• Illustrations that provide high support<br>• Consistent placement of print<br>• Familiar objects and actions | • *Cat on the Mat* (Brian Wildsmith, 2001)<br>• *I Went Walking* (Sue Williams, 1996) |

In formulating this scale, Fountas and Pinnell used criteria that include the following:

- Length and number of words in the book
- Size and layout of the print
- Vocabulary and concepts, themes and ideas
- Language structure, literary features
- Text structure and genre
- Predictability/pattern of language
- Support from illustrations

To understand this system, it may help to know some general "benchmarks." Books classified as levels A–C are generally suitable for very beginning readers (kindergarteners or early first graders); books at levels I–M are appropriate for typically developing second graders; and books at levels Q–S are appropriate for more fluent readers at the fourth-grade level. See Figure 5.1 for characteristics and sample titles of books that have been leveled for beginning readers at level C or D. Books that are appropriate for levels L and M have other characteristics; see Figure 5.2. Using these and other criteria, Fountas and Pinnell (2005) have compiled extensive lists of leveled books, and these lists are readily available.

Additional leveling systems to investigate include R. C. Owens's (www.rcowens.com) and Brenda Weaver's (2000) *Leveling Books K–6: Matching Readers to Text*.

You don't always have to rely on books whose levels were determined by experts and publishers, though. Teachers can level books on their own using guidelines and criteria from the systems described above. Many schools create their own systems of categorizing the classroom library or school "book room" to "match" children with books that meet their strengths and needs as readers. In addition, not all books need to be leveled; having *all* books in a

FIGURE 5.2  **Characteristics of Leveled Books at Middle to End of Grade 2**

| Characteristics of Books at Levels L, M: Typically Used with Children Reading at Middle to End of Grade 2 | Sample "Benchmark" Titles |
| --- | --- |
| • Literary language<br>• Extended descriptions<br>• Elaborated episodes and events<br>• More unusual, challenging vocabulary<br>• Illustrations that provide low support | • *The Littles Go to School* (John Peterson, 1994)<br>• *The Secrets at the Polk Street School* (Patricia Reilly Giff, 1990) |

classroom library leveled can constrain children's choices, and possibly make them think that they are allowed only to pick up books marked "C" or "D," or books with a yellow sticker on the spine.

*Readability.* Other texts are categorized according to difficulty by using readability formulas. A wide variety of readability formulas are available, and all attempt to determine the reading difficulty level of a particular text. Readability formulas such as the Fry Readability Formula (Fry, 1997) use 100-word samples to assess the readability of various grade-level texts. To identify a particular readability level, the formulas may factor in the number of words per sentence or the number of syllables per sentence. Most readability systems yield a reading level that is represented in terms of grade level and month, such as 1.5 (which indicates 1st grade, 5th month). However, it is not at all uncommon for a particular text to yield widely different readability scores according to different formulas. Other publishers follow alternate systems such as the Lexile Framework, which uses scales to measure text difficulty based on word frequency and sentence length; these scales are also used to measure and report individual children's reading ability.

*Other Approaches to Leveling.* Books listed by grade level in commercially published (basal) programs are often categorized by readability formulas and a variety of other criteria. Commercial publishers of "basal" reading series frequently arrange their books by grade level and sometimes subcategorize them by quarter or semester (e.g., 1.1, 2.1, 2.2). Many of these publishers use readability formulas and additional criteria to select passages for children's anthologies or supplementary reading books.

It is important to note that some degree of variability, judgment, and approximation is always present, both in readability formulas and in leveling books. Text-leveling systems can sometimes be frustrating because many publishers and authors create their own systems. Most schools (or, ideally, districts) decide on *one* system so that their teachers use common language. Figure 5.3 provides a comparison chart that allows you to convert from one text-leveling system to another.

## Understanding Oral Reading Accuracy

Looking at the difficulty of a book itself is just one part of the "how well do children read?" puzzle. Most assessment tools that attempt to track children's progress in this area look closely at the *oral reading accuracy* of what children read. Reading accuracy sounds pretty straightforward, but from a beginning reader's perspective, a lot goes into it. Children need to use decoding skills (linking letters/clusters of letters and patterns with sounds) to figure out words, and they also need to recognize sight words that they can't easily decode (words such as *want* or *said*). How is oral reading accuracy determined? How "perfectly" does a child need to read in order to be considered an accurate reader?

Interestingly, it depends on the way a child will use a book. In other words, if a child is going to read a book on his own, he needs a high degree (usually 95% or higher) of accuracy. If support from a teacher will be present and the book will be used for teaching, a slightly lower percentage of accuracy is expected. Determining whether or not a book is at a child's level is very important in order to provide instruction in the student's *zone of proximal development* (Vygotsky, 1978). If the texts children are reading are too hard, they will be unable to use the skills they have learned, and texts that are too easy won't present them with enough opportunities to solve problems and extend their

For more information on the Lexile Framework, go to www.lexile.com. Also, the Flesh-Kincaid formula is available to everyone who uses Microsoft Word; you should be able to access it (under "Tools") after completing a spelling and grammar check.

FIGURE 5.3  **Combination Text Levels Chart**

| Grade Level | Reading Recovery | DRA levels | Fountas and Pinnell | RCOwen Guided Levels |
|---|---|---|---|---|
| K | | A | | Em* |
| K | 1 | 1 | A | Em |
| K | 2 | 2 | B | Em |
| Preprimer | 3 | 3 | B | Em |
| Preprimer | 4 | 4 | C | E1 |
| Primer | 6 | 6 | D | E1 |
| Primer | 8 | 8 | E | E1 |
| 1st | 10 | 10 | F | E2 |
| 1st | 12 | 12 | G | E2 |
| 1st | 14 | 14 | H | E3 |
| 1st | 16 | 16 | I | E4 |
| 2nd | 18 | 18 | J | F1 |
| 2nd | 20 | 20 | K | F2 |
| 2nd | | 24 | L | F3 |
| 2nd | | 28 | M | F4 |
| 3rd | | 30 | N | ⌉ |
| 3rd | | 34 | O | |
| 3rd | | 38 | P | (Leveled for Concepts) |
| 4th | | 40 | Q, R | |
| 5th | | 44 | S, T | |
| 6th | | | U, V | ⌋ |

*Em = emergent; E = early; F = fluent.
Based on *Reading recovery* (Clay, 1991); *Developmental reading assessment K–3* (Beaver, 2006); *Leveled books K–8: Matching texts to readers for effective teaching* (Fountas & Pinnell, 2005); and Books for young learners (www.RCOwen.com).

skills and knowledge. Generally, in the field of reading, the terms listed in Figure 5.4 are used to identify a student's reading performance on particular books or other text material. It should be noted, however, that educators and researchers differ in terms of these performance expectations, although most agree that the frustration level occurs at or below 90% accuracy.

## Understanding Reading Fluency

Reading fluency, another hallmark of a child's progress in reading, strongly contributes to overall success in comprehension as well as to overall reading

FIGURE 5.4  Reading Performance Levels and Descriptions

| Level | Percent of Accuracy of Oral Reading | Description |
|---|---|---|
| Independent (Easy) | 98–100% | Books that the child can read on his/her own. Phrasing and expression convey meaning. |
| Instructional (Just Right) | 90–97% | Books that are appropriate for use with teacher support. Phrasing and expression convey some meaning. |
| Frustration (Too Hard) | Below 90% | Books that are very challenging, and there is little phrasing or expression during reading. Should be used only when significant support is present (e.g., read aloud, with an audiotape or CD). |

*Note:* The figures for percent of accuracy are quite broad in this chart, and are based on a variety of sources. Some researchers (e.g., Betts, 1946) specify instructional level more narrowly, at 95–98%.

achievement (National Reading Panel, 2000). Only within the past 10 or 15 years or so has fluency received greater attention as an important component of beginning reading. Some tend to think of fluency as synonymous with "speed of reading," and interestingly, when primary-level children are asked to name someone who is a good reader, they often name a classmate who reads quickly. Fluency actually has several dimensions, however:

- Automaticity
- Phrasing and expression
- Rate (Rasinski, 2003)

Fluent oral readers display all of these characteristics, not just one or two of them.

***Automaticity.*** The term *automaticity* refers to the ability to recognize words quickly, without pausing. Students who demonstrate automaticity at a certain level have moved beyond sounding out and blending words and instead read words almost effortlessly (Pressley, 2002). There is a good deal of evidence that when automaticity is in place, the brain can focus more easily on the meaning of what is read (LaBerge & Samuels, 1974). For example, think about a time when you have attempted to read a text with a large number of unfamiliar words. Usually your understanding is limited because you are focusing on figuring how to pronounce the difficult words.

***Phrasing and Expression.*** In addition to automaticity, other factors involved in fluency include phrasing as well as intonation and expression, which are sometimes referred to as "prosody." Rasinski (2000) explains that when readers demonstrate prosody, they not only show their understanding of syntax and phrasing, but they also are more likely to read with comprehension. Reading with prosody also involves paying attention to punctuation so that words are grouped into units that make sense (Rasinski, 2000).

When children read with appropriate phrasing, they group together words that belong together. Clay and Imlach (1971) conducted a study of 100 beginning readers and found that the children who made the least amount of progress read in segments of one or two words, while those who made the most progress read phrases of five to seven words. It is also important that students read words that are grouped in *meaningful* phrases. For example, a child with good phrasing might read, "/ Under the tree / the little skunk sat / and wondered why everyone was running away/." A student with poor phrasing might read the same sentence accurately but as follows: "/ Under / the tree the little / skunk sat and / wondered why everyone was / running / away/." In addition, reading in phrases or "chunks" allows one to read faster.

Expression and intonation, other important aspects of fluency, refer to how a voice reflects feeling or emphasis. Children who particularly struggle often read in a "flat" voice, with little expression, while others might pay little attention to phrase boundaries or punctuation. Teachers must also remember that children who are learning English as a second language often translate "inside their heads," and as a result, limited expression, lack of intonation, and slower rates of reading may occur.

*Rate of Reading.* Rate is perhaps the most obvious but also the trickiest aspect of fluency. On the one hand, rate is easy to measure and provides a reliable way to track progress over time. But faster word reading is not always better. Some children read at a very high rate but "run through" punctuation or tend not to notice phrase groupings that help signal meaning, which negatively affects their comprehension.

Others read at a slow rate compared to that of other children at their age or grade. Slow reading does have some serious consequences for many students. Schumm (2006) explains that problems with rate of reading are "associated with poor comprehension, poor overall reading performance and eventual reading frustration" (p. 193).

Be sure not to confuse rate (speed of reading) with overall fluency (Rasinski, 2003), because rate is only one dimension of fluency. However, it *is* helpful for teachers to have a sense of what rates are appropriate for children at different ages and stages of development. Several research studies have identified the rates that successful readers display at different grade levels (Hasbrouck & Tindal, 1992; Rasinski, 2003), and even though the different studies do not always agree about exact rates, it is still possible for teachers to set approximate targets. See Figure 5.5 for guidelines concerning expected rates of reading.

**FIGURE 5.5  Frequently Listed Targets for Rate of Oral Reading at Increasing Grade Levels**

|  | Late Grade 1 | Late Grade 2 | Late Grade 3 | Late Grade 4 |
|---|---|---|---|---|
| Rate of reading* | 50–80 words correct per minute | 85–110 words correct per minute | 100–125 words correct per minute | 120–150 words correct per minute |

*Targets listed are drawn from a variety of sources, including Hasbrouck and Tindal (1992), Rasinski (2003), and grade-level expectations in several states.

To appropriately use these targets, keep the following points in mind:

- Rate is *only one* aspect of fluency.
- Particularly when children read more complex text material, their rate should be slower.
- The lower number in each box in Figure 5.5 represents a target. If a child's rate of reading is slightly below that target, it may not be a cause for immediate concern, but might have more to do with a particular text or situation.

A student's rate that is significantly below the target might indicate that she would benefit from regular monitoring of her reading rate and intervention in this aspect of fluency.

### Summary of Accuracy and Rate of Reading at Increasing Text Levels

This section provided some background information concerning text levels, reading accuracy, and fluency. Text level is a complex and critical concept that involves word difficulty, syntax, and the features of printed text. A variety of different approaches have been used to categorize books so that children can be matched with books at appropriate levels of challenge.

We also clarified expectations concerning developing readers' accuracy and stressed the importance of noticing the various aspects of fluency, not just rate of reading. It is important to keep in mind that fluency and accuracy, as well as text level, interact with each other to influence a child's performance. Particularly when a child tackles a more challenging text or a different genre, it may seem as though he or she is taking a step backward; but it is important to remember that it takes time for a child to develop accuracy and fluency when reading more challenging texts, similar to the challenges involved in climbing a higher mountain peak or trying to play a more difficult piece on the piano.

In the next section we turn to some methods of assessing accuracy and fluency, which are critically important indicators of children's progress on the road to proficiency.

## ASSESSING READER ACCURACY AND FLUENCY

Many tools assess oral reading accuracy and fluency; some are formal and published, while others are informal and can be used continuously. When measuring a child's oral reading accuracy, the goal is usually to determine the percentage of words (e.g., 88%, 93%, 97%) that the child can read correctly. This information allows the teacher not only to gauge whether or not a text is appropriate for a child and for a particular reading purpose, but also to look at children's developing reading behaviors. Typically, these reading behaviors include positive, strategic behaviors such as rereading or looking carefully at an ending, and also miscues, the errors students make when reading. Miscues were described in more detail in chapter 4; see Figure 5.6 for a list of miscues that do and do not "count" as errors when calculating reading accuracy. When assessing fluency, the goal is to evaluate the degree to which the child is developing the various aspects of fluency: automaticity, rate, phrasing, and expression. As you read about some of the methods of assessing fluency, ask yourself which dimension or dimensions of fluency are being assessed.

FIGURE 5.6  **Common Types of Miscues to Look for When Observing Oral Reading Accuracy**

| Common Types of Miscues | Description | Count as Error? |
|---|---|---|
| Substitution | Child reads a different word in place of text. | Yes |
| Omission | Child leaves out a word of text. | Yes |
| Insertion | Child adds a word that does not appear in the text. | Yes |
| Transposition | Child switches the order of words in the text. | Yes (count as two errors) |
| Repetition | Child repeats a word or phrase. | No |
| Self-Correction | Child goes back to fix an error. | No |
| Mispronunciation | Child articulates the word incorrectly (e.g., "pasgetti" for "spaghetti"). | Depends upon degree of mispronunciation |

## Formal or Published Assessment Tools for Accuracy and Fluency

Several commercially published assessment tools include subtests that assess students' reading fluency and accuracy. Some of the most frequently used assessments at the current time include DIBELS (Dynamic Indicators of Basic Elements of Literacy; University of Oregon, 2007), PALS (Phonological Awareness Literacy Screening; Invernizzi, Meier, & Juel, 2005), and the Developmental Reading Assessment (DRA K–3; Beaver, 2006).

***DIBELS.***  The DIBELS Oral Reading Fluency subtest, which involves individual children reading aloud from a short passage for 1 minute, may be downloaded at no charge from the following Web site: http://dibels.uoregon.edu. The teacher records the number of words read accurately within that minute and compares the child's performance with target scores. A number of text selections (for Grades 1, 2, and 3) are available at each level, and benchmark indicators (for the beginning, middle, and end of the year) are included to indicate whether a student is "at risk," "some risk," or "low risk" based on his/her performance.

***PALS.***  PALS (Phonological Awareness Literacy Screening) also includes passages appropriate for children in Grades 1 through 3. This assessment is administered to all students in the state of Virginia, and includes optional comprehension questions. It also involves having individual children read orally to the teacher, but be aware that oral reading errors are not counted on the PALS fluency assessment.

***Developmental Reading Assessment, K–3.***  This assessment, which involves teachers hearing individual students read and retell short books, has recently been updated to include expository text passages. Teachers select a starting reading level for the child and collect information concerning her or his reading accuracy, miscues, and fluency. A grid is provided to calculate accuracy, and teachers use a checklist to note reading behaviors and strategies. When assessing comprehension through the retelling and some follow-up questions, the teacher uses a rubric to evaluate responses. Children's scores are translated into reading levels described as "intervention," "instructional," "independent," and "advanced."

***Three-Minute Fluency Assessment.*** Rasinski and Padak (2005) have developed an efficient tool for monitoring children's fluency development: the Three-Minute Fluency Assessment. They compiled passages at grade levels from 1 through 6 and collected data on students' reading accuracy, rates of reading, as well as phrasing and expression. To use this tool, teachers listen to individual children read and compare children's results with tables of expectations (using end-of-year targets) in order to determine if a child is below, at, or above expectations for a particular grade level. The passages can be administered three times a year, and the authors provide tables to help teachers notice whether a child is making appropriate progress toward the end-of-year targets.

***Diagnostic Assessments, Including Informal Reading Inventories.*** Other published assessments are more commonly used for diagnostic purposes. The GORT (Gray Oral Reading Test; Wiederholt & Bryant, 2001) is a norm-referenced, individually administered assessment that is appropriate for children in Grades 2 and up. It uses grade-level passages and is sometimes employed as part of a comprehensive evaluation process to determine whether a child needs special education services. Informal reading inventories such as the Analytical Reading Inventory (Woods & Moe, 2003), the Basic Reading Inventory (Johns, 2005), and the Qualitative Reading Inventory IV (Leslie & Caldwell, 2006) are among those that reading specialists and teachers use to obtain an estimate of a child's instructional and independent reading levels. These assessments also indicate the child's strengths and needs (e.g., attention to punctuation, or accurately reading the inflected endings of words such as *played* or *brightest*). Sometimes informal reading inventories are also used to provide a way to monitor a child's progress from the beginning of the year to the end of the year.

### Informal Measures for Assessing Oral Reading Accuracy and Fluency

In addition to the assessments we have mentioned so far, teachers can use a variety of informal methods to record and determine oral reading accuracy. The most commonly used are running records, records of oral reading, and anecdotal records; we will also describe a few other approaches that are practical for either classroom use or in remedial reading/special education programs.

***Running Records and Records of Oral Reading.*** Running records, developed by Marie Clay (1985), involve recording and analyzing a child's reading behaviors and strategies during oral reading. In chapter 4 we discussed how to take and analyze a running record and provided a sample. Remember that while taking a running record, the teacher does not correct the child's errors; rather, he or she takes on the role of observer. The teacher can, however, provide a "told" (i.e., provide the correct word) if the child is struggling for more than 4 seconds or if the child asks for the word.

Closely related to running records are records of oral reading. The key difference between the two is that records of oral reading involve the use of printed scripts of the actual text, while running records are taken on blank or lined paper. Some assessment tools come with scripts already typed up; in other cases, teachers simply photocopy a page or two of text to have on hand. When a record of oral reading is taken, instead of placing a check mark on a blank sheet of paper, the teacher simply makes a check mark above or below the appropriate word. Generally, the other recording symbols are similar to the notations shown in Figure 5.6.

***Benchmark Books.***   Some schools ask teachers to regularly assess students by taking running records or records of oral reading using "benchmark" books. "Benchmark" in this context refers to a book that is indicative of proficient reading at a particular level. For example, the books listed in each column of the "Reading Accuracy and Fluency" strand of the Literacy Profile might be used as benchmark books because they are the books that are generally considered to have the level of difficulty appropriate for children at that grade level/stage of development. At the end of the school year, a first-grade teacher might take a running record of a student using the text *Little Bear* (Minarik & Sendak 1992). If the child's accuracy is less than 90% and fluency is limited, then the book at the next lower text, *Five Little Monkeys* (Christelow, 2006), might be tried. If the child reads with at least 90% accuracy (and some fluency), then the informal assessment would indicate the child's stage of development with respect to reading accuracy and fluency. Alternatively, a school might select other books that are more commonly used in that region or state. Using benchmark books provides a degree of uniformity that is helpful in promoting shared and uniform expectations across classrooms (Lipson & Wixson, 2003).

Because leveling systems vary from one school or district to another, we have not used a specific system in the Literacy Profile; instead, we have listed books that are often "benchmark" books at different levels. However, at the individual school level, it may be helpful to decide on *one* system and to use that system to fill in "targets" in terms of levels or benchmark books for Strand 5 of the Literacy Profile. For example, Booth Elementary School uses the DRA K–3 assessment (Beaver, 2006) leveling system and has set targets of level 16 for the end of Grade 1/beginning of Grade 2, and level 28 for the end of Grade 2. Jocelyn Primary School, on the other hand, uses the Fountas and Pinnell levels (2005), with a target of H–I for the end of Grade 1 and M for the end of Grade 2. Those targets, then, could be listed on the blanks provided on the Literacy Profile in order to provide shared expectations across classrooms.

***Anecdotal Records.***   Observation is often the most appropriate tool when teachers need to gather information about accuracy at very early levels of reading. For example, when a kindergartener begins to "pick out" the label "Cheerios" at the grocery store, or finds his name among others listed on the "cubbies" that contain jackets and mittens, he clearly recognizes "environmental print." Keeping a dated log of such events is an appropriate assessment tool.

In keeping anecdotal records, specificity is important—such as noting the language the child used or the conditions when you noticed the behavior. You can also use the Literacy Profile as a source of specific, descriptive language. For example, you might intentionally make anecdotal observations about kindergarteners' attention to signs, labels, symbols or other environmental print (as listed in the Profile) during a free choice or explore time. You will need to develop a technique to systematically record these notes so that you can use them later to make instructional decisions. Consider, for example, the following anecdotal note one kindergarten teacher wrote:

> 1/7/08 During circle time today Joshua pointed to the label "FISH" on the aquarium, and said, "That's a letter 'F' like my dad's name Fred!" (I was impressed that he knew F and knew that it was called a letter; until now he only knew "J is for Joshua"!)

Particularly at the very earliest stages of reading, such as at ages 5 or 6, children sometimes "read" a very familiar book with a high degree of what sounds like accuracy. Often, they are actually using their knowledge of the

McKenna and Stahl (2003) have a particularly useful tool called the Emergent Storybook Reading Scale that they adapted from Elizabeth Sulzby (1995). This would be an excellent resource for those who teach at the kindergarten level.

story, their memory of how "story language" sounds, and the pictures to help them "sound like" a reader. Sulzby (1995) has closely studied the stages of this "emergent reading" period and encourages both professionals and parents to value this "pretend" reading behavior, because it indicates the child's development toward print-based, or more conventional, reading. Interestingly, as children move toward the stage of print-focused reading, their degree of "accuracy" may actually decrease, and sometimes they will even refuse to read stories that they have previously "read" in an emergent manner.

***Fluency Rubrics.***    Most of us are quite familiar with rubrics, scoring guides that include clear descriptions of what is being evaluated. When evaluating the phrasing and expression aspects of fluency, rubrics can be particularly helpful. One of the most widely known tools for evaluating fluency is the NAEP Fluency Scale, shown in Figure 5.7. Researchers who worked on the NAEP Fluency study (Pinnell et al., 1995) found that children who performed at levels 3 and 4 scored highest in a silent reading comprehension test. In other words, fluency was clearly correlated with reading achievement. To use this rubric, as you listen to the child read aloud, you circle the number on the rubric that best reflects the child's performance. You can also highlight the phrases that describe the child's reading and leave blank those that the child doesn't show yet.

Sometimes it is preferable, however, to differentiate between the different aspects or dimensions of reading fluency. The "Three-Way" rubric (see Appendix A-16) does just that by providing different ratings of phrasing and expression, accuracy, and rate. Because the language in the "three-way" rubric is relatively user-friendly, it can be used by a teacher, a volunteer, a

**FIGURE 5.7  The NAEP Oral Reading Fluency Scale, Adapted**

| Levels of Fluency | Descriptors of Students' Oral Reading |
|---|---|
| Level 1 | • Reads primarily word by word.<br>• Occasional two- or three-word phrases may occur, but these are infrequent and/or they do not preserve meaningful syntax. |
| Level 2 | • Reads primarily in two-word phrases with some three- or four-word groupings.<br>• Some word-by-word reading may be present.<br>• Word groupings may seem awkward and unrelated to the larger context of sentence or passage. |
| Level 3 | • Reads primarily in three- or four-word phrase groups.<br>• Some smaller groupings may be present.<br>• However, the majority of phrasing seems appropriate and preserves the syntax of the author.<br>• Little or no expressive interpretation is present. |
| Level 4 | • Reads primarily in larger, meaningful phrase groups.<br>• Although some regressions, repetitions, and deviations from text may be present, they do not appear to detract from the overall structure of the story.<br>• Preservation of the author's syntax is consistent. Some or most of the story is read with expressive interpretation. |

(U.S. Department of Education, National Center for Education Statistics, 1995, p. 15.)

student "partner," or by older students in Grades 3 and 4 as a self-assessment tool. To use it, simply circle the appropriate description of the child's phrasing and expression, accuracy, and rate. A teacher might time the child's reading to help mark the "rate" aspect of the rubric. The rubric may be used by itself to evaluate a child's fluency when she reads a particular text (see the example about Willa later in this chapter). Or the rubric may be used in conjunction with the record-keeping chart that accompanies it to record progress during repeated readings. To use the record-keeping chart, transfer the numbers from the rubric to the chart each time the child reads (and rereads) the selection.

**Timed Readings.** Assessing the *rate* aspect of fluency is important, especially when children's fluency is developing, usually during Grades 1 and 2. You might notice that the Literacy. Profile does not mention rate until the end of Grade 1, but you may decide to monitor rate before then, particularly if you are concerned about a student's slow rate of reading. The simplest way to assess the rate aspect of fluency involves a stopwatch or watch with a second hand, a text selection, and, of course, the child. With practice, it is very easy to monitor a child's rate. To determine the number of words a child reads correctly per minute (rate of reading):

1. Ask the child to read the text aloud and explain that you will not be helping him (or her).
2. Note the starting time (e.g., 11:06:30) or use a 1-minute stopwatch.
3. As the child reads, tally any errors. (Do not count self-corrections as errors.)
4. After exactly 1 minute (11:07:30), note the word the child read last.
5. At a suitable stopping place (such as the end of the next sentence), thank the child for his/her reading.
6. Count the number of words the child read in the passage, and subtract the number of errors. The resulting number is the child's reading rate, or "words correct per minute" (wcpm).

Alternatively, if you want to evaluate a more sustained amount of reading, you can have the student read for 2 minutes and then divide the total number of words by 2. Refer back to Figure 5.5 for a range of commonly used rates of reading. Be aware, however, that different sources vary in the rates they recommend as targets. Also, keep in mind that the eventual goal is for children to read *silently* with fluency. Transitioning to silent reading is sometimes a challenge for children, and, although measuring silent reading fluency is less exact and precise than measuring oral reading fluency, monitoring silent reading fluency of some children may be helpful.

**Quick Text-Level Check-In.** When students progress to a third-grade level of reading or above and are fluent enough that keeping up with their oral reading fluency is a challenge, some teachers prefer to administer the "Quick Text-Level Check-In" (Biggam & Thompson, 2005). This tool is similar to both a running record and a record of oral reading, but includes a rubric for evaluating fluency as well as a scale to assess the child's "surface-level" comprehension of the particular text read. See Appendix A-17 for a printable copy of the recording sheet and directions for administration and scoring. One benefit of this tool is its ease of use; while conducting an individual conference with a child, a teacher can complete this informal assessment within 5 to 10 minutes and gain valuable information about the appropriateness of the particular text for the student's level of development.

### Summary of Assessing Oral Reading Accuracy and Fluency

A wide range of both formal and informal tools and approaches are available for teachers to determine how well children's accuracy and fluency are progressing. These include running records, informal inventories, rubrics for collecting information about different aspects of fluency, and many other tools. For older children, an informal tool such as the Quick Text-Level Check-In may be helpful because of its flexibility. As soon as the teacher collects information about a child's accuracy and fluency, she should consider instructional approaches.

## INSTRUCTIONAL APPROACHES FOR BUILDING ACCURACY AND FLUENCY AT INCREASING TEXT LEVELS

After assessment information has been collected, it is important to determine the next steps to take to support children as they read harder books. Some approaches are appropriate to use with all children, while others are more appropriate to use with individual children or groups of children who share the same characteristics (as determined through assessment and observation). For example, while all children need to grow in the area of fluency, careful assessment can reveal that one child has greater needs in phrasing and expression, while another has greater needs in automaticity and rate. In addition, it is important to sort out teaching priorities. If a child needs help in both automaticity and phrasing, in most cases the teacher will want to address automaticity first because unless the child's automaticity improves, phrasing will be difficult to work on.

### Instructional Approaches for Building Accuracy and Fluency at Increasing Text Levels for All Students

Ample opportunities to read and reread a variety of inviting books and other text materials, along with high-quality, explicit instruction in decoding and strategy use and supported feedback are key ingredients for supporting student growth in the area of accuracy (Pressley, Gaskins, & Fingeret, 2006). Overall, for promoting fluency, teacher-guided oral reading with feedback (National Reading Panel, 2000) and repeated reading (Samuels, 1979) are probably the two most frequently used practices, and both are supported strongly by research. Rasinski (2003) outlines four ways to build reading accuracy and fluency: modeling good oral reading, providing oral support to children, offering plenty of practice opportunities, and encouraging fluency through phrasing. First we will consider what is involved in promoting ample reading opportunities.

> Echo reading involves having the teacher read a sentence or two, with the child reading the same sentence immediately afterward.

***Opportunity to Read in a Supportive Reading Community.*** It sounds overly simple, but it is clearly true: in order to get better at reading,   children need to practice reading! Particularly in Grades 1 and 2, much of that practice takes place in small teacher-led guided-reading groups that include opportunities for active teaching. Choral (shared) reading, echo reading, taped reading, and partner reading are excellent ways to include time for reading.  However, it is also important to provide other settings and opportunities for reading, especially time for independent reading. Making sure that at least some of these opportunities involve feedback from a more skilled reader is key because otherwise, children may end up practicing reading *in*accurately or *dis*fluently. We would also like to add a word of caution about round-robin reading, in which the teacher calls on different children to read successive sentences or paragraphs. Although round-robin reading sometimes feels like an efficient management tool, it clearly limits the amount of actual reading that children do, because only one child reads at a time and the other children are often not engaged in reading (Opitz & Rasinski, 1998).

Independent reading, which takes a variety of forms in the early years, is critical as well. Although some educators cite the report of the National Reading Panel (2000) as *not* supporting independent reading, in fact, the findings indicated that there was not sufficient evidence from *experimental* research to support using sustained silent reading to improve oral reading fluency. Others (Allington, 2006; Pressley et al., 2006; Rasinski, 2003) have pointed out that several other (nonexperimental) studies provide evidence of a strong relationship between the amount of independent reading and overall reading achievement.

In many kindergarten and first-grade classrooms, independent reading does not look or sound like "silent reading time," but instead involves partner reading and/or "whisper-reading." Some children may be moving around the classroom with a pointer, "reading the room" by pointing to signs and labels attached to objects such as the flag, the gerbil's cage, or the sink. Other children might be rereading the list of children's names or the lyrics of the "Happy Birthday" song that is on a chart. In later grades, independent reading often takes a variety of forms and has a variety of labels, from "DEAR" (drop everything and read) time to "SSR" (sustained silent reading) time to "Quiet Reading Time."

An excellent approach that definitely increases the amount of text children read and is also highly engaging is Readers' Theater. Readers' Theater involves repeated reading of a text selection that has several characters or "parts." For example, a teacher might obtain a script of "The Three Billy Goats Gruff" and have five different groups of children take on the parts of the three billy goats, the troll, and the narrator. The teacher assists the children in identifying their parts, models what fluent reading sounds like, and provides time for practice. Then children "perform" the story—usually with no props. Ideally there is an opportunity to debrief after the "performance"—to discuss what went well and what parts might have been read with more expression, better phrasing, or different intonation. Some teachers at the third- or fourth-grade level use the NAEP fluency scale (included earlier in this chapter as Figure 5.7) as an aid for this kind of debriefing. Many resources for Readers' Theater, including scripts for plays, can easily be found online. Techniques such as Readers' Theater clearly involve a good deal of repeated reading, along with extensive opportunity to read in a supportive community.

> An excellent source of (free) Readers' Theater scripts that you might want to investigate is www.aaronshep.com

***Explicit Teaching.*** Teachers need to provide ample opportunities for direct, explicit teaching of reading accurately and fluently. As noted previously, researchers have shown repeatedly that teacher-guided oral reading is directly linked with increases in children's fluency (National Reading Panel, 2000). However, explicit whole-class instruction is also important and efficient, particularly when introducing key grade-level expectations such as noticing punctuation marks, using "chunks" to identify words during reading, self-correcting, etc. Explicit instruction involves the use of a gradual release of responsibility model (i.e., explaining and modeling, providing guided practice and then independent practice) (Pearson & Gallagher, 1983). Teachers should especially make sure that guided practice and independent practice include ample opportunities for reading "connected" text (stories, informational books or articles, etc.) as opposed to relying primarily on practice with single words or sentences on worksheets or other basic-skills activities (Allington, 2006).

***Supportive Feedback.*** Supportive feedback or coaching during oral reading is also critical to ensure that children generalize their newly learned skills and strategies. Practice that involves feedback and coaching will be particularly effective when children have a meaningful reason to practice reading aloud and a real audience as well (Rasinski, 2003). If small groups of children practice a poem or story and prepare to share it within their classroom reading community, with family members, or with children in other grades or classes, they usually have greater interest and more motivation than if they are simply practicing because the teacher has given them an assignment on practicing their reading. In addition, it's important to ensure that the environment for sharing feels safe enough for them to present their fluent (or nearly fluent) reading.

### Instructional Approaches for Building Accuracy and Fluency for Students with Specific Needs

As Richard Allington, in *What Really Matters for Struggling Readers* (2006), points out, children who are struggling:

- Need to read a lot
- Need books they *can* read
- Need to learn to read fluently
- Need to develop thoughtful literacy

We suggest that *all* children have these needs but that those children who have specific needs in building accuracy and fluency are in a unique situation. In order to catch up to their peers, they need to read *more* than children who are able to handle grade-level text.

This need to increase the sheer amount of reading to be done calls for some creative planning on the part of teachers. Although sometimes challenging, it can be accomplished through strategies such as scheduling extra teacher-guided reading groups, shared reading, and interactive/shared writing, and using books on CD-ROM or tape, partner reading, book clubs, and home-reading contracts, to name a few. One approach that several schools and districts use to build reading accuracy and fluency is the Accelerated Reader program (www.rosenpublishing.com/acreader.cfm). In this approach, children take quizzes on the computer as they finish each book. Sometimes incentives are offered to prompt children to increase the number of books they read. Some schools have found the approach to be quite successful, but if your school decides to use the program, be sure that it is only one part of a balanced literacy program.

Paired Reading (Topping, 1987), which is sometimes confused with partner reading, is actually a specific technique that has been shown to be especially effective in strengthening fluency and that parents, volunteers, peer tutors, and others can use. Topping explains that this technique involves a tutor and a "tutee" first reading aloud together, with the tutor adjusting his or her pace to match the tutee's. If errors occur, the tutor reads the word correctly, and the tutee repeats it. When the tutee feels confident enough to read independently, he gives a signal (a tap or nudge) to the tutor and reads alone, while the tutor listens and is ready to provide help as needed. If the tutee makes an error, the tutor joins back in and the two read together until the tutee signals that he is again ready to read independently. Throughout the reading, the tutor provides encouragement and periodically pauses to discuss the meaning of the text. With beginning readers, often the tutor will first read the book aloud to the tutee, followed by paired reading.

While the approaches listed above are excellent for most children who need further work to improve their accuracy and fluency, some children have very particular and persistent needs. Some sample approaches for addressing those specific needs in phrasing and expression, rate, and accuracy are listed below; we will describe some of them in more detail.

***Gaps in Reading Accuracy.*** To begin, it is important to make sure that students with specific needs in the area of reading accuracy have many, many opportunities to read text that is at an appropriate level. With "just right" (instructional-level) text, supportive and specific feedback (e.g., "Try that again" or "What else could you try?") from teachers or other partners who listen to reading is also important. You may want to refer back to Figure 4.8 for some sample prompts to use when listening to children read. Using such "coaching" language tells children that they have the capacity to problem-solve and decreases the tendency of some struggling children to depend on the teacher to "fix" their errors. Taylor, Pearson, Clark, and Walpole (1999) found that in high-poverty schools, the most effective teachers frequently use this kind of coaching and scaffolding.

The Talking Dictionary approach (Ballard, 1978, as cited in Lipson & Wixson, 2003) is a specific, individualized technique that is appropriate for children who need to work on their reading accuracy, from second grade on. The child works side by side with a teacher, parent, or para-educator, following these steps:

1. The child selects a "just right" book and reads aloud for 1 minute.
2. When the child comes to a word she does not know, she says, "Word, please" to the "listener" working with her. *Note:* The listener acts as a "Talking Dictionary" since he/she provides the word. The listener also keeps track of the time and tallies the errors.
3. At the end of 2 minutes, the reading ends and the total number of words read correctly is counted and graphed. (Divide by 2 to obtain the number of correct words per minute.) It's important to do the charting/graphing *with* the child. The teacher might also select one or two of the words to review with the child.
4. The child reads the same text (starting in the same place) two *more* times in the same day, and the same procedure is followed. The number of words read correctly should increase each time, and the child should be able to read farther into the passage as well. With this technique, a child is almost *always* successful, which certainly boosts motivation to practice reading!
5. The following day, choose the NEXT passage in the same book. Figure 5.8 provides a sample of a completed Talking Dictionary chart.

***Gaps in Rate of Reading.*** Children with needs in this area generally benefit from various forms of repeated reading (e.g., choral reading, echo reading, partner reading, tape recording of oral reading) that use instructional or independent-level text. Timed readings may also be used, but teachers must be sure not to overemphasize rate at the expense of comprehension.

FIGURE 5.8  **Talking Dictionary Sample**

Student's Name: *Miranda*
Book Title: *Green Eggs and Ham*

| Number of words read correctly in 2 minutes | Date: 9/19 | | | Date: 9/20 | | |
|---|---|---|---|---|---|---|
| | 1st read | 2nd read | 3rd read | 1st read | 2nd read | 3rd try |
| 80 | | | | | | |
| 78 | | | | | | |
| 76 | | | | | | |
| 74 | | | | | | |
| 72 | | | | | | |
| 70 | | | | | | |
| 68 | | | | | | |
| 66 | | | | | | ▓ |
| 64 | | | ▓ | | | ▓ |
| 62 | | | ▓ | | ▓ | ▓ |
| 60 | | ▓ | ▓ | | ▓ | ▓ |
| 58 | ▓ | ▓ | ▓ | ▓ | ▓ | ▓ |
| 56 | ▓ | ▓ | ▓ | ▓ | ▓ | ▓ |
| 54 | ▓ | ▓ | ▓ | ▓ | ▓ | ▓ |
| 52 | ▓ | ▓ | ▓ | ▓ | ▓ | ▓ |
| 50 | ▓ | ▓ | ▓ | ▓ | ▓ | ▓ |

From Lipson and Wixson (2003); based on Ballard (1978).

Most approaches for increasing reading rate emphasize the use of text that is easy or just right, but one very effective approach uses text that is more challenging (closer to grade-level text). This approach, called FORI (Fluency Oriented Reading Instruction), was originally developed by Stahl and Heubach (2005) but has been expanded by Kuhn et al. (2006) to include a variation called "wide reading." If you use this technique, be sure to use text material that is interesting, include discussion of what the child reads, and periodically time the child's rate of reading to monitor his or her progress:

- **Day 1:** Teacher read-aloud, with discussion, of text that may be somewhat challenging for the group. Students follow along.
- **Day 2:** Echo reading of same text (teacher reads one sentence or two; then students read the same text aloud), with discussion.
- **Day 3:** Choral reading of same text (teacher and students' voices together), with discussion.
- **Day 4:** Partner reading of same text, with discussion.
- **Day 5:** Extension activities for some, fluency check for others.

*Gaps in Phrasing or Expression.*  Students with needs in this area benefit from observing a skilled reader model how to read "like someone is talking." Many teachers use "high-frequency phrase cards," which combine high-frequency words (as described in chapter 3) into two- and three-word phrases (Rasinski, 2003). Children work in pairs reading the flash cards until they can read them fluently. One adaptation we have recently used involves an additional feature that provides opportunity for application and language expansion. After practicing with the high-frequency phrases, children are asked to pick one of their favorite phrases, make up a sentence that includes that phrase, and practice reading that sentence fluently, with expression. For example, one child might read the phrase "behind the door" and then make up the sentence, "In my dream I saw the monster sneaking behind the door."

*Phrased text lessons* (Rasinski, 2003) are also beneficial for children. To use this technique, mark the phrases in a text passage with slashes and use modeling and guided practice as you read the text two or three times with the child. For example, if you are working with a third- or fourth-grade student who has difficulty with phrasing, you might use a pencil to mark the phrase boundaries as shown in the following sentence: "As the hurricane approached / people were asked to leave their homes, / and then go to a shelter, / or stay with relatives or friends / away from the low-lying areas." You could then support the child's reading of the sentence, perhaps with assistance such as "scooping" under each phrase with your finger or a pointer as needed. The child should read the sentence independently before the session is over. On the next day, erase the slashes to help the child transfer her understanding of phrased reading to conventional text. The goal, of course, is to have the student eventually generalize her skills in orally reading meaningful phrases to independent, silent reading.

## Summary of Instructional Approaches for Reading Accuracy and Fluency

Explicit instruction, along with opportunities for wide reading and support from teachers or other skilled readers, are all critical elements for promoting children's growth in accurate and fluent reading. In this section we reviewed practices that benefit all students as well as some techniques that can be used specifically with students who need extra help in this area. The importance of linking assessment information with instruction is particularly critical in this area of literacy, because knowing a student's instructional reading level is important in planning proper instruction. If a child is regularly reading material that is at his/her frustration level, negative practice takes place (in other words, children practice being inaccurate and nonfluent), and progress is easily hampered.

Some examples of instructional practices discussed include repeated reading, reading poetry, and Readers' Theater, along with techniques such as FORI (Fluency Oriented Reading Instruction), Paired Reading, and the "Talking Dictionary" approach. Especially in the area of fluency, it is important to identify the specific needs when working with children whose fluency is not coming along as expected. For example, some students need particular support in the area of rate of reading, while others need work with phrasing or expression. Finally, it is important to keep in mind that rate is only one aspect of fluency; while it is a critical factor, it shouldn't be the sole focus of fluency work or overemphasized at the expense of a child's comprehension.

## LOOKING CLOSELY AT ONE CHILD'S ASSESSMENTS FROM STRAND 5 OF THE LITERACY PROFILE

Willa's assessments for reading accuracy and fluency included a record of oral reading and a fluency rubric, which were administered in early May. In this section we describe the information obtained and the next steps to consider for Willa's continued development as a reader.

Review the Combination Text Levels Chart in Figure 5.3 to locate the level of difficulty of level H books.

Willa's use of strategies was discussed more fully in chapter 4.

## Assessment Results Regarding Reading Accuracy and Fluency

To find out how accurately and fluently Willa is able to read, she was asked to read *Pepper's Adventure*, a level H book. This level of text was selected because all indications were that Willa is generally able to read books at approximately a late Grade 1 level. Willa demonstrated good accuracy and fluency at this level and read the text with both confidence and interest.

*Accuracy.* On this text, Willa's oral reading accuracy was calculated to be 94%, which is within the "instructional" range. The errors she made tended to be on small words ("the" substituted for "a," "in" substituted for "to"). Willa also omitted and inserted words, but generally her errors did not disrupt either the flow or the meaning of her reading, and she self-corrected often. However, her errors showed a fairly consistent pattern of misreading "little words" and a possible overemphasis on her use of structure and meaning cues.

Willa's accuracy is in the instructional, not independent, range at this point. She is a reader who has good skills and uses self-correction effectively. However, her accuracy is not particularly high at this level, and the level of text she read is on the lower end of what is expected of children at the end of first grade. We think she is ready for some "acceleration" in order to help her pay greater attention to print and self-monitor her reading accuracy. So the next steps for Willa might include introducing her to text that's a bit more challenging. This should prompt her to read more carefully in order to understand the content, and we think that informational text might be particularly useful for this purpose. As Willa takes on more challenging texts, and begins to read more books silently, teachers should periodically check her reading (by listening to her read aloud and taking records of oral reading or periodic Quick Text-Level Check-Ins) to notice whether she is omitting or substituting small words, which might end up interfering with her comprehension. This might easily take place during individual conferences, such as the model described in chapter 4 and displayed in Appendix A-12. If needed, after taking a record of oral reading, some "debriefing" of strategies used and not used might be helpful.

*Fluency.* Willa's oral reading fluency is strong at this level. She read the text with an oral reading rate of 70.6 words per minute. This is above commonly used targets for the end of Grade 1. When errors were counted, her rate was 66.39 words correct per minute, but this, too, is well within the "targeted" range for the end of first grade. It certainly does not appear that rate of reading is a problem area for Willa.

Willa's reading demonstrated attention to phrase boundaries, as evidenced by her reading the following sentence, with phrase boundaries marked as she read them: "/One day / Dad came home / with two pet mice / in a little cage/." Willa also used appropriate expression as she read, using her voice to indicate emotion and pauses as required by the punctuation. The teacher who administered the assessment asked Willa to read the book a second time and used the "three-way" fluency rubric to note changes in her reading as she reread. The first time Willa read, she was scored a "2" in phrasing and expression, a "3" in rate, and a "2" in accuracy. The second time Willa read, she was rated as "2 plus" in phrasing and expression as well as accuracy, and again as a "3" in rate. To see how the information from these and other assessments was recorded on the Literacy Profile, look at Figure 5.9.

## FIGURE 5.9 Willa's Profile for Reading Accuracy and Fluency at Increasing Text Levels

Note: This figure has been excerpted from the full Literacy Profile chart for illustrative purposes. Please consult the full pull-out chart to identify the column headings and development phases.

| Strand *Question & Sample Assessment Tools* | Late K | Early–Mid Grade 1 | Late Grade 1–Early Grade 2 |
|---|---|---|---|
| **5. Reading Accuracy and Fluency at Increasing Text Levels** *To what degree is the child reading books of increasing complexity with accuracy and fluency?* **Sample Assessment Tools** • Running records • Records of oral reading using benchmark books • Quick Text Level Check-In • Oral Reading Fluency (DIBELS) • Three-Way Fluency Rubric **Text Leveling approach used:** *Fountas & Pinnell* | Reads simple, predictable, or decodable books (previously introduced), such as *Have You Seen My Cat* and *Monster Sandwich* <br><br> Text Level Target: ___B___ | Independently reads books, such as *Five Little Monkeys* and *All by Myself* (previously introduced) with acceptable accuracy <br><br> Text Level Target: ___D/E___ | Independently reads books, such as *Little Bear* and *Frog and Toad Are Friends* with acceptable accuracy and developing fluency <br><br> *[Read level H with 94% accuracy— instructional level. Fluency is strong, with good phrasing and expression.] KI* <br><br> Text Level Target: ___I/J___ |

Gray areas represent highlighting added by the teacher, preferably using a different color for each year (e.g., yellow highlights for Late K, orange highlights for Early–Mid Grade 1, etc.).
Bracketed material represents teacher/examiner comments from June, Grade 1.

## Summary of Willa's Development in Reading Accuracy and Fluency

In general, Willa's development in the areas of accuracy and fluency is coming along appropriately. With ample opportunities to read a variety of texts, including text materials that require her to concentrate, and encouragement to monitor her accuracy in reading "little" words, Willa should be able to read increasingly complex books with accuracy, fluency, and confidence.

## REFERENCES

Adams, M. J. (1995). *Beginning to read: Thinking and learning about print*. Cambridge, MA: MIT Press.

Allington, R. (2003). You can't learn much from books you can't read. *Educational Leadership, 60,* 16–19.

Allington, R. (2006). *What really matters for struggling readers*. Boston: Pearson Education.

Anderson, R. C., & Pearson, P. D. (1984). A schema-theoretic view of basic processes in reading. In P. D. Pearson (Ed.), *Handbook of reading research* (pp. 255–291). New York: Longman.

Beaver, J. (2006). *Developmental reading assessment, K–3* (2nd ed.). Columbus, OH: Pearson Learning.

Betts, E. A. (1946). *Foundations of reading instruction*. New York: American Books.

Biggam, S., & Thompson, E. A. (2005). "The QT" quick text-level check-in: A practical tool for classroom-based reading assessment in the intermediate grades. *New England Reading Association Journal, 41*(1), 35–39.

Christelow, E. (2006). *Five little monkeys*. New York: Clarion Books.

Clay, M. M. (1985). *The early detection of reading difficulties*. Aukland, New Zealand: Heinemann.

Clay M. M., & Imlach, R. (1971). Juncture, pitch and stress as reading behavior variables. *Journal of Verbal Learning and Verbal Behavior, 10,* 133–139.

Clay, M. M. (1991). *Becoming literate: The construction of inner control*. Portsmouth, NH: Heinemann.

Dowhower, S. L. (1994). Repeated reading revisited: Research into practice. *Reading and Writing Quarterly: Overcoming Learning Difficulties, 10*(4), pp. 343–358.

Dynamic Indicators of Basic Early Literacy Skills DIBELS (2007). http://dibels.uoregon.edu/benchmarkgoals.pdf

Fountas, I., & Pinnell, G. S. (1996). *Guided reading: Good first teaching for all children.* Portsmouth, NH: Heinemann.

Fountas, I., & Pinnell, G. S. (2001). *Guiding readers and writers, grades 3–6. Teaching comprehension, genre and content literacy.* Portsmouth, NH: Heinemann.

Fountas, I., & Pinnell, G. S. (2005). *Leveled books K–8: Matching texts to readers for effective teaching.* Portsmouth, NH: Heinemann.

Fry. E. (1997). *Elementary reading instruction.* New York: McGraw-Hill.

Fry, E. B. (2002). Readability versus leveling. *The Reading Teacher, 56*(3), 286–291.

Hasbrouck, J. E., & Tindal, G. (1992, Spring). Curriculum-based oral reading fluency norms for students in grades 2 through 5. *Teaching Exceptional Children,* 41–44.

Johns, J. L. (2005). *Basic reading inventory* (9th ed.). Dubuque, IA: Kendall Hunt.

Invernnizzi, M., Meier, J., & Juel, C. (2005). *Phonological awareness literacy screening.* Charlottesville, VA: University of Virginia.

Kuhn, M., Schwanenflugel, P., Morris, D., Morrow, L., Woo, D., Mersinger, M., et al. (2006). Teaching children to become fluent and automatic readers. *Journal of Literacy Research, 38*(4), 357–387.

LaBerge, D., & Samuels, S. J. (1974). Toward a theory of automatic information processing in reading. *Cognitive Psychology, 6,* 293–323.

Leslie, L., & Caldwell, J. C. (2006). *Qualitative reading inventory* (4th ed.). Reading, WA: Allyn and Bacon.

Lipson, M. Y., & Wixson, K. K. (2003). *Assessment and instruction of reading and writing difficulty.* Boston: Allyn & Bacon.

McKenna, M., & Stahl, S. (2003). *Assessment for reading instruction.* New York: Guilford Press.

Minarik, E. H., & Sendak, M. (1992). *Little bear.* New York: Harper Trophy Books.

National Reading Panel. (2000). *Teaching children to read: An evidence based assessment of the scientific research literature on reading and its implications for reading instruction.* Rockville, MD: National Institute of Child Health and Human Development.

Opitz, M., & Rasinski, T. (1998). *Goodbye round robin.* New York: Scholastic.

Pearson. P. D., & Gallagher, M. (1983). The instruction of reading comprehension. *Contemporary Educational Psychology, 8,* 317–344.

Pinnell, G. S., Pikulski, J. J., Wixson, K. K., Campbell, J. R., Gough, P. B., & Beatty, A. S. (1995). *Listening to children read aloud: Data from NAEP's integrated reading performance record (IRPR) at Grade 4.* Washington, DC: Office of Educational Research and Improvement, U.S. Department of Education.

Pressley, M. (2002). *Reading instruction that works: The case for balanced teaching.* New York: Guilford Press.

Pressley, M., Gaskins, I. W., & Fingeret, L. (2006). Instruction and development of reading fluency in struggling readers. In S. J. Samuels & A. E. Farstrup (Eds.), *What research has to say about fluency instruction.* Newark, DE: International Reading Association.

Rasinski, T. (2000) Speed does matter in reading. *The Reading Teacher, 54*(2), 146–151.

Rasinski, T. (2003). *The fluent reader: Oral reading strategies for building word recognition, fluency and comprehension.* New York: Scholastic.

Rasinski, T., & Padak, N. (2005). *Three minute reading assessments: Word recognition, fluency and comprehension.* New York: Scholastic.

Samuels, J. (1979). The method of repeated readings. *The Reading Teacher. 50,* 376–382.

Scharer, P., Pinnell, G. S., Lyons, C., & Fountas, I. (2005). Becoming an engaged reader. *Educational Leadership, 63*(2), 24–29.

Schumm, J. S. (2006). *Reading assessment and instruction for all learners.* New York: The Guilford Press.

Seuss, Dr. (1960). *Green eggs and ham.* New York: Random House.

Stahl, S. A., & Heubach, K. (2005). Fluency oriented reading instruction. *Journal of Literacy Research, 37,* 25–60.

Sulzby, E. (1995). *Emergent reading and writing in 5 and 6 year olds: A longitudinal study.* Norwood, NJ: Ablex Publishing.

Taylor, B. M., Pearson, P. D., Clark, K. F., & Walpole, S. (1999). *Beating the odds in teaching all children to read* (CIERA Report No. 2–006). Ann Arbor: Center for the Improvement of Early Reading Achievement, University of Michigan.

Topping, K. (1987). Paired reading: A powerful technique for parent use. *The Reading Teacher, 40,* 608–614.

U.S Department of Education, National Center for Education Statistics. (1995). *Listening to children read aloud.* Washington, DC: Author.

Vygotsky, L. (1978). *Mind in society.* Cambridge, MA: Harvard University Press.

Weaver, B. M. (2000). *Leveling books K–6: Matching readers to text.* Newark, DE: International Reading Association.

Wiederholt, J. C., & Bryant, B. (2001). *Gray oral reading test.* Austin, TX: Pro-Ed.

Woods, M. L., & Moe, A. (2003). *Analytical reading inventory.* Upper Saddle River, NJ: Merrill/Prentice Hall.

Zutell, J., & Rasinski, T. V. (1991). Training teachers to attend to their students' oral reading fluency. *Theory into Practice, 30,* 211–217.

# CHAPTER SIX

# Comprehension and Reading Response

> ── CORE QUESTION
>
> How is the child developing an ability to understand text and demonstrate thoughtful responses to text?

How many of us have "read" a page, a chapter, a newspaper article, or a poem and said to ourselves, "Did I really read that? I have no idea what it said!" On the Literacy Profile, "comprehension" might very well be displayed in neon, large font, or at least **bold print**! Comprehension is, after all, the real *point* of reading, because *without* understanding what we read, the act of reading is, "meaningless." One highly regarded researcher, Dolores Durkin (1980), once commented, "If there is no comprehension, there is no reading" (p. 191).

While comprehension generally translates to "understanding" what we read, response to text is often more broadly thought of as a range of ways of connecting to or representing a reaction, feeling, or thought. A person can respond to a text in a wide variety of ways: through discussion, writing, music, dance, drawing, and other forms of art. Sometimes these responses demonstrate comprehension (understanding); other times they reveal a more emotional, aesthetic, or evaluative kind of reaction. The kinds of responses that students display depend very much on the range of opportunities their teachers provide for them.

In fact, both comprehension and reading response are critical areas of focus even for kindergarteners. We now know that if teachers focus *only* on the mechanics of reading and writing (for example, decoding, phonological awareness, spelling, handwriting, and other conventions) during the early primary (and later) grades and do not intentionally build comprehension, many students' reading achievement will suffer (Duke & Pearson, 2002). Also, because early reading instruction tends to emphasize word recognition rather than comprehension, classroom teachers often don't notice the less skilled comprehenders in their classrooms (Snow, Burns, & Griffin, 1998).

Chall and Jacobs (1990) documented what has come to be referred to as the "fourth-grade slump," an apparently sudden drop-off in reading comprehension among low-income children between third and fourth grades. We now know that this drop-off actually begins earlier, with its roots in language gaps as well as instructional practices, and that the gaps are not evident *only* in low-income children but are more widespread. (Hirsch, 2003). In this chapter we will first discuss some key concepts related to comprehension and reading response, and then we will turn to assessment practices and considerations for instruction.

**LITERACY PROFILE**
Be sure to have your Literacy Profile available as you read through this chapter, referring to the question in the left-hand column and the indicators across the columns for Strand 6.

## UNDERLYING PRINCIPLES OF COMPREHENSION AND READING RESPONSE

What actually *is* comprehension? In general, we think of comprehension as evidence of understanding what has been read. The Rand Reading Study Group defined reading comprehension as "the process of simultaneously extracting and constructing meaning" (2002, p. xiii). In other words, when readers comprehend, they "get" meaning from text, but they also "make their own meaning" by connecting their background knowledge with what is in the text. Comprehension of text can range from a basic "grasping of the meaning" of a sentence or an idea, to synthesizing, inferring, critiquing, and evaluating a particular text or multiple texts. We are using the term "reading response" to describe readers' personal connections with what they have read.

One way to think about what is involved in comprehension is to consider what readers need to "orchestrate" in order to understand a text. In addition to being able to decode the text with accuracy and fluency and understand the meanings of words in the text, a reader also needs to use comprehension strategies, some background knowledge, and knowledge about text itself. Motivation and engagement are also critical, particularly in influencing reader response. In this section we will briefly describe these influential factors:

- Strategies
- Background knowledge
- Knowledge about text
- Motivation/engagement

### Understanding Comprehension Strategies

Comprehension strategies are cognitive (or mental) processes that people use to help them think as they read. As discussed in chapter 4, the National Reading Panel (2000) listed six strategies that improve reading comprehension:

- Monitoring comprehension (noticing when understanding is disrupted, and using "fix-up" strategies such as rereading or "chunking" to remedy the situation)
- Using graphic organizers (maps, webs, charts)
- Answering questions (explicit and implicit)
- Generating questions to process information (when children ask questions before, during, and after reading)
- Recognizing story structure
- Summarizing central ideas

It is important to keep in mind that strategies such as these will be used flexibly and variably, depending upon the child, the type of text the child will read, and the context, task, or situation. Strategies are *tools* that people use to support their understanding of what they are reading; they are not goals by themselves. Because reading comprehension strategies were discussed at some length in chapter 4, we suggest that you review that chapter if needed at this time.

## Understanding Background Knowledge

Children also need *background knowledge* or *schema* to understand what they are reading. Comprehension has sometimes been referred to as "building bridges between the new and the known" (Pearson & Johnson, 1978, p. 24). Clearly, if a person knows very little about a topic he or she is reading, that "bridge" will be insecure, and comprehension will be hampered. Research indicates that prior knowledge influences "what students attend to, what inferences they make and what they remember after reading" (Reutzel, Camperell, & Smith, 2002, p. 324). At the same time, prior knowledge might interfere with comprehension, such as when a child has an incorrect or incomplete understanding of something he or she is reading about. For example, some children have heard that all snakes are poisonous; as a result, they may read with that assumption in mind and ignore new text information that conflicts with their original beliefs. Finding out what children already know about a topic is critical. In addition, we need to teach children to refer to their own background knowledge while they read—for example, by thinking, "This is about dolphins; I already know that they are smart!"

## Understanding Knowledge About Text

Background knowledge and strategies are critical for comprehension, but they aren't enough! Children also need *knowledge about text itself*:

- Text types/genres (e.g., narratives, poetry, biographies, informational text)
- Text structures (e.g., character, problem, solution in narrative text; compare-contrast, sequential, classification structures in informational text)
- Authors' purposes (to inform, entertain, persuade, etc.)

Knowledge of text features (discussed in chapter 2), such as headings, subheadings, bold print, and captions, and other aspects of authors' craft, such as repetition, exaggeration, or imagery, is also important to aid comprehension and reader response (Lipson & Cooper, 2002; Ray, 2004). Teachers sometimes overlook these "contributors" to comprehension (knowledge of text structures, features, purposes, and authors' craft) when dealing with young readers. But children's comprehension is hindered when they have had only limited experiences with text. Imagine a first or second grader who has never encountered a book of riddles or a recipe book. Both kinds of texts require different knowledge of how the author "put the text together" in order for the reader to understand it. Having a basic knowledge of text structures, features of text, and authors' craft helps children pay attention to what is important (or intentional) in text.

Experience with and knowledge about texts and their structures become evident during assessment. Children who have learned that stories have key elements (i.e., characters, a setting, a problem, and a solution) tend to produce better retellings or summaries of stories than children who have not learned this basic story structure (Block & Pressley, 2001). Similarly, a third- or fourth-grade student who is familiar with the "classification" or "compare-contrast" text structures that are hallmarks of informational text will more likely be able to summarize or answer questions about passages that have those patterns.

**LITERACY PROFILE** Notice in Strand 6 of the Literacy Profile that different aspects of comprehension are listed for narrative and informational text. You may also want to refer back to chapter 4 for more information about patterns or structures of informational text.

## Understanding Motivation and Engagement

Motivation clearly impacts reader response; unfortunately, motivation to read generally declines over the elementary school years (Wigfield et al., 1997). Pressley (2002) pointed out that motivation is a multifaceted concept that includes reader self-efficacy (the belief that one can read well), a particular book's challenge level, reading curiosity, the belief that reading is important, reader goals, and social reasons for reading. Interestingly, primary-level children believe more than intermediate-level children that effort pays off. Intermediate–grade children tend to believe that success is more a result of how "smart" a person is, rather than how much effort a person puts into learning something.

## Understanding Other Related Factors That Impact Comprehension

Comprehension is affected by other factors as well. Two that particularly stand out are listening comprehension and attention. Listening comprehension (understanding while someone else is reading a text aloud) and reading comprehension are closely related. Biemiller (2003) contends that oral (listening) comprehension *sets the ceiling* of reading comprehension. In other words, children are able to understand a higher level of text when someone reads aloud to them than the level of text they can understand when they read independently. This is usually true of children up through the middle grades (Grades 7 and 8). Biemiller stresses that teachers should use read-alouds to build children's understanding of grade-level (and beyond) vocabulary, especially during the primary and elementary grades, because read-alouds strengthen listening skills and the language skills necessary for comprehension.

In addition, attention, memory, and general cognitive ability contribute to comprehension (Rand Reading Study Group, 2002). Children need both the ability and the willingness to focus on what they read, and they also need to be able to "hold" at least some of what they read in their working memories. As children get older and enter the intermediate grades, they usually develop more of a range of strategies to organize information and remember what is important.

General thinking abilities also contribute to comprehension, particularly when understanding a text requires analytical or inferential thinking. When teachers ask children to "think between the lines," draw conclusions, or come up with generalizations, themes, or judgments, children need to use the higher-order thinking skills of analysis and inference. Students with very limited cognitive abilities, therefore, often struggle with tasks that require a lot of analysis and inference (such as identifying a theme or forming a judgment supported by evidence in the text); however, it is important not to limit their opportunities to engage in higher-order thinking. All children need to know that reading involves thinking!

## Summary of Underlying Principles of Comprehension and Reading Response

Because comprehension is at the heart of reading, we have emphasized the complex nature of reading comprehension and reading response, and argued that without comprehension, "real reading" does not take place. In this section we have stressed the importance of considering four factors that influence comprehension: reading comprehension strategies, background knowledge, knowledge about text itself, and motivation and engagement. Other factors such as attention and cognitive level play a role in supporting comprehension as well. In the next section we turn our attention to specific ways of assessing comprehension and reading response.

## ASSESSING COMPREHENSION AND READING RESPONSE

A wide range of assessment tools, some formal, some informal, is available to gather information about children's reading comprehension and reading response. An important point to keep in mind is that because comprehension and reader response are multifaceted, assessment should be multifaceted as well. One assessment will not "do it all."

At the earliest stages of literacy development, evaluating *listening* comprehension and response to what the teacher has read aloud makes the most sense. What the child reads independently at these early stages of reading is usually *very* simple and straightforward (e.g., stop signs, labels on cereal boxes, or simple, patterned books). Needless to say, these types of texts do not provide the teacher much opportunity to notice a child's ability to think about the meaning of what she or he read, so teachers need to use more complex texts, usually presented through teacher read-alouds, to support children's development of comprehension (Lipson & Cooper, 2002).

### Formal or Published Measures for Assessing Comprehension and Reader Response

A variety of published assessment tools provide information about children's reading comprehension at different levels. Some formal assessments focus specifically on comprehension; others include comprehension along with other aspects of reading. First we will consider tools that assess broad outcomes or monitor student progress, and then we will discuss a few tools that can diagnose students' areas of strength and weakness.

***Comprehension Measures Used for Assessing Broad Outcomes, Screening, or Monitoring Student Progress.*** From Grade 2 or 3 on, a number of schools use formal, standardized assessment tools such as the Iowa Test of Basic Skills (2001) or the Degrees of Reading Power (Koslin, Koslin, Zeno, & Ovens, 1989) tests. These paper-and-pencil assessments measure children's reading comprehension (often along with other areas of achievement) and provide overall *program evaluation* data to determine how well children are achieving broad outcomes of comprehension, or "understanding what is read." Many standardized tests use a multiple-choice format; others use a "cloze" format, in which students fill in words missing from a passage. Particularly for Grades 3 and 4, states often require standardized tests (either norm-referenced or standards-based) in order for schools to be in compliance with the federal No Child Left Behind Act, known as NCLB. Standards-based assessments provide a way for teachers to determine the degree to which children are achieving agreed-upon standards for a particular grade; norm-referenced assessments, on the other hand, provide information about how well children performed on a test administered to a large "normative sample" of children at their grade level, in relation to the other children who took the test. Sometimes the tests states select are "off-the-shelf" products; in other cases they are designed by assessment companies for individual states, and are (ideally) closely aligned with the state's standards or grade-level expectations.

Other assessments are primarily used for *screening*—to identify students who need a "closer look." For example, the Gates-MacGinitie test (MacGinitie, MacGinitie, Maria, & Dreyer, 2000), which includes subtests for both vocabulary and comprehension, is often used to identify children who might be achieving below others at their grade level across the country. Some schools use reading comprehension measures even more

The No Child Left Behind Act (2002) is a U.S. federal law that aimed to increase the performance of primary and secondary schools by increasing standards of accountability for states, districts, and schools. NCLB strongly emphasizes student testing, teacher quality, and the use of "scientifically based research."

frequently, such as several times a year, to *monitor student progress*. Some examples of tools used for this purpose include the Rigby Benchmark Assessment Kit (2007), the Developmental Reading Assessment K–3, (Beaver, 2006), and benchmark book reading assessments (described by Lipson & Wixson, 2003).

All of these assessments involve teachers listening to individual children read leveled text selections aloud, recording the child's accuracy, and noticing strategies the child does or doesn't use. The teacher uses retellings or questions (or both) to evaluate comprehension. In addition, some teachers (and schools) use periodic "unit" or "theme" assessments that are part of a comprehensive published program and are usually administered to the whole class.

For students in grades 4 and above, an upper-grade version of the Developmental Reading Assessment is available: DRA 4–8 (Carter & Beaver, 2003).

### Comprehension Measures Used to Diagnose Strengths and Needs.

Formal *diagnostic* assessments that are frequently used include the Woodcock-Johnson III Diagnostic Reading Battery (Woodcock, Mather, & Schrank, 2004) and the Test of Reading Comprehension (or TORC; Brown, Hammill, & Wiederholt, 1995). These assessments provide a detailed look at individual student's comprehension through a variety of tasks, and yield information as to children's relative strengths and areas of weakness. In many cases, teachers use these measures as part of a comprehensive evaluation to determine whether a child is eligible for special education services, but in other situations a reading specialist might administer one or more assessments to find out what might be influencing or hampering a child's comprehension. One relatively new, group-administered assessment is GRADE (Group Reading Assessment and Diagnostic Evaluation; Williams, 2002), which includes listening comprehension, sentence comprehension, and passage comprehension.

Informal reading inventories (also known as IRIs) are published assessments that include several components: word lists, passages, and comprehension questions or retelling probes at different grade levels. One of the most well known is the Qualitative Reading Inventory IV (published by Pearson/ Allyn & Bacon, 2006), which includes questions designed to evaluate a child's background knowledge about a specific topic. IRIs are frequently used at Grades 2, 3, 4, and beyond, and usually include both narrative and expository text passages. They are individually administered and provide information regarding the text level a particular child can read with accuracy and comprehension. IRIs can also yield more detailed information depending upon the expertise and training of the person using the assessment. The comprehension component of most IRIs involves the child providing an oral response to comprehension questions, although some IRIs use a retelling format as well.

See chapter 5 for titles of some commonly used informal reading inventories.

To evaluate children's comprehension of informational text, Nell Duke and her colleagues at Michigan State University have recently developed a set of criterion-referenced assessments for first- and second-grade students. The two assessments are called the Concepts of Comprehension Assessment (COCA) and the Strategic Cloze Assessment, which will be available free of charge and online at www.msularc.org. "Cloze" is an assessment (and sometimes instructional) technique where a sentence or series of sentences is provided, and children need to fill in the word that makes sense. Designed to measure different "feeders" to comprehension, including comprehension strategy use, informational text feature knowledge, understanding of graphics, vocabulary knowledge, and vocabulary strategy use, the assessments take only about 15 minutes to administer.

Keep in mind that many of the tools mentioned in the previous section, such as the Developmental Reading Assessment, Rigby Benchmark Assessment Kit, and informal reading inventories, can provide valuable diagnostic information as well. For example, teachers can learn children's relative strengths and weaknesses as they respond to different types of questions, different levels of questions, or different types of text. One child might show strong responses to questions asked orally, but have a difficult time when asked to respond in writing to a constructed-response question. Another child might answer literal, text-based questions easily but demonstrate a good deal of difficulty when the teacher asks inferential or critical thinking questions. Still other children may show strong comprehension of narrative text, but find informational text challenging. In addition, teachers can also obtain a good deal of information about children's comprehension from ongoing, informal assessment.

### Informal Measures for Assessing Comprehension

A variety of informal tools and tests are available to obtain information about children's comprehension on an ongoing basis. Because comprehension is such an important goal of reading instruction during the K–4 years, it is critical for teachers to have a broad repertoire of tools available to help inform and adjust their instruction. First we will discuss observation and documentation, and then we will consider other classroom-based tools.

***Observation and Documentation.*** Observations of students' developing comprehension can provide extremely valuable information, and they're also highly flexible. Such observations can happen "on the spot" or can be more strategically planned. An example of an "on-the-spot" observation might be a teacher noticing (and recording) statements or questions that first-grade children might offer in response to a teacher read-aloud of *A Pocket for Corduroy* (Freeman, 1978). See Figure 6.1 for two examples.

The teacher can use the information obtained from Tasha ("Corduroy wanted to get himself a pocket just like Lisa's!") to mark her Literacy Profile, documenting evidence of her developing comprehension. The same teacher might use the information from Jerome ("Corduroy got put into the dryer!") to determine an area where Jerome needs practice (identifying the beginning of a story), and to make decisions in planning a small-group lesson or an individual conference to focus on how stories begin.

**FIGURE 6.1  Sample Anecdotal Notes on Students' Comprehension During Teacher Read-Aloud**

| **Name:** *Jerome T.*<br>**Date:**  *Feb. 5*<br>**Focus:** *beginning/middle/end of story* | **Name:** *Tasha M.*<br>**Date:**   *Feb. 5*<br>**Focus:** *beginning/middle/end of story* |
|---|---|
| *After reading A Pocket for Corduroy I asked the group: "So—how did this story get started?"*<br><br>*Jerome said, "Corduroy got put into the dryer!"*<br><br>*—I need to make sure he understands the notion of "how stories get started," as another way to think about the beginning of the story?* | *Tasha's response to my  question:*<br><br><br>*"Corduroy wanted to get  himself a pocket just like Lisa's!"*<br><br>*She really thought back to the beginning!* |

Other observations might be conducted with the whole class. A kindergarten teacher might ask children to draw a "before" and "after" picture (for example, before and after a teacher read-aloud of *The Carrot Seed*; Krauss, 2004) and use that as an assessment opportunity. A third- or fourth-grade teacher focusing on literary devices and author's craft with a small group of students reading *Cloudy with a Chance of Meatballs* (Barrett, 1982) might provide each participant with four specific "discussion cards" (Caldwell, 2002). For this particular book, the cards might be labeled "exaggeration," "imagery," "descriptive language," and "humor." The teacher then asks each student to select one card on which to base his/her comments, and the teacher can then observe (and record) the content of the students' discussion in order to evaluate the children's understanding of the literary elements that he has taught them.

In "observational" situations such as these, it is essential that the teacher has some *criteria* for what she or he is observing and records the observations accordingly. Sometimes a teacher uses a scoring guide (a checklist, scale, or rubric), but at other times the teacher might simply take notes that document what the child said (or drew, danced, etc.) in response to the text. For example, in the case of the *A Pocket for Corduroy* discussion, the teacher would write down notes to record what she noticed in terms of desired outcomes such as "identifying beginning, middle, or end of stories." This information, of course, could contribute to evidence used to mark those indicators for that student's Literacy Profile.

In addition, teachers need to have a *method of recording* the student's "product" or "performance" (versus hoping to remember it). The anecdotal notes form in Figure 6.1 provides one example of intentional and focused recording, and Appendix A-20 provides another format: a sample checklist for observing children as they read informational text.

***Other Informal Tools for Assessing Comprehension and Reader Response.***
Many other informal tools are available to evaluate children's comprehension and response to reading as well. We will describe several listed on the Literacy Profile: the Quick Text-Level Check-In, individual conferences, think-alouds, retellings/summaries, assessment of reader responses including journals, and teacher-posed questions, including constructed responses.

*Quick Text-Level Check-In.* We discussed this tool (Biggam & Thompson, 2005), also called the "QT" (see Appendix A-17), in chapter 5, but we include it here because it can provide (from the end of Grade 2 onward) a useful way for a teacher to monitor a child's comprehension of a *particular* text he or she is reading. In Part 2 of the QT assessment, the teacher asks the child to silently read a designated segment of text and tells the child, "When you are finished, I will ask you to tell me about the part you read." After the teacher writes down the "gist" of what the student says, she then judges the quality of what the student said (how well does it match the key points of the text?), and marks "limited," "some," "acceptable," or "strong." This informal assessment provides a simple measure of "surface" comprehension that can be useful for on-the-spot adjustments to instruction, but for other purposes (placement, grading, screening, etc.), the teacher should supplement this assessment with other measures.

*Individual Student Conferences.* As children begin to read independently (often at mid to late Grade 1 but sometimes before or after that), it is important for teachers to know whether a child is gaining meaning from what she is reading. It is not uncommon for children to select a book for their independent reading that is a popular title, one that a friend has recommended, or one that has been previously read aloud—but clearly a text that is too difficult for the child to read independently. (Remember—in most cases, a child should be able to read a text with at least 98% accuracy for him or her to be considered at an "independent" reading level.) Conferences can provide a valuable opportunity to make sure that children are selecting appropriate books for independent reading.

A teacher-student conference can serve other important purposes (beyond finding out whether a book is at a child's independent reading level and whether the child understands it or not); a conference can also provide an opportunity to find out connections the child may have made, questions the text might have raised, personal responses the text generated, and so on. The individual conference form introduced in chapter 4 (see Appendix A-12) includes some prompts to help evaluate children's comprehension.

*Think-Alouds.* A think-aloud is a technique that a teacher can use either for instruction or for assessment. When used as an assessment tool, it involves asking the child to talk about the reading strategies he used during reading (for example, whether he used any fix-up strategies when he didn't understand something) and the content of what he read. While possible to use with younger children, think-alouds are probably most appropriate for children in Grades 3, 4, and up. Lipson and Wixson (2003) outline the following steps for constructing a think-aloud:

- Select a text (generally about 200 words or a little longer).
- Segment the text and mark it so that the student will stop at predetermined spots.
- As the student reads and stops at the marked places, ask the student to think aloud about the text or her thoughts. Use language such as, "Tell me what you were *doing* and *thinking* as you read that part."

There are a variety of ways to evaluate children's think-alouds, but one simple method suggested by Caldwell (2002) involves designating appropriate stopping points in the text and then making a three-column chart with the headings "Retelling," "Inferring," and "Other" along with a row for each stopping point marked. After each think-aloud opportunity, the teacher simply notes (on the chart) the kind of think-aloud the child produced, or leaves the columns blank if the child was unable to verbalize what she was "thinking or doing."

Wilhelm (2001) advises teachers to remember that the reports of thinking they obtain through think-alouds will often be partial, and will rarely reveal all of the child's thoughts or feelings. However, think-alouds *can* provide a very helpful "window" into a child's thinking during reading and can provide direction for needed instruction. For example, children who only retell and rarely infer will likely need further modeling and guided practice in how to infer during reading. Afflerbach, Pearson, and Paris (2008) make the point that asking students to explain their thinking during or after reading provides important insights for both teachers and students. This can take place in a variety of settings, such as during shared reading and small-group reading lessons.

*Retellings and Summaries.* During the primary grades another method of informally assessing comprehension that teachers commonly use is having the student retell a story that he or she read. A retelling should not be complete verbal recounting of the full text; rather, the child is expected to include, mostly in his or her own words, just the *key* elements of the story that he or she read. Even as early as kindergarten, children can begin to retell stories that teachers have read aloud to them, providing a valuable window for teachers to understand how much children understand from the text as well as their ability to use the text structure to organize and retain information (Moss, 2004).

If the teacher read a narrative story, the key points a child should include in a retelling are the elements of a narrative: characters, problem, key events, and the solution. But for very young children (kindergarteners and early first graders), beginning retellings are usually much simpler; as noted in the Literacy Profile, by mid-first grade, teachers should encourage (and expect) children to tell what happened at the beginning, the middle, and

A teacher listens to Willa as she retells a story she just read.

the end of the story. More "advanced" narrative retellings at the late-second-grade level should include (in addition to the key elements listed above) the initiating event (what happened to get the story started) and the main character's goal (what did she or he want? what was she or he after?). In addition, depending upon the story and the age/level of the children, a retelling by children at the second- or early third-grade level might also include a theme or message (what was the author trying to tell us in this story?). It is important to keep in mind, though, that primary-level children often understand and remember only parts of some stories—particularly actions and action-driven events—and often omit emotions or motivations when retelling a story (Lipson, Mosenthal, & Mekkelsen, 1999).

If what the child read was informational text, his or her retelling will generally include one or two very important "big ideas" and some details that are connected to those "big ideas." Remember, though, that in order to evaluate what a student says during a retelling, using a scoring guide is key. Figure 6.2 provides one version of a scoring guide for narrative retellings that might be appropriate for a child at a typical Grade 1/early Grade 2 stage of development. You might adapt this to reflect the expectations of children at different levels. Teachers can create their own scoring guides for retellings as well. If using a narrative text, you should first read the story and and then create a story map (perhaps accompanied by icons or graphic representations such as those suggested below) to chart the key elements:

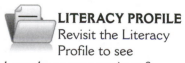

**LITERACY PROFILE**
Revisit the Literacy Profile to see how these expectations for students' retellings develop over time.

- Initiating event (sunrise or arrow)
- Characters (faces or stick figures to represent people or animals)
- Goal (telescope or goalpost)
- Problem (question mark or storm cloud)
- Key events (steps or footprints)
- Solution or resolution (sunset, smiley face, or !)

If using informational text, look for the main idea and key details. Next, decide which key elements (big ideas—not little details) are absolutely critical

**FIGURE 6.2  Sample Retelling Scoring Guide for Narrative Text (Grade 1–Early Grade 2)**

| Student: *Tammy K.* | | Teacher:<br>Grade: | | |
|---|---|---|---|---|
| Retelling included: | Date: *11/08*<br>Story: *Gingerbread Boy* | Date:<br>Story: | Date:<br>Story: | Date:<br>Story: |
| Important characters | ✓ | | | |
| Problem | *?*<br>*(vague)* | | | |
| Important events | ✓ | | | |
| Solution | ✓ | | | |

to understanding that particular story, and make a checklist to use while you listen to children's retellings. Piloting the scoring guide for the retelling will be important, as we tend to learn much from listening to children tell us what *they* think is important! In other words, after you record several students' retellings of a given story, use the scoring guide to evaluate their understanding of the story, and then check to make sure that the scoring guide reflects what the students who demonstrated strong comprehension said. If not, revise the scoring guide accordingly.

Retellings are not the same as a full summary, which generally includes some kind of main idea, theme, or generalization and less detail; full summaries are definitely more challenging for children to produce, even in Grades 3 and 4. When children begin to construct summaries of narrative or informational text that they have read, it is important to share with them some clear expectations about what constitutes a good summary. Displaying those expectations in a "student-friendly" scoring guide makes enormous sense so that children can use the guidelines for self-assessment and teachers can use them for ongoing assessment as well. A checklist for children to self-assess their own summaries of informational text is provided in Appendix A-19; this format is probably most appropriate for children in Grades 3 or 4.

*Reading Responses/Journals.*  Another informal, classroom-based approach for assessing students' understanding of what they read is a response notebook or journal. Formats for reading responses and response journals can range from very simple to more complex (see Figures 6.3 and 6.4) and can either involve student choice or be teacher-directed. In the first format, which might be used in first grade, children are expected to choose from a variety of possible prompts and provide evidence from the text to support their responses. The second example (which is more appropriate in third or fourth grade) takes the form of a letter that students write to their teacher and also includes evidence from the text to support their response. Other teachers use different options such as having children write a book recommendation to be posted on a bulletin board or a book review to be placed in a collection of reviews to be shared with another classroom. Important factors to keep in mind about reading responses or reading journals are *variety* and *authenticity*

FIGURE 6.3  **Sample Reading-Response Format for Kindergarten
or Grade 1**

| Name: | Date: |
|---|---|
| I read: | |

Choose two:
☐ Tell what you liked about the book.
☐ Make a picture of your favorite part.
☐ Write two new words you learned.
☐ Who else might like this book? Why?

| | |
|---|---|
| | |

so that the mode of response does not become tedious. Consider this: if most of us were required to write the same type of journal response every time we read a chapter of a book we were (voluntarily) reading, we might very well decide to stop reading!

*Questions, Including Constructed Responses.*  Perhaps the most commonly used technique to assess reading comprehension is asking questions. To use questions well, it is important to consider the types and levels of questions you

FIGURE 6.4  **Sample Fourth Grader's Response Letter
to a Teacher**

Dear Ms. B.,

   I just finished reading <u>Bats</u> by Gail Gibbons and I wish it was not over. I really liked learning all the cool details about bats. I already knew some of them but here are some that I bet you did not know.

   Did you know that the oldest bat fossil is 50 million years old? That means they have been around a really long time! Bats have this neat thing called echolocation that helps them move around at night. They send out beeping sounds that people can't hear but when the sound waves hit an insect then the waves bounce back to the bat and then the bat can catch the insect! They help keep the number of insects down. But one problem is that in some places bats are endangered, because people kill bats and also because of pollution and pesticides. If there aren't enough bats the number of insects will probably go up.

   I think I know a couple of kids who might like to read this book, because it has great illustrations and lots of good information. You might not like it, though, because I have a feeling you do not like bats!

Your friend,
Jamie F.

ask, the method of response you're expecting, and how you'll evaluate students' responses to the questions.

There are a variety of ways to think about the types of questions that you ask. One involves thinking about *what* you are questioning: content, process, or response. "Content" questions ask about the substance of what the child read. One example of a content question from the widely read book *Caps for Sale* might be, "What is this monkey trying to do?" "Process" questions try to find out the strategies the student used during reading. Questions to find out about a child's processes might be, "How did you figure out that word 'peddler'?" or "What clues did you use to make that prediction?" Finally, "response" questions elicit a personal reaction from a child either during or after reading. An example of a "response" question that a teacher might pose to a child who read *Caps for Sale* could be, "What would you have done if you were the peddler?" or "Which part of this story did you like the best? Why?" Keep in mind that, as teachers, we tend to primarily ask content–focused questions, but process questions can be very useful in promoting or assessing strategy use. Finally, response questions can be particularly helpful in assessing (as well as promoting) children's engagement in what they read.

We can also differentiate questions according to *level*. Generally we think about three or four levels: literal, inferential, and evaluative or critical thinking types of questions. The last three types are generally considered "higher-level" questions that call for children to engage in deeper thinking. Raphael, Highfield, and Au (2006) have outlined a highly useful and practical framework, Question-Answer Relationships (or QAR), to provide a "common way of thinking about and talking about sources of information for answering questions" (p. 14). This student-friendly method of categorizing the relationship between questions and where children can find the answers includes four categories:

- Right There
- Think and Search
- Author and Me
- On My Own

See Figure 6.5 for a more detailed description of each category; we will discuss more uses of QAR later in this chapter. Using approaches such as QAR can not only help teachers monitor their use of a range of questions but can also help children consider the type of thinking they need when various questions are posed.

The *format* of questions is important to consider as well. Questions may be oral or written, and may involve a "selected response" in which students must choose among options provided (usually multiple choice or true–false) or a "constructed response" in which students have to come up with (and write) their own answers. Constructed-response questions can be quite simple, such as having children complete a chart of characteristics or qualities (of a character, for example), or more complex, as when children must write a paragraph explaining what message they think the author was trying to get across, supporting their thinking with evidence from the text. See Figure 6.6 for an example of a constructed-response question that teachers might ask of third or fourth graders and a scoring guide that teachers might use to score the children's responses. Paying attention to the *way* children answer questions is also important. Clearly,

For more information about Question-Answer Relationships (QAR), the resource *QAR NOW* by Raphael, Highfield, and Au (2006) is very helpful.

An excellent resource for finding sample constructed-response questions in reading (for third or fourth graders) is the Web site of the National Assessment of Educational Progress, or NAEP: http://nces.ed.gov/nationsreportcard/reading/

FIGURE 6.5  QAR (Question-Answer Relationship) Categories

| In the Book | | In My Head | |
|---|---|---|---|
| The answer will be found in the book. | | The answer will be found in my own head. | |
| Right There | Think and Search | Author and Me | On My Own |
| The answer is in one place in the text. Words from the question and words that answer the question are often "right there" in the same sentence or a couple of sentences next to each other. | The answer is in the text. Readers need to "think and search" or put together different parts of the text to find the answer. The answer can be within a paragraph, across paragraphs, or even across chapters and books. | The answer is not in the text. To answer the question, readers need to think about how the text and what they already know fit together. | The answer is not in the text. Readers need to use their own ideas and experiences to answer the question. They do not have to read the book to answer the question. |

Adapted chart from QAR NOW by Taffy Raphael, Kathy Highfield, and Kathy Au. Copyright © 2006 by Taffy Raphael, Kathy Highfield, and Kathy Au. Reprinted by permission of Scholastic Inc.

some questions have a straightforward, right or wrong answer, but many do not. Beyond checking whether the answer is simply right or wrong, it can be very useful to dig a little deeper and probe children's responses to figure out what might have influenced their answers.

Rubrics and scales are especially useful for evaluating children's responses to constructed-response questions, and one resource that can be particularly helpful for evaluating text-based constructed responses is the QuEEC self-monitoring tool (Biggam, 2006). The acronym QuEEC stands for "**Qu**estion, **E**nough, **E**vidence, and **C**lear & Correct." Using QuEEC, children and/or teachers check responses to see:

- Whether the child understood the **question** and whether the child used part of the question stem in the response
- Whether the response provided **enough** to answer all parts of the question

FIGURE 6.6  Sample Constructed-Response Question and Scoring Guide (for Third or Fourth Graders)

**Question**: From what you just read about bats, what are two important things the author wants to make sure you know? Explain why they are important, using details from the article to support your answer.

**Scoring Guide**:
4. The response includes two relevant facts about bats from the article, and clearly explains their importance.
3. The response includes two facts, but one is not important or explained clearly.
2. The response includes one or two facts about bats, but they are not explained.
1. The response does not include facts about bats, or the response is irrelevant.

- Whether the response provided **evidence** from the text, or whether the child used his own **experience**
- Whether the child reread the question and response to see whether the answer was **clear** and **correct**.

This tool (see Appendix A-20) is most appropriate for children in Grades 3 and 4, and, to use it effectively (either for assessment or for instruction), teachers should provide ample opportunities for modeling and guided practice *before* having children use it as a self-monitoring tool.

*Anticipation Guides.* A highly effective approach to finding out children's background knowledge before reading, and then following up after reading, is the use of Anticipation Guides (Buehl, 2001; Herber, 1978). Most often used with informational text, the technique simply involves having children "respond to several statements that challenge or support preconceived ideas about key concepts in the passage" (Buehl, 2001, p. 28). For example, before reading an article about planets, some statements to present to second- or third-grade students might include:

- *Planets are bodies that revolve around the earth.*
- *The moon is not a planet.*
- *Earth is a planet.*
- *We can see all the planets when we look at the stars at night.*

Students are asked to check off "strongly disagree," "disagree," "agree," or "strongly agree" beside each statement and then talk about their responses during small-group or whole-class discussions. Later, after they have read the text, children return to their previous responses, revise them as needed, and engage in discussion once more. By closely observing children's initial *and* final responses, teachers can gain extremely valuable information about children's background knowledge and also about children's understanding of what they have read. Teachers can then use this information to plan the next steps for instruction—for example, guiding the teacher in forming small groups of children who need a more "guided-reading" experience and more building of their background knowledge. Like QuEEC, this tool can be useful for both instruction and assessment, since children are activating their prior knowledge while using Anticipation Guides and then revisiting (and perhaps revising) their knowledge after reading.

*Drama/Movement or Other Non-Print-Based Response Formats.* We can learn a great deal about how much children have understood from either independent reading or a teacher read-aloud through non-print-based responses such as music, visual arts, movement, or dramatic play. For example, after reading a story that involves a character whose goal or motive drives the story, you might have two children interview each other, using props (such as a dollar-store "microphone") if possible. This technique of "character interviews" can provide a valuable, engaging, and interactive way to determine whether children understand a character's goal or motive.

Other informal assessment activities that use drama and movement involve having children interpret the text through pantomime, or asking children to demonstrate the sequence of emotions a character experiences at the beginning, middle, and end of a story. Other children can then try to guess the particular emotions or attributes their classmates are acting out. For this kind of activity to be useful as an assessment, you need to have some sort of scoring guide or method of systematic observation to evaluate the children's responses.

### Summary of Assessing Reading Comprehension and Reading Response

We have described a variety of formal and informal approaches to assessing children's comprehension and reading response, including tools for measuring outcomes, screening, monitoring progress, and diagnosing children's strengths and areas of need. When assessing comprehension, it is especially important to keep in mind that comprehension is multifaceted. Because of this, using a variety of different types of assessment formats and kinds of questions is recommended, because they can reveal different aspects of children's comprehension and provide valuable information to inform and differentiate instruction.

Teachers should also use informal assessments to gain information about children's background knowledge as well as their response to what they have read. These informal assessments can take a variety of forms, such as individual conferences, constructed response questions, think-alouds, and reading response options that use dramatic play, movement, or other art forms.

## INSTRUCTIONAL APPROACHES FOR BUILDING READING COMPREHENSION AND READING RESPONSE

Sometimes it is tempting to think that as long as children can decode the text at hand, their comprehension of that text will automatically follow. We know, however, that most children need both explicit instruction and supported practice in order to become better at comprehending (Duke & Pearson, 2002; Lipson, 2007). Keeping in mind that expectations for comprehension have increased, now that we live in an information-rich era that requires an educational climate of high standards and accountability (Smith, 1998), teachers need to provide ample opportunities for children to become thoughtful and skillful comprehenders. In addition, many children need specifically tailored instruction to support their developing comprehension; therefore, we must carefully match our differentiated instructional approaches to what children need.

Comprehension assessment results can reveal general and particular patterns of need. First we will briefly discuss some general approaches that all or most children need, and then we will consider possible gaps in comprehension and sample approaches to help children who exhibit those needs.

### Instructional Approaches for Building Comprehension and Reading Response for All Students

Before considering what children need to strengthen their reading comprehension, let's think back to the factors that influence comprehension. In addition to text that children can read, developing readers also need ample opportunities to expand their strategies, background knowledge (including vocabulary), understandings about text, motivation, and attention. Within the classroom, approaches and techniques used to build these aspects of comprehension generally fall into the broad categories of explicit instruction and supportive practice.

***Explicit Instruction in Comprehension.*** Comprehension *does* need to be "taught," not just "caught"! In other words, comprehension is not simply a by-product of reading or an ability that some readers just "have" and others do not. In addition, it's important not to mistake *checking* for comprehension with actually *teaching* children how to comprehend by providing them with the knowledge and tools they need to understand a variety of texts. Asking comprehension questions is not the same as actually *teaching* children how to comprehend. When, where, and how might this explicit teaching take place? Teaching comprehension strategies and background knowledge frequently takes place during intentionally planned teacher read-alouds, mini-lessons, or lessons using text selections from a basal anthology or other grade-appropriate text selection. Children also need to learn about the nature of text itself, and how to demonstrate their understanding of what they read. Santoro, Chard, Howard, and Baker (2008) designed and implemented a read-aloud curriculum for first grade that includes daily 20- to 30-minute lessons with an emphasis on text structure, multiple readings of both informational and narrative text, vocabulary exploration, higher-order questions, and peer discussion. The results of their study revealed that "students in the read-aloud classrooms had longer retellings than students from classrooms that did not follow read-aloud lessons and procedures" (p. 407). In addition, students in the project's read-aloud classrooms produced retellings that included more text-based evidence and examples.

*Developing Comprehension Strategies.*  Whole-class mini-lessons and teacher-guided reading lessons are key opportunities to explicitly teach comprehension strategies. For example, a teacher might decide to use some of the books by Cynthia Rylant (e.g., *The Relatives Came*, 1993) to teach the strategy of making connections. The same teacher might then use another of Cynthia Rylant's books and spend a few days working with a small group of children who need even more modeling and explanation of that strategy.

You can find more information concerning mini-lessons and guided reading lessons in chapter 4, on reading strategies.

While you *can* teach comprehension strategies one at a time, it is essential to move toward having children use the strategies flexibly and as a "set" (Pressley, 2002). One of the most well-researched and effective approaches for helping students apply comprehension strategies is Reciprocal Teaching (Palinscar & Brown, 1985); this approach often includes both explicit teaching and supported practice.

See chapter 4 for a description of the reciprocal teaching approach.

*Building Background Knowledge.*  In order to build children's background knowledge, techniques such as discussion and mapping what children know through graphic organizers (which are visual representations or templates that show the organization of text) such as the frequently used Know-Want-Learn (KWL) template (Ogle, 1986) are particularly helpful. The National Reading Panel (2000) specifically cites the use of graphic organizers and focused discussion as being highly effective in promoting comprehension.

The K-W-L technique, which is most appropriate for informational text, provides a systematic way of eliciting children's background knowledge (which sometimes is accurate but at other times may be off-the-mark) as well as generating questions and ideas concerning what children will learn. See Figure 6.7 for an example of a partially completed K-W/E-L chart, which is adapted from the original KWL model. In this case the teacher had students generate what they already *knew* about tornadoes, along with what they *wanted* and *expected* to learn, based on a teacher-led preview of the text. We know that building background knowledge through discussion is key, and teachers often have children "think-pair-share" after the teacher has posed an initiating question or "think-pair-pair-share," which involves pairs of children sharing with other pairs. This sort of interaction is powerful because other children's background knowledge is often one of the most helpful resources available! Other ways to build background knowledge include teacher read-alouds of related texts and bringing in artifacts related to what children will read.

FIGURE 6.7  Sample K-W/E-L Chart, Partially Completed Before Reading

| K (What we know or think we know) | W/E (What we want to find out or expect to learn) | L (What we have learned) |
|---|---|---|
| • *Tornadoes can wreck houses and trailers.*  • *There is a lot of wind and it goes around in a circle.*  • *There was one in* The Wizard of Oz. | • *Where do they happen?*  • *What makes them begin?*  • *Can they happen here?*  • *What should we do if one comes?* | |

Ogle, D. M. (1986, February). K-W-L: A teaching model tht develops active reading of expository text. *The Reading Teacher, 39*(6), 564–570. (adapted by authors)

*Developing Knowledge About Text and Skill in Demonstrating Comprehension.* As mentioned earlier, the QAR (Question-Answer Relationships) framework is highly useful for helping both teachers and students think about levels of questions and what kinds of thinking the questions require. Teachers can also use this framework to provide useful language for children to think about before, during, and after reading. For example, you might remind children to do some "on-my-own" thinking before they read and to do some "thinking and searching" at various points in the text. Once children are familiar with all of the QAR categories (most likely in third or fourth grade), they can generate "Author and Me" questions for book groups. We have found that "Author and Me" questions do the best job of stimulating discussion because they are the ones children *want* to talk about. For example, consider which of these questions children would rather talk about together:

- Would you have done the same thing as Toby did if you were in the same situation? Why? (Author and Me)
- Where did Toby live? (Right There)
- What did his teacher have to do to find out about Toby's problem? (Think and Search)

When children need instruction about text itself (e.g., characteristics of different genres, text structures, text features, or author's craft), teachers usually provide it in whole-class lessons or mini-lessons, using sample (sometimes called "mentor") texts—perhaps photocopied onto overhead transparencies—as examples. Previewing the text structure of informational texts is quite helpful, as is providing visual/graphic displays to map the content. By "text structure" we mean the organizational formats that authors use to get their points across. Common text structures include, but are not limited to, the following:

- Classification (sometimes called label-list, because the structure includes providing a label, or category, for the group and then including a list of examples, such as "continents: Asia, Africa, etc.")
- Sequence

- Compare-contrast
- Problem-solution
- Explanation

For example, a third- or fourth-grade teacher might post a Venn diagram (interlocking circles) when reading a text about butterflies and moths that primarily utilizes the compare-contrast pattern. On the other hand, when reading text about how laws are made, a teacher might use a "ladder" visual display because the piece probably has a sequential pattern. Many different varieties of graphic organizers have been developed, several of which are available online at sites such as www.thinkingmaps.com. Other online resources are listed in chapter 4. Graphic organizers such as these help children see text patterns and organize their thinking as they read. In addition, teachers often help children notice the signal words that authors use to indicate organization, such as (in the case of the compare–contrast text structure) "however," "on the other hand," "different," etc.

Most students also need explicit instruction in how to *demonstrate* their knowledge about text, such as when they must infer character traits using evidence from the text or make generalizations about main ideas. Figure 6.8 shows a template that teachers can use to teach children how to infer character traits. You can see that this template includes a sample that you could use for modeling, some scaffolding, and the opportunity for children to come up with their own character traits and supporting evidence. You might also notice on the Literacy Profile that the Strand 6 indicators for Grades 2, 3, and 4 gradually increase in terms of expectations related to children's thinking about character traits and locating supporting evidence.

***Supported Practice in Comprehension and Reader Response.*** Beyond modeling and guided practice, supported practice and feedback are also essential to build children's comprehension (Pearson & Gallagher, 1983).

You can find an excellent list of sample texts for teaching primary-level children about authors' craft in *About the Authors* by Katie Wood Ray (2004).

**FIGURE 6.8  Characters and Clues: Finding Evidence for Character Traits**

| CHARACTERS AND CLUES | |
|---|---|
| Name:<br>Book:<br>Character: | |
| **Character Trait**<br>(what the character is like) | **Clues, or evidence in the**<br>text (what makes me think that…) |
| SAMPLE:<br>(from *Tacky the Penguin*)<br><br>*Tacky is odd.* | *Tacky sings weird songs like "How many toes does a fish have?"*<br><br>*He does cannonballs instead of dives.* |
| *Tacky is brave.* | |
| *Tacky is _____.* | |

To ensure that children's use of skills, knowledge, and strategy can be generalized, it is important to give children opportunities to apply these strategies across a variety of genres and types of text. Such supported practice can take place before, during, and after reading. Before reading, practices such as "story impressions" (McGinley & Denner, 1987), in which the teacher lists on the board 8 to 10 words from a passage and then children talk about (or write about) what they think the passage will be about, are very helpful in triggering children's background knowledge and fostering a readiness to pay attention during reading. During reading, practices such as the Directed-Reading-Thinking-Approach (DR-TA) (Stauffer, 1969) foster children's active use of strategies such as predicting and confirming. This approach involves the teacher and students making predictions of upcoming sections of text; they would then periodically stop to evaluate their predictions and locate evidence that confirmed or disconfirmed those predictions. Finally, an example of an "after-reading" approach is asking children to talk together in partners to come up with an alternate title for what they just read—and to explain why they came up with that title.

Children also need supported practice in learning about text itself. Some teachers have third- or fourth-grade children use a section of their Readers' Notebooks to keep track of what they have learned about text genres, authors' craft, and text structures or features. Other teachers have children become "text structure detectives," asking them to search for and then jot down on Post-its specific examples of an author's use of organizational patterns and signal words, and then attach those examples on charts labeled "compare-contrast," "classification," etc. Books with predictable patterns are best for this kind of exploration.

> For guidance about implementing the Directed-Reading-Thinking-Approach, refer to Blachowicz and Ogle's (2001) *Reading Comprehension: Strategies for Independent Learners*.

> Two excellent resources for locating books with expository text patterns include Barbara Moss's (2003) *Exploring the Literature of Fact: Children's Nonfiction Trade Books in the Elementary Classroom* and Linda Hoyt's (2002) *Make It Real: Strategies for Success with Informational Texts*.

Providing supported practice and scaffolding are also important for strengthening reader response. As children move from the early primary grades to the intermediate grades, teachers usually expect them to demonstrate an increasing ability to respond in thoughtful ways to what they read. Children's responses should show developing reflection or careful thinking, have a basis in the text that they read, and show personal involvement, if appropriate.

Some examples of "response to reading" opportunities that might be appropriate in K–4 classrooms include:

- Drawing and labeling pictures, using clay, making cartoons, and making collages, mobiles, and book covers
- Presenting an oral review of a book or planning a book talk
- Marking a book log with a happy face or a sad face
- Roleplaying a story with a partner, participating in Readers' Theater, using puppets
- Making an "investigations" poster, contributing to a class newspaper, and making a "wanted" poster, an advertisement, and a "report card" for a book, etc.
- Keeping notes in a Reader's Notebook or literature discussion log for later use during a literature discussion group or "book club"

## Instructional Approaches for Building Comprehension and Reading Response for Students with Specific Needs

While the approaches listed above are an excellent foundation for nearly all students, some students have very particular and persistent needs and require some more tailored instruction. Duke and Pearson (2002) stress that differentiated instruction with children is essential to truly meet the needs of diverse learners, and they argue that more work is needed to make this kind of support available for struggling readers. In order to differentiate, however, teachers need to look closely at assessment results and then either locate or design an "intervention" to deal with the particular source of the child's difficulty. At the same time, teachers should also build on children's strengths.

Looking closely at how children respond to comprehension questions can provide some useful guidance for intervention. Dewitz and Dewitz (2003) found that closely analyzing children's responses to questions on the Qualitative Reading Inventory (Leslie & Caldwell, 2006) yields some helpful patterns. Some children demonstrate difficulty with "relational" inference questions that call for them to link one part of the text with another part; a different pattern reflects children's difficulty with "causal" inference questions. For example, a "relational" inference question might be, "What do you think of this character now?" while a "causal" inference question might be, "Why was the pilot worried that morning?" Other patterns the researchers in the Dewitz study noticed include difficulty in understanding the syntax (sentence structure) of what the child reads and lack of understanding what the question is asking. By noting the particular types of patterns that children demonstrate, the teacher (or literacy specialist) can then design a series of focused lessons that involve modeling, guided practice, and feedback.

Valencia and Buly (2004), in their study of second graders who had failed a state-level performance assessment, identified six different "varieties" of struggling readers: automatic word callers, struggling word callers, word stumblers, slow comprehenders, slow word callers, and disabled readers. All categories except that of the "slow comprehenders" involved specific issues in comprehension, and some of the recommended approaches for these children include:

- Extensive teacher modeling of the use of comprehension strategies, including self-monitoring strategies
- Emphasis on building vocabulary, including understanding of "academic" vocabulary (e.g., *compare, solution, topic*)
- Intentional work on building background knowledge and familiarity with a wider range of genres and their structures

Massey (2007) identified several barriers to comprehension—prior knowledge, distraction techniques, and word identification—and proposed some approaches to assist children who display these difficulties. She suggests working intensively on Question-Answer Relationships (discussed previously in this chapter and also in chapter 4) to help children who overrely on often-inaccurate or unrelated prior knowledge instead of actually using the text to respond to comprehension questions. For children who use "distraction" as an avoidance technique, Massey recommends having children use a comprehension checklist to build metacognition (thinking about one's own thinking). For example, such a checklist might include items like these: "I read every sentence." "I tried not to think about other things as I read." "I stopped and thought about it when something did not make sense."

To help children who need guided practice in a particular aspect of answering constructed-response questions (e.g., using part of the question stem in their answer), a teacher might form a small group. Using the QuEEC self-monitoring tool (described earlier in this chapter), the teacher might provide repeated modeling and guided practice and keep data on the progress the children are making.

Another helpful approach for third- or fourth-grade children who have difficulty focusing on what they read is the Read-Pause-Retell-Reread technique (Robb, 2006) in which the teacher models the approach by reading a section of text, pauses, and then attempts to retell the "gist" of what she read.

The teacher (with possible input from the children) then judges whether the retelling was acceptable. If the retelling does not appear to be adequate, the teacher then rereads and attempts to retell a second time. As necessary, the rereading and retelling take place again. Children then follow the same procedure in pairs. The listener should read the same text as the reader so that he or she can also reflect on the acceptability of the retelling. Two benefits of this approach are that children learn to recognize the power of rereading as a strategy that supports comprehension, and that they also learn to use retelling as a self-monitoring tool to check their own understanding of what they read.

Finally, some specific programs are available for children who have comprehension difficulties. In chapter 4 we mentioned two that are commonly used: Soar to Success and Visualizing and Verbalizing. Often teachers use these programs, which should supplement a balanced literacy program, in small-group settings. We still have much to learn about supporting children who have difficulties in the area of comprehension, though, and interventions in this area often take a substantial amount of time to make a difference. The "fourth-grade slump" has its roots before fourth grade, and its effects often last well beyond fourth grade.

### Summary of Instructional Approaches for Building Reading Comprehension and Reading Response

In this section we discussed some key ingredients for supporting comprehension: explicit teaching and supportive practice. Areas that need attention include developing comprehension strategies, strengthening background knowledge and vocabulary, building understandings of text, and fostering motivation and attention. Several areas of instructional focus were described such as the "Question-Answer Relationship" (or QAR) framework, QuEEC, and the "Character Clues" template. We also emphasized the importance of closely matching comprehension interventions with children's specific areas of need (as identified from assessment and observation).

In addition, we described a few specific instructional techniques and programs that teachers might use with children who have specific areas of need, such as "Read-Pause-Retell-Reread," Soar to Success, and Visualizing and Verbalizing. In the next section we will look at how Willa's performance was assessed and how her Literacy Profile was marked and annotated.

## LOOKING CLOSELY AT ONE CHILD'S ASSESSMENTS FROM STRAND 6 OF THE LITERACY PROFILE

To find out about Willa's comprehension and response to reading, several assessment tools were used. These included a retelling following her record of oral reading (described in chapter 4), a reading-response task, and some informal questions from the teacher. You can see how Willa's progress was recorded and annotated in Figure 6.9.

Willa's comprehension was assessed after she read *Pepper's Adventure*, a short book at level H (Randell, 1995), which is approximately a late-first-grade level. After she read the book orally, the teacher asked her to retell what she had just read, and then the teacher asked Willa a few follow-up questions to see whether she could "fill in" some story elements that she had not included in her retelling. Willa gave a very succinct, but not elaborate, retelling of the key elements of the story, showing that she understood the characters, the problem in the story, and how it ended. When the teacher asked further questions, Willa added additional details that showed her ability to link what she had read with her own background knowledge, and to think beyond what the text clearly stated. Because

FIGURE 6.9  **Willa's Profile for Comprehension and Reading Response**

Note: This figure has been excerpted from the full Literacy Profile chart for illustrative purposes.

| TEACHER TIP: Date, initial, and color code each of your entries. | EMERGENT | EARLY | |
| --- | --- | --- | --- |
| **Strand** *Question & Sample Assessment Tools* | **Late K** | **Early–Mid Grade 1** | **Late Grade 1–Early Grade 2** |
| **6. Comprehension and Reading Response** *How is the child developing an ability to understand text and demonstrate thoughtful responses to text?* **Sample Assessment Tools** · Gates MacGinitie Test · Developmental Reading Assessment · Discussions · Retellings · Journals · Drawings · Observation notes · Performances · Conferences · Constructed Responses | Connects what is read to background knowledge   Begins to retell parts of stories | Communicates basic "gist" of story line through drawings, story maps, or other representations   Identifies main characters of narrative text   Retells the beginning, middle, and end of story   Tells what was learned from informational text | Retelling and responses show developing understanding of story elements: character, problem, and solution   Identifies some key ideas and details after reading informational text   Answers both literal and basic inferential questions in response to text read   *[Her retellings are concise and efficient; Willa gets to the point quickly! She could benefit from instruction in including more detail, and also in responding to inferential questions.] KI* |

Gray areas represent highlighting added by the teacher, preferably using a different color for each year (e.g., yellow highlights for Late K, orange highlights for Early–Mid Grade 1, etc.).
Bracketed material represents teacher/examiner comments from June, Grade 1.

Willa responded only partially to two of the follow-up comprehension questions, the teacher scored this level of text as "instructional." Because Willa clearly understands the structure of narrative text, we highlighted the part of the Literacy Profile that indicates, "Retellings and responses show developing understanding of story elements: character, problem, and solution." We did *not* highlight the section about responding to inferential questions even though we think that Willa may very well have this capacity at this time. Because we did not have current evidence, though, we kept it unhighlighted. Next steps for Willa might be encouraging her to include some additional, elaborating details when she retells, such as the initiating event, or what happened to get the story started. Using a story map or retelling chart with icons (described earlier in this chapter) might be a useful teaching aid to help Willa incorporate more story elements in her retellings.

We used an informational text about "concrete" to observe Willa's development in responding to text. After Willa read the book, the teacher gave her a response sheet (see Figure 6.3) that offered her the opportunity to choose two out of four response options. Willa chose to write two words that she learned, and she also drew a picture of her favorite part. After reading this book, which had concepts that were mostly familiar, Willa was able to find only one word that was new to her: *gravel*. When she made a picture of her favorite part, she drew a picture much like the one on the last page of the book—a dog sitting on a concrete driveway. When the teacher engaged Willa in a brief follow-up conversation, Willa added that she would recommend the book to two of her friends because "both of them are smart about doing stuff." This response reveals that Willa was aware of the (informational) purpose of the text she read and how different readers might view it.

Willa's comprehension and response to reading are both coming along well. With ample opportunities to read and discuss a variety of high-quality texts and further support in producing more elaborated retellings, she should flourish into a thoughtful and engaged reader.

# REFERENCES

Afflerbach, P., Pearson, P. D., & Paris, S. G. ( 2008). Clarifying differences between reading skills and reading strategies. *The Reading Teacher, 61*(5), 364–373.

Barrett, J. (1982). *Cloudy with a chance of meatballs*. New York: Aladdin.

Beaver, J. (2006). *Developmental reading assessment K–3* (2nd ed.). New York: Pearson Learning.

Beaver, J., & Carter, M. (2003). *Developmental reading assessment 4–8*. New York: Pearson Learning.

Biemiller, A. (2003). Vocabulary: Needed if more children are to read well. *Reading Psychology, 24,* 323–335.

Biggam, S. C. (2006). Supporting students in responding to constructed response tasks in reading. *VT Council on Reading Journal, 13*(4), 27–29.

Biggam, S. C., & Thompson, E. A. (2005). The "QT" quick text-level check-in: A practical tool for classroom based reading assessment in the intermediate grades. *New England Reading Association Journal, 41*(1), 35–39.

Blachowicz, C., & Ogle, D. (2001). *Reading comprehension: strategies for independent learners*. New York: The Guilford Press.

Block, C., & Pressley, M. (Eds.). (2001). *Comprehension instruction: Research-based best practices*. New York: Guilford Press.

Brown, V. L., Hammill, D. D., & Wiederholt, J. L. (1995). *Test of reading comprehension* (3rd ed.). Austin, TX: PRO-ED.

Buehl, D. (2001). *Classroom strategies for interactive learning*. Newark, DE: International Reading Association.

Caldwell, J. (2002). *Reading assessment: A primer for teachers and tutors*. New York: The Guilford Press.

Chall, J. S., & Jacobs, V. A. (1990). *The reading crisis: Why poor children fall behind*. Cambridge, MA: Harvard University Press.

Dewitz, P., & Dewitz, P. K. (2003). They can read the words, but they can't understand: Refining comprehension assessment. *The Reading Teacher, 56*(5), 422–435.

Duke, N. K., & Pearson, P. D. (2002). Effective practices for developing reading comprehension. In A. E. Farstrup & S. J. Samuels (Eds.), *What research has to say about reading instruction* (3rd ed., pp. 205–242). Newark, DE: International Reading Association.

Durkin, D. (1980). *Teaching young children to read* (3rd ed.). Boston: Allyn & Bacon.

Freeman, D. (1978). *A pocket for Corduroy*. New York: Viking Juvenile.

Guthrie, J. T., & Ozgungor, S. (2002). Instructional contexts for reading engagement. In C. Block & M. Pressley (Eds.). *Comprehension instruction: Research-based practices*. New York: Guilford Press.

Herber, H. (1978). *Teaching reading in content areas* (2nd ed.). Englewood Cliffs, NJ: Prentice-Hall.

Hirsch, E. (2003, Spring). Reading comprehension requires knowledge—of words and the world. *American Educator*, 10–43.

Holdoway, D. (1980). *Independence in reading: A handbook on individualized procedures*. Gosford, NSW: Ashton Scholastic.

Hoyt, L. (2002). *Make it real: Strategies for success with informational texts*. Portsmouth, NH: Heinemann.

Iowa Test of Basic Skills. (2001). Rolling Meadows, IL: Riverside.

Javernick, E. (2001). *Concrete*. Katonah, NY: RC Owens.

Koslin, B. L., Koslin, S., Zeno, S. M., & Ovens, S. H. (1989). *The degrees of reading power test*. Brewster, NY: Touchstone Applied Science Associates.

Krauss, R. (2004). *The carrot seed*. New York: Harper Trophy.

Leslie, L., & Caldwell, J. (2006). *Qualitative reading assessment* (4th ed.). Boston: Pearson Learning.

Lipson, M. Y. (2007). *Reading beyond the primary grades*. New York: Scholastic.

Lipson, M. Y. (2007). *Teaching reading beyond the primary grades*. New York: Scholastic.

Lipson, M., & Cooper, J. D. (2002). *Current research in reading-language arts: Understanding and supporting comprehension development in the elementary and middle grades*. New York: Houghton Mifflin Co.

Lipson, M., Mosenthal, J., & Mekkelsen, J. (1999). The nature of comprehension among grade 2 children: Variability in retellings as function of development, text and task. In T. Shanahan & F. V. Rodriguez-Brown (Eds.), *Forty-eighth yearbook of the National Reading Conference* (pp. 104–119). Chicago: National Reading Conference.

Lipson, M. Y., & Wixson, K. K. (2003). *Assessment and instruction of reading and writing difficulty*. Boston: Pearson Education.

MacGinitie, W. H., MacGinitie, R. K., Maria, K., & Dreyer, L. G. (2000). *Gates-MacGinitie reading test*. Itasca, IL: Riverside Publishing.

Massey, D. D. (2007). "The Discovery Channel said so" and other barriers to comprehension. *The Reading Teacher, 60*(7), 656–666.

McGinley, W. J., & Denner, P. R. (1987). Story impressions: A prereading/writing activity. *Journal of Reading, 31*, 248–253.

Moss, B. (2003). *Exploring the literature of fact: Children's nonfiction trade books in the elementary classroom*. New York: The Guilford Press.

Moss, B. (2004). Teaching expository text structures through information trade book retellings. *The Reading Teacher, 57*(8), 710–718.

National Reading Panel. (2000). *Teaching children to read: An evidence based assessment of the scientific research literature on reading and its implications for reading instruction*. Rockville, MD: National Institute of Child Health and Human Development.

Ogle, D. M. (1986). K-W-L: A teaching model that develops active reading of expository text. *The Reading Teacher, 39*(6), 564–570.

Palinscar, A. S., & Brown, A. L. (1985). Reciprocal teaching: Activities to promote read(ing) with your mind. In T. L. Harris & E. J. Cooper (Eds.), *Reading, thinking and concept development: Strategies for the classroom*. New York: The College Board.

Pearson, P. D., & Gallagher, M. (1983). The instruction of reading comprehension. *Contemporary Educational Psychology, 8*, 317–344.

Pearson, P. D., & Johnson, D. (1978). *Teaching reading comprehension*. New York: Holt, Rinehart and Winston.

Pressley, M. (2002). *Reading instruction that works: The case for balanced teaching*. New York: The Guilford Press.

Randell, B. (1995). *Pepper's adventures*. Orlando, FL: Rigby, PM Story Books.

Raphael, T. E., Highfield, K., & Au, K. H. (2006). *QAR NOW*. New York: Scholastic.

Ray, K. W. (2004). *About the authors: Writing workshop with our youngest writers*. Portsmouth, NH: Heinemann.

Reutzel, D. R., Camperell, K., & Smith, J. A. (2002). Hitting the wall: Helping struggling readers comprehend. In L. Gambrell, C. C. Block, & M. Pressley (Eds.), *Improving comprehension instruction* (pp. 321–353). San Francisco: Jossey-Bass.

Rigby benchmark assessment kit. (2007). Orlando, FL: Rigby.

Robb, L. (2006). *Teaching reading: A complete resource for grades 4 and up*. New York: Scholastic.

Rylant, C. (1993). *The relatives came*. New York: Aladdin.

Santoro, L. E., Chard, D. J. , Howard, L., & Baker, S. K. (2008). Making the very most of classroom read-alouds to promote comprehension and vocabulary. *The Reading Teacher, 61*(5), 396–408.

Smith, M. C. (Ed.). (1998). *Literacy for the twenty-first century: Research, policy, practices, and the National Adult Literacy Survey*. New York: Praeger.

Snow, C., Burns, P., & Griffin, P. (Eds.). (1998). *Preventing reading difficulties in young children*. Washington, DC: National Academy Press.

Snow, C. E. (2002). *Reading for understanding: Toward an R&D program in reading comprehension.* Santa Monica, CA: Rand.

Stauffer, R. G. (1969). *Directing reading maturity as a cognitive process.* New York: Harper and Row.

Valencia, S. W., & Buly, M. R. (2004). Behind test scores: What struggling readers really need. *The Reading Teacher, 57*(6), 520–531.

Wigfield, A., Eccles, J. S., Yoon, K. S., Harold, R. D., Arbreton, A. J. A., Freedman-Doan, C., & Blumenfeld, P. C. (1997). Change in children's competence beliefs and subjective task values across the elementary school years: A 3 year study. *Journal of Educational Psychology, 89*(3), 451–469.

Wilhelm, J. D. (2001). *Improving comprehension with think-aloud strategies.* New York: Scholastic.

Williams, K. T. (2002). *Group reading assessment and diagnostic evaluation.* Circle Pines, MN: American Guidance Service.

Woodcock, R., Mather, N., & Schrank, F. A. (2004). *Woodcock-Johnson III diagnostic reading battery.* Allen, TX: DLM Teaching Resources.

# CHAPTER SEVEN

# Writing Strategies, Processes, and Dispositions

## CORE QUESTION

To what extent does the child use the processes of writing? How engaged is the child with writing?

"I don't know what to write," declares a third-grade child at the start of writer's workshop. Do these words sound familiar? On the surface, choosing a topic may seem rather straightforward, but when we stop to think about it, we realize that making the leap from thinking to writing is no small feat! Generating topic ideas requires strategic thinking, mentally sorting through a range of possibilities and then settling on one. How do writers go about doing this? In this chapter we will look at the "how" of writing, examining the processes writers use and the strategies that are available to them.

We will also consider how a child's attitude, or disposition, about writing develops. If children have successful and satisfying early writing experiences, they are more apt to feel positively about themselves as writers, thus influencing their growth in writing development (Bandura, 1977; Bottomley, Henk, & Melnick, 1997/1998; Routman, 2005). Later, in chapter 8, we will focus on the quality or effectiveness of children's writing. Chapters 9 and 10 will explore the conventions we use in writing, including spelling, mechanics, grammar, and punctuation.

**LITERACY PROFILE**
Consult your Literacy Profile as you read through this chapter, referring to the question and indicators for Strand 7.

## UNDERLYING PRINCIPLES OF WRITING STRATEGIES, PROCESSES, AND DISPOSITIONS

Many children enter school with some experiential background in writing (Clay, 1991; Ferreiro & Teberosky, 1982; Teale & Sulzby, 1986). Even the youngest children have undoubtedly seen adults, peers, and siblings engage in the act of writing; and probably most have done some of their own "message making" as well. Technology has also brought new forms of writing into children's lives through interactive computer software and the Internet (Leu, 2001). Donald Graves (2003) believes that children naturally want to write, and he implores teachers to give them ample opportunities to do so. If the desire to write is indeed inherent in young children, how can we help nurture and support their positive writing development as they move through the grades?

In the following section, we will first consider the factors that influence children's developing attitudes about writing. Next, we will describe the writing process itself, highlighting the many decisions that writers make as they compose. Keep in mind that writing is one of the language arts and, like any art form, should not be viewed as a lockstep process (Bertrand & Stice, 2002; Graves, 2003). Calkins (1994) reports that although most writers follow the same general "process of craft" (p. 22), they vary widely in their implementation of the various stages. Similar to reading strategies, writing strategies can be viewed as *personalized* thinking tools that writers apply flexibly and variably based on their own styles and the genre of writing they are crafting. As you introduce writing strategies, be sure to honor each child's developing style, sensitively balancing requirements and choices within your writing instruction.

## Writing Dispositions

When a child enters kindergarten, he already has formulated some beliefs about his writing capabilities; in fact, "ninety percent of children come to school believing they can write" (Calkins, 1994, p. 62). Yet Routman states that "as early as first grade, many children already dislike writing" (2005, p. 20). How does this happen? Routman believes that in many cases, "we kill off their writing spirit and energy" through some of our well-intentioned instructional techniques and the additional pressure of high-stakes testing (2005, p. 20). Let's review some of the natural sequences that children experience before they begin formal schooling.

Children learn to write naturally under the same conditions they learn to talk: immersion, demonstration, expectation, responsibility, use, approximation, and response (Cambourne, 1995). Similar to learning to talk and learning to read, learning to write is a gradual, emerging process that begins early in a child's life, with new skills building incrementally in small steps, each discovery making way for new understandings (Clay, 1975; Strickland & Morrow, 1989; Teale & Sulzby, 1986). And writing development, like all language learning, proceeds most positively when children have opportunities to engage in meaningful writing experiences during this emerging and, we hope, lifelong process (Calkins, 1991; Graves, 2003; Routman, 2005).

In their earliest years, children first begin drawing or creating visual representations that delight their families and friends. Eventually children add squiggles, scribbles, or letter-like shapes to their creations, often imitating the writing they have seen in their environments, perhaps not even yet realizing that print is a tool for recording their own thoughts (Clay, 1975; Ferreiro & Teberosky, 1982; Harste, Woodward, & Burke, 1984). For instance, after finishing a paper sprinkled with drawings and letter-like squiggles, a child may ask an adult to read it back to her, thus demonstrating a belief that "print" holds a message, as Marie Clay notes in her book *What Did I Write?* (1975). The responses a child receives from adults during these early writing attempts play an influential role in her developing beliefs about her capability to write, also known as self-efficacy (Bandura, 1977).

Self-efficacy is important because a child's beliefs about her ability to write will influence whether she chooses to write, how much effort she is willing to put forth when she writes, and how persistent she will be when trying to accomplish a written task (Bandura, 1986; Schunk, 1990). Bandura and Schunk identify four factors that influence a writer's growing self-efficacy: (1) Performance (Was I able to accomplish my goals?); (2) Observational comparison (How does my writing compare to others' writing?); (3) Social feedback (What do others think of my writing?); and (4) Physiological states (How do I feel inside when I write?). If most children enter school believing that they are writers, we are off to a good start! Keeping in mind the interplay of the four factors that have influenced and will continue to influence a child's developing self-perception, we want to nurture this positive stance as young writers navigate the increasing complexities of writing.

Writing performance, a factor that influences self-perception, is rather complex. Students' perceived performance is related to a broad range of variables including past successes, required effort, amount of support needed, difficulty of the task, amount of persistence needed to complete the task, and confidence in instructional support (Bottomley et al., 1997/1998). These performance skills are tied to a child's developing ability to write. Writers learn how to write by writing, so children will need many opportunities to write in school, establishing a regular time and place so that children internalize the habits and skills of a writer (Anderson, 2000). The Literacy Profile lists some behaviors that can serve as indicators of a child's unfolding attitude about writing. For instance, developing writers are able to sustain their concentration for longer periods of time as they become more independent and self-reliant. Also, with encouragement, young writers will try out new genres and forms of writing, broadening their repertoire of writing topics.

Developing writers also begin to understand that writing is not all joy. Ultimately, they appreciate that the process requires time, effort, persistence, resilience, and patience in order to bring a piece to a satisfying culmination. Attitude and growth as a writer can be perceived as an interdependent relationship. When children define themselves as writers, their personal engagement during writer's workshops and other integrated writing activities helps them fully experience the instructional opportunities, supporting growth in skill development that in turn fosters stronger identity as writers. In the following sections, we will describe a writing process approach that builds on meaningful, authentic experiences by intentionally re-creating the conditions that are in place when natural language learning occurs, which in turn supports children's growing identities as writers.

## Writing as a Strategic Process

We can examine the writing process through three broad stages: before writing, during writing, and after writing (Turbill & Bean, 2006). "Before writing" represents the time period that lasts from the moment the *idea* of a piece is assigned or generated and continues throughout the entire planning process. The "during writing phase" is the actual construction of the piece and includes the first draft right through the final editing and publishing of the piece. (Publishing can vary widely—from placing a piece on colored paper and hanging it on the wall to typing a piece and making it into a book.) Finally, the "after writing" phase is when the child shares the work with the intended audience. See Figure 7.1 for an excellent visual of the recursive writing process (Ministry of Education, 1992). Be sure to refer back to this circular model often as we describe each phase of writing throughout this chapter. Before turning our attention to separate stages, we must remember not to lose sight of the "bigger picture." Although we conveniently describe writing as a generalized process, keep

FIGURE 7.1  **Recursive Model of Writing Process**

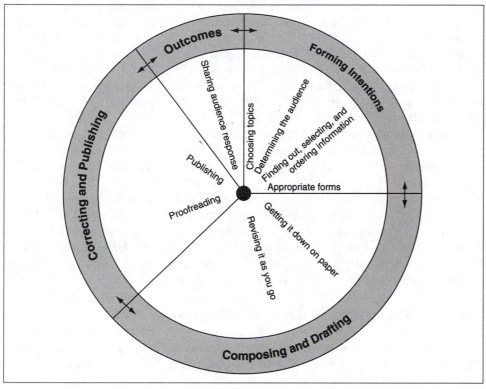

Material from *Dancing with the Pen, the Learner as Writer—Diagram of the "Writing Process"* on p. 23 is reproduced by permission of the publishers Learning Media Limited, PO Box 3293, Wellington, New Zealand. © Crown, 1996.

the following points in mind: (1) writing influences reading and reading influences writing; (2) writing is recursive; (3) writing is not a prescribed set of procedures.

*Writing influences reading and reading influences writing* (Smith, 1988). Children who define themselves as writers begin to read in a different way, acknowledging the craft behind the words or paying attention to the construction of a particular piece knowing that they too are potential users of the technique of written form (Cambourne, 1995; Ray, 1999; Smith, 1988). For instance, a child might seek out and read a short skit if it's the first time he is trying to write a play of his own, "reading like a writer" as he slows down and studies the various text structures and language devices (Smith, 1988, p. 26). When children write, it is helpful if they are immersed in books and text of all kinds and can easily access them as needed (Graves, 2003).

*Writing is recursive* (Emig, 1971; Ministry of Education, 1992; Turnbill & Bean, 2006). Within each of the three broad categories of writing, children generally follow a series of steps,  although not in a linear fashion. The writing process is recursive in nature, meaning that we think and clarify as we write, often moving from one stage to another, forward and backward, as new ideas come to us. Writing often takes knowledge and ideas to a deeper level for the writer, requiring a reworking of sentences or organization, sometimes necessitating more reading or researching for information or structural support. Writers may return to planning, reading, researching, revising, or editing during any stage of the writing process, including the final stage, the publishing stage.

*Writing is not a prescribed set of procedures* (Graves, 2003). Although we can describe the writing process through a general series of steps, each writer has a personal style that guides her or his process (Ray, 1999). Graves describes writing as a "messy" endeavor, reminding us that we cannot predict the length of the intervals from beginning to end of the process (2003, p. xi). The purpose of a writing task also influences a writer's decision-making process. For instance, when using writing as a tool for gathering research information, it is rare to see extensive evidence of writing stages, which is also true of journal writing.

Each writer brings his own set of values, his own background experiences, and his own way of thinking to each task. The amount of time he spends within each stage and the decisions he makes about how to manage the process are personal choices. Richard Sterling, executive director of the National Writing Project, suggests that we help children explore different processes and allow them to discover what works best (Freeman, 2007). In the upcoming sections, we will explore some of the underlying thinking processes that are not always visible as the process unfolds. Although writing is complex, with support and encouragement even the youngest of our students can experience the satisfaction of a finished product.

***Before Writing.***  Preceding the actual act of writing a first draft is usually a period of time known as "forming intentions" or prewriting (Ministry of Education, 1992, p. 24; Turbill & Bean, 2006). Prewriting is when writers ponder ideas, determine audience and purpose, and gather information. This stage also includes planning and organizing ideas based on the preliminary conceptualization of the end product. Donald Murray (1982) refers to prewriting as a rehearsal and suggests that a person should spend a large percentage of her writing time in this stage. Notice in Figure 7.2 the number of steps in the process column for prewriting, and look at all the types of strategies that a person might use during the rehearsal stage.

At the top of the strategy list is "Thinking and pondering." Much of the writing process is internal. As Murray reminds us, children need time to daydream, imagine, and remember; simply put, they need time to think. Continuing down that list of strategies, you'll find various types of talking. When children form intentions for writing, they need time and space for conversation. Britton (1970a) describes oral language as the foundation for writing success with these words: "Writing floats on a sea of talk" (p. 164). But prewriting is not only oral or mental; it can also include some important written work as well. Let's consider the variables that a writer needs to take into account during this "rehearsal" period.

*Topic, Audience, Purpose (TAP).*  Children might begin their writing process by *choosing a topic,* something that interests them or is important to them. Remember at the beginning of this chapter when we mentioned the challenges associated with choosing a topic? Although children must learn how to write when their teacher assigns topics, children also need opportunities to develop the strategies to self-select a topic. Selecting a topic requires some self-reflection—a personal review of priorities, interests, and meaningful events. Nancie Atwell (1987) reminds us that choosing a topic implies a certain level of responsibility for the outcome. No wonder a child may be reluctant to settle on a self-selected topic!

A parallel consideration when forming intentions is designating *the audience,* the eventual receiver (or reader) of the written piece. Again, it is important to remember that there is not one specific sequence for moving

FIGURE 7.2  **Stages, Steps, and Writing Strategies**

| Broad Stage of Writing | Steps of Writing Process | Possible Strategies Used |
|---|---|---|
| Before writing | Selecting a topic<br>Determining audience<br>Identifying purpose<br>Making a plan<br>Sequencing information<br>Choosing a form | Thinking and pondering<br>Remembering past experiences<br>Visualizing<br>Talking and discussing ideas<br>Brainstorming ideas<br>Reading for more information<br>Studying and sharing other writers' processes<br>Observing<br>Drawing<br>Jotting down information<br>Categorizing<br>Charting<br>Creating<br>Expanding ideas<br>Narrowing ideas<br>Evaluating ideas<br>Selecting ideas |
| During writing | Drafting and composing<br>Revising<br>Editing<br>Publishing | Thinking and pondering<br>Searching for language to represent thoughts<br>Choosing the most appropriate words<br>Self-monitoring<br>Adding information<br>Deleting information<br>Restating ideas<br>Expanding ideas<br>Reorganizing ideas<br>Elaborating on ideas<br>Stepping away to gain distance<br>Proofreading for spelling<br>Proofreading for punctuation<br>Rereading aloud to hear intonation<br>Evaluating quality and appropriateness<br>Reading to others for input<br>Listening to feedback<br>Discussing ideas |
| After writing | Sharing | Reading aloud to audience<br>Sending material to audience<br>Reflecting and self-evaluating |

through the steps of writing. Sometimes audience choice precedes identifying a topic. For instance, a child may first decide to write something beautiful for a friend and then determine the topic of the piece. Sometimes, though, a topic is the starting point, and then the child must determine the audience. Suppose a child decides to write about pandas. It will be important for the child to identify who will be reading the end product. Word choice, sentence length, and depth of information are quite different when the intended audience is a preschooler, a fourth-grade peer, or a caretaker at a zoo.

Also central to the prewriting stage is *identifying the purpose* of the writing. This is the "why" of the writing piece. The primary strategy a child uses at this point is self-questioning: Why am I writing this piece? What am I trying to accomplish with these words? Am I writing to inform, to inspire, to entertain, or for some other reason? Purpose is the crux of this stage because it helps the writer gather the necessary tools to achieve the writing's goals. Similar to choosing a topic and determining an audience, setting a purpose for the writing operates as a parallel, but not necessarily sequential, process. For instance, a child can begin with an established purpose and work from there. Consider a fourth grader who wants to inform others about pandas because she knows so much about them and wants to share her knowledge. Because her purpose is to inform, her piece may require some research and clarification of facts. But if the purpose of the piece is to entertain, she might need to review story structure, especially setting, plot, and characterization. But what if her purpose is to alert others that pandas are an endangered species? In that case, she would try to persuade the reader to help save pandas, which would require her to locate specific, factual research to support the argument.

Identifying these three factors (topic, audience, and purpose) is part of the prewriting process. Although a writer may decide on each factor early in the process, he very likely will revisit and change any one of these factors as the process unfolds. Also, each writer's prewriting process may differ greatly. For some writers, prewriting may consist merely of talking to a classmate, reading, or rereading a book (Routman, 2005). Others may put ideas down on paper to plan their written piece.

*Planning.* At some point in the prewriting process, many children prefer to make a written plan. Routman (2005) reminds us that planning can often be a very quick process that involves only a few words or a short list. Kindergarten and Grade 1 children often begin the planning process by making a sketch or a series of sketches. Eventually they begin to add words and labels to the sketches. As writing becomes more complex, written plans can serve as a visual thinking and organizing map. A plan can help the child identify the areas that need more research or allow the child to step back and consider the overall structure of the piece. The written plan can take a variety of forms, including:

- Webbing of ideas
- An outline
- A series a questions
- A chart
- A single sketch or a series of sketches
- A list
- A freewrite, recording thoughts as they come and noticing where they lead without worrying about conventions; also known as a quickwrite (Elbow, 1998)
- Any combination or variation of these techniques, including that the writer simply begins writing to see where the writing takes her (Fletcher, 2007)

Children must make another important decision sometime during the prewriting stage: the genre of writing and the form. Let's review the difference between genre and form. A *genre* is a broad category of literature linked by similar characteristics or features (Galda & Cullinan, 2006). For example, futuristic stories based on scientific possibilities are grouped together into the genre of "science fiction"; realistic stories set in the past are called "historical fiction." The *form* is the structure or organization of the piece (Mooney, 2001), and even within the same genre, the author can choose from a variety of forms. For instance, both science fiction and historical fiction can take the form of a diary, a series of letters, or a story.

Here's an example of what the decision-making process might entail during the planning stage of prewriting. Suppose the fourth grader who selected the topic of pandas did so because she loves pandas. Next she decides that she wants to inform other fourth graders about pandas and also learn more about pandas herself in the process. Her "TAP" (Duncan, 1994; Ministry of Education, 1992) includes the following:

T (topic): pandas

A (audience): classmates and teacher

P (purpose): to tell others all the interesting facts about pandas

Notice that purpose can actually determine genre. In this case, writing to inform narrows the genre to nonfiction; yet the child still hasn't identified the form that her final product will take. Settling on the form is not always necessary at this point in the writing process since form may emerge later based on the type of information that the writer/researcher discovers in the prewriting process. Nonfiction writing can take many different forms. Some possibilities for informing a fourth-grade audience about pandas include a poster presentation, an ABC book about pandas, a nonfiction picture book, a multimedia presentation on the computer, or a written report with illustrations. Selecting a form will narrow the author's planning to an appropriate organizational structure based on the eventual product.

*Planning Conferences.* Some teachers require children to check in with an adult or a peer support group after they have created a written plan. In kindergarten or early Grade 1, this "conference" might be a brief chat with either a teacher or a peer about a sketch or series of pictures to provide some additional support, essentially offering a short oral rehearsal before children begin writing. Graves (2003) describes conferences as an opportunity for teachers to listen to what children have to say, intelligently reacting as the writer takes the lead. Calkins (1994) describes three roles of a teacher during a conference: researching (simply listening to the student writer); deciding (determining what part of the process to focus on); and teaching (guiding the child toward self-reflection and independence by helping the child identify ways to strengthen the piece). Some interactions that might take place during planning conferences include:

- Orally rehearsing the language and vocabulary that the genre requires
- Clarifying through guiding questions, helping the child consider the eventual reader of the piece
- Identifying the text features expected in the chosen genre of the material
- Ordering and reorganizing the ideas through a numbering or sequencing system
- Determining ways to expand the child's ideas through reading or research (Ministry of Education, 1992).

Children enjoy talking about their writing plans, and these short conferences can help them bring clarity to their work. You'll find that student writers are much less resistant to structural revisions during this stage, as they have not yet invested a lot of time into composing.

**During Writing.** After a child has formed an intention and made a plan, it is time for her to compose. In this phase, children complete four specific actions: drafting, revising, editing/proofreading, and publishing (Turbill & Bean, 2006).

*Drafting.* Because the child "incubated" many of the ideas and structures for the piece of writing during the prewriting period, all of her focus can now go toward choosing the best words to carry out the goals of the selected topic (Britton, 1970b). Her voice and style will unfold as she attempts to construct meaningful passages, writing with a consciousness of the intended audience. Although writers are encouraged to compose first drafts without being too concerned about details such as spelling and grammar, it makes sense to persuade even beginning writers to use what they know about writing and to keep in mind that the writing is for someone else to read. Even though the emphasis is on the creation of meaning, you should expect to see improvement in spellings and conventions over time during first-draft writings as these conventions become more and more automatic (Graves, 1994).

Beginning writers often find themselves in situations where neither they nor anyone else can read their draft. To alleviate this problem, kindergarten and first-grade teachers often move through the classroom during independent writing sessions and briefly confer with each child. If the child's writing would not be decipherable at a later time, the teacher might note the conventional spelling of words above (or below) the child's approximations to "hold" the stories for later publishing; other teachers might choose to write the intended message in a corner of the page (Calkins, 1994; Machado, 2003).

During the drafting stage, children need time and space to work independently without interruption unless they need assistance. The focus at this stage is on the craft, the careful choice of words and inventive use of language that will best satisfy the purpose and address the specific audience.

*Revising.* The act of revising involves going back to consider an idea again, perhaps changing a word or sentence to make it clearer or stronger, reorganizing information, or even deleting words or portions of text. Also described as "reseeing" (Graves, 1994, p. 160), revising requires a child to be able to listen carefully to his own words through the lens of a reader (Calkins, 1994). Through his writing research, Graves (1994) has identified a "rough" developmental revision sequence that children often follow:

1. Adding to the ending
2. Pointing out within the writing where to place other events, in the order in which they occurred
3. Inserting new information
4. Identifying the main idea within text that leads up to and then follows the important part of the story—stories that are often called "morning to night" or "bed to bed" (p. 233)
5. Understanding that first drafts are flexible starting points, not ending points

Gradually children discover that revision can also include deleting words, sentences, or even paragraphs to make their writing more succinct. Revision can even mean going back to the original plan and rethinking the entire structure of the piece, possibly changing it far into the composing process, which might occur if a particular form is not working or the voices of the characters seem ineffective. For instance, in the case of the panda story, the fourth grader may decide that an ABC book is too cumbersome and go back to writing a nonfiction picture book with labels, illustrations, and drawings to support the text. Or a child might change the third-person point of view (*she*) to first person (*I*) if he decides to have the main character rather than an outsider tell the story. Drafting and revising go hand in hand as a child moves back and forth among these processes, but learning the art of revision takes time and scaffolded practice.

Look back at Figure 7.2 and read through the list of strategies a child might use during this stage. As you read through this section, try to think of other strategies you might add.

Many teachers incorporate a second conference into the writing process during this stage to make the revision process visible and supportive. Lucy Calkins (1994) describes conferring to be at the heart of writing because children learn to take the lead in their own writing by requesting input from teachers and peers with a primary focus on meaning. At a revision conference, a child presents his writing to a sample audience before he moves through the remainder of the process. Some children prefer to receive feedback after working on a small piece of the whole project; others wait until they've completed the first draft. During a revision conference, which can be a one-to-one interaction or a small-group gathering, the child usually reads a portion of the piece aloud and then requests a response. It is important to begin any response session with a validation of the child's intention and also an identification of something positive about the piece (Routman, 2005). Besides offering direct support to the writer, revision conferences also have indirect benefits. Graves believes that when children listen to the writing of others, remember what the other children read, and then participate through active questioning, they learn how to listen to their own writing better and eventually internalize the revision process (1994).

For the emergent and early writer, revision might occur as the teacher walks through the classroom and confers briefly with each child. A simple question from the teacher might suggest that the child could add more to his story: "What else did you do? Can you add that?" It's often the case that the child will answer "no" to this question, though, because young writers are often perfectly pleased with what they have created. A child's unwillingness to revise might indicate the developmental stage of the child, possible issues with the child's motor skills, or the child's lack of familiarity with the process, topic, or genre (Graves, 1994). Eventually, with frequent opportunities to write and immersion in a supported writing community that fosters meaningful writing, you will see signs that a child is beginning to incorporate revisions into the drafting stage, thinking about what a reader may still want to know, and independently adding clarity and depth to her writing.

*Editing and Proofreading.* After the composition and revision stages are completed to the writer's satisfaction, it is time for her to pay particular attention to conventions of written language. This stage of writing is really about audience courtesy and ensuring that someone else will be able to read and understand the piece without confusion from the surface features of the written text (Ministry of Education, 1992). Children must learn to attend to the details of capitalization, punctuation, and language use, which for young writers is often a tall order.

Children can learn proofreading and editing in incremental steps that are based on the developmental level of each child. You will want to help children manage spelling, mechanics, grammar, and handwriting in ways that are not overwhelming but always moving toward more conventional levels. An editing conference can be a short, succinct session that is designed to support a child's growing awareness of the various conventions of our written language. Graves reminds us not to "overteach" during the brief sessions, but rather to focus on only one teaching point (1994). Because we want children to consider their audience, even early writers can begin to develop strategies such as rereading for accurate placement of punctuation so that reader knows when to stop. Other strategies at this stage may include checking resources for spelling accuracy.

After a child has completed the proofreading process, you will need to decide how to manage the next stage of writing. Some teachers treat the final editing process much like it is in the publishing world, with the teacher serving as the copy editor. The underlying message of this technique is that writing must meet certain standards if it will be distributed to the intended audience. In other classrooms, teachers may choose to keep the child's final edited version of a draft and allow her to polish the finished work as her skill level permits. In either case, this is a wonderful opportunity to assess a child's independent proofreading skills. We will describe editing more thoroughly in chapters 8 and 10.

*Publishing.* Once the proofreading process is completed, the preparation shifts to sharing or presenting (Ministry of Education, 1992). Again, the child has many decisions to make such as:

- How will this writing be printed?
- Will it be typed or handwritten? If typed, what style and size of font will I use?
- How will I orient the paper, as a landscape or portrait?
- What size paper will I use?
- Should I use photographs, collage, drawings, paintings, or some combination?
- How will I lay out the text and supporting illustrations?
- Will I use a border or bubble letters for the cover page?

As you can see, there are many decisions to make even after the actual writing has been completed. After all of the child's hard work in planning, composing, revising, and editing, this final stage can be extremely fulfilling as the child prepares the product for the intended audience.

In many early primary classrooms, teachers frequently use a "quick publish" routine in which children select ready-made booklets that will hold their stories. (You can prepare many sizes and shapes in advance by stapling a construction paper cover to precut pages.) After a child has completed her rough draft, she rereads it to the teacher, the teacher prints the child's language onto the empty pages, and presto, the child is ready for the illustration phase.

***After Writing.*** After a child has taken a topic from an idea to a finished product, it's time for him or her to share the written piece with an audience (Ministry of Education, 1992; Turbill & Bean, 2006). This is the moment that helps a beginning writer discover the power of the written form. One effective sharing technique is an author's circle in which the author sits in a special sharing chair and reads the completed work to the class. After he or she reads each page, the author pauses and turns the book toward the audience, showing them the accompanying illustrations. The class listens carefully and comments on things they really liked as listeners and viewers.

Often a teacher will model appropriate comments by also raising her hand to give genuine responses. Authors politely call on several audience members to hear their reactions. Responses can range from content to delivery such as, "I really like the way your illustrations added more details to your story," "I like the way you used dialogue to make your characters talk," and "I like the way you read your story out loud with a clear voice." Sometimes children will make a connection to the text and say, "Your story reminded me of a time when that also happened to me." Since the book is already finished, this is not the time for classmates to make recommendations.

Once the child has shared the piece publicly, it can be placed in the classroom library for interested classmates to reread. Writing can be shared in numerous ways relating to the planning stage when the writer identified the audience. A few examples of ways to share include placing the piece in a class book, reading it to a parent, posting it on a class bulletin board, or mailing it to the intended recipient.

Besides the author's circle, children receive feedback in other ways as well. They receive feedback when they see other children reading their texts or when they become known as the resident panda expert. Sometimes students who send letters receive authentic responses from pen pals, published authors, and sometimes even the President of the United States!

In the end, it is the child who determines whether or not the writing process went well and achieved the intended goal. Teachers need to build time for self-reflection into children's writing programs through brief conversations with an adult or through reflection sheets that are placed in writing portfolios or notebooks. When children define themselves as writers and are able to observe their own growth over time, writing engagement becomes quite evident.

## Summary of Writing Process and Engagement

Reading and writing development are closely linked, each one supporting the development of the other. We can help our student writers develop a wide array of strategies by exposing them to a range of genres and forms as they learn to "read like writers" and, conversely, write with an eventual reader in mind (Smith, 1988, 1994). Through frequent, meaningful, and supported writing experiences, teachers can guide children toward forming the habits and attitudes of a writer, moving naturally through the writing process, not because it's required, but because it makes sense. We will also want to attend to our developing writers' dispositions because children need perseverance, commitment, and confidence to follow a piece of writing through to completion.

# ASSESSING DEVELOPMENT OF WRITING STRATEGIES, PROCESSES, AND DISPOSITIONS

An effective way to track children's development of strategies throughout the writing process is by noticing them in the act of writing during a variety of experiences and situations. A teacher can monitor a child's developing attitude about writing not only during writing periods but also throughout the school day. It is also useful to examine the written products at each stage of the writing process—including the plans, the drafts, the revisions, and the proofreading—to monitor the child's increasing use of strategic processes.

## Formal or Published Measures for Assessing Writing Strategies, Processes, and Dispositions

One standardized writing survey that measures children's attitudes about writing is the Writing Attitude Survey (Kear, Coffman, McKenna, & Ambrosio, 2000). This 28-item survey can be read to younger children and administered to a whole class or an individual child. Similar to the Reading Attitude Survey mentioned in chapter 4, a child answers each question by circling one of four pictures of Garfield, the cartoon cat, displaying an emotion ranging from very happy to very upset. The teacher can use the results as a before and after measure of a child's attitude about writing, and the teacher can use the results to help plan instruction.

Another tool that measures a child's self-efficacy is the Writer Self-Perception Scale (Bottomley et al., 1997/1998), which was designed for

For a copy of the survey, see Kear, D. K., Coffman, G. A., McKenna, M. G., & Ambrosio, A. L. (2000). "Measuring Attitude Toward Writing: A New Tool for Teachers." *The Reading Teacher, 54*, 10–23.

This survey is available by locating the article "Assessing Children's Views about Themselves as Writers Using the Writer Self-Perception Scale" by Bottomley, D. M., Henk, W. A., & Melnick, S. A. (1997/1998). *Reading Teacher, 51,*(4), 286–297.

children in Grades 4 through 6 and can be administered in a whole-class, small-group, or individualized format. The Writer Self-Perception Scale is comprised of 38 sentences that children respond to on a scale ranging from "strongly agree" to "strongly disagree." It is structured around the factors of self-efficacy described earlier in this chapter. The authors state that the results are an "estimate of how children feel about themselves as writers" (p. 286).

Most formal writing assessments are constructed to measure children's writing effectiveness rather than their ability to use strategies within the stages of the writing process or their attitude about writing. Although some tests do look for evidence that a writer has followed the steps of the writing process, the results are usually embedded within the overall evaluation of the final product. We will describe these instruments in chapter 8.

## Informal Measures for Assessing Writing Strategies, Processes, and Dispositions

Lucy Calkins suggests that informed teaching decisions depend on teachers' abilities to "read the room, to read our students' ambitions and intentions and fears and strengths and habits of thought" (1994, p. 314). Informal assessments can help us begin to know our students as writers. These assessments might include (but are not limited to) anecdotal notes from our conversations with children, notes from focused observations during writer's workshops, and a systematic way to collect children's writing and interpret the strategies that children are using within a range of genres and forms.

In the beginning of the year, it is useful to conduct informal interviews, which allows teachers to have some individual time with each child (Atwell, 1987). Besides establishing a caring rapport, this short interaction can supply an abundance of information about the child's past experiences with writing, the child's interests (for possible writing topics), and the child's feelings about writing. See Appendix A-21 for a sample writing interview. Some teachers write letters to parents early in the year, either inviting them to respond to a survey about their child's writing habits or asking them to write a letter describing their child's interest in literacy (Calkins, 1991, 1994). Behind each of these actions is the desire to understand previous writing experiences that may have contributed to the child's self-efficacy.

Anecdotal record keeping can also help you discover a child's attitude about writing by noting behaviors that reveal a level of engagement with writing (Graves, 2003). For instance, you might note that with a prompt, one first-grade child is willing to add onto her weekend story, whereas another child might respond to a similar prompt by saying, "I don't want to." If you record this information systematically, you will be able to notice when a child begins to add information; this should allow you to recognize the student's growth in using revising as a tool. For the child who independently begins to add more information at the end of the story, you might encourage revision by teaching him how to add an insertion earlier in the story, a "next step" in the developmental revision process (Graves, 1994).

A teacher can also use anecdotal records to systematically focus on specific strategy use that he introduced during a whole-class session. For instance, the teacher can note each child's ability to generate new topics independently if this is a strategy he introduced and is now monitoring. He will also want to keep track of the topics and forms of writing that a child has attempted, which he can do through a simple record-keeping

## FIGURE 7.3  Sample Record of Claire's Writing

| Date | Topic | Genre | Form |
|------|-------|-------|------|
| 4 / 11 | Pandas | Nonfiction | Poster |
| 5 / 03 | Birthday present | Functional writing | Thank you letter |
| 5 / 05 | Vacation memories | Poetry | Free verse |
| 6 / 01 | Taking care of my dog, Sprout | Informational/procedural | Manual |

instrument such as the one shown in Figure 7.3. Many school systems use their state's curriculum frameworks to assign specific genres and forms to different grade levels, thoughtfully broadening developing writers' awareness and competence across a range of types of writing in a supported manner. You might also want to track your students' progress using a whole-class record-keeping system that is also known as "status of the class" to identify what stage of writing children are in over a sequential period of time; see Figure 7.4 (Graves, 2003). Careful record keeping can alert you to whole-class and individual children's needs. For example, you might notice that some third- and fourth-grade students are writing only fantasy or that they are "stuck" in the drafting stage, with little evidence of revision.

## FIGURE 7.4  Sample "Status of the Class" Chart for Writing

| Names of Students | Monday 2/3 | Tuesday 2/4 | Wednesday 2/5 | Thursday 2/6 | Friday 2/7 |
|-------------------|------------|-------------|---------------|--------------|------------|
| Annie T: broken ankle | Revising | Revising | Revising | Proofreading | |
| Bonnie T: princess story | Planning | Planning | Absent | Planning | |
| Chase T: letter to pen pal | Drafting | Drafting | Drafting | Drafting | |
| Claire T: Sprout, her dog | Publishing | Publishing | Planning | Drafting | |
| Craig T: land of gnomes | Drafting | Revising | Revising | Revising | |
| David T: favorite cars | Planning | Drafting | Drafting | Revising | |
| Kyle T: snowboarding | Absent | Drafting | Drafting | Revising | |

*Note:* You can also use an abbreviated system for keeping track by assigning letters or numbers to the various stages or steps.

Portfolios are authentic assessment tools that can provide a record of a child's writing history (Calkins, 1994). Portfolios can take many forms, ranging from a simple file of writing samples from various time periods or in various genres to a sophisticated organization of children's work that includes work samples, teacher evaluation notes, and children's self-reflections (Winograd, Flores-Dueñas, & Arrington, 2003). Portfolios can "follow the child" through the grades and document various benchmark skills and processes the child learns, providing opportunities for both the child and the teacher to examine writing development over time. In many cases the portfolio includes a copy of the final piece as well as earlier drafts and evidence of brainstorming, mapping, and other forms of planning. This is especially important if the finished product includes final editing by the teacher and thus does not reflect the child's independent skills in editing and proofreading.

For younger children, a portfolio might simply contain the draft writing notebook and a list of "published" topics, but with guided support from teachers, even Grade 1 children can learn to self-select their own "best pieces" based on criteria the class generates to evaluate successful writing (Winograd et al., 2003). When a portfolio includes pieces that children select themselves and their self-reflections, children are encouraged to monitor their own growth by identifying the specific criteria they use to judge the success of a piece of writing. See Appendix A-22 for a sample self-evaluation checklist that focuses primarily on the process of writing. Children can also reflect on their topic choices, the variety of writing forms they are using, and their overall writing progress. See chapter 8 for discussion about portfolio development that focuses on writing effectiveness.

### Summary of Assessment Tools for the Development of Writing Strategies, Processes, and Dispositions

A teacher can assess a child's strategy use and independent control over the steps of the writing process using a variety of informal methods. Many teachers use a combination of focused observations during children's implementation of the writing curriculum and collections of children's writing to document a child's growing control over the writing process. Students can also participate in the assessment process through compiling portfolios and using self-reflection tools that specifically identify criteria to help evaluate growth. Some dispositional surveys have been standardized to measure the growing attitudes of young writers, but interviews, self-evaluation forms, and parent input can also be very informative.

## INSTRUCTIONAL APPROACHES FOR TEACHING WRITING STRATEGIES, PROCESSES, AND DISPOSITIONS

Key to successful writing instruction is fostering student engagement (Cambourne, 1995). In school, children need to write often, but they also need to be personally invested in the process. When writing instruction occurs across the disciplines and is coupled with a writing workshop approach, children begin to understand that:

- Writing has utility for many life functions.
- Writing can assist in the learning process.
- Writing can enhance the quality of life (Bertrand & Stice, 2002; Calkins, 1994, 1991; Graves, 1994).

Writing research has led educators to seek a balance between teaching children how to use the writing process, teaching children the strategies to use during various stages of the process, and teaching children the skills they need to create a successful piece of writing (Tompkins, 2008). In this section, we will examine ways to design a writer's workshop that focuses on process and strategies while also considering children's engagement and their developing self-efficacy. Next we will turn our attention to ways we can support children who have difficulty developing effective writing strategies or who dislike or avoid writing.

## Instructional Approaches for Building Writing Strategies, Processes, and Dispositions in All Students

Early in the school year, it is important to create a safe and supportive writer's community so that children can try out various strategies as they refine their writing skills (Bertrand & Stice, 2002). Many teachers implement a writing workshop that supports children at all levels of writing development in a collaborative rather than an evaluative atmosphere. A writer's workshop can offer time and space for authentic writing with built-in levels of and support for children as they learn to manage the stages of the writing process. Within a writer's workshop, teachers incorporate a variety of explicit and implicit teaching approaches that include whole-class mini-lessons, read-alouds, writing demonstrations, small-group lessons, and individualized focused instruction. After describing ways to develop a writer's community, we will use Margaret Mooney's (1990) reading model of To, With, and By as a framework to differentiate some key components of writing instruction: *To* (modeled writing), *With* (shared or guided writing), and *By* (independent writing).

***Creating a Writer's Community.***  Open, guided discussions can help launch a yearlong exploration into the process and purposes of writing. Some discussion starters might include:

- What is writing?
- Why do we write?
- For whom do we write?
- When do we write?
- What kinds of writing exist?

Children must learn not only to value the importance of writing but also to discover their own writing potential and believe that they have something worth writing about. You can support the development of a writer's community by carefully crafting discussions and lessons about strategic writing. Useful investigations can include:

- Journaling as a way to generate topics
- Exploring the processes of various writers
- Exploring and trying out various genres and forms
- Using graphic organizers to help plan a piece of writing
- Reading like a writer

*Journaling to Generate Topics.*  In *The Art of Teaching Writing,* Lucy Calkins (1994) passionately describes how writing serves as a tool to help her view life more deeply. She encourages teachers to help children look at their own lives as sources for writing topics. Through her work with Donald Murray and, later, with teachers and children, she contends, "Writing does not begin with deskwork but with lifework" (p. 3).

Diaries, writer's notebooks, and writer's journals can provide rich sources of material to closely examine things that matter in our lives (Buckner, 2005;

Calkins, 1991; Fletcher, 1996). In *Living Between the Lines* (1991), Calkins and Harwayne describe how the use of writer's notebooks can transform the quality of writing for teachers and students by teaching them to pay closer attention to their lives. Journals can be simple composition books that teachers and children personalize by including words, phrases, paragraphs, or freewrites. Journals can also be used for sketching ideas or taping in special remembrances such as ticket stubs and fortunes from cookies. If teachers stress the value of a journal in their own lives, children are more likely to keep journals as springboards for writing.

*Exploring the Processes of Various Writers.* By having children study the processes of other writers, we can help them discover how seasoned writers continually mull over potential topics (Calkins, 1994; Ray, 1999). Authors describe many sources of writing topics, including newspaper articles, radio stories, personal stories, and sometimes an overheard conversation. At a children's literature conference for teachers, one famous author described pulling off the road when she was driving in order to jot down a catchy phrase she had heard on a radio ad. Others have shared times when they've scribbled a word or a phrase on napkins or other handy objects in order to "preserve" the possibility for further consideration. When writers share secrets about their own writing processes, they help young writers understand that there is more than one way to successfully compose and publish a piece of writing.

*Exploring and Trying Out Various Genres and Forms.* Children must learn how to write within a variety of genres and use a variety of forms. When we read to children from a broad range of written genres, we help them expand their possibilities for selecting topics, genres, and forms and identifying purposes for writing. Reading aloud provides opportunities to bring attention to the construction of the writing behind the story or text (Ray, 1999; Smith, 1988). But conversations, journals, and read-alouds might not be enough to nudge a child toward trying out different types of writing. Sometimes teachers need to direct children to try out a new form of writing and not give them a choice.

Also, students need to learn how to respond to an assigned topic for academic and testing purposes. Routman (2005) calls this type of writing *demand writing* and recommends that, beginning in second grade, teachers offer some practice sessions throughout the year. Besides the development of a high-quality writing program across the curriculum, she encourages teachers to use focused freewrites, which are simply 5- to 10-minute writing periods when children are required to respond to a prompt provided by the teacher. Clearly, when children have internalized a writing process that makes sense to them, they will be better equipped to respond to external assignments and prompts.

*Using Graphic Organizers to Help Structure Planning.* The use of organizing structures such as Venn diagrams and "T charts" can clarify prewriting stages, both to record while gathering information and to organize for presenting information. Together, teachers and children can also use graphic organizers to deconstruct a piece of writing, examining its underlying structure. Later, using the knowledge of the structure or form of writing, a child may be able to construct a plan within the same genre of writing.

*Reading Like a Writer.* Although we initially want children to respond to reading by focusing on the author's message, we can also teach children to examine text construction through the eyes of a writer. Katie Wood Ray (2004), author of *About the Authors*, describes how to help children look closely at authors' craft.

See Richard C. Owen Publishers for a series of books called *Meet the Author*. The collection contains 35 autobiographies written for children by popular children's authors. Most of the authors describe their own writing process and include photographs of their writing studios and materials.

Initially, the teacher helps children identify an aspect of craft that the author intentionally used (e.g., repeating the words "fortunately" and "unfortunately"), and then they think about why the author used that technique. Next children name the technique, and then they "envision" how they might use a similar technique in their own writing. Beck, McKeown, Hamilton, & Kucan (1997) designed a technique known as "Questioning the Author" in which children are encouraged to think about why writers made the various decisions they did as they constructed their text. When teachers bring attention to the writing aspect during reading lessons, children can begin to think about using some of these same techniques in their own writing as they think about who will be reading their writing.

### Writing Demonstrations: Writing "to" Children.

The work of Lucy Calkins (1986) and Donald Graves (1994) highlights how important it is for teachers to identify themselves as writers in order to fully appreciate the process of writing. Their work concurs with the Conditions for Learning model described in the Introduction of this book (Cambourne, 1995). Children need to be immersed in all kinds of writing forms and genres; they also benefit when the teacher demonstrates the writing process by actually moving through the steps of writing. If the first two conditions, immersion and demonstration, are in place within a classroom community, the writing process becomes demystified, and children can then appreciate the labor that is behind polished written products.

Modeled writing begins with the teacher "thinking aloud" at the prewriting stage. You can begin this process by developing a topic list in front of the children: "Let's see, what are some of the things I would like to write about? What are some of the things I need to write about?" As children observe your pondering, decision-making, and recording methods, invite them to begin thinking about the creation of their own topic lists. You can use a large easel pad or an overhead projector to list your ideas, which will help all children feel connected to the process, much like reading a "big book." There is no one recipe for modeling the writing process. The important consideration is to describe your thinking as you move through the steps while holding the children's interest and engagement intact.

Routman (2005) reminds us to adjust our teacher demonstrations to the developmental ages of the children and to model what is within the children's zone of proximal development in both length of writing and topic choices. For instance, when working with kindergarten or early Grade 1 children, your demonstrations might include a one-picture sketch for the plan and then a few sentences for the writing. The following day, you can reread the story and show the children how you will prepare the final copy for your audience. Eventually you can add other steps of the process, such as revising by adding on and rewording some sentences to increase clarity.

When working with older children, the demonstration part may take several writing sessions. After selecting a topic and narrowing it down, you can "think out loud" about the audience and purpose. Some teachers begin by recording the "TAP" on an easel to visually keep the thinking steps in mind and then continue on to some form of planning. The next day, the process continues by first revisiting the previous day's work and then continuing through the entire writing process in front of the children until the piece of writing is completed. The children thus witness the teacher's full writing process, from how a writer begins a new project and all the way up to the completed piece. No amount of teacher demonstration will be helpful, though, unless children are engaged in the process. Listed below are some helpful suggestions to consider.

Teachers can also use a word processor with a projected screen so that children can see the writing process unfold through technological processes. The teacher should remain in close proximity to the children, always able to keep their level of engagement in view.

1. Setting a timer for a 7- to 10-minute demonstration helps even the "squirmiest" children understand that they will not be kept "on the rug" indefinitely.
2. When you move through the steps of the process the first time, you can write each specific step on a large classroom chart for display. This way, the children have a visual way to identify the steps as they mentally rehearse their own process (Tomkins & Zurnwalt, 2005).
3. Make the "think-aloud" part genuine, demonstrating the actual decision making and mental pondering that makes up the thinking process. If you occasionally invite children to give suggestions, you will also be modeling when it is useful for writers to talk to others for support.
4. Be sure also to model the publication process to help children appreciate the number of decisions that are made at this stage of writing.
5. When the timer reminds you to end your demonstration, invite the children to share what they noticed. Ask them to name something that you did as a writer—doing so might help them as they write. This reflection session reminds children that by engaging in the demonstration process, they become potential "doers" of this process (Cambourne, 1995).

***Writing "with" Children.***    Three different instructional approaches for writing "with" children involve varying levels of adult support. You can choose shared writing, interactive writing, and guided writing, depending on the needs of your students.

*Shared Writing.*    Shared writing involves the teacher doing the writing while the children help construct the piece by providing ideas and words. Shared writing can take place in whole-group, small-group, or one-on-one settings and can also involve any subject area throughout the school day. For instance, shared writing could result in the creation of a class book modeled after a read-aloud, or it could be done during content studies such as a K-W-L chart. Shared writing could also take the form a group letter written to thank a guest speaker or a list of classroom rules that everyone agrees to follow. Many opportunities warrant these "class collaborations" (Tompkins, 2008, p. 41).

Let's explore the creation of a class book through a shared writing approach. In Mem Fox's book *Tough Boris*, the author introduces the main character on page 1 in simple language: "Once upon a time, there was a pirate named Boris Van der Borch." Beginning on page 2, the lines in the story repeat over and over, adding descriptions. "He was_____. All pirates are_____." After reading the story of *Tough Boris*, you might lead the class through the publication of their own book using this format, recording the children's words as they offer their ideas.

Near Thanksgiving, one kindergarten class wrote a story about a female superhero turkey. "Once upon a time there was a turkey named Super Turkey von der Borch." The class collectively contributed ideas for describing the character traits of the turkey as the teacher recorded the story. One example was, "She was strong. All superhero turkeys are strong." The teacher helped the children create a twist at the end in which the turkey fled to a vegetarian farm for Thanksgiving dinner. That evening, the teacher typed the story, and the next day the children each received a page to illustrate. The finished publication was placed in the classroom library, and the children read it again and again over the course of the year, immersing the children in the repetitive story structure that had a twist at the end.

During content studies, teachers frequently record children's thinking on a K-W-L chart, which is a form of shared writing. K stands for "What we think we know," W stands for "What we want to know," and L stands for "What we learned" (Ogle, 1986).

The Language Experience Approach (LEA) is another form of shared writing (Ashton-Warner, 1965; Stauffer, 1970; Van Allen, 1976). Although it was initially developed to support beginning reading, it reinforces all of the language processes: speaking, listening, reading, and writing. The LEA is based on the belief that a child is more likely to be able to read materials that she composes from her own experiences than those others have written. This approach can be used individually, in small groups, or as a whole-class experience. In LEA, the teacher records the children's experiences as they report them. For instance, after a field trip, you could record each child's special memory about the trip on separate pages and then distribute each page to the eager illustrators in your class. Within a short period of time, the book will be published and available for children to read and reread in the classroom library.

Shared writing has many benefits for children, but the most important is that they actually experience all of the steps of the writing process in a non-threatening, "apprenticeship" format. The process of creating and then reading and rereading class books reinforces all aspects of the language arts. It also ensures full class engagement.

*Interactive Writing.* Interactive writing is a form of writing in which children "share the pen" with the teacher (Button, Johnson, & Furgerson, 1996; McCarrier, Pinnell, & Fountas, 2000). Teachers frequently use this model of writing to support the development of phonics (from sound to letter), spelling of sight words, and the mechanics of writing. For instance, early in the school year, when kindergarten children arrive at school, the teacher may have a prewritten message on the whiteboard that looks like this: "Good _orning. Today is _onday. We have _usic today." After the children are assembled for the morning messages, they can help decide which letters represent the missing sounds. With support, one child then goes to the whiteboard and writes the missing letter. The interactive writing can become increasingly more varied and use longer words, full sentences, and punctuation symbols as appropriate. You can provide the children with individual whiteboards or clipboards so that everyone else can attempt to write the text as an individual child fills in the large chart paper (Tompkins, 2008). You can also effectively use this model in small-group formats that are geared to the individual needs of the learners.

*Guided Writing.* Guided writing allows children to take more control of the actual composition process while the teacher still provides needed support. The children do their own writing, but like guided reading, the teacher provides a "safety net" as the children venture into new territory. The supports can include a structured sentence format or guided discussions as needed during various stages of the process. For instance, at the kindergarten level, such as in the turkey story mentioned in the shared writing section, the teacher could take a guided approach and invite children to use a predeveloped structure to write their own creative lines. "She was _____. All superhero turkeys are _____." The beginning and ending of the story could still be done as a shared approach, with the teacher doing the writing and varying the level of support based on the children's developmental needs.

Guided writing frequently occurs in small-group settings as well. Teachers meet with a group of children who need more guidance; however, each child composes her own work. For example, if the children are learning how to write a plan for a beginning, middle, and end of a personal memoir, you can help each member of the small group identify an individual TAP through a small-group discussion. After the children talk together, share their intentions, and record their individual TAP, you can then structure the planning process, which could include a predeveloped graphic organizer such as a simple story mapping device or a self-designed graphic organizer such as a series of three boxes that encourage the planning of beginning, middle, and end. The teacher remains with the group as each child sketches out a plan and then discusses his ideas. (It is important to remember that when writers begin the process, they do not always know how a written piece will end. Thus the third box can simply have a question mark space holder for when the idea comes.)

Once the children have had this guidance at the planning stage, including the oral rehearsal, you could leave the small group and let the children develop the beginning of their story, referring back to their written plan as they write. Group members can support each other as they write, and with short "check-ins," you can determine how much more support each child will need as the composition process continues.

Writing "with" children refers to both the teacher's role and the children's role, with the level of support varying among the approaches of shared, interactive, and guided writing based on the learners' specific needs. The goal is to *gradually release the responsibility* to the children as they are able to increasingly manage each new phase of writing (Pearson & Gallagher, 1983).

***Writing "by" Children.*** The primary goal of a writing program is to create competent, independent writers; this means that children need time to write independently and try out their developing strategies and skills. A writer's workshop is designed to include ample time and space for independent practice. A writer's community works best when the Conditions for Learning are in place:

- *Expectation:* Children know that there is an expectation that they will write every day.
- *Responsibility:* Even though there will be some assigned topics, children have some choice in what topics they will write about, and they have decision-making power in the revision process.
- *Use:* Children are given time to write every day.
- *Approximation:* Children are encouraged to try out new strategies, processes, and forms and don't need to fear failure or criticism.
- *Response:* Children are given appropriate responses throughout the writing process so that they can continue to develop their product with confidence and assurance. Their eventual audience provides the most meaningful response when they receive the writing (Camborne, 1995).

For emergent and early writers, the independent portion of the workshop is a time when they can use their developing skills as writers even if they are just learning how to make a sound-to-letter connection. Beginning writers often use picture/letter cards that alphabetically list each lowercase letter and a corresponding picture such as "a" printed in a box with an apple, "b" with a book, etc. Of course, like anything else, you will need to demonstrate how to use these cards to locate the appropriate sound, but you can do this in whole-class writing demonstrations and then reinforce the skill as you move throughout the class supporting each child. For example, after a child independently draws a sketch of something that happened over the weekend, you can encourage the child to stretch out the sounds in each word that tells the story. If the child says, "I went to the mall with my mom," the teacher could prompt the child to find the /w/ sound by locating a picture of a watch on the letter-sound card. Some children will be ready to hear and record the /t/ sound at the end of *went* by finding the picture of a turtle, but others may move on to the next word, recording only beginning consonants.

Writer's workshop is an active but structured instructional setting that includes all of the language arts: speaking, listening, reading, writing, viewing, and visually representing ideas. With full immersion in a natural writer's community, children learn to appreciate and value the hard, but satisfying work that needs to be invested in a polished, finished product as they develop the attitudes and habits of writers.

## Instructional Approaches for Building Writing Strategies, Processes, and Dispositions for Students with Specific Needs

For children who struggle with writing, you can use the same practices that we have described for the general classroom writing program. The difference in instructional practices lies in the amount of support that children may need at any one specific point in the process. Good assessment procedures will alert you to the needs of the learners, thus allowing you to adjust your support accordingly. Some types of specific learning needs and suggestions follow:

- *Remember the steps of the process to be followed.* Make a checklist and keep it in the child's writing folder. The child can keep track of each step of the process by checking them off along the way. You can specifically match these steps to the procedures you have set up in your classroom. See Appendix A-23 for an example.
- *Manage writing time.* You can assist a child who does not stay on task by creating a list together of two things the child will do during the writer's workshop. Be sure to include what the child can do while waiting for a teacher conference. See Figure 7.5 for a sample planning sheet.

> You can purchase alphabet cards (sound-to-letter cards) for emergent writers in bulk from various publishing companies such as Richard C. Owen Publishers, Inc., or you could photocopy them from texts such as Fountas and Pinnell's *Guided Reading*, (1996).

### FIGURE 7.5 **Sample Planning Sheet**

Name : Claire

Date  : June 1

The topic I am working on today is: Taking care of my dog, Sprout

I plan to use the two following steps in the writing
process if I have enough time:

_____    Brainstorm ideas

_____    Read other manuals to see what they look like

If I finish or am waiting for a conference, I plan to:
_____    read by myself
__X__    read with a partner
_____    go to the listening center
_____    practice my spelling words
_____    illustrate another story
_____    start making my book cover
__X__    go to the library

- *Indentify the physical writing environment.* Children can use keyboards and word processing programs. You might also use the language experience model to provide scaffolding to help children complete more sophisticated stories.
- *Practice fluent reading of the final written piece.* You can provide reading practice of the finished product in a one-to-one setting. Then during author's circle, sit next to the author's chair so that you can add voice support to ensure the writer's oral reading fluency and the audience's enjoyment.
- *Organize materials.* Some children need help keeping the various materials including loose papers organized, and if this is the case, you might want to use a bound writer's notebook. Designated folders for editing supports and pencil cases for writer's tools can help organize other items.
- *Avoid difficulty skipping lines or moving in a return sweep.* You can place a green dot on the appropriate lines on the drafting paper to alert beginning writers to move to the left in a return sweep or to skip every other line if this is a convention in the classroom.
- *Scaffold difficulty with sentence structure.* You can use sentence and story frames to provide scaffolding for children who need support in this area. For example, a frame for a child who is struggling to write a compare-contrast piece might look like this: "_____ and _____ are alike in some ways. To begin with, they both _____. They also are alike because _____. But they are different too. On the one hand, _____ is _____. Also, _____ is _____. You can see how _____ and _____ are pretty different!"

Tools that support learners by using technology are sometimes referred to as assistive technology. See the author's website, www.kathyitterly.com, and click on "Tools for Assistive Technology" to access an excellent resource compiled by Dr. Windy Schweder of the South Caroline Aiken.

Technology can be especially useful for striving writers. Word processing programs help children who have handwriting difficulties, and the spell-check tool can help to build confidence. Many software programs provide structured prompting for planning and expanding ideas, and others specifically support children with special needs in literacy skills. Some computer programs actually record voices, and others read back the stories that children write. If you do not have access to these forms of technology, you can use an old-fashioned tape recorder during planning or after writing, enabling children to tape-record themselves and then listen to a playback to self-assess or reconsider ideas. Check with your special education department to identify the hardware and software that are available in your school.

Writing takes hard work, and children who struggle with reading and writing tasks may become easily discouraged since they already use so much mental energy to stay engaged in the requirements of day-to-day schoolwork. You will want to carefully match the level of support with the needs of the child in order to ensure success and build confidence for these challenged writers.

English Language Learners (ELLs) often have unique writing needs too. Teachers should immerse ELLs in meaningful writing experiences from the very start of their educational experiences regardless of their command of English. You can encourage them to draw visual representations of their thinking during the planning stages. During the rehearsal stage, some ELLs prefer to use their primary language to brainstorm ideas and label sketches. You can check in often with these learners and offer the English translation to support the developing English vocabulary of the learner. You should also encourage them to share their writing in the author's circle, perhaps using your voice in a shared reading approach to support them as they read their stories aloud. All student writers need to experience the satisfaction of successfully completing writing projects.

Nothing encourages children more than a growing portfolio of meaningful and successfully written material.

## LOOKING CLOSELY AT ONE CHILD'S ASSESSMENTS FROM STRAND 7 OF THE LITERACY PROFILE

The following synopsis is based on three pieces of writing that Willa completed. She wrote two of them, a self-selected topic and an assigned topic, in school during early June of Grade 1. She wrote the third piece, a story about a duck and a fox, spontaneously while the examiner watched and listened to her. Figure 7.6 shows Willa's "duck and fox" story and accompanying illustration. The teacher gathered other information during a one-to-one writing interview with Willa, a short interview with her mother, and an oral self-assessment/interview the teacher conducted using the "Self-Assessment for Writing Process and Strategies." Appendices A-21 and A-23 offer samples of the writing interview and the self-assessment. Refer to Figure 7.7 to see how Willa's use of writing strategies, her processes, and her dispositions are

FIGURE 7.6 **Willa's Draft of a Self-Selected Writing Topic, a "Duck and Fox" Story**

FIGURE 7.6  (Continued)

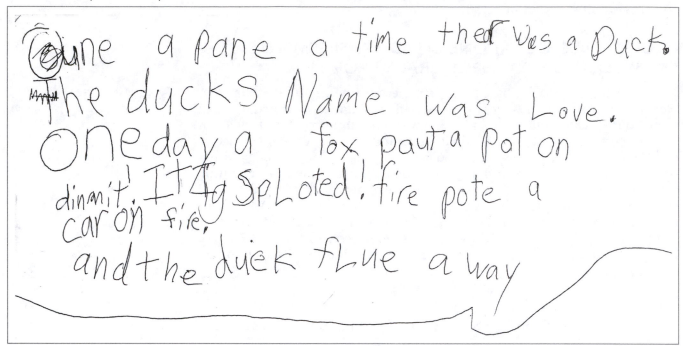

recorded on Strand 7 of the Literacy Profile. Notice the additional information the examiner's comments provided.

Willa's attitude about writing is generally favorable. She stated that she likes to write only when she's in a happy mood. It is clear that she is developing habits supported by the instructional program in her first-grade classroom. For instance, she asked the evaluator how many sentences had to be in her story when she was partially finished with her self-selected topic. Willa wrote her story and then drew a picture. When asked if she usually writes before she draws, she responded, "We have to." In the parent interview, her mother stated that at home, Willa writes often, never worries about length, and usually draws first.

As far as managing the writing process, Willa is able to generate her own topics and respond to an assigned topic. Willa's "duck and fox" story ended without a resolution, but after being prompted with the question, "What happened to the duck?", she willingly added an ending. Willa is developing independent proofreading skills, as noted when she went back to add capital letters and a period after writing two of the sentences. Willa understands that writing is meant to be shared, and after illustrating with great attention to detail, she was excited to share her story with her mom. Willa described her personal writing goal as, "to be able to think of more things to write about." As Willa hears more informational texts read aloud and is encouraged to read more informational texts (as suggested at the ends of chapters 2 and 5), she will expand her familiarity with different genres, which should help her generate new ideas and topics for writing. This will also provide models for writing in different genres.

Regarding instructional next steps, Willa could use some guidance in applying prewriting strategies (brainstorming, mapping, organizing) so that her creativity can flow more freely during the drafting stage of writing. Overall, Willa's use of writing strategies is developmentally on track, and her attitude toward writing is positive.

## FIGURE 7.7  Willa's Profile for Writing Strategies, Processes, and Dispositions

Note: This figure has been excerpted from the full Literacy Profile chart for illustrative purposes. Please consult the full pull-out chart to identify the column headings and development phases.

| Strand *Question & Sample Assessment Tools* | Late K | Early–Mid Grade 1 | Late Grade 1–Early Grade 2 |
|---|---|---|---|
| **7. Writing Strategies, Processes, and Dispositions** *To what extent does the child use the processes of writing? How engaged is the child with writing?* **Sample Assessment Tools** · Elementary Writing Attitude Survey · Portfolios · Writing samples · Interviews · Self-evaluation | Draws, labels, and writes to express ideas<br><br>Often generates original ideas and responds to others' prompts<br><br>Participates in shared writing activities | Writes with increasing independence<br><br>Uses resources such as word walls and letter-sound visuals for support *[looks around room for words as she is writing] KI*<br><br>With support, will reread what has been written *[Although she lost her place at times, she was willing to reread story to me and later to her mother.] KI* | With support, uses prewriting strategies, such as making a plan, sketch, or map. *[Examiner: "Do you usually write and then draw?" Willa: "We have to." Mother reports at home she draws first.] KI*<br><br>Writes independently *["when I'm in a happy mood"] KI*<br><br>Adds on to what is written when prompted *[when I asked, "What happened to the duck?" she added a sentence to have the duck fly away safely] KI* |

Gray areas represent highlighting added by the teacher, preferably using a different color for each year (e.g., yellow highlights for Late K, orange highlights for Early–Mid Grade I, etc.).
Bracketed material represents teacher/examiner comments from June, Grade I.

# REFERENCES

Anderson, C. (2000). *How's it going? A practical guide to conferring with student writers.* Portsmouth, NH: Heinemann.

Ashton-Warner, S. (1965). *Teacher.* New York: Simon & Schuster.

Atwell, N. (1987). *In the middle: Writing, reading, and learning with adolescents.* Montclair, NJ: Boynton/Cook Publishers.

Bandura, A. (1977). Self-efficacy: Toward a unifying theory of behavioral change. *Psychological Review, 84,* 191–215.

Bandura, A. (1986). *Social foundations of thought and action: A social cognitive theory.* Englewood Cliffs, NJ: Prentice Hall.

Beck, I. L., McKeown, M. G., Hamilton, R. L., & Kucan, L. (1997). *Questioning the author: An approach for enhancing student engagement with text.* Newark, DE: International Reading Association.

Bertrand, N. P., & Stice, C. F. (2002). *Good teaching: An integrated approach to language, literacy, and learning.* Portsmouth, NH: Heinemann.

Bottomley, D. M., Henk, W. A., & Melnick, S. A. (1997/1998). Assessing children's views about themselves as writers using the writer self-perception scale. *Reading Teacher, 51*(4), 286–297.

Britton, J. (1970a). *Language and learning.* Harmondsworth, Middlesex: Penguin.

Britton, J. (1970b). *Language and thought.* Harmondsworth, Middlesex: Penguin.

Buckner, A. (2005). *Notebook know-how.* Portland, ME: Stenhouse.

Button, K., Johnson, M. J., & Furgerson, P. (1996). Interactive writing in a primary classroom. *The Reading Teacher, 49,* 446–454.

Calkins, L. M. (1986, 1994). *The art of teaching writing.* Portsmouth, NH: Heinemann.

Calkins, L. M. (1991). *Living between the lines.* Portsmouth, NH: Heinemann.

Cambourne, B. (1995). Toward an educationally relevant theory of literacy learning: Twenty years of inquiry. *The Reading Teacher, 49*(3), 182–190.

Clay, M. M. (1975). *What did I write? Beginning writing behavior.* Portsmouth, NH: Heinemann.

Clay, M. M. (1991). *Becoming literate: The construction of inner control.* Portsmouth, NH: Heinemann.

Duncan, J. (1994). Presented during formal mentoring sessions through the *Learning Network*. Katonah, NY: Richard C. Owen.

Elbow, P. (1998). *Writing with power* (2nd ed.). New York: Oxford University Press.

Emig, J. (1971). *The composing process of twelfth graders*. Urbana, IL: National Council of Teachers of English.

Ferreiro, E., & Teberosky, A. (1982). *Literacy before schooling*. Portsmouth, NH: Heinemann.

Fletcher, R. (1996). *A writer's notebook: Unlocking the writer within you*. Portsmouth, NH: Heinemann.

Fletcher, R. (2007). Stated during online TLN author conversations. Katonah, NY: Richard. C. Owens, Pub. Retrieved from tln@listserve.com

Fountas, I. C., & Pinnell, G. S. (1996). *Guided reading: Good first teaching for all children*. Portsmouth, NH: Heinemann.

Freeman, M. (2007). National writing project's time-tested approach evolves and adapts to a new millennium. *Reading Today, 24*(6), 41.

Galda, L., & Cullinan, B. E. (2006). *Literature and the child* (6th ed.). Belmont, CA: Wadsworth/Thomson Learning.

Graves, D. (1994). *A fresh look at writing*. Portsmouth, NH: Heinemann.

Graves, D. (2003). *Writing: Teachers and children at work* (20th-anniversary ed.). Portsmouth, NH: Heinemann.

Harste, J. C., Woodward, V. A., & Burke, C. L. (1984). *Language stories and literacy lessons*. Portsmouth, NH: Heinemann.

Kear, D. K., Coffman, G. A., McKenna, M. G., & Ambrosio, A. L. (2000). Measuring attitude toward writing: A new tool for teachers. *The Reading Teacher, 54*, 10–23.

Leu, D. (2001). Exploring literacy on the Internet: Preparing students for new literacies in a global village. *The Reading Teacher, 54*(6), 568–572.

Machado, J. M. (2003). *Early childhood experiences in language arts: Emerging literacy* (7th ed.). Belmont, CA: Wadsworth/Thomson Learning.

McCarrier, A., Pinnell, G. S., & Fountas, I. C. (2000). *Interactive Writing: How language and literacy come together, K–2*. Portsmouth, NH: Heinemann.

Ministry of Education. (1992). *Dancing with the pen*. Wellington, New Zealand: Author.

Mooney, M. E. (1990). *Reading to, with, and by, children*. Katonah, NY: Richard C. Owen.

Mooney, M. E. (2001). *Text forms and features: A resource for intentional teaching*. Katonah, NY: Richard C. Owens Publishers, Inc.

Murray, D. M. (1982). *Learning by teaching*. Montclair, NJ: Boynton/Cook.

Ogle, D. (1986). K-W-L: A teaching model that develops active reading of expository text. *The Reading Teacher, 39*, 564–570.

Pearson, P. D., & Gallagher, M. C. (1983). The instruction of reading comprehension. *Contemporary Educational Psychology, 8*, 317–344.

Ray, K. W. (1999). *Wondrous words*. Urbana, IL: National Council of Teachers of English.

Ray, K. W. (2004). *About the authors*. Portsmouth, NH: Heinemann.

Routman, R. (2005). *Writing essentials: Raising expectations and results while simplifying teaching*. Portsmouth, NH: Heinemann.

Schunk, D. H. (1990). Goal setting and self-efficacy during self-regulated learning. *Educational Psychologist, 25*(1), 71–86.

Smith, F. (1988). *Joining the literacy club: Further essays in education*. Portsmouth, NH: Heinemann.

Smith, F. (1994). *Writing and the writer* (2nd ed.). Hillsdale, NJ: Erlbaum.

Stauffer, R. G. (1970). *The language-experience approach to the teaching of reading*. New York: Harper & Row.

Strickland, D., & Morrow, L. (1989). *Emerging literacy: Young children learn to read and write*. Newark, DE: International Reading Association.

Teale, W. H., & Sulzby, E. (1986). *Emergent literacy: Writing and reading*. Norwood, NJ: Ablex.

Tompkins, G. E. (2008). *Teaching writing: Balancing process and product*. Upper Saddle River, NJ: Merrill/Prentice Hall.

Tompkins, G., & Zumwalt, S. (2005). Process posters: Making the writing process visible. In G. E. Tompkins & C. Blanchfield (Eds.), *50 ways to develop strategic writers* (pp. 92–94). Upper Saddle River, NJ: Merrill/Prentice Hall.

Turbill, J., & Bean, W. (2006). *Writing instruction K–6: Understanding process, purpose, audience*. Katonah, NY: Richard C. Owens.

Van Allen, R. (1976). *Language experiences in communication*. Boston: Houghton Mifflin.

Winograd, P., Flores-Dueñas, L. F., & Arrington, H. (2003). Best practices in literacy assessment. In L. M. Morrow, L. B. Gambrel, & M. Pressley (Eds.), *Best practices in literacy instruction* (2nd ed., pp. 201–240). New York: Guilford Press.

# CHAPTER EIGHT

# Writing Effectiveness

### CORE QUESTION

How is the child's independent writing developing with regard to purpose, organization, details, and voice/tone?

"I went to the park. It was fun. Then I went home." This short story has the format of beginning, middle, and end; yet it clearly lacks details. How can we help children write more interesting and thoughtful pieces? First, the creation of an interactive, engaging reading program sets the stage for good writing instruction. Children gain insights about effective writing as they learn to appreciate the interconnectedness between reading and writing.

Second, an effective writing program includes many occasions for children to write across the curriculum and within a variety of genres. Frequent writing opportunities permit children to try out and improve their developing skills. These are good starting points, but children need more than just reading and writing opportunities to develop into competent writers.

Developing writers have a complex process to navigate as they attempt to put their thoughts into print. In addition to managing the writing process itself (described in the previous chapter), they must synthesize other tasks ranging from the physical requirements of holding a pencil (chapter 10), the cognitive requirements of linking sounds and letters to spell words (chapter 9), and the ultimate goal of creating a meaningful and effective piece of writing (this chapter). We will highlight a variety of ways to describe, measure, evaluate, and teach writing effectiveness by focusing on the following qualities of effective writing: purpose, organization, details, and voice/tone.

**LITERACY PROFILE**
Consult your Literacy Profile as you read through this chapter, referring to the question and indicators for Strand 8. Notice the relationships among the neighboring Strands 7, 9, and 10.

# UNDERLYING PRINCIPLES OF WRITING EFFECTIVENESS

Donald Graves (1994) describes writing as a social act that requires a sense of authorship, not only in how we craft written text but also in how we view the world. He reminds us that we can become more effective teachers of writing by putting ourselves into the role of a writer and also by responding to students' writing through the "listening ears" of a writer. Routman, too, encourages teachers to write and examine their own attitudes, processes, and beliefs about writing (2005). She has identified 12 writing essentials that apply to children in all grade levels, stating that "the skills and strategies that writers use are the same across the grade levels; their depth and sophistication are what increase" (2005, p. 13). As you read over the 12 essentials in Figure 8.1, think about the writing strategies and processes that you use when you write. The first "essential" is that writers define their audience and purpose; and the second essential is that writers determine an appropriate topic. Recall the discussion in chapter 7 about identifying topic, audience, and purpose. These three factors will resurface in this chapter because they also play an important role in how well a piece of writing accomplishes the writer's goal.

## Writing Effectiveness Through Purpose, Organization, Details, and Voice/Tone

Young children use oral language naturally to create stories, retell interesting tales, or convey information. In this section, we will identify ways to build on what children already know and are able to do, thus assisting their performance as they become skillful, confident, and competent writers who use a variety of forms. We will also describe ways to help student writers regulate the quality of their own writing by considering how well a piece of writing accomplishes their writing goals.

One way to judge the effectiveness of a piece of writing is to examine a child's ability to maintain purpose, develop a coherent organization, provide details that support a topic, and develop a personal voice and tone (Lane, 1992). These four areas are embedded in Routman's 12 writing essentials and can be applied throughout all levels of writing development.

FIGURE 8.1  **Routman's 12 Writing Essentials**

- Writing for a specific reader and meaningful purpose
- Determining an appropriate topic
- Presenting ideas clearly with a logical, well-organized flow
- Elaborating on ideas
- Embracing language
- Creating engaging leads
- Composing satisfying endings
- Crafting an authentic voice
- Rereading, rethinking, and revising while composing
- Applying correct conventions and form
- Reading widely and deeply and from a writer's perspective
- Taking responsibility for producing effective writing

***Maintaining Purpose.***  Purpose is really about intention: What is it I am trying to accomplish as a writer? Audience reaction is why we write for others, so as writers, we need to consider our eventual readers. Unlike oral storytelling, response to writing is delayed; therefore, teachers need to help young writers build this awareness as they consider the end product (Graves, 1994). Often, though, for our youngest writers, the delay is short. The beginning writer may receive on-the-spot feedback when creating a story as an adult writes it down, or a child may give the teacher a written story and wait expectantly for the teacher's reaction. These early experiences begin to spur the intentional thinking process: "Oh, if I say this, my mom will laugh." Conversely, if the teacher or parent becomes confused by something in the child's writing, the child learns that clarity is important in order to receive the desired response.

If our goal is for children to become self-reflective, it may be useful to develop a guide that will help them identify what experienced writers seem to accomplish so effortlessly. Our first consideration of effective writing, maintaining purpose, is evident when the writer:

- Stays on topic
- Works with a manageable topic (one that is not too broad or too narrow)
- Uses interesting leads to draw in a reader
- Consciously tries to "hold" a reader's interest
- Completely develops a topic (compiled from a variety of sources including Ministry of Education, 1992; Routman, 2005; Spandel, 2004; Turbill & Bean, 2006).

In other words, these criteria can help guide a child in accomplishing a writing goal or purpose. Making these criteria "visible" and understandable in "kid-friendly" language can help provide a structure for setting goals and discussing the quality of a written product. In addition to writing with a clear purpose in mind, children also need to organize their ideas in a logical format.

***Developing Coherent Organization.***  The "short story" at the beginning of this chapter includes a beginning, middle, and end, which indicates that the writer developed a basic structure for organizing ideas. This is a great starting place for early writers, but by studying the many forms of writing available, children can also learn to present ideas in a logical order that is creative and varied. Here is where teachers can bring the reading and writing connection to the forefront. Through a guided exploration of a variety of text structures, children can essentially learn to "read like writers" and more capably plan a coherent design for their own writing (Calkins, 1994; Graves, 2003; Ray, 1999; Smith, 1988).

Narrative texts are presented in one body of structural shapes, and informational texts have another body of shapes (Duke & Bennett-Armistead, 2003; Hoyt, 2002; Mooney, 2001). Poetry is another wide-ranging category of writing that deserves special consideration (Heard, 1989; Mooney, 2001). An increasing awareness of different literary forms helps promote experimentation; and if we provide support starting at the planning stage and give them assistance as needed as they branch out into new genres and forms, children can learn to write within their "zone of proximal development" (Vygotsky, 1978). Let's review various structural patterns of narrative, informational, and poetic text. Following a short description of each of these text structures, we will examine other considerations such as forms and features within genres and, on a narrower level, the various forms of paragraphs.

*Narrative Story Structures.* Narrative story structure includes the development of setting, character, plot, theme, and style. You can choose read-aloud books that will introduce children to a variety of plot development structures:

- Circular stories such as *The Oxcart Man* (Hall, 1983)
- Cumulative stories such as *The Napping House* (Wood & Wood, 1984)
- Stories with repetitive plots such as *Brown Bear, Brown Bear What Do You See?* (Martin, 1992)
- Stories with a twist at the end such as *The Sweetest Fig* (Van Allsburg, 1993)
- Linear, chronological accounts such as *The Carrot Seed* (Krauss, 1989)
- Stories with problem, climax, and resolution such as *Hey Al* (Yorinks, 2001)
- Stories with cliffhangers such as *Hey, Little Ant* (Hoose & Hoose, 1998)
- Stories with flashbacks such as *A Chair for My Mother* (Williams, 1984)

(There are many other variations of plot structures. Begin to collect your favorites. This list was adapted from Hennings, 2002.)

Children enjoy creating plot structures based on stories they've heard, and often these structures will lead to creative explorations into new forms of story writing. See chapter 6 for more information on narrative story structures.

*Informational Text Structures.* Once children begin to notice the underlying structures of informational text, they will be more capable of trying out these structures themselves (Mooney, 2001). Here are a few informational text structures, but keep in mind that the forms within each text type range in variety, depending on audience and purpose:

- Letter writing
- Expository text
- Functional text
- Journals

See Figure 8.2 for a chart that clarifies some of the types of nonfiction texts, their forms, and the possible purposes for writing them. Each piece of writing contains specific features that may relate to that particular form, but there is no limit to the creative uses of forms across text types and genres (Graves, 1989; Stead, 2002). For instance, a recipe usually includes a title, ingredients, and directions, but a writer might choose to use this form to describe the "recipe for happiness." As complex as all of this may sound, you can teach children to manage the organizational structures successfully by considering the audience and purpose of the piece and giving them opportunities to read and discuss the various forms (Mooney, 2001; Stead, 2002). Awareness of audience and purpose causes the child to think logically about what will make sense to the identified audience, and determining the order in which to divulge this information will become a logical and, often, creative process.

For an excellent description of more than 70 text forms and their accompanying features, see *Text Forms and Features: A Resource for Intentional Teaching* (Mooney, 2001).

One popular structure taught in many intermediate and middle school classrooms is the five-paragraph essay. As a rule, most published writers do not follow this structure, but many teachers begin with this structure, helping young writers understand this tried-and-true form for supplying enough details to support topic development when writing an essay in response to a prompt.

*Poetry.* We highlight poetry as a broad category of writing to emphasize its importance in writing programs. Be aware that poetry can also be story-like or informational. Although poetry takes many forms, most fall under the

FIGURE 8.2  Informational Text Types and an Accompanying Menu
of Forms and Purposes

| Text Type | Text Form | Purposes of Form |
|---|---|---|
| Letter writing | Friendly letters<br>Business letters<br>Invitations<br>Thank you notes<br>Letters to the editor<br>E-mails | To inform<br>To communicate<br>To share<br>To announce<br>To complain<br>To request<br>To express (gratitude,<br>  sympathy)<br>To invite<br>To clarify<br>To persuade |
| Expository text | ABC books<br>Reports<br>News articles<br>Magazine articles<br>Essays<br>Movie or book reviews<br>Summaries<br>Multimedia presentations<br>Autobiographies | To inform<br>To describe<br>To summarize<br>To report<br>To explain<br>To offer opinions<br>To share |
| Functional writing | Recipes<br>Menus<br>Lists<br>Book jackets<br>Advertisements<br>Notices, flyers<br>Memos<br>Manuals<br>Job descriptions<br>Schedules<br>Résumés<br>Web pages | To inform<br>To give instructions<br>To organize<br>To remember<br>To market items<br>To sell<br>To request<br>To invite<br>To guide<br>To promote |
| Journals | Personal journals<br>Diaries<br>Literature response journals<br>Plan books<br>Logs | To inform<br>To reflect<br>To keep track<br>To record<br>To account for<br>To communicate<br>To plan |

category of free verse (Galda & Cullinan, 2002). Except when introducing new forms of poetry, teachers shouldn't emphasize structure over purpose when encouraging children to write poetry (Routman, 2005). Graves describes poetry as a way of "uncovering the ordinary world" (1994, p. 327) and recommends that we help children "read the world for sources of poems to write" (p. 328). A poem's form is simply a way for the writer to accomplish the purpose of the piece. Besides free verse, other poetic forms include haiku, cinquain, limericks, list poems, and couplets.

*Organizational Structures Embedded Within Text Forms.* Some text forms contain organizational features that are central to the defining structure (Galda & Cullinan, 2002). For instance, if a child begins a story with "Once upon a time . . .," the reader already knows that the story occurred in the past. The reader next anticipates the structure of problem, climax, and solution. All of this results just from those four opening words. Even young children seem able to go from retelling fairy tales to writing personal versions of fairy tales with ease.

Early writers also begin to understand the importance of selecting a title for a story or informational piece, knowing that the wording of a title contributes important information. Organizing details also include transitional words throughout a piece of writing. Children learn to use words and phrases such as "Next" and "The following day" to help the reader understand the development of topic ideas or plot.

Finally, the child also learns about clustering ideas through paragraph development. Early, simplified versions of paragraphs generally follow the structure of a main idea supported by important details. When writing informational paragraphs, children can begin to analyze some simple examples of paragraphing and text structures that appear in expository text and eventually choose the one that best matches the purpose of their writing:

- *Enumeration:* listing ideas in a first-to-last or numbered format
- *Description-examples:* making a statement and supporting it with examples
- *Comparison-contrast:* describing the similarities and/or differences between two ideas
- *Cause-effect:* making a statement about something that happened and then explaining some probable reason
- *Problem-solution:* stating a problem, the possible causes, and a possible solution (Allen, 2002; Moore, 1995)

Later in the instructional section, we will discuss ways that teachers can support young writers as they begin to experiment with these tools and add the important details that support their main-idea statements.

Children begin to understand that unlike oral language, the end product of writing does not interact with the originator, which means that the responsibility for clarity falls squarely on the writer. One way to ensure clarity is through the use of details.

**Providing Details That Support a Topic.** Returning once again to the opening "story," we can see that a writer can stay on topic, have a solid organizational structure, and still not satisfy the reader. Good writing provides enough details to ensure that the piece achieves the writer's intention, whether it is to convey an appreciation of an experience, contribute to the reader's existing body of information, or some other purpose (Routman, 2005; Spandel, 2004). To examine the effective use of details, we will discuss:

- Sufficient information to support the topic
- Overall word choice, including richness of vocabulary and descriptive phrases and passages

Let's begin by examining the amount of information that is needed to thoroughly address a topic.

Appendix A-14 includes a chart that identifies text structures and signal words, along with a space to add additional signal words.

*Sufficient Information to Support a Topic.*  Children need to consciously consider the amount of information the reader needs, temporarily stepping outside the writing process and becoming an objective reader and listener (Ministry of Education, 1992). Depending on the piece being written, this might consist of thinking about what information to include so that the reader can understand the message, deciding what information the reader can infer from a character's actions, identifying what information may be redundant, and determining what information is needed to draw an aesthetic response from the reader. This is quite a lot to consider!

Routman believes that storytelling can be an important link between oral language and written language because active storytelling sessions help children learn the language and structures of stories when they listen, tell, dramatize, and draw stories. Storytelling helps children learn to consider what information is important to communicate to their audience (2005). The tricky part of writing stories is deciding which words will elicit the desired response from the reader, because the interactive component of oral storytelling is absent from written storytelling.

Writers learn to anticipate the questions a reader might have when they share their writing with others, sometimes in revision conferences and sometimes through one-to-one conversations with a peer or teacher. Eventually children internalize the revision voice. As children read and reread their own writing, they begin to ask themselves questions such as, "Is there anything I'm leaving out that is important?" "Will my reader understand what I'm trying to explain?" Evidence that a writer has learned to "stand outside" her writing is apparent when she begins revising drafts independently, adding, inserting, deleting, or making other changes that clarify or elaborate her ideas (Ministry of Education, 1992, p. 57).

*Overall Word Choice.*  Generally, when young children tell stories about their lives, they use basic, everyday vocabulary (what Beck, McKeon, & Kucan, 2002 refer to as "Tier One words"), creating sentences such as, "My hands were cold. I left my mittens at home." Through interactive read-alouds and guided-discovery lessons, you can help children begin to notice the language of books (words known as "Tier Two words"), reinforcing new vocabulary development through writing demonstrations (Ray, 1999). The sentences listed above might shift to incrementally more descriptive language, such as, "My fingers felt like icicles because I had forgotten my mittens at home." Tier Three words (words that are used more specifically within particular disciplines) become integrated through content-area writing and informational text writing. For instance, if a child is writing a daily weather report, he might include terms such as *temperature* and *forecast*. As discussed in chapter 1, it is important to encourage children to move from a passive awareness of new words to an active use of them. Writing gives children a perfect opportunity to do so.

Word choice is only one example of writer's craft. Katie Wood Ray (1999) describes how we can all learn to write more deliberately and creatively by studying the writing styles of others through an inquiry approach. Ray defines writer's craft as "a knowledge that a writer has about *how* to do something" and suggests that we explore "author's craft" by looking at the processes a writer uses and also by examining the variety of text structures, language structures, and word choices a writer employs (p. 25). For instance, we can model how to "read like a writer" when we guide children to ponder, "I wonder why Eric Carle chose to say this sentence in this particular way" or "Let's examine how Eric Carle organized this text in a way that helped us follow the story so easily." By reading and discussing the works of authors through the lens of a writer, children can imagine themselves using these same writer's tools (Ray, 1999; Smith, 1988).

As a class you can also have children study a wide variety of literary devices depending on their developmental level. Some of these include onomatopoeia, metaphor, dialogue, word pictures, hyperbole, and other figurative language. Many teachers collect children's books or poems that are good examples of particular literacy devices corresponding to the standards of the learners' specific grade level. For instance, *Owl Moon* contains rich language metaphors that second- and third-grade children easily understand (Yolen, 1987). In studying a variety of authors' techniques, young writers will be more likely to add interesting phrases to their own writing or experiment with playful language to make their own writing more interesting, and often children will begin to identify these techniques in the writing of their classmates. In the following section we will consider how writers stay true to their own voice and consider the overall tone of a piece.

***Developing Personal Voice/Tone.*** Storytellers do not usually need reminders to use their own voice because they are telling their own stories or sharing information that matters to them. Routman (2005, p. 13) describes using voice as writing "in a style that illuminates the writer's personality." Tone, although related, is different from voice. It can be described as the overall feeling that an author conveys through her or his word choice and other deliberate literary devices (Tompkins, 2008). Voice and tone go beyond adding details, however; their use indicates that the writer is conveying feelings and connecting with the reader in a personal way. Children's use of voice and tone appears in their descriptive word pictures, in text features such as boldface and underlining, and in their experimenting with punctuation such as exclamation points. Voice and tone are also evident in the overall effect that the writer creates. For instance, the child may try to build suspense and in doing so add some foreshadowing, or perhaps the story is a humorous one and the child uses exaggeration purposefully and effectively.

Children can begin to recognize authors' particular patterns and even favorite topics through author studies (Ray, 1999). Some writers prefer to tell stories using animal characters and lots of dialogue (such as Cronin, *Click Clack Moo: Cows That Type*, 2000), whereas others may use animal characters, speech bubbles, and illustrations to tell stories (such as Willems, *Don't Let the Pigeon Drive the Bus*, 2003). Sometimes writers prefer the first-person point of view, others talk directly to the reader, and still others choose to take on the third-person role of storyteller. Children also learn that authors use different styles in different books but that through noticing particular word choices and literary devices, it is often possible to identify writers by their voice and tone. For instance, in an author study of Robert Munsch, first- and second-grade children can begin to identify and expect some level of repetition, humor, exaggeration, and onomatopoeia. Go to http://robertmunsch.com/ to find a list of his books.

Children will experiment with many borrowed techniques, eventually finding comfort in their own personal style. Over time, as they receive meaningful responses from readers, and hear what moved the reader and what worked well, young writers learn to identify the techniques that make their writing work (Ministry of Education, 1992). Within the writer's community, children soon begin to identify not only the stylistic devices of published authors but also the individual voices of classmates, which validates the uniqueness of each child's developing interests and style (Miller, 2002).

### Summary of Underlying Principles of Writing Effectiveness

The effectiveness of a piece of writing can be described by how well a writer maintains purpose, develops a coherent organization, provides details that support the topic, and uses personal voice and tone. The audience of the writing and the intention of the writer guide the overall development of each of the four factors. The next section will describe assessment procedures that enable teachers to monitor a child's increasing understanding about effective writing and how he or she can observe these elements in his or her own writing "products."

## ASSESSING WRITING EFFECTIVENESS

In order to assess student writing, it is important to determine the knowledge and skills that students are expected to gain as they take increasing control over the writing process. Keep in mind that this developmental process does not always occur in a linear path. As children take on more complex topics and experiment with new forms of writing, they may seem to regress in their control of writing elements that appeared "solid." In fact, this regression often represents a mental "renegotiation" of how prior knowledge relates to new situations. Like a student driver who is trying to drive for the first time on a major highway, the student writer may require assistance to fully integrate a previously "solid" concept or skill in novel, more complex ways.

In other words, don't panic if you find a learner moving backward to a previously identified skill on the Literacy Profile; simply stop and analyze the situation. In doing so, you may be able to identify a new opportunity to support the learner within the "zone of proximal development" that has presented itself through assessment procedures. For instance, if a second-grade child effectively uses a solid organizational structure such as "beginning, middle, and end" and then composes a story that seems disorganized, closer inspection might reveal that the writer is attempting a newer, more complex structure that involves multiple characters or dialogue. When you recognize and support this new development, the child will gain confidence to try out more complex structures as he also gains competence (Routman, 2005).

Both formal and informal measures are available to assess a child's developing skills in writing effectively. Each form of assessment provides important information that you can use as you track a child's growth. In the following sections we will offer a sample of assessment tools.

### Formal or Published Measures for Assessing Writing Effectiveness

Teachers often assess writing effectiveness through the use of a rubric, a scoring guide that describes desired performance. Rubrics come in two "varieties," holistic and analytic. Holistic rubrics are simpler, combining criteria into single descriptions of performance at increasing levels of proficiency. Holistic rubrics can have several performance levels, ranging from 2 to even 5 or 6. Analytic rubrics include several criteria or categories (e.g., purpose, details, organization), and for each category, provide descriptors of increasing proficiency, listed horizontally and usually in a numerical sequence. Formal measures for evaluating writing effectiveness have been developed for use at national, state, district, and schoolwide levels. Most of the time, formal measures of writing effectiveness involve rubrics.

***Holistic Scoring Rubrics.*** Holistic measures are usually employed when it is necessary to score large numbers of writing samples and the goal is to determine generally where the writing falls within the identified numerical

FIGURE 8.3 Sample from Massachusetts English Language Arts Composition Scoring Guide

| Massachusetts English Language Arts Composition Scoring Guide | | | | | |
|---|---|---|---|---|---|
| Topic Development | | | | | |
| 1 | 2 | 3 | 4 | 5 | 6 |
| • Little topic/idea development, organization, and/or details<br>• Little or no awareness of audience and/or task | • Limited or weak topic/idea development, organization, and/or details<br>• Limited awareness of audience and/or task | • Rudimentary topic/idea development and/or organization<br>• Basic supporting details<br>• Simplistic language | • Moderate topic/idea development and organization<br>• Adequate, relevant details<br>• Some variety in language | • Full topic/idea development<br>• Logical organization<br>• Strong details<br>• Appropriate use of language | • Rich topic/idea development<br>• Careful and/or subtle organization<br>• Effective/rich use of language |

Used by permission from the Massachusetts Department of Elementary and Secondary Education.

score. The ratings are often placed in 4- or 6-point scales to prevent too many "middle ground" scores (Tompkins, 2008). These scores can also be converted into word descriptors such as "advanced," "proficient," "needs improvement," and "warning." Many states have implemented assessment programs that examine children's writing progress at particular grades. For instance, in Massachusetts, elementary students are assessed in writing during the spring of their fourth-grade year. The holistic scoring guide for the Massachusetts Comprehensive Assessment System (MCAS) is divided into two areas, Topic/Idea Development and Standard English Conventions. See Figure 8.3 for a sample of the 6-point scale used for topic and idea development.

In Vermont, New Hampshire, and Rhode Island, writing is evaluated in Grades 5 and 8 through holistic rubrics based on grade-level expectations, which include attention to purpose, organization, details, and voice/tone. These rubrics are used to evaluate both children's short responses and their extended responses. Be sure to research your own state's scoring system in order to help your students become familiar with the state's expectations for writing and scoring procedures.

The national assessment tool known as the National Assessment of Educational Progress (NAEP) is administered to randomly selected Grade 4 students in every state, but only once every 4 years. The purpose of this test is to look at American children's progress over time. Children are required to write in response to three different prompts, each representing a different purpose. See Figure 8.4 for a sample of the descriptors and prompts in this holistic scoring system.

Finally, some school districts and individual schools develop their own holistic scoring guides based on the curriculum frameworks or grade-level expectations in their respective states. These assessments often use a preselected writing prompt administered at specified times throughout the year, often at every grade level in order to track children's progress several times a year at every grade level. Teams of teachers usually score the assessments and record the scores, building common expectations for writing.

FIGURE 8.4  **Samples from National Assessment of Educational Progress Grade 4**

| 300-point scale that supplies one of six ratings | Narrative | Informative | Persuasive |
|---|---|---|---|
| | Sample Prompt: "Write about a very unusual day." | Sample Prompt: "Describe lunchtime on a usual day." | Sample Prompt: "Convince the school librarian to replace a missing book." |
| Excellent | | | |
| Skillful | | | |
| Sufficient | | | |
| Uneven | | | |
| Insufficient | | | |
| Unsatisfactory | | | |

Taken from http://nces.ed.gov/nationsreportcard/writing/results2002/itemmapgrade4.asp.

See *Creating Young Writers: Using the Six Traits to Enrich Writing Process in Primary Classrooms* (Spandel, 2004) for a guide that applies to K–3 writers.

***Analytic Scoring Rubrics.***  Schools and districts often use analytic rubrics that supply more precise information about children's progress. Common analytic rubrics are often designed around the "Six-Trait Model" descriptors. A group of 17 teachers in the Beaverton, Oregon, school district originally developed this model in 1984 to provide teachers with consistent language for discussing effective writing (Harp & Brewer, 2005; Spandel, 2004). The original rubrics applied to children in Grades 3 and up, but many have been adapted to describe younger children's writing effectiveness.

Each of the original six traits has descriptors at levels 1, 3, and 5 to help evaluators and children determine their strengths and also to set goals in the areas of ideas and content, organization, voice, word choice, sentence fluency, and conventions. Go to http://www.nwrel.org/assessment/pdfRubrics/6plus1traits.PDF for a list of each trait and the corresponding descriptors. School districts have also developed rubrics that combine the curriculum standards established by their state and the language of the six-trait model. To assist teachers in judging various qualities of a paper, anchor papers are often included in the scoring guides. See Appendix A-23 for an example of an analytic writing rubric that describes purpose, organization, details, and voice/tone (Biggam, Herman, & Trubisz, 1996).

### Informal Measures for Assessing Writing Effectiveness

Writing assessment should ideally involve both the teacher and the children, thus enabling them to identify the characteristics of effective writing (Oglan, 2003). Informal writing assessments may include anecdotal record keeping, writing samples with accompanying rubrics and/or checklists, portfolios with student and teacher reflection sheets, and student self-reflection tools. Teachers can use these assessments to inform classroom instruction at both the individual level and the whole-class level, and teachers can also use them to help children set realistic goals.

***Anecdotal Record Keeping.***  Some teachers carry a clipboard to record observations during writing periods and often keep the clipboard handy to add comments throughout the day. As described in earlier chapters, this type of note taking is the most informative when the teacher uses specific language centered around an identified focus area and when the teacher transfers the information to a working document for each individual child. For instance, you might make an anecdotal note about a child's use of concepts or skills after a mini-lesson you'd conducted earlier that week: "*5/13 Annalise used chart of 'said words' to add more variety to her dialogue.*" Note that it's important to include a date so that, when you add this note to other notes, you can see Annalise's pattern of development over time, in this case signifying Annalise's willingness to use resources to strengthen her writing.

Individual monitoring files can take the form of loose-leaf sheets, file folders, or some other management system you create. Besides identifying patterns of an individual writer's development, anecdotal notes can also provide information that informs whole-class lessons or mini-lessons for specific children. For instance, you may see many children overusing words like "good," in which case you might decide to conduct a whole-class lesson on descriptive word use.

*Writing Samples with Accompanying Rubrics and Checklists.*  Some school systems require teachers to keep benchmark writing samples from specific time periods of the school year such as September, January, and May. Collecting these samples is the first step in the assessment process, but you will also want to evaluate each sample using an identified set of criteria, possibly through checklists or rubrics.

Teams of teachers can work together to create rubrics or checklists that are appropriate for each grade level, or perhaps your school district might use evaluation materials that have been developed through a published program. You can collect the writing samples from teacher prompts or student-generated topics, depending on the purpose of the assessment. Teachers often develop checklists to determine whether a child has applied a set of features to a particular writing form. You can tailor each checklist to the specific writing forms taught at different grade levels. A checklist, which can include a wide range of skills that may or may not be evident, is most useful when a "yes" or "no" response adequately describes a set of criteria. See Figure 8.5 for an example of a second-grade thank you letter checklist.

Rubrics, on the other hand, can show finer gradations of skill development. If their language is clear and understandable, they can also supply useful information to children and parents about a child's developing control of writing effectiveness. See Figure 8.6 for an example of a second-grade letter-writing rubric.

You can also find an analytic rubric in Appendix A-24 for overall writing effectiveness in primary grades. Remember that it isn't necessary to use a

FIGURE 8.5  **Sample Checklist for Evaluating a Second Grader's Use of Effective Writing Strategies in a Thank You Letter**

```
____ Included a greeting such as Dear_____
____ Indicated why the letter was being written
____ Clearly thanked recipient for the specific item or gift
____ Included some personal response to the item or gift
____ Ideas flowed in a logical manner
____ Included some creative use of language or words
____ Included a closing
____ Included a signature
```

FIGURE 8.6 **Sample Rubric for Second-Grade Letter-Writing Unit**

| Area to Evaluate | Clear Command of Form | Getting There | Starting Out | Not Yet | Comments |
|---|---|---|---|---|---|
| Purpose: Content | Clearly states purpose for writing, stays on topic | Purpose is partially established; some attempt is made to stay on topic | Strays from topic; little evidence of the why of writing the letter | Fails to address topic | |
| Organization: Letter form | Supplies date, greeting, body of letter, closing, and signature in appropriate places | Partially supplies features, includes at least three of four: greeting, body, closing, or signature | Only slight evidence that writing is a letter, includes at least two of four defining features | No evidence of letter-writing format, could be any form | |
| Details that support topic | Ideas flow smoothly; language is rich and varied; sentences are varied | A sprinkling of variety in sentences, letter makes sense to reader, some interesting word choice | Choppy presentation of ideas, words don't vary | Ideas hard to follow, word choice is limited | |
| Voice/tone | Clearly engages with intended recipient using personal style | Shows some interactive quality with the intended recipient | States information in distant tone, not much personality shows through | No personal engagement, simply a mechanical listing of information | |

rubric for every writing sample that you evaluate; however, rubrics can be useful for large projects or summative descriptors at the end of a unit of study.

One important consideration when using checklists or rubrics is that children will want to know what criteria you are using to describe their writing. Many teachers choose to create rubrics or checklists *with* children, allowing them some input into the process and using student-friendly language as descriptors (Routman, 2005). Children can then use this tool to evaluate their own work and carefully consider their use of agreed-upon standards. When the expectations are clear to children, they are better able to manage the multiple requirements of writing effectiveness, writing conventions, and the entire writing process. A writing or literacy portfolio is also useful for recording the child's progress over time.

***Portfolios with Student and Teacher Reflection Sheets.*** One of the most authentic and supportive ways to help children take an active role in their growth as writers is to use a portfolio approach. Although there are various types of portfolios, each holds collections of children's work over time, ranging from decorated cereal boxes to hanging file folders (Graves, 1994). Writing portfolios may include student-selected pieces, teacher-selected pieces, a combination of pieces that both have selected, or every piece of writing a child composes at school.

See Geoff Hewitt's *A Portfolio Primer* (1995) for more information on portfolio development.

Graves (1994) believes that children should decide on a writing piece to include and then justify its selection, which adds insights into what a child values in her own writing. Many teachers ask children to attach a self-reflection form to the selected writing sample, but with younger children you might want to record their reasoning. Self-reflections encourage children to stop and consider their work, identifying strengths and goals for further work. See Appendix A-25 for reproducible portfolio slips that you can use as a starting place (Biggam et al., 1996).

***General Self-Reflection Sheets.*** Of course, not all teachers use a portfolio approach, but children can still learn to reflect on their own writing. Children need time to ponder and consider their progress throughout the school year. Even young children enjoy thinking about their successes and goals. Appendix A-26 contains a reflection sheet to support this process (Biggam et al., 1996). You might want to use this form as an interview template if the children have not yet developed independent reading and writing skills.

### Summary of Assessing Writing Effectiveness

Students should have an active role in evaluating and setting goals for themselves as writers (Graves, 1994; Routman, 2005; Turbill & Bean, 2006). Teachers and children can collaboratively analyze and discuss writing samples or finished products to begin these conversations. Teachers can also collect systematic observations and use recording tools to inform their teaching and support their learners. In addition, it is important to carefully consider the results from large-scale writing prompts or state-level writing assessments, which could help guide the development of your overall writing program.

## INSTRUCTIONAL APPROACHES FOR ASSESSING WRITING EFFECTIVENESS

"The Teaching and Learning Cycle" model described in the Introductory chapter of this book sets a clear framework for writing instruction: assess, evaluate, plan for instruction, teach, and then assess again (Owen, 2001). After collecting assessment samples and evaluating individual children's work, you can analyze the status of the whole class to determine your instructional goals. Next you will want to plan instruction based on what a child can do and what a child is attempting to do. But which teaching points should you choose? Which approaches work best?

As outlined in previous chapters, the "to, with, and by" reading model works well within the structure of a writing workshop, supporting developmentally appropriate, authentic lessons (Mooney, 1990). This model, similar to the gradual release of responsibility model (Pearson & Gallagher, 1983), can be applied by demonstrating new ways to think about the craft of writing (*to*), supporting children as they try out new ideas (*with*), and then observing and celebrating as children gain competence and independence (*by*). In this section, we will look at some explicit teaching methods that support the overall development of effective writing.

### Instructional Approaches for Writing Effectiveness in All Students

Students learn literacy best when they learn it in the context of real reading and writing, activities often described in school settings as authentic literacy (Goodman, 1986). Duke, Purcell-Gates, Hall, and Tower define authentic literacy as "reading and writing activities that occur in the lives of people outside of a learning-to–read-and-write context and purpose" (2006/2007, p. 346). Let's take a closer look at how you can apply the learning models described in the previous section in a classroom setting using meaningful reading and writing.

Writing demonstrations provide opportunities for children to see their teacher as a writer and observe the authentic process of writing by a more "expert other." You can use these demonstrations to introduce children to new writing ideas. For instance, if you notice that children are well versed in the story structure of beginning, middle, and end, you might decide to teach them a new structure such as a circular structure. Begin by selecting a children's book that illustrates this structure, such as *Rosie's Walk* by Pat Hutchins (1968). Read, enjoy, and then analyze this story's structure, letting the children know that you are going to try this structure for a story idea of your own. After modeling the creation of your own circular story, you can assist the children as they try out this new structure to create a circular story in a whole-class shared writing experience. This collaborative class project can then be published as a class book. Later, when you notice a child attempting to apply this structure on his own, you can provide support through an individual conference or, if several children are trying it out, you might form a guided writing group to help them use this new idea in their writing. Children who attempt this skill receive encouragement as they share their story with others; meanwhile, they are also reinforcing the idea that the structure can be applied in future writing projects.

The circular story example combines two effective teaching strategies: mini-lessons and shared writing. These instructional models work effectively within the context of a writer's workshop, and each approach can be used both in whole-class and small-group instructional settings. You will also want to conduct individual conferences to provide focused lessons when you observe children who are struggling with writing effectiveness.

***Mini-Lessons.*** A mini-lesson is an effective way to identify and discuss specific writing strategies or to teach specific writing skills (Calkins, 1994; Fletcher, 1992; Routman, 2005). In this approach, the teacher selects an instructional objective (for example, adding descriptive details) and then creates a lesson to "teach" the idea using authentic reading and writing materials through the gradual release of responsibility model. The reading-writing connection is important here: finding good printed-text examples of a particular writing feature can help children "see" that feature in action. Listed below is one framework that you might find useful.

*Step I.* To set the groundwork for the instruction, the teacher explicitly sets an objective and selects either a real text or a piece of writing that applies to the objective.

*Step II.* The teacher identifies the way an author uses the particular skill or strategy and then demonstrates using the strategy or skill through a guided-discovery process, helping the students identify the skill or craft.

*Step III.* The teacher provides guided practice through a shared experience.

*Step IV.* The children work together in partnerships or in small groups to try out the new strategy or skills with teacher support.

*Step V.* The class comes back together to discuss their new discoveries and think about how they can apply this new strategy or skill to future writing (adapted from a compilation of ideas from Calkins, 1994; Miller, 2002; Routman, 2005; Spandel, 2004; Tompkins, 2008).

Calkins (1994) cautions us to avoid requiring children to immediately apply the new skill in their personal writing; rather, she suggests that we encourage children to apply the strategy or skill when it is appropriate for them to do so, for instance, if a child in your class is writing a business letter. Otherwise, mini-lessons can be developed to support each of the areas of effective writing that we've discussed in this chapter, including how well a child maintains purpose, develops a coherent organization, provides details to support the topic, and develops a personal voice and tone. In the following section, we provide a few examples of how you can apply mini-lessons in each of the four broad areas.

*Mini-Lessons for Maintaining Purpose.*  Even young children can begin to think about the purpose of a piece of writing. We can begin this process as we read stories out loud and discuss our responses to the stories' words. "Oh, this story made me laugh" or "This book helped me learn more about pandas." By helping children directly link the texts they hear to their own potential writing experiences, we plant the seeds for them to think about how writers successfully accomplish their goals.

Mini-lessons go beyond building awareness, actually creating opportunities for children to begin applying new ideas to a sample piece of writing. The mini-lesson in Figure 8.7 is a sample first-grade lesson that demonstrates how writers stay on topic. Some of the possible mini-lessons in maintaining purpose include:

- Identifying how writers stay on topic
- Working with a manageable topic (one that is not too broad or too narrow)
- Using interesting leads to draw in a reader
- Consciously trying to "hold" a reader's interest
- Completely developing a topic

### FIGURE 8.7  Sample Mini-Lesson for Staying on Topic, Grade 1

**Step I.** *Setting an objective:* Students will identify how writers stay focused on one topic and then apply this idea. *Materials:* Short book about worms entitled *Wonderful Worms* (Glaser, 1994)

**Step II.** *Opening demonstration:* Read the entire book about worms to the class (or small group), focusing on meaning. After reading it, discuss the idea of staying on topic. Reread the first sentence in the book to see whether the author stayed on the topic of worms as identified by the title. Ask the children to state out loud either a "yes" or "no" if they think the author stayed on topic.

**Step III.** *Shared experience:* Ask the class to help as you continue rereading each page, by showing a "thumbs up" or "thumbs down" (to reflect whether the sentence stayed "on topic" or not) after you read each sentence. Now choose a topic that you are studying in class and in a shared demonstration, write a few sentences together about this topic.

**Step IV.** *Supported practice with peers:* Invite the children to work in partnerships to write a few sentences about a topic you have studied together. Give them adequate time to compose a few sentences.

**Step V.** *Closure:* Bring the class back to a whole-class grouping and ask for volunteers to read their short piece about the topic they chose. Ask them how this skill will help them as they go back to their independent writing projects.

*Mini-Lessons for Developing a Coherent Organization.* As discussed earlier, young writers can best develop a coherent organization if they are aware of the underlying structures that exist in various written forms. You can help them through a mini-lesson that focuses on a sample text, analyzing it together to identify the author's organization of events or thoughts. You can use the same process to examine narrative, nonfiction, or poetic forms. Simply use the mini-lesson structure to design a lesson. See Figure 8.8 for a sample mini-lesson on the narrative structure of memoirs.

Mini-lessons can offer explicit teaching opportunities to demonstrate and isolate the variety of ways writers organize their delivery of information. For instance, to teach the use of enumeration, you may want to develop a mini-lesson that uses a text that shows how to list the order of a procedure. Try to choose something that is of high interest to the children, such as a short paragraph about how to successfully eat an ice cream cone on a hot summer day. You can then choose something relevant to the whole class in order to give them a bit of shared practice, such as written guidelines for a substitute teacher on how the class prepares to go home each day.

*Mini-Lessons for Providing Details That Support a Topic.* In order to explicitly teach how writers add details to support a topic, it will be helpful for you to decide which genres and forms to explore with the entire class, especially because each form requires different skills and different levels of detail. Let's revisit the two broad areas of ways to provide details:

- Sufficient information to support the topic
- Overall word choice, including richness of vocabulary and descriptive phrases and passages

You can teach each of these skills through the mini-lesson format. For instance, if you've been noticing that many children are writing using only the words

## FIGURE 8.8  Sample Mini-Lesson for Organizational Structure of Memoirs for Grade 3

**Step I.** *Setting an objective:* Students will identify the development of a plot structure in a memoir and then apply this idea to a planning structure of their own. *Materials:* A sample of a memoir from an author's life, such as *When I Was Young in the Mountains* (Rylant, 1982)

**Step II.** *Opening demonstration:* Read Rylant's book about when she was young to the class (or small group). Discuss the organization of the text and then reread the first page of the book to see how the author began her story. After rereading, ask the class what they noticed about the beginning and sketch an organizational graphic on a large sheet of chart paper to record the idea.

**Step III.** *Shared experience:* Ask the class to help as you continue rereading each page, working together to create a graphic representation of the story's development. Model a quick representation of a short story from your life.

**Step IV.** *Supported practice with peers:* Invite the children to work in partnerships to sketch out a plan for retelling a story the class experienced together. Give them adequate time to compose a written graphic plan.

**Step V.** *Closure:* Bring the class back to a whole-class grouping and ask for volunteers to share their design for the plan. Ask them how this skill will help them as they go back to their independent writing projects.

they know how to spell independently, you can design a mini-lesson to emphasize choosing rich words. After you introduce the idea of using interesting vocabulary, point out a few examples from the first page of a carefully selected text, perhaps *Sylvester and the Magic Pebble* (Steig, 1969), and then send the children off into small groups with a photocopied sample of a few more pages of the author's text and a highlighter. Children love using highlighters to identify author's craft, and highlighted passages help them quickly refer back to their thinking. If you give them the actual text, you can provide little Post-it notes or flags to allow them to mark their thinking.

After the discussion, ask the children to place their *rich word discoveries* onto a sheet of paper or in their writer's notebooks for their own personal reference. Talk to children about strategies they might use if they want to use a word they know but cannot yet spell correctly, such as writing a temporary spelling that uses the individual sounds within each syllable. Model this process by revisiting one of your own drafts from a previous writing demonstration. Finally, invite the children to take out any of their previously written pieces to see whether they can add richer vocabulary. They might even like using a special-colored pencil to highlight the richer word choices they made. Other mini-lesson ideas in the category of word choice include using descriptive language or stronger action verbs, eliminating bland words, using figurative language, and including dialogue.

Finally, you can also use mini-lessons to help students think about other ways they can add details to support their topic. For instance, in narrative pieces, you can help children analyze character development by creating webs that identify the ways an author talks about a character. Hennings (2002) names three ways that authors develop characters: through explicit descriptions, through the deeds the character performs, and through dialogue, including self-talk and words they exchange with others. A mini-lesson on identifying character traits can help children realize that readers learn about characters in a variety of ways. The *Henry and Mudge* series by Cynthia Rylant (1996) is a wonderful resource for helping first- and second-grade children think about character development. The more visible we make authors' techniques, the more accessible the techniques become to our young writers.

*Mini-Lessons for Developing Voice/Tone.* Voice and tone are deeply linked to purpose and audience. Even though young children might tell wonderful stories orally, they may have difficulty capturing that oral storytelling voice when they begin to write independently, often because of the challenges of spelling and handwriting (Clay, 1975). For instance, when early writers stop to use an alphabet card to locate the letter that represents the first sound in the word *went,* they may lose their concentration and forget what they wanted to say. You can support their development of voice and style by blending independent and shared writing approaches. Allow a child to start out independently, and then in an individual conference, provide support by writing additional words or phrases that the child supplies. Young children who are just learning to connect sounds and letters will be more likely to use their own "voice" if an adult is willing to transcribe as they dictate or revise.

For older children, mini-lessons can focus on their own styles as you identify the uniqueness of one author's voice or tone in several works. Katie Wood Ray encourages teachers to select a few of their favorite authors and then to read their work extensively. Get to know the style of these authors "like the back of your hand" (1999, p. 41), Ray suggests, allowing these authors to guide you and your students. Children will hear your excitement as you examine the writing of authors you love, and they, too, will begin to identify personal favorites. Children can be encouraged to read multiple works by the same author, reread favorite stories or pieces, and identify familiar stylistic devices. In this way their favorite author can become a "writing mentor" (Ray, 1999, p. 41).

Teaching voice and tone through mini-lessons that use a variety of forms and genres will be most effective when it occurs in a meaningful context. For instance, if a child is writing a letter to persuade the principal to change a lunchroom procedure, she will be more inclined to read a sample persuasive letter and examine that author's style and effectiveness. See Appendix A-26 for a template that will help you design effective mini-lessons.

***Shared Writing Demonstrations.*** Routman (2005) emphasizes "efficiency of context" (p. 70) in explicit teaching, which means that once we have established a writer's community, we can take advantage of this structure to create purposeful writing for real audiences. She contends that such instruction makes writing more "explicit, effective, and enjoyable" (p. 70). Shared writing takes place when the teacher transcribes and orchestrates the writing but the entire group helps plan and compose the writing. A shared writing demonstration can work at all grade levels if the selected topics are meaningful to the children and if there is a real audience and purpose for the writing—in other words, incorporating authentic literacy practices.

Routman reminds us that shared writing works best when the teacher displays enthusiasm and passion for the topic and when the pace is quick and lively (2005). Children can use shared writing to practice writing within new genres, to manage new forms of writing, and even to try out new writing styles. Because the teacher does the actual writing, the focus is on idea making and collaboration around the chosen writing objective. Shared writing can be done on an easel or on a projected computer screen. One example of a shared writing experience is writing a book review.

1. Read an interesting book to the class.
2. Next, suggest that the class write a review of the book together to post in an upcoming class newsletter or on the class Web site.
3. Read a few actual book reviews from other children's Web sites. Identify the features that make the reviews effective. Make an anchor chart for writing a book review.
4. Next, plan ways to get started on your own review. Reread the book you plan to review. Have students share their ideas out loud about an interesting lead—to "hook" the reader.
5. Accept a couple ideas and then craft the sentence, saying the words out loud as you write them.
6. Keep the whole class actively involved by inviting children to reread certain lines or help with spelling a word as you write or revise.
7. Keep posing questions about the structure out loud, modeling for children and pondering how to effectively state the ideas for the piece as you combine or restate words that children provide.
8. Think about how to end the piece. You might even give children a chance to turn to a neighbor and try out several ideas.
9. After rereading and revising, type out the piece of writing so that it becomes a collective classroom piece. Be sure to actually publish it in the newsletter or on your Web site.

Shared writing demonstrations can be used to explicitly teach any form. They can also be effective for turning some of the topics you covered in mini-lessons into meaningfully crafted group writing.

## Instructional Approaches for Writing Effectiveness for Students with Specific Needs

Gunning (2006) reminds us that in order to close the literacy achievement gap for our striving readers and writers, we need to set realistic goals but also hold our learners to high standards. While it is realistic to expect all children to write every day, the amount of writing and the levels of support children need may vary widely. Gunning also suggests that literacy programs include an affective element. Routman reminds us that kindness counts, adding that offering "one honest compliment" can help turn a child's self-perception into that of a budding writer (2005, p. 79). In order to really help our striving writers become more capable, effective writers, Graves recommends that we get to know them, really know them, as people (1994). Children need to trust that you care enough about them as individuals, which will help you guide them by building on their interests and their strengths.

A learner-centered program can provide the affective supports that are recommended and also target specific developmental "next steps," such as assisting a child as he gains competence and confidence. It may be necessary, though, to "provide more hand holding" within the identified areas of need (Routman, 2005, p. 76) to ensure success for our more reluctant writers. In this section, we will share a few ideas for providing additional support, primarily through supported and focused small-group and individualized instruction, to children who are having difficulty in various areas of writing effectiveness.

***When Writing Lacks Purpose.*** Clearly, a child who has heard many stories and has been exposed to a broad range of informational text is at an advantage when constructing stories and identifying topics of interest that can further her goals in life. Children who have difficulty choosing and then staying on topic may have this trouble because they haven't learned how to select a meaningful topic that is personally engaging. They may select a topic that is too big or too small. Or you might need to help them *build* the background knowledge that is a prerequisite for the topic, particular genre or writing form. One way to support a child who does not stay on topic or does not write clearly is to provide a supported, individualized, or small-group conversational exchange. Brainstorm together, and once a child "lights up" and settles on a topic, you can begin to plan together.

For a child who is just learning how to stay on topic, a planning conference can take the form of an individualized, interactive planning session, "sharing the pen," helping a child hold onto the ideas through sketches and written phrases that you both take turns recording. Once the plan is established, again invite the child to "tell" the story, rehearsing and either adding or deleting ideas from the plan as she practices the storytelling aspect. If a child needs more background experience, you can locate texts within his independent reading level to encourage more rehearsal through reading.

Revision conferences also support the development of purpose. If a writer hears from an eventual reader in a small revision group that an area was confusing, the teacher can support the revision process through an individualized conference directly afterward, helping the child decide how to clarify his writing for the reader. Through individualized, supportive conversations, a child can learn to stick to a topic and not get discouraged, and eventually bring a written piece to completion.

A dialogue journal, a written conversation between you and a student, is another useful tool you can use to encourage writing and keep up a supportive idea exchange with students who need more writing support. By sending written messages back and forth, you can support the use of writing to communicate even as you help the writer discover interesting possibilities for writing topics. Dialogue journals are particularly helpful for children who are learning English as a second language (Gunning, 2006). For instance, if you keep up a written dialogue with an English Language Learner, you provide the extra "think time" for the writer to exchange ideas, and your responses also model the syntactic structure of written communication.

***When Writing Lacks Organization.*** One effective intervention for a child whose writing lacks organization is a linear planning format. Help the child orally rehearse the story or topic and provide a supported conversation. Graves (1994) suggests that we repeat the story by saying things like, "Let me see if I have this right. You said . . ." and then repeating what you think the child has said. Once the structure of the story is somewhat clear, use an interactive or guided-writing model to record the plan.

As the child begins to write, encourage a checking-off system in which you carefully consider each planned event and check them off as she writes. If you have already modeled the form of writing the child is using, review your planning structure with the child and demonstrate how you used a plan to organize your story or letter. Require the child to keep the planning sheet visible during the composition process. As the child ventures out and begins to use various planning structures, demonstrate ways to sequentially number the ideas as the child orally rehearses the story.

When second graders begin to experiment with webbing, it often resembles more of a brainstorming session. You might see a wide array of ideas scattered about the main topic, each connected independently to the center of the web. Using colored pencils, you can help the child circle the ideas that relate to the same subcategories. After your clustering discussion, you can number each colored subgroup in a sequential order to represent the story structure, and the child can check off the ideas as he writes.

If a child is having difficulty with the organizational structures of paragraphs or sentences, you might use a structured language experience approach, which is similar to the framed paragraphs we highlighted in the previous chapter but can also be used to specifically support syntactical structures. For instance, you might discover that a child is trying to write a story about her cat. A structured approach might include a framework for paragraph development that follows the child's series of sketches. "My pet cat's name is ____. One day my cat ____. My cat is special because ____." This technique works particularly well with children who are learning English as a second language (Gunning, 2006).

***When Writing Lacks Details.*** When a child simply lists events or retells a story, the final piece can be rather dull. To encourage a striving writer to add details, having a meaningful conversation with him or her can help illuminate the underlying and interesting facts or descriptions in the story. Small-group oral rehearsals also work, again using an interactive writing format in which you jot down some of the interesting words and phrases and encourage the child to write some as well.

By showing a true interest in the child's topic through your own curiosity and engagement, you can help a child believe that the extra effort of adding details has a payoff for the audience. Some young writers can add details later, through their illustrations. A Post-it note or revision slip stapled into the writing notebook can serve as a reminder for when the child gets to the publishing stage.

It is also helpful to point out when a child has effectively used descriptive writing (Elbow, 1998). For instance, "Lonnie, when you wrote that your cat stares at you by closing one eye and sticking out its tongue, it made me laugh because I could just picture that so well." Commenting on specific passages helps children understand exactly what they are doing well as writers. It also helps them learn that additional details bring readers into the scene and allows them to have a more satisfying experience.

***When Writing Lacks Voice/Tone.***    When teachers give children the opportunity to write about topics that are meaningful, they will be more personally invested in their product. The TAP structure that we introduced in the previous chapter consistently reminds children to grapple with the questions of "Why? Why am I writing this? Who is my audience? What am I hoping to achieve?" If even our youngest writers know that their writing is destined to go to a specific audience, they will be more likely to care about the finished product. Donald Graves (1994) encourages teachers to have frequent conferences with children to help them identify their writings' themes. He suggests that we ask children to identify the one sentence that points out the underlying theme, beyond the "bed-to-bed" recount. "What is this story about? What is this story *really* about?"

If a child is having difficulty producing writing with emotion, ask her to read her story out loud to you. If you can hear places in the story where emotion is coming through, point them out to her and discuss ways that the text might show this feeling. For instance, if the child writes, "I played tag all night until my mom called me in for dinner" and uses intonation on the "all," demonstrate how the child can underline or "stretch" out the word to show the length you heard in the spoken version. This small step indicates that you are listening carefully to what she is trying to say and building on her ideas rather than adding your own voice to her writing (Calkins, 1994; Graves, 1994). Graves (1994) reminds us that children who struggle do not need unfocused praise; rather, they need to believe that they have something worth saying. By providing specific responses, teachers can help children learn to identify for themselves what makes writing work successfully. It is also important to use quality children's literature as models when you are working in small groups so children can have more opportunity to participate and notice the author's craft.

***Supportive Techniques for Individualizing.***    One way to provide developmentally focused instructional support is to conduct one-to-one sessions or focused small-group instruction. To help the child (and yourself) keep track of these lessons, you can create a chart based on what the individual child has learned and is attempting to control independently. The authors of *Dancing with the Pen* (Ministry of Education, 1992) developed a simple form called "I Am Learning/ I Can." This recording sheet is simply a three-column chart that lists the date of the explicit instruction on the left, the skills and strategies that a child is learning in the middle, and a blank column on the right for recording when the child accomplishes the goal independently. You should date the skill in the "I Can" column only when the teacher and child are able to identify that the child is using the skill or convention consistently. This list is useful because it is tailored to the individual child and written using the child's own language. Some teachers make this sheet a double-sided form, with one side used by the child during planning, composing, and revising and the other side used during proofreading. One example of a recorded entry for organization might read, "I am learning to make a list to plan my story" or for details, "I am learning to add interesting details to my story."

To see an example of this chart, turn to chapter 10, Figure 10.4, or go to Appendix A-30 for a reproducible blank form.

When striving learners take part in large-scale writing assessments that are generally prompt-driven, they can become discouraged if they feel unprepared. It is thus important to help children learn to respond to prompts through focused practice sessions. You can begin sessions by teaching children how to read the prompt carefully to understand the directions. Help the children specifically identify the topic, audience, and purpose. Children are often surprised when they picture the evaluative setting where their stories will end up and visualize the actual "readers" as retired teachers or volunteer teachers who leave their classrooms for a few days to help with the evaluations.

After giving the children practice with prompt reading, support them by creating written plans with a basic, reliable structure that children can follow to build the required written form. The next steps can be oral rehearsals, or small-group shared writing. Practice these skills until children respond to the format of the prompt automatically. This will allow striving writers to develop confidence, and perhaps even allow more time for them to expend mental energy on creating stronger writing to support their structured plan. These small-group sessions can be engaging and interactive, and with well-selected prompts, you can also promote the development of higher-order critical thinking skills and, yes, even the standard five-paragraph essay.

Although we have described a variety of instructional approaches for all types of learners, it is important to honor each child's background experiences and skill level in order to plan a manageable instructional program that builds on what the learner can do and is now attempting to do with support. You can best do this through an active, engaging, and authentic writing program.

## LOOKING CLOSELY AT ONE CHILD'S ASSESSMENTS FROM STRAND 8 OF THE LITERACY PROFILE

The following synopsis is based on three pieces of Willa's writing. These are the same pieces that we mentioned in chapter 7. She developed one story after selecting her own topic and the other two from assigned topics. Other information concerning Willa's writing effectiveness was gathered through a teacher-student discussion using the format found in Appendix A-26, "What We Noticed About My Writing—Together." Refer to Figure 8.11 to see how Willa's writing effectiveness is recorded on Strand 8 of the Literacy Profile.

Willa can clearly maintain focus when writing about a topic, whether it is self-generated or teacher selected. Her self-selected topic was a fantasy story about a duck and a fox (see Figure 7.7 in chapter 7). Her assigned topics included a story about penguins (see Figure 8.9) and a story about an important person (see Figure 8.10). The penguin story came about because of a science unit on penguins. The second assignment involved a worksheet that instructed the children to "Draw a picture inside this coin of a person who is important to you. Then write 6 or 7 sentences about that person."

Willa begins both narratives with the familiar opening "Once upon a time," clearly demonstrating her knowledge of the typical structure of past tense narratives. In the story about the duck and the fox, Willa includes a duck as the main character and a fox as the antagonist. In her assigned story about penguins, Willa included both a protagonist and an antagonist: the human is a threatening character.

In Willa's informational piece, she has an effective lead that introduces her sister as an important person by stating, "I love my sister Camlyn." She adds a list of six things that she and her sister like to do together, ending with "and we also play jump off the bed and make our moms nuts." All three pieces show evidence of a developing sense of underlying structure both in

FIGURE 8.9 **Willa's Penguin Story**

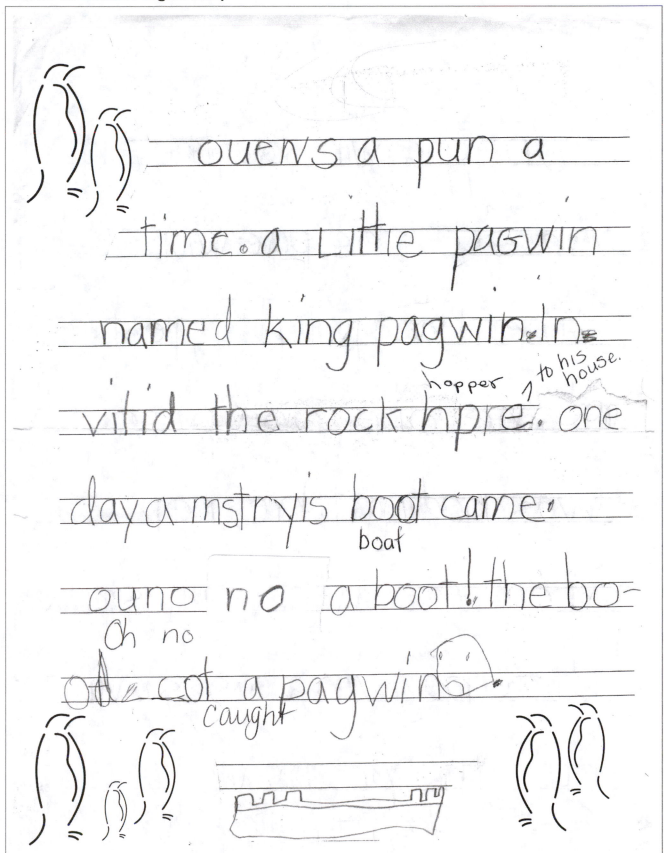

ouens a pun a
time. a little pagwin
named king pagwin. In
vitid the rock hpre. one
*hopper* *to his house.*
day a mstryis boot came.
*boat*
ouno no a boot! the bo-
*Oh no*
ot cot a pagwin
*caught*

FIGURE 8.9 (Continued)

one pagwin saw the pag-

wig old the pagwig sawa
all

one hae jumpt jest on
the

time ole one prson
only

was hoding the rop

vfom fast asca wik splaw
wink

the pagwin was savd

but the prsons whose
was hoding the rop drdid didn't get him crowded

FIGURE 8.10 Willa's I Love My Sister Story

Name: Willa            Date: 3-21-07

### Create Your Own Coin

**Directions:** Draw a picture inside this coin of a person who is important to you. Then write 6 or 7 sentences about that person.

I Love my sistr Cam-
Lyn, we Like to play
wrestling
Wrestling-ing. and guard and
Warm Wee com M. and snow-
Warm

221

FIGURE 8.10 (Continued)

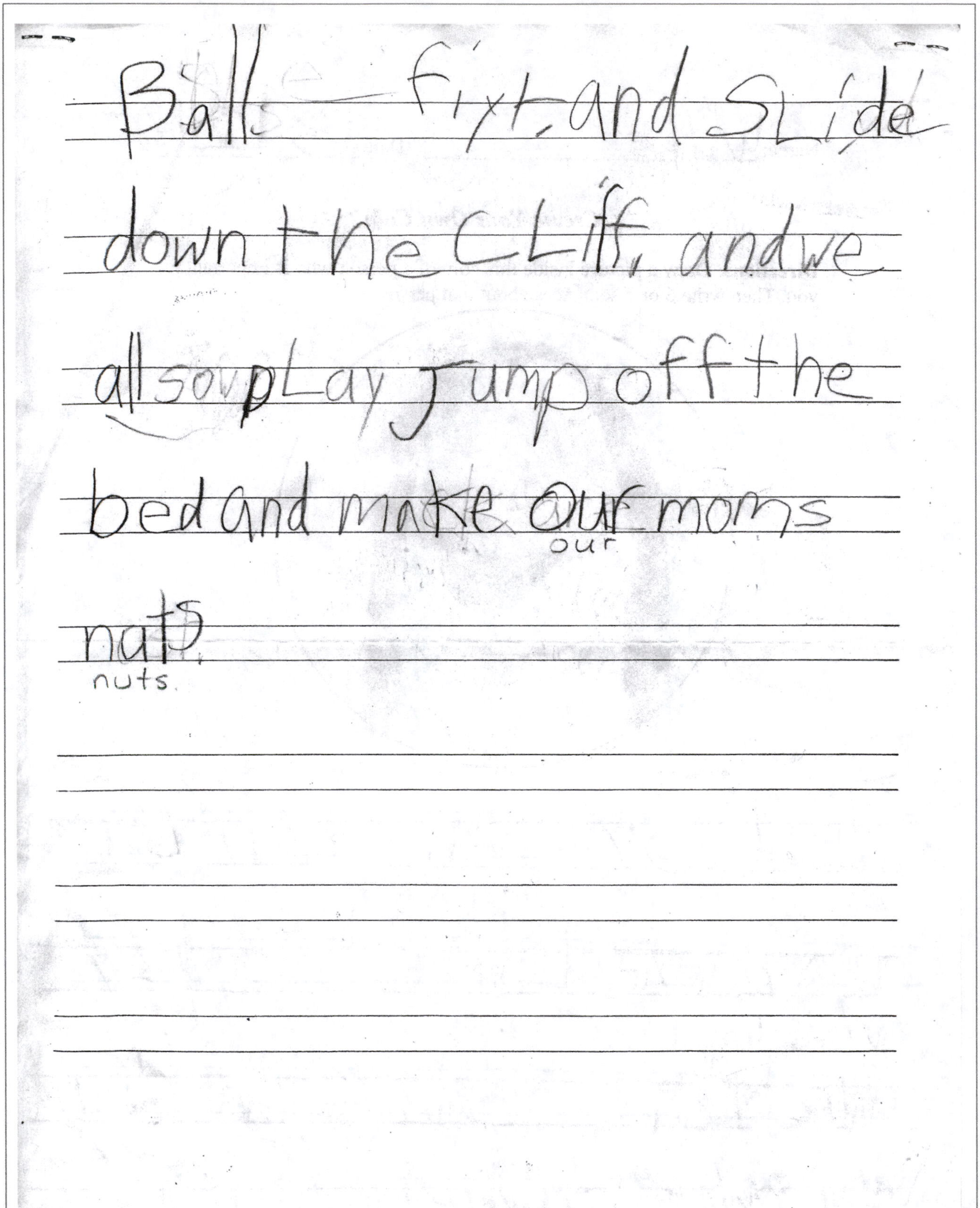

Ball fixt, and slide down the cliff, and we allso play jump off the bed and make our moms

our

nuts.

nuts.

FIGURE 8.11  **Willa's Profile for Writing Effectiveness**

Note: This figure has been excerpted from the full Literacy Profile chart for illustrative purposes. Please consult the full pull-out chart to identify the column headings and development phases.

| Strand *Question & Sample Assessment Tools* | Late Grade 1–Early Grade 2 | Late Grade 2–Early Grade 3 | Late Grade 3–Early Grade 4 |
|---|---|---|---|
| **8. Writing Effectiveness**<br>*How is the child's independent writing developing with regard to purpose, organization, details, and voice/tone?*<br>**Sample Assessment Tools**<br>· Writing samples (prompted and/or independent writing) with checklists, scales, rubrics, or portfolios | Writes three to four understandable sentences on a single topic — to communicate information or tell a story | Writes a narrative with a beginning, middle, and end<br><br>Writes a simple procedure<br><br>When provided with a structure, writes short informational pieces including details relevant to the topic<br><br>With some support, writes poetry as a form of expression, using simple poetic form<br><br>*[Some interesting words used are: mysterious, exploded. She also used the phrase, "Once upon a time" to start her story. Exclamations and a sad face were used to show expression.] KI* | Writes narratives that include more than one character, details, and some dialogue<br><br>Writes procedures with steps, materials, and relevant vocabulary<br><br>Writes informational pieces with appropriate organization and relevant details<br><br>Writes poetry as a form of expression, using simple poetic forms |

Gray areas represent highlighting added by the teacher, preferably using a different color for each year (e.g., yellow highlights for Late K, orange highlights for Early–Mid Grade 1, etc.).
Bracketed material represents teacher/examiner comments from June, Grade 1.

narrative writing and in nonfiction. There is a setting, a problem, and a solution in both narratives. (In her self-selected duck and fox story in chapter 7, she needed prompting to add the ending, but she easily did so.) In the nonfiction piece, Willa includes a topic sentence, and then in her own style, adds a list of the things that she and her sister do together. She adds a bit of humor in the end, letting the reader know that she and her sister often get a reaction from their moms when they jump off their bed.

Willa's transfer into her own writing of descriptive book language and other literacy devices that authors use is evident when she adds phrases such as, "Oh no! A boat!" and "One day a mysterious boat came." Another interesting phrase that Willa uses is, "Just in time," indicating tension and excitement. In her duck and fox story, Willa added details about a car's explosion to add further dramatic effects. In describing her story, Willa talked about the car as another character and as something she was proud to have included. She explained, "I have lots of characters, like the car is just sitting around, waiting to get exploded." Her writing also has appropriate voice/tone, showing feelings and emotion in each of her writing samples as well as varied sentence structures. For instance, after the penguin was caught, she drew a sad face next to the sentence, indicating her emotions as she wrote. She used punctuation to show emotions, too, when she added one exclamation point in each of the narrative stories.

Overall, Willa's writing effectiveness is strong. As she adds new forms of writing to her repertoire, she will need to develop a greater variety of organizational techniques along with greater elaboration and detail.

## REFERENCES

Allen, J. (2002). *On the same page*. Portland, ME: Stenhouse.

Beck, I. L., McKeon, M. G., & Kucan, L. (2002). *Bringing words to life*. New York: Guilford.

Biggam, S. C., Herman, N., & Trubisz, S. (1996). *Primary and 2–4 literacy/communication profiles: Resource guide*. Unpublished manuscript.

Calkins, L. M. (1994). *The art of teaching writing* (new ed.). Portsmouth, NH: Heinemann.

Clay, M. M. (1975). *What did I write? Beginning writing behavior.* Portsmouth, NH: Heinemann.

Cronin, D. (2000). *Click clack moo: Cows that type.* New York: Simon & Schuster Children's Publishing.

Duke, N. K., & Bennett-Armistead, V. S. (2003). *Reading and writing informational text in the primary grades: Research-based practices.* New York: Scholastic.

Duke, N. K., Purcell-Gates, V., Hall, L. A., & Tower, C. (2006/2007). Authentic literacy activities for developing comprehension and writing. *The Reading Teacher, 60*(4), 344–355.

Elbow, P. (1998). *Writing with power* (2nd ed.). New York: Oxford University Press.

Fletcher, R. (1992). *What a writer needs.* Portsmouth, NH: Heinemann.

Galda, L., & Cullinan, B. (2002). *Literature and the child* (6th ed.). Belmont, CA: Wadsworth/Thompson Learning.

Glaser, L. (1994). *Wonderful worms.* Minneapolis, MN: Millbrook Press.

Goodman, K. (1986). *What's whole in whole language? A parent/teacher guide to children's learning.* Portsmouth, NH: Heinemann.

Graves, D. H. (1989). *Investigate nonfiction.* Portsmouth, NH: Heinemann.

Graves, D. H. (1994). *A fresh look at writing.* Portsmouth, NH: Heinemann.

Graves, D. H. (2003). *Writing: Teachers and children at work* (20th anniversary ed.). Portsmouth, NH: Heinemann.

Gunning, T. G. (2006) *Assessing and correcting reading and writing difficulties.* Boston: Pearson.

Hall, D. (1983). *The oxcart man.* New York: Puffin.

Harp, B., & Brewer, J. A. (2005). *The informed reading teacher: Research-based practice.* Upper Saddle River, NJ: Pearson/Merrill Prentice Hall.

Heard, G. (1989). *For the good of the earth and sun: Teaching poetry.* Portsmouth, NH: Heinemann.

Hennings, D. G. (2002). *Communication in action: Teaching literature-based language arts.* Boston: Houghton Mifflin.

Hewitt, G. (1995). *A portfolio primer.* Portsmouth, NH: Heinemann.

Hoose, P. M., & Hoose, H. (1998). *Hey, little ant.* Berkeley, CA: Tricycle Press.

Hoyt, L. (2002). *Make it real: Strategies for success with informational text.* Portsmouth, NH: Heinemann.

Hutchins, P. (1988). *Rosie's walk.* New York: Macmillan.

Krauss, R. (1989). *The carrot seed.* Hempstead, TX: Sagebrush.

Lane, B. (1992). *After "The End": Teaching and learning creative revision.* Portsmouth, NH: Heinemann.

Martin, B., Jr. (1992). *Brown bear, brown bear, what do you see?* Austin, TX: Holt.

Miller, D. (2002). *Reading with meaning.* Portland, ME: Stenhouse.

Ministry of Education. (1992). *Dancing with the pen.* Wellington, New Zealand: Author.

Mooney, M. E., (1990). *Reading to, with, and by.* Katonah, NY: Richard C. Owen Publishers.

Mooney, M. E. (2001). *Text forms and features: A resource for intentional teaching.* Katonah, NY: Richard C. Owen Publishers.

Moore, S. (1995, December). Questions for research into reading-writing relationships and text-structure knowledge. *Language Arts, 72,* 598–606.

Oglan, G. R. (2003). *Write, right, rite.* Boston: Pearson.

Owen, R. C. (2001). *Literacy learning in the classroom.* Katonah, NY: Richard C. Owen Publishers.

Pearson, P. D., & Gallagher, M. C. (1983). The instruction of reading comprehension. *Contemporary Educational Psychology, 8,* 317–345.

Ray, K. W. (1999). *Wondrous words: Writers and writing in the elementary classroom.* Urbana, IL: National Council of Teachers of English.

Routman, R. (2005). *Writing essentials: Raising expectations and results while simplifying teaching.* Portsmouth, NH: Heinemann.

Rylant, C. (1982). *When I was young in the mountains.* New York: E. P. Dutton.

Rylant, C. (1996) *Henry and Mudge: The first book.* New York: Aladdin.

Smith, F. (1988). *Joining the literacy club: Further essays in education.* Portsmouth, NH: Heinemann.

Spandel, V. (2004). *Creating young writers: Using the six traits to enrich writing process in primary classrooms.* Boston: Pearson Education, Inc.

Stead, T. (2002). *Is that a fact? Teaching nonfiction writing K–3.* Portland, ME: Stenhouse.

Steig, W. (1969). *Sylvester and the magic pebble.* New York: Simon and Schuster.

Tompkins, G. E. (2008). *Teaching writing: Balancing process and product.* Upper Saddle River, NJ: Pearson/Merrill Prentice Hall.

Turbill, J., & Bean, W. (2006). *Writing instruction K–6: Understanding process, purpose, audience.* Katonah, NY: Richard C. Owen Publishers.

Van Allsburg, C. (1993). *The sweetest fig.* New York: Houghton Mifflin.

Vygotsky, L. (1978). *Mind in society: The development of higher psychological processes* (M. Cole, V. John-Steiner, S. Scribner, & E. Souberman, Eds. & Trans.). Cambridge, MA: Harvard University Press.

Willems, M. (2003). *Don't let the pigeon drive the bus.* New York: Hyperion Books for Children.

Williams, V. A. (1984). *A chair for my mother.* New York: Harper Collins.

Wood, D., & Wood, A. (1984). *The napping house.* New York: Harcourt.

Yolen, J. (1987). *Owl moon.* New York: Philomel/Penguin Group.

Yorinks, A. (2001). *Hey, Al.* New York: Farrar, Straus & Giroux, Inc.

# CHAPTER NINE

# Spelling

─────────────────────────── CORE QUESTION

How is the child's spelling developing, including application in independent writing?

Nearly every day, teachers or parents hear the question, "How do you spell ____?", as children begin to figure out the many, many different ways that words can be spelled. The adults who attempt to respond to this question often find themselves in a quandary, trying to decide whether to spell the word for the child, help the child with some strategies or clues, or just suggest that the child try it on his/her own by using "invented spelling."

Fortunately, we now know a lot more about spelling than we did 50 years ago. From the 1970s through the 1990s, Read (1975), Henderson (1981), Templeton and Bear (1992), Ehri (1997), and others conducted exciting research into children's spelling errors and found them to provide a wealth of information about children's emerging understandings of how words work. They also found that evaluating children's attempts at spelling could guide teachers in differentiating word study for children and providing timely, effective instruction. Bear, Invernizzi, Templeton, and Johnston (2008) explain:

> Students' spellings provide a direct window into how they think the system works. By interpreting what students do when they spell, educators can target a specific student's "zone of proximal development." (p. 8)

In this chapter we will explain some key principles of spelling development and word study, describe some formal and informal methods of assessing spelling, and provide some instructional techniques that can support children's development of spelling concepts and skills. Finally, we will describe Willa's spelling development, how it has been represented on the Literacy Profile, and what next steps might make sense for her continued growth in the area of spelling and word study. You will find in this chapter that we discuss many of the same concepts we discussed in chapter 3 on decoding and word analysis, since decoding and encoding (spelling) are so closely linked.

## UNDERLYING PRINCIPLES OF SPELLING

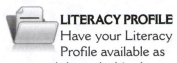

**LITERACY PROFILE**
Have your Literacy Profile available as you read through this chapter, referring to the question and indicators for Strand 9.

Spelling is complex but also intriguing. Initially, spelling involves figuring out that there is a way to move from speech (what we say) to print (how we write what we say) and learning to represent sounds (phonemes) with letters (graphemes) in a sequence that corresponds to those sounds. When children demonstrate this important understanding—that letters represent speech sounds—we say that they have learned the "alphabetic principle." Later, spelling involves skills in using word patterns, structural analysis, and word origins, along with other strategies.

Knowledge about spelling is often referred to as "orthography," which is the writing system of a language using a correct sequence of letters. Orthography in English has three layers: alphabet, pattern, and meaning. Good spelling instruction addresses all three of those layers, but in a developmental sequence geared to the spelling stage of the child who is learning how to spell. Knowing the child's developmental level provides powerful information to obtain and use; Templeton and Morris (1999) describe orthographic knowledge as the *engine* that drives both reading and writing.

Clearly, children's early spelling progress can indicate their overall literacy development, although other indicators such as comprehension and vocabulary are critical as well (Ehri, 1997; Gentry, 2004). In this section we will describe what goes into the development of spelling and how children's stages of spelling shift over time.

### Understanding the Nature of Spelling

Learning how to spell in English is an accomplishment that depends on several different kinds of skills and knowledge, such as phonological awareness (the ability to detect and manipulate speech sounds in language), the concept of "word" as a unit, phonics (control over sound-symbol relationships and patterns), and automaticity when spelling high-frequency or irregularly spelled words.

Earlier in this chapter we mentioned that spelling is complex but intriguing. As an indication of this complexity, consider the following: English has 44 phonemes (or sounds), but more than 1,000 different graphemes (letters or letter combinations) that can represent these sounds. For example, the long /a/ sound can be spelled with "-ay" as in *play,* "-ai" as in *rain,* "a_e" as in *make,* or "-eigh" as in *freight*—and these aren't the only ways to spell the long /a/ sound! In contrast, Italian has 25 phonemes and only 33 graphemes (spelling combinations) for these sounds. Not surprisingly, there are many fewer instances of spelling and reading difficulty in Italy than in the United States! (Gentry, 2004).

So helping children learn to spell takes time, and teachers need to intentionally plan this instruction. To do so, it is particularly helpful for teachers to understand the three layers (alphabet, pattern, and meaning) of English orthography mentioned previously.

***Alphabet.*** The first layer involves the relationship between letters and sounds, which, as explained earlier, is not neat and tidy. Sounds in English can be represented by a variety of letters and letter combinations. As children gain knowledge at this level, they often "use their alphabet knowledge quite literally, relying on the sound embedded in the names of the letters to represent the sounds they are trying to represent" (Bear et al., 2008, p. 5). For example, a child who wants his mother to buy more ice cream at the store might write a note saying, "BI MR IS KREM." This form of writing is often called "invented spelling," and actually, it is not only a key step in learning to spell, but it also assists reading development because it helps students a learn to unlock the "code" of reading (Gentry, 2007).

Children at this stage often have difficulty distinguishing among short vowels as well and frequently spell a word with a vowel sound that is articulated (in the mouth) close to the correct one. For example, a child might spell "sick" as "SEK." At this level, children need many experiences with building phonological awareness and learning the sound-symbol correspondences of consonants and short vowels.

*Pattern.*  This layer involves studying the common patterns in single-syllable and multisyllable words. Such patterns help the speller (and reader) notice consistency in how sounds are represented by different combinations of letters (such as the different ways to spell long *e*, as in *seat, free, key, me*). This is also an important time for children to study the patterns that result from different arrangements of consonants and vowels and also how syllables are put together. For example, CVC (consonant-vowel-consonant) words such as *cap* have short vowel sounds, but CVCe words such as *cape* in most cases have a long vowel sound.

*Meaning.*  The meaning layer is particularly interesting because it helps explain some spellings that children might have thought of as unusual, irregular, or just plain odd. This layer involves studying roots, prefixes, suffixes, and word origins. A basic principle of this layer is that words that are related in meaning will also have related spelling patterns (Bear et al., 2008). For example, *trio* is spelled with the prefix "tri-" because it means "a group of three." (A student who is not yet ready to explore the meaning layer might spell "trio" as "treeo" or "treo.") In most cases, only children in the upper grades will explore this layer, although some advanced spellers at the third- or fourth-grade level might do so.

## Understanding Stages of Spelling Development

Figuring out a child's stage of development in spelling is critical to understand how to support him or her in reaching the next step of spelling development. In this section we will describe two commonly used approaches for categorizing stages or phases of spelling development. Understanding these categories will be very helpful as we explore spelling assessment and ways to plan instruction based on assessment results. Both approaches focus on what children can control in their writing as well as what they "use but confuse."

*Two Phases, with Four Initial Levels in Phase One.*  Gentry (2004) clearly distinguishes between two separate phases of spelling development: learning *how to spell* and *becoming an automatic and correct speller*. Learning *how to spell* generally occurs in kindergarten through the end of Grade 1, while the process of *becoming a good speller* develops gradually from Grade 2 through Grade 8. This is particularly important to keep in mind when working with children in Grades 2, 3, or 4 who, for one reason or another, have not yet learned how to spell. Teaching them advanced word patterns would be an ineffective use of time because these children are functioning at an earlier level of spelling development.

*Phase One: Learning to Spell.* A lot goes on during the first phase of spelling, which involves learning how the alphabetic system works, or how to represent sounds and words with letters. At the very beginning of this phase, much of what children produce may be hard to think of as "spelling," but their spelling attempts are definitely laying the foundation of learning to spell. This phase takes approximately 2 years in most cases, but can occur much more quickly or take more time. Gentry (2004) describes the stages that children go through during this phase (see Figure 9.1).

Let's consider what children's writing at the different stages within phase one might look like. Imagine a kindergarten classroom in which five different children are trying to write the word "snowman." A child functioning at Gentry's level 0 might represent "snowman" with a series of scribbles or loops, or a picture with no label.

A child functioning at Gentry's level 1 (precommunicative) stage might accompany a picture of a snowman with letters (*E i V*), but the letters are basically random and don't represent any of the sounds in *snowman*. Children at this level do not yet demonstrate phonemic awareness, and even though they know something about writing, they haven't yet learned the alphabetic principle about the relationship between sounds and letters.

Another child, functioning at Gentry's level 2 (semi-phonetic spelling), might represent *snowman* with "S M N" or even "SOMN," demonstrating her early development of phonemic awareness. When children demonstrate this degree of competence by the end of kindergarten, it is a promising sign and an indication that they are in the process of learning the alphabetic principle.

Still another child in the same kindergarten class might be functioning at Gentry's level 3 (phonetic spelling). This child might represent *snowman* as "S N O M E N," which clearly demonstrates his control of the alphabetic principle, by writing a letter for each sound he heard, including vowels. Note that children's representation at this stage is not always correct (the child wrote "O" instead of "OW" and "E" instead of "A"), but the child was definitely attempting to systematically and sequentially represent the sounds in the word with letters or letter combinations.

Finally, a child might already be functioning at Gentry's level 4 (transitional spelling) stage. That child might represent *snowman* as "SNOEMAN." Clearly this child is trying out more advanced spelling patterns even though her spelling is not yet "conventional." Needless to say, the five children described above will need different approaches to help them get to the next step.

*Phase Two.* Gentry (2004) describes this phase as the period when children work on spelling correctly and automatically, "fine-tuning their word-specific knowledge" and concentrating on "adding entries to the dictionary in the brain" (p. 16). This phase generally spans second through eighth

### Figure 9.1 Stages of Development in Phase One: Learning to Spell

| Gentry's Levels of Writing and Stages of Spelling Development |
| --- |
| Level 0: No ability to use invented spelling |
| Level 1: Use of letters with no matches to sound. Precommunicative spelling |
| Level 2: Use of partial letter-sound matches. Semi-phonetic spelling |
| Level 3: Use of one letter for each sound. Phonetic spelling |
| Level 4: Use of chunks of phonic patterns. Transitional spelling |

Another researcher who uses the same developmental spelling stages as Bear et al. (2008) is Kathy Ganske, author of *Word Journeys* (2000). There are some slight differences in the labels she uses (*syllable juncture* instead of *syllables and affixes*, and *derivational constancy* instead of *derivational relations*), but the stages are actually identical to those Bear et al. list.

grade, and during this time, the percentage of words that children misspell should decrease dramatically. Gentry indicates that at the beginning of second grade, even children who have reached level 4 typically still misspell up to a third of the words they use in independent writing, but this should decrease to 10% by the end of Grade 3; by Grade 6 the percentage should be very small. During both phases (phase 1 and phase 2), while children are building their spelling knowledge and skill, it is critical for them to study spelling patterns appropriate for their developmental stage along with high-frequency words.

***Five Developmental Stages of Spelling.***  Other researchers have divided the stages of spelling somewhat differently, although the underlying principles are really the same. The labels Bear et al. (2008) use are based on the work of Henderson (1990); see Figure 9.2 for an outline of these stages. One benefit of the model Bear et al. and Ganske use is the degree of detail all five levels of spelling provide. Let's look more closely at each stage.

*Emergent Stage.*  Children are at the emergent stage of spelling when they are writing with symbols, random strings of letters, or letter-like figures that have no connection to the sounds in the words they are trying to write. Some children only draw and use no symbols or letters at all. For example, a child at the emergent stage might spell "vacation" as "T E S" or perhaps draw a roller coaster as a scribble. This stage may be evident in children from preK up to the middle of Grade 1, or from ages 1 to 7.

*Letter-Name Stage.*  Letter-name or alphabetic spellers rely on the sounds they hear to spell, although they may not represent all of the phonemes in a word yet. Also, they often rely on the names of letters to help them spell, not always successfully. A child at the letter-name stage might spell *vacation* as "FAKSHN." Letter-name spelling is evident in most first- and second-grade classrooms, or in the spelling of children from ages 4 to 9.

*Within-Word Stage.*  Children at this stage can spell most short vowel, single-syllable words correctly and have control over most consonant blends and digraphs. Learning about silent *e*, vowel combinations such as "ou," "ay," and "oi," and "*r*-controlled" vowels are important areas to focus on at this stage, which is most frequently evident from Grade 2 to Grade 4, or from ages 6 to 12. A child at the within-word stage might spell *vacation* as "vakashin"

*Syllables and Affixes Stage.*  By the time children reach this stage, they spell most single-syllable words correctly and are ready to concentrate on multisyllabic words. Areas of focus include when to double consonants when adding endings, when to drop a final *e*, and how to spell using common prefixes and suffixes. A child working at the syllables and affixes stage might spell *vacation* as "vacasion." This stage can range from Grades 3 to 8, or ages 8 to 12.

*Derivational Relations Stage.*  Even though very few students in the lower grades function at this level, it is good for teachers to know about it nevertheless. At the derivational relations stage, children apply the principle that words with similar meanings share similar spelling patterns. Children also explore word origins, including Greek and Latin roots and affixes. A child at the derivational relations stage is likely to spell *vacation* conventionally. A few fourth-grade children may be at this stage, but usually it's evident in children in Grades 5 to 8, or ages 10 and up.

FIGURE 9.2  **Stages of Developmental Spelling**

| Stage | Key Features of the Stage: What the Student Does When Spelling | Sample of Student Writing/Spelling |
|---|---|---|
| Emergent | • Often scribbles, or uses drawings only<br>• May use random letters<br>• No sound-letter correspondence | |
| Letter-name | • Uses letters to represent sounds (demonstrates alphabetic principle)<br>• Gains control over consonants, blends, digraphs, and short vowels | *KR*<br>(for "car") |
| Within-word | • Spells most single-syllable, short vowel words correctly<br>• Gains control over vowel patterns within single-syllable words | *croud*<br>(for "crowd") |
| Syllables and affixes | • Spells most single-syllable words correctly<br>• Gains control over when to drop silent *e*, when to double consonants, etc.<br>• Learns to use common prefixes and suffixes in multisyllable words | *stoping*<br>(for "stopping") |
| Derivational relations | • Explores words that are spelled similarly because their meaning is similar<br>• Expands control over words with Greek and Latin roots, prefixes, and suffixes | *compasition*<br>(for "composition") |

Source: Bear, Donald R., Invernizzi, Marcia, Templeton, Shane R., & Johnston, Francine. *Words Their Way: Word Study for Phonics, Vocabulary, and Spelling Instruction*, 4th ed. © 2008, pp. 22–24. Reprinted by permission of Pearson Education, Inc. Upper Saddle River, NJ.

## Summary of Understanding Spelling

Learning how to spell is complex but predictable in most cases. In this section we considered factors involved in learning how to spell, along with two commonly used approaches to understanding the stages of spelling development: Gentry's two-phase approach, with five levels in Phase One, and Bear et al.'s five developmental spelling stages. Both ways of thinking about children's development in spelling and word study have a common foundation: a child develops spelling knowledge and skill in a predictable sequence, and trying to teach spelling skills that are beyond the child's current stage does little to help the child. Knowing a child's stage of spelling development, however, provides invaluable information to teachers as they plan the next steps for helping the child move to the next level, not only in spelling but also in reading. In the next section we will discuss both formal and informal approaches to spelling assessment.

## ASSESSING SPELLING

For most of us, our school-based experience with spelling assessment was limited to the Friday spelling test. The information the teacher gained from that test often had limited value in evaluating our spelling skills, though, because we could memorize the words on the test (and would often forget them by the next Monday). Now, however, teachers have several ways to assess children's progress in becoming competent spellers, and in this section we will discuss both formal and informal measures that teachers might use in K–4 classrooms.

### Formal or Published Measures for Assessing Spelling

A variety of formal measures are available for assessing spelling progress. In this section we will consider developmental spelling assessments and other published tools.

***Developmental Spelling Assessments.*** A noted researcher in the area of spelling, Moats (1995), particularly recommends using assessments that are sensitive to changes in children's developmental spelling levels during the early stages of learning how to spell—because the information gained can be useful in guiding instruction. To find out children's individual spelling stages, several options are available. Three tests that are used frequently include Gentry's Monster Test (2004), Bear et al.'s Primary and Elementary Spelling Inventories (2008), and Ganske's Developmental Spelling Analysis (2000). We will briefly describe each test, and at the end of this chapter, we will refer back to the Primary Spelling Inventory because it was used to help determine Willa's stage of spelling and to plan the next steps.

*Monster Test.* This simple 10-word assessment developed by Gentry (2004) reflects the "two-phase" categories we described earlier. The Monster Test is administered much like any other spelling test, and Gentry provides a chart that indicates the kind of spelling that a child at each stage would likely produce. For example, a child might spell the word "eagle":

- With random letters (at the precommunicative/level 1 stage)
- As "EL" (at the semi-phonetic/level 2 stage)
- As "EGL" (at the phonetic/level 3 stage)
- As "EGUL" (at the transitional/level 4 stage)
- As "Eagle" (at the conventional level)

To determine a child's predominant spelling stage, teachers simply calculate the percentage of words in each stage; usually a child's responses primarily indicate one stage, but it is also helpful for teachers to see when children are "edging" into the next category. For example, 70% of a particular child's responses might reveal semi-phonetic spelling, but the remaining 30% might be phonetic, indicating that the child is beginning to gain control over phonemic awareness and the alphabetic principle.

*Primary and Elementary Spelling Inventories.*  These inventories, developed by Bear et al. (2008), provide a reliable and valid way not only to determine a child's spelling stage but also to determine specifically which orthographic features the child already has control over, and which ones will be appropriate to focus on next.

The Primary Spelling Inventory includes 26 words and is appropriate for most children in K–3, while the Elementary Spelling Inventory may be used in Grades 1–6. Some schools opt to use the Elementary Spelling Inventory for all grades as a shared (schoolwide) assessment tool, but the Primary Spelling Inventory will yield more detailed information for most children in K–2, which is why we recommend using it for those grade levels. If you use the Primary Spelling Inventory with kindergarteners or other emergent readers, you will most likely use only the first five words.

Administering both inventories simply involves dictating words to the group of children. To score the assessment, teachers first count the number of words spelled correctly to obtain a "power score," which indicates each child's stage of spelling development. Next teachers check off particular features (e.g., short vowels, consonant digraphs, *r*-controlled vowels) that were spelled correctly and confirm the predominant spelling stage. This will be the stage where most of the features are checked. A Feature Guide is provided so that teachers can tally up the number of points for each feature and gauge what each child has *some* control over, and what the child is "using but confusing." The teacher then has helpful information to determine the next steps for instruction.

> You can find both inventories in Bear et al.'s *Words Their Way* (2008), which also includes assessment resources on CD and DVD.

*Developmental Spelling Analysis (DSA).*  This assessment, available in *Word Journeys* (Ganske, 2000), is very similar to the Elementary Spelling Inventory but can provide more detailed information regarding specific spelling features that children seem to have control over and gaps that their responses indicate. The assessment has two parts, a broad Screening Assessment and more detailed Feature Inventories (for four different spelling stages). Consisting of 20 words, the Screening Assessment determines a child's apparent stage of spelling development so that the teacher can select an appropriate Feature Inventory to test the child.

One benefit of the DSA's two-step process is that the Screening Assessment allows a teacher to "zoom in" on the particular stage where a student is functioning, and then the teacher can obtain much more detailed information from the appropriate Feature Inventory. For example, if a teacher administers the Feature Inventory for the within-word stage, the teacher administers five words for *each* of the following features:

- Long vowels (Vce)
- *R*-controlled vowels
- Other common long vowels
- Complex consonants
- Abstract vowels

Because of the number of items for any particular feature, teachers can feel quite confident when they tailor instruction based on this information. The DSA is slightly more time-consuming than the Elementary Spelling Inventory, so some schools decide to administer the Elementary Spelling Inventory or the Primary Spelling Inventory to *all* students, and then individual teachers or specialists administer the Developmental Spelling Analysis to diagnose the spelling difficulties of children who need a "closer look."

***Other Published Spelling Assessment Tools.*** In addition to the assessments described above, other assessments are available to screen, diagnose, or monitor a child's progress. The Test of Written Spelling (Larsen, Hammill, & Moats, 1999) takes about 10 or 15 minutes to administer and involves students spelling words that have predictable patterns and words that have unpredictable patterns. Lists are organized by grade level, and the assessment yields grade-equivalent scores along with percentiles and "spelling ages." Some schools use this as a screening tool; it might be most appropriately used with children at or above Grade 1. In addition, many commercial spelling programs contain their own assessments, and norm-referenced tests often have a spelling subtest as well.

## Informal Measures for Assessing Spelling

Looking at children's ongoing, everyday progress in spelling competence is also important. Weekly spelling tests can provide some information about spelling progress, but too often (unless teachers include "transfer" words on a test), children can do quite well on these tests by simply memorizing the words. The challenge for teachers, of course, is finding efficient and effective ways beyond the Friday test to assess spelling. We will discuss a few options that can provide valuable information.

***Reviewing Spelling from Independent Writing Samples.*** As the old adage says, "The proof is in the pudding." In other words, if children do just fine on a weekly spelling test but don't use their skills in their everyday writing, what's the actual result of testing them? One approach that teachers might use is scheduling spelling "dipstick" assessments that look at children's daily writing. Once each week, you might collect two samples of independent writing from two or three children. (That way, you can assess each child's independent writing perhaps three times each year.) Using the selected samples, first determine the percentage of correctly spelled words. You might do this by reviewing two or three different 20-word sections of student writing. Remember earlier in this chapter that we noted some benchmarks Gentry (2004) recommends. At the beginning of second grade, a child who has reached level 4 (transitional spelling) should correctly spell up to 66% of the words used in independent (first-draft) writing; by the end of third grade, that percentage should be closer to 90%. These benchmarks should help gauge children's progress, but they will also be influenced by the child's degree of risk taking and the climate of the classroom as well.

Next, you might take a closer look at some (perhaps four or five) of the errors the child made, and use a "Spelling Application Grid" like the one in Figure 9.3 to analyze the child's spelling in terms of stage and features used and/or confused. To gain the most information from this approach, teachers should select words that are in the child's "zone," as opposed to words that are well beyond what one could reasonably expect the child to spell, given his or her stage of spelling development. It will also be helpful to use the Comments section of this form to note patterns that you see. For example, you may have noticed that a particular child does quite well with "regular" words that fit into patterns that he or she has learned but is having more difficulty spelling irregular high-frequency words such as *thought* and *because*, and may benefit from some regular review of how to spell these words and tips for remembering the "tricky parts."

FIGURE 9.3  Spelling Application Grid: Reviewing Spelling in
Independent Writing

**Student:** *Joey*                    **Gr:** *3*                    **Date:** *Oct 5*
**Writing samples:** *Journal, weekly letter home*

**Percentage of words spelled correctly:** *92%*
  *Note*: Gentry's (2004) benchmarks for extended
    independent writing:
      • 66% words correctly spelled at beginning of Grade 2
      • 90% words correctly spelled at end of Grade 3

**Comments:**

| Word | Correct Spelling | Emergent | Letter-Name | Within-Word | Syllables and Affixes | Derivational Relations | Features to Be Worked on (or used but confused) |
|------|------------------|----------|-------------|-------------|-----------------------|------------------------|-------------------------------------------------|
| *wint* | *went* | | x | | | | *Short vowel e–i* |
| *grabed* | *grabbed* | | | | x | | *Doubling* |
| *houled* | *howled* | | | x | | | *ou  ow* |
| *suprised* | *surprised* | | | x | | | *ur* |
| *crak* | *crack* | | x | | | | *Ck at end of word* |

**Notes for Next Steps:**

*Clear up short vowel confusion;*
*work on sorts that highlight ck at end of words*

Using this type of informal assessment a few times a year should provide a helpful picture of children's progress over time. What is key is keeping the process manageable. You might consider reviewing strong spellers' independent writing only twice a year but more frequently reviewing the writing of children who struggle with spelling. Appendix A-28 provides blank copy of the "Spelling Application Grid." With children in Grades 3 or 4, you might ask them to locate errors within their own writing; this practice definitely builds children's self-reflection and reduces "spelling passivity."

***Student Self-Assessment and Self-Monitoring.*** Very young children probably won't be able to self-assess their own spelling, but by the time children are in third or fourth grade, they may be able to self-assess their spelling by reviewing their independent writing. What can be tricky is finding a balance between focusing too much and focusing too little on spelling correctness when children are writing independently. As early as first or second grade, though, teachers can certainly ask children to look over their independent writing to find two or three words that they tried to spell but have questions about. This practice promotes self-reflection and self-monitoring, which are very important aspects of spelling "consciousness." Checklists and rubrics may also be useful, but it's best to develop them *with* the children to make sure the language is familiar to them. For example, some items in a checklist for late first graders or early second graders might include:

_____I try to spell unknown words.

_____I try to write the sounds I hear in a word.

_____I check my own writing.

_____I use what I already know to help me spell.

With third or fourth graders, teachers might use a promising approach called Thoughtful Editing (Wheatley, 2005). When a child is almost ready for the editing and proofreading phases of the writing process, the teacher reviews the draft and locates 5 to 10 errors that he/she would like the child to find and correct. (Be sure to choose errors that the child *should* have control over, given his/her stage of development and previous instruction.) The teacher simply writes the *number* of errors at the top of the page and does *not* identify them. The child then finds, underlines, and corrects the errors. Because the teacher can vary the number according to children's level of spelling awareness, the approach is very flexible. Again, this practice promotes spelling consciousness, which is critical for children as they move up the grades.

### Summary of Assessing Spelling

Spelling assessment should involve much more than the "Friday test." Developmental spelling assessments such as the Primary and Elementary Spelling Inventories are very useful, particularly because the information they provide can inform the next steps in instruction. Other assessment options include formal/commercial assessments as well as informal approaches such as looking at children's writing samples and children's self-assessments. What's essential at this point is to consider how to use this information to inform and guide instruction.

## INSTRUCTIONAL APPROACHES FOR SPELLING

Some people think that spelling is "caught," not taught, or that children learn to spell by reading, but research (Ehri, 1997; Gentry, 2004) tells us that is not the case. In fact, instruction *does* matter, and instruction that is based on careful assessment and observation of where children are developmentally is particularly effective. In this section we first address common instructional approaches for teaching spelling to the general population of children, and then we turn to more specialized approaches for children with specific spelling difficulties.

Approaches to spelling instruction vary widely, and many people have very strong opinions about what works, and what doesn't. Some emphasize memorizing spelling rules; others favor a multisensory approach; and still others claim success by focusing primarily on visual cues. That said, most agree that the overall goal is for children to develop the strategies and skills of competent spellers, but also to know that their writing is valued even if they struggle with spelling.

### Instructional Approaches for Supporting Spelling Development in All Students

Developing competence as a speller requires time, good instruction, and a supportive environment that includes the encouragement to take risks and use available resources. In addition, children need instruction that is tailored to their developmental stage of spelling (Fresch & Wheaton, 2002; Zutell, 1996). In this section we will describe the qualities and principles of good spelling instruction, some frequently used approaches, and a few specific techniques for supporting spelling development.

***Qualities and Principles of Good Spelling Instruction.***  Although there certainly are a variety of approaches to spelling instruction, it is helpful to agree upon some best practices. Snowball and Bolton (1999) provide a list of key principles and practices to foster effective spelling development. Their key points include:

- Encouraging risk taking
- Linking spelling to reading and writing
- Guiding children in a process of inquiry and discovery
- Using children's writing to demonstrate strategies
- Providing a resource–rich classroom environment
- Informing parents
- Keeping spelling in perspective

***Frequently Used Approaches to Teaching Spelling.***  Some schools utilize a comprehensive reading-language arts program (basal) that frequently includes a spelling component. While this may seem efficient, sometimes the words and patterns being taught and assessed do not match children's specific needs.

Other schools use an independent commercial spelling program. These programs differ widely in how they address spelling. Most present word lists arranged by spelling patterns that are appropriate for each grade level and include a range of activities for children to complete during the week. Some (such as Spelling Mastery from SRA) include more explicit instruction from the teacher; others (such as Rebecca Sitton's approach) focus primarily on high-frequency words that are appropriate to each grade level. Sitton's approach emphasizes the development of a core of spelling words, approximately 100 words per year. The program supports the development of word study skills and student accountability for the correct spelling of words previously taught throughout the grades. Teachers choose their own skill-building lessons from resource books that offer ready-to-teach lessons, blackline masters, and a menu of optional lesson ideas. One unique feature of this approach is the cloze assessments (fill-in-the-blank stories) that incorporate words from all previous grade levels as well as the newly introduced words. Children receive word lists of previously taught words to focus their attention on spelling accuracy during proofreading.

As mentioned earlier in this chapter, one persistent challenge that teachers face is differentiating spelling instruction according to children's needs. Some programs, such as Spelling for Writers from Great Source, provide opportunities for differentiation among children. In Spelling for Writers, children take a pretest, and depending on their pretest score, they select words from supplemental lists that are appropriate to their level of performance.

Some commercial programs such as Fundations (from Wilson Language Systems) integrate phonics and decoding with spelling. Fundations, a classroom adaptation of a Wilson program that was developed for older children with reading and spelling disabilities, may be useful when a consistent and "direct" approach is needed.

Still other schools use a developmental spelling approach. Using the assessment and word-sorting routines from *Words Their Way* (Bear et al., 2008) or *Word Journeys* (Ganske, 2000), teachers divide the class into two or three groups according to children's predominant spelling stage. On the first day, teachers introduce the children in one group to a specific feature, and then the children practice sorting words and applying their new learning during the rest of the week. Teachers introduce different sorts to other groups on succeeding days. Keeping word sorts organized can be a challenge, but publishers provide management resources to help teachers. This is very much in line with a developmental approach to spelling, along with other key principles and practices (Snowball & Bolton, 1999) listed previously.

Finally, teachers in some schools address spelling on an individual basis. While teachers may provide excellent spelling instruction, the inherent danger is that there is often very little common language or shared expectations among children's spelling. In some cases, using a common spelling assessment can at least provide a first step toward building a common approach to spelling and word study.

***Specific Techniques.*** A variety of techniques are effective for supporting children as they develop into competent spellers. Many of these techniques, such as word sorting, spelling conferences, and keeping a spelling notebook or personal dictionary of "tricky" words, are useful for children at most spelling stages. To learn high-frequency words, children commonly use the "look-say-name-cover-write-check" strategy, in which first children look closely at the word to be studied, particularly noticing familiar or tricky parts within the word. Then children say the word and name the letters in the word. Next, children cover the word, picture it in their minds, and write the word from that mental picture. Finally, children check to see whether they wrote the word correctly.

Some techniques, such as using Elkonin (1973) boxes (described in chapter 1), are most effective with emergent and letter-name spellers, while others, such as "Homophone Rummy" (Ganske, 2000), are more appropriate for children who are at the within-word stage or are just beginning the syllables and affixes stage. Interestingly, homonym errors (e.g., *maid, made*) are the most common spelling error of all. Children's confusions about word usage (discussed more in chapter 10) contribute to this situation.

The "I Can/I Am Learning To" resource described in chapter 10 can also be very useful to support children at almost any level as they gain control over spelling patterns that they have been taught *and* that are within their reach. In addition, for children who are at the syllables and affixes stage or even the derivational relations stage, having them make word webs or word clusters can be particularly useful. Children at this stage benefit from exploring words that have common roots (e.g., "port" is a common root for words like *portable, report, export, porter,* and so forth). One particularly engaging and flexible resource that allows children to create word webs as well as other types of visual displays is a computer (software) program called Kidspiration. Next we will briefly describe three of the techniques listed above: word sorting, word operations, and spelling conferences.

See www.kidspiration.com to find out about this resource that uses visual tools to help children combine pictures, text, and spoken words.

***Word Sorting.*** From an early age, children can sort objects and pictures and then words. Sorting simply involves grouping similar things together and eventually making generalizations about the noticeable traits of different groups. There are several kinds of sorts: closed sorts, open sorts, blind sorts, concept sorts, buddy sorts, and others. Sorts can also be organized by pattern, by sound, or by sound and pattern.

Here is an example of a word sort. A teacher of fourth-grade children who are at the syllables and affixes stage might lead a closed word sort that includes words ending in "-le," "-al," and "-el." To begin this sort, the teacher would place three "header" cards (with "bushel," "puddle," and "final") in a row. Next, she would model placing several additional cards ("funnel," "able," "medical," "cradle," "model") under the header card that matches the spelling at the end of each word. Children would then do the same sorting with the remaining cards, after which the class would discuss any patterns they noticed. In this case, children should come to realize that words ending in "-al" are usually adjectives, and that many more words end in "-le" than in "-el." Children then practice the sort with their own set of cards and receive feedback from the teacher.

*Word Operations.* Ganske (2000) describes the simple activity "Word Operations," which helps children generate additional words from a given word. This practice is highly useful because it helps build what Gentry (2004) calls the child's *mental spelling dictionary*. Children choose four or five words at their developmental stage (teachers need to arrange folders or boxes of word cards by stage). Children then add, subtract, or add and subtract word elements to "operate on" or make a new word. For example, if a letter-name speller chose the word "bat," he or she might "operate" on it by subtracting the "b" and adding "fl" to make a new word, "flat." Children record the new word in their word-study notebooks, and sometimes teachers ask them to underline the change.

*Spelling Conferences.* Another way to "nudge" children toward the next step in their spelling development is through an individual spelling conference. This approach, based on the work of Dahl et al. (2004) is probably most appropriate for children in Grades 2, 3, or 4, and might be used periodically in place of a regular reading or writing conference. Basically, the teacher identifies a few words (in the child's "zone") from the child's independent writing and meets with him to look at what strategies (in addition to the ones the child already tried) might be helpful in the future when he tries to spell that word again, or others like it. The spelling conference form in Figure 9.4 is a

FIGURE 9.4 **Spelling Conference Form**

**Spelling Conference Form**

Name: *Sara B.*  Grade: *3*

Date: *Oct. 5*

| How I spelled the word | Correct spelling | What OTHER strategy might be good to use that would help me spell that word conventionally/correctly? |
|---|---|---|
| *stoping* | *stopping* | *Remembering the pattern (double the consonant when the vowel is short—like a CVC word such as hop)* |
| *olny* | *only* | *Stretching the word and saying it slowly and reflecting/checking the order of sounds* |
| *frend* | *friend* | *Remembering the cover of Best Friends for Frances, and thinking, "I am with my friend"* |
| *furst* | *first* | *Picturing the word in the word sorts we've done, and remembering that "ur" is not that common* |

sample of how this might work for Sara B., a third grader who is at the later within-word stage but is beginning to work on syllables and affixes. You'll notice that some of the strategies listed refer to previous instruction (i.e., remembering the consonant doubling pattern); others are more personalized and metacognitive, such as the reminder about the presence of "i" in "friend." Appendix A-29 provides a blank copy of the Spelling Conference Form.

### Instructional Approaches for Supporting Spelling Development for Students with Specific Needs

Spelling difficulties are important to address as soon as you identify them so that children do not avoid writing. Several possible factors can contribute to spelling issues, including limited phonological awareness, gaps in instruction, visual processing issues, and others. Two major avenues are used to help children with specific difficulties: remediating the source of difficulty, and compensatory approaches, which involve providing resources so that the child's spelling difficulty does not get in the way of his or her writing.

***Remedial Approaches.***   Careful spelling assessment can often help isolate the source of a child's spelling difficulty, and can also provide guidance for teachers and specialists in selecting approaches for remediation. After the teacher has determined the child's spelling stage, the teacher might use closer analysis (e.g., using the Developmental Spelling Analysis from Ganske) to more closely isolate specific areas of the child's need. For example, a child who seems "stuck" in the late letter-name stage and does not appear to be acquiring phonemic awareness may benefit from an approach called Phoneme-Grapheme Mapping (Grace, 2006). In this approach, teachers use a grid to help children spell one phoneme at a time. Children learn that different letters or letter combinations (graphemes) represent phonemes and gain valuable practice in saying words slowly to spell each phoneme. See Figure 9.5 for an example of phoneme-grapheme mapping, along with basic directions for using this approach.

A helpful resource that outlines a full sequence of steps for phoneme-grapheme mapping is Kathryn Grace's *Phonics and Spelling Through Phoneme-Grapheme Mapping* (2006).

Gentry (2004, 2007) describes several techniques that are useful in supporting very early writers or those with spelling challenges, including finger spelling (holding up a finger for each phoneme), stretching out sounds in a word (using stretchy fabric), and adult underwriting, in which the adult writes directly under the child's production of the word or sentence, modeling letter formation, concept of word, and conventional spelling. The purpose of adult underwriting is not to criticize the child's spelling but to give the teacher an opportunity to point out some "conventional" features that the child is already using. For example, if a child writes, "RD SKS" (for "Red Sox"), the teacher first admires the "kid writing" and then says to the child, "I'll show you how 'Red Sox' looks in adult writing . . . here it is." Then, after the teacher has written the correct spelling under the child's attempt, the teacher and child reread the adult "underwriting" and later practice reading it again. This provides an important model for children who have some grasp of the alphabetic principle but are still at a beginning stage of spelling.

Bedrova and Leong (1998) offer another helpful approach that they call *scaffolded writing* for beginning writers. First, the child chooses a topic, draws a picture, and says some words (or a sentence) that go with the picture. Next, the child draws lines with a highlighter for each word in the story/message. The teacher might need to provide some assistance in counting the words. Then the child uses private speech to rehearse the sentence she will write by saying the sentence out loud and pointing to the line where she will write the words. The child says each word and writes it on the line to whatever degree she is able. This technique helps build the student's independence as a speller.

## FIGURE 9.5  Phoneme-Grapheme Mapping

**Purpose: To help students listen for the sequence of phonemes (sounds) in words, and represent the phonemes with graphemes (letters or combinations of letters)**

**Directions:**
* Write the grapheme for one sound (phoneme) per square.
* Silent *e* "sits" in the lower right corner of a box—you can draw a line/arrow from the "e" to the vowel it affects.
* If two sounds are part of one grapheme (e.g., /k/ /s/ for *x*), put the grapheme (x) on the line between two squares.
* When writing "ng" use one box.
* When writing "er" (or "ir," etc.), use one box.
* To guide students in using this approach ask: "What do we hear?" followed by "How can we write that?"

**Sample:**

| | | | | |
|---|---|---|---|---|
| s | n | a | p | |
| c | ur | l | | |
| f | l | ew | | |
| sh | a | k<br>e | | |

*Phonics and Spelling Through Phoneme-Grapheme Mapping*, by Kathi Grace, copyright 2007, Sopris West; reprinted with permission from Sopris West.

The Fernald method (Fernald, 1943), which uses multisensory techniques, is sometimes known as "V-A-K-T" because the senses involved are visual, auditory, kinesthetic, and tactile. In this approach the teacher first models writing the word with a marker, crayon, or chalk and then has the child trace the word with his finger while saying it out loud three times and then copy the word three times. Finally, the child writes the word from memory, also three times.

***Compensatory Approaches.***  For children who seriously struggle with spelling, technology can be useful. In addition to tape recorders, the spell-checking tool on computers, and electronic spelling dictionaries, other tools increasingly include "talking" word processors and word predictors, which display words based on frequency and recency of use as well as grammatical correctness.

### Summary of Instructional Approaches for Spelling

To learn how to spell, children need many supportive opportunities to write and use invented spelling, and they also need explicit instruction that corresponds to their developmental stage. Once children have the "basics" of spelling and are able to use their phonemic awareness skills to write letters for each phoneme, they are on their way to being competent spellers. But they still need to acquire knowledge about the many different patterns present in English spelling, and eventually they will need to learn about how meaning affects spelling. In this section we reviewed some key principles, commonly used approaches, and a few specific techniques that teachers can use to support children's growth as spellers. Now let's look at Willa's spelling development and think about what next steps will be useful for her as her spelling skills and strategies grow.

## LOOKING CLOSELY AT ONE CHILD'S ASSESSMENTS FROM STRAND 9 OF THE LITERACY PROFILE

Willa is clearly well on her way to becoming a confident speller. To evaluate her progress in spelling, we administered the Primary Spelling Inventory (Bear et al., 2008) and also reviewed her spelling in several samples of her "everyday" writing. Figure 9.6 shows how Willa's developing skills are recorded and annotated on Strand 9 of the Literacy Profile. Willa spelled five words correctly on the Primary Spelling Inventory, which yielded a power score of 5. According to Bear et al. (2008), this power score predicts a predominant spelling stage close to the late letter-name stage of spelling. Since Bear et al. consider the grade levels at which children demonstrate letter-name spelling to be from kindergarten through early Grade 3, Willa's performance certainly appears on target.

By using the Feature Guide for the Primary Spelling Inventory, we were able to confirm the predicted stage/level and also identify specific features that Willa has control over (initial and final consonants and short vowels, except for short *u*), those she has *some* control over (digraphs and blends), and those she is *not yet* ready for (long vowels with consonant-*e* and other vowel patterns). With regard to the blends and digraphs, Willa definitely showed that she knows about blends and digraphs and how they work, but she seems not always to hear all of the sounds and record them accurately. For example, she spelled *coach* as "choch" and *fright* as "frit." This information is quite consistent with what we learned about her phonics knowledge (in chapter 3) as well as her ability to segment phonemes (as described in chapter 1).

Looking at Willa's writing samples was illuminating as well. Overall, she demonstrated an impressive range of spelling strategies and skills in all the pieces she wrote. By looking back at Figure 7.6 (Willa's story about a fox and a duck), we can learn a good deal about her evolving progress in learning to spell. Willa's willingness to take risks in spelling challenging multisyllabic words such as *dynamite* (spelled "dinmit") and *exploded* (spelled "igsploded") is clearly evident here and further confirms her current developmental spelling stage. Along with her readiness to spell words the way they sound, Willa's "using but confusing" spelling of words with vowel combinations (e.g., *flue* for *flew*) shows that she is nearly ready to explore long vowel sounds and other vowel combinations.

As to specific next steps for Willa, some continued work on consonant blends and digraphs will be useful for her at this point in time. Some quick clarifications about how to spell words with the short /u/ sound would also make sense. After she has blends and digraphs under control, Willa will be ready to enter the world of "within-word" patterns, first exploring long vowel patterns including vowel-consonant-e, and later moving on to other vowel combinations such as *ea, ai, ou*, etc.

## FIGURE 9.6  Profile of Willa's Spelling Development

Note: This figure has been excerpted from the full Literacy Profile chart for illustrative purposes. Please consult the full pull-out chart to identify the column headings and development phases.

| Strand *Question & Sample Assessment Tools* | Late K | Early–Mid Grade 1 | Late Grade 1–Early Grade 2 |
|---|---|---|---|
| **9. Spelling**<br>*How is the child's spelling developing in independent writing?*<br>**Sample Assessment Tools**<br>· Writing samples (prompted and independent writing) with scales, rubrics, or checklists<br>· Elementary Spelling Inventory<br>· Developmental Spelling Analysis | Uses beginning and ending consonants to spell some words, demonstrating some sound-symbol correspondence (*KT* for *CAT*) | Represents each phoneme in a word with a grapheme (*LUV* for *love*); beginning to use some short vowels | Represents most beginning and ending consonants, most consonant digraphs, and regular short vowels<br><br>*[Represents many blends]* KI<br><br>Begins to spell silent *e* words<br><br>Spells grade-appropriate high-frequency words<br><br>*[Spells multisyllabic words with invented spelling; showing strong phonemic awareness!]* KI<br><br>*[Ready to explore within-word patterns...]* KI |

Gray areas represent highlighting added by the teacher, preferably using a different color for each year (e.g., yellow highlights for Late K, orange highlights for Early–Mid Grade 1, etc.).
Bracketed material represents teacher/examiner comments from June, Grade 1.

In second grade, Willa will need to learn to proofread her spelling by rereading and circling a few words that she is not sure of but thinks she *almost* spelled correctly. Overall, Willa's spelling is moving along nicely, and reflects her development as a reader.

## REFERENCES

Bear, D. R., Invernizzi, M., Templeton, S., & Johnston, F. (2008). *Words their way.* Upper Saddle River, NJ: Pearson Education.

Bedrova, E., & Leong, D. J. (1998). Scaffolding emergent writing in the zone of proximal development. *Literacy Teaching and Learning, 3*(2), 1–18.

Dahl, K., Barto, A., Bonfils, A., Carasello, M., Christopher, J., Davis, R., et al. (2004). Connecting developmental word study with classroom writing: Children's descriptions of spelling strategies. *The Reading Teacher, 57*(4).

Ehri, L. C. (1997). Learning to read and learning to spell are one and the same, almost. In C. A. Perfetti, L. Rieben, & M. Fayol (Eds.), *Learning to spell* (pp. 237–269). London: Lawrence Erlbaum Associates.

Elkonin, D. B. (1973). In J. Downing (Ed.), *Comparative reading* (pp. 551–579). New York: Macmillan.

Fernald, G. M. (1943). *Remedial techniques in basic school subjects.* New York: McGraw Hill.

Fresch, M. J., & Wheaton, A. (2002). *Teaching and assessing spelling.* New York: Scholastic.

Ganske, K. (2000). *Word journeys.* New York: Guilford Press.

Gentry, R. (2004). *The science of spelling.* Portsmouth, NH: Heinemann.

Gentry, R. (2007). *Breakthrough in beginning reading and writing.* New York: Scholastic.

Grace, K. (2006). *Phonics and spelling through phoneme-grapheme mapping.* Natick, MA: Cambium Learning.

Henderson, E. H. (1981). *Learning to read and spell: The child's knowledge of words.* DeKalb: Northern Illinois Press.

Henderson, E. H. (1990). *Teaching spelling.* Boston: Houghton Mifflin.

Larsen S. C., Hammill, D. D., & Moats L. C. (1999). *Test of written spelling* (4th. ed.). Austin, TX: Pro Ed.

Moats, L. C. (1995). *Spelling: Development, disability and instruction.* Baltimore: York Press.

Read, C. (1975). *Children's categorization of speech sounds in English* (Research Report No. 17). Urbana, IL: NCTE.

Sitton, R. (1996). *Seminar handbook* (7th ed.). Cambridge, MA: Educators Publishing Service.

Snowball, D., & Bolton, F. (1999). *Spelling K–8: Planning and teaching.* York, ME: Stenhouse.

Templeton, S., & Bear, D. (Eds.). (1992). *Development of orthographic knowledge and the foundation of literacy: A memorial Festschrift for Edmund H. Henderson.* Hillsdale, NJ: Lawrence Erlbaum.

Templeton, S., & Morris, D. (1999). Questions teachers ask about spelling. *Reading Research Quarterly, 34*(1) 102–112.

Wheatley, J. (2005). *Strategic spelling: Moving beyond memorization in the middle grades.* Newark, DE: International Reading Association.

Zutell, J. (1996). The directed spelling-thinking approach: Providing an effective balance in word study programs. *The Reading Teacher, 50*(2), 98–108.

# CHAPTER TEN

# Writing Conventions and Handwriting

**CORE QUESTION**

To what degree does the child use acceptable conventions of grammar, usage, and mechanics in written language? How is handwriting developing?

"Remember that sentences start with an uppercase letter," Mrs. Conz reminds her first graders before she sends them off to write in their draft-writing notebooks. The implication, of course, is that the children are using all lowercase letters when they write. Mrs. Conz has been working hard during daily explicit handwriting lessons to teach her young writers how to form lowercase letters. She is now encouraging her students to use lowercase letters unless they have a reason not to, emphasizing that capitalization carries meaning. Similar to letter identification, learning how to form the lower- and uppercase of each letter requires practice to bring the skill to a level of automaticity, which enables a child to invest more mental effort in spelling, capitalization, punctuation, and, most importantly, the message.

In this chapter, we will take a closer look at handwriting development and also the conventions of our language including grammar, usage, and mechanics. It is essential to keep in mind the overall profile of a child and carefully consider how the child's language and reading skills are developing in relation to written language. You may particularly notice that children often experiment with the same print concepts in their writing that they identify in text they read, directly linking Strands 2 and 10.

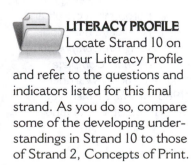

**LITERACY PROFILE** Locate Strand 10 on your Literacy Profile and refer to the questions and indicators listed for this final strand. As you do so, compare some of the developing understandings in Strand 10 to those of Strand 2, Concepts of Print.

## UNDERLYING PRINCIPLES OF WRITING CONVENTIONS, INCLUDING HANDWRITING

A convention is defined as "a customary practice, rule, method; a general agreement on the usages and practices of social life" (Neufeldt & Guralnik, 1991). Written conventions can also be thought of as "audience courtesy."

In using agreed-upon sentence structures, letter formations, and punctuation, writers show special consideration for the intended reader, making written communication more accessible. Vicki Spandel reminds us that "conventions are ever changing," which is surely evident when we examine documents from the past (2004, p. 11). Take a look at the punctuation in children's books from the past few decades and compare them to present-day children's books. You'll find that contemporary authors often use "unconventional" conventions such as three exclamation points instead of one, or an ellipsis on every other page of text, whereas in the past, authors used punctuation more traditionally. Since reading influences writing, you will frequently notice children using much of the same punctuation in their writing that they have seen in the print around them. In this chapter, we will describe the audience courtesies that are sometimes called the "GUM" of writing: grammar, usage, and mechanics. We will also discuss handwriting as it affects writing development.

## Understanding How Grammar Impacts Writing Development

Grammar describes how words and sentences are put together into a logical order to create meaning, a concept also known as "syntax" (Freeman & Freeman, 2004). Traditionally, people studied grammar in isolation from writing, primarily using textbooks and worksheets. Researchers haven't been able to find any significant link between improved writing and grammar lessons; however, they have found improvements when teachers link grammar lessons to children's own writing (Cotton, 2002; Hillocks, 1986; Weaver, 1996). In particular, the proofreading stage (used interchangeably with editing in this Handbook) of the writing process can provide a perfect opportunity for children to focus on constructing sentences and on using the standard conventions for the particular form of writing they are creating. Using the writing process model, children learn to focus first on meaning and later, during editing, on audience courtesy (Calkins, 1994; Ministry of Education, 1992). Teachers can assess and teach grammatical concepts through meaningful literacy activities that help children integrate their developing awareness of grammar and usage directly into their writing.

The language of conventions is one of several things children need to learn in order to consider and discuss how the surface features influence their written messages. As children learn *about* their language (Halliday, 1984) through grammar studies, they will discover many new terms for conventions, such as "singular," "plural," or "exclamation point." These are examples of what Beck, McKeon, and Kucan (2002) describe as "Tier Three words," content-specific words from the field of linguistics. (See chapter 1 for more information about the three tiers of words.) They are also examples of what is often called "academic language." In the following section, we review two aspects of grammar: parts of speech and sentence structures. Compare your own background of grammar instruction to the ideas presented in this chapter.

If you need to review grammar more thoroughly, consult an English language handbook such as *English Composition and Grammar: Complete Course* by John Warriner (1988) or *The Elements of Style* by William Strunk Jr. and E. B. White (2000).

***Parts of Speech.***    Children can learn to name and identify the seven parts of speech—noun, verb, adjective, adverb, preposition, conjunction, and pronoun—within the context of writing, eventually using the parts of speech as tools for building clearer or more creative sentences (Polette, 2008). Although children do not need to identify a word's part of speech in order to write effectively, knowing these terms provides a foundation for discussing and improving the structure of sentences.

Early grammar investigations often begin with identifying subjects and predicates. Children are then soon able to name the noun phrases (and pronouns) that make up subjects and the verb phrases (including the auxiliary verbs) that make up predicates. Later, children learn to identify direct objects and prepositional phrases. Being able to identify the parts of speech and their functions within a sentence serves as a building block for further language explorations, helping children add more resources to their writing "toolboxes."

***Sentence Structures.***   A teacher can identify a child's developing awareness of sentences by examining how spacing and punctuation are being used in writing samples (Clay, 1991). Early writing often consists of simple and repetitive sentences that frequently begin with the word "I." As writing becomes more fluent, simple sentences often lead to long lists of ideas that children connect rather loosely with the conjunction "and," which creates the common run-on sentence (Hunt & O'Donnell, 1970). Also, sentences begin to have a wider variety of forms: declarative, interrogative, imperative, and exclamatory. Varied sentence structures and a child's active interest in punctuation often go hand in hand, each one influencing the other. For instance, a child experimenting with dialogue might write the following sentence:

> My mom said, "Chase, you must clean your room."

Writing this sentence requires the child to look at the structure of dialogue and the punctuation used to convey a speaker's direct words.

Reading a wide range of texts directly influences children's writing development and, within that, their use of more complex sentence structures as well. As children develop stronger reading skills, you will often find them trying out more sophisticated ways to convey information in their writing (Stahl & Pagnucco, 1996). They eventually begin to use sentence structures that include more than a simple subject and predicate, including compound subjects and predicates, compound sentences, and complex sentences. Even though a child's previous writing may have been fully conventional, you might notice that she is suddenly writing incomplete sentences and using inappropriately placed punctuation marks. Complex sentence structures such as clauses often confuse children as they try to decide whether or not a group of words is a "complete thought." After all, clauses such as, "When we sat down for dinner last night" do appear to have a subject and a predicate. But following rules doesn't always work, and thus children need to use critical thinking skills such as, "Does this group of words make sense on its own?" to determine whether a group of words is a complete sentence or not.

Other children may need a nudge before they will experiment with varied structures. You can teach them how to combine simple sentence structures by having them examine sentences from read-aloud books or their classmates' writing samples. Through guided discussions and supported practice, young writers can learn to appreciate the usefulness of varied structures such as compound subjects, compound predicates, compound sentences, complex sentences, and sentences with a series of words or phrases.

## Understanding How Language Usage Impacts Writing Development

Often children rely on what "sounds right" in order to determine word choice and correct grammar. However, this is not always sufficient to produce standard English because we often speak more casually than we write. Although going by what sounds right can be a good starting place when children first begin to make decisions regarding usage, this strategy will be less effective for children who are not native English speakers. English grammar can be diffi-cult for English Language Learners because their mental grammar—the rules that have been internalized—does not necessarily resemble that used by native English speakers (P. K. Matsuda, as cited in Collier, 2007, p. 4). In this section we will describe some of the common usage hurdles that children in the early grades encounter, such as subject-verb agreement, verb tense agreement, proper pronoun use, and choosing correct homophones based on usage.

Be sure to review your state and district curriculum frameworks to determine at which grade levels these ideas are specifically introduced; you will also want to take your cues from the children themselves, building on their existing knowl-edge in an incremental way that makes sense based on their background. As we describe potential "trouble spots" for children, you will notice that it is often hard to separate spelling conventions from usage issues. In these cases, under-standing one will support the development of the other.

***Subject-Verb Agreement.*** In order for students to understand subject-verb agreement, they will need to learn the academic vocabulary of singular and plural nouns. Initially, they will be able to identify this morphemic structure by searching for either an "s" or an "es" at the end of common nouns. Because children already know the concepts of "one" and "more than one," they should easily be able to assimilate the language of singular and plural, with assistance from the teacher. Later, children can learn to identify plural nouns that change form, such as *goose* and *geese*, and those that stay the same, such as *deer* and *deer*.

Generally, oral language development precedes written language develop-ment, and the carryover will be automatic in commonly used words and sentences. An example is, "My dog plays. Our dogs play." As children begin to use more creative sentence structures, subject-verb agreement might become a little "cloudier." For example, "My friends and my dog play together after school." In this case, it will be necessary for you to provide more explicit instruction as well as decision-making support (e.g., posters on walls) for children to use. Subject-verb agreement is an area in which spelling confusion and usage often overlap. Verbs might need the addition of an "s," or they might need "es" (*The car crashes*) or "ies" after dropping the "y" (*The boy studies*).

***Verb Tense Agreement.*** Children tell many stories that have already taken place, and this requires them use to past tense verbs. Initially, children begin to experiment with verbs using "-ed" or "-d" endings or some that require changing the "y" to an "i" and adding "ed." As we described in chapter 1, "Phonological Awareness and Oral Language Development," you will often find that young children carry over to writing the language structures they use in speech such as, "I goed to my friend's house." When you support early writers, you will need to decide whether to make the writing grammatically correct during the editing stage.

Some writing experts believe that published kindergarten and first-grade writing should use the child's own language, to encourage risk taking and writing fluency (Betrand & Stice, 2002; Fletcher, 2007; Graves, 2003). In describing what he calls guidelines for dealing with children's errors, Donald Graves states, "Syntax remains unchanged. This is the child's own language" (2003, p. 58). Others believe that writing should be published in a more standardized format such as, "I went to my friend's house," to reinforce conventional usage when the child reads his writing to the audience or when the teacher places the published writing in the classroom library. When teachers become the final editors, it is important that they discuss the options with the child and ultimately allow the child to decide how to finalize the published work even if the child's choice is unconventional (Ministry of Education, 1992).

Children often learn about verb tense shifts when they try out new text structures and experiment with various plots and styles such as point of view, stories embedded within other stories, and time shifts. In your reading and writing demonstrations, you can model a writer's deliberate decision making when he or she decides which form of a verb is needed based on the structure of a piece of writing. For instance, if you are writing a repetitive and lyrical piece in the present tense but on the last page shift to future tense, even young children will notice the change from "She is the millennium baby, now isn't she fine?" to "As the years go on and on, she will always be my millennium baby." Children enjoy expanding their repertoires of conventions when it is meaningful and serves them as writers (Graves, 1994).

***Proper Pronoun Use.***  Although we use pronouns frequently in oral language, they can be rather abstract for young children. Pronouns carry meaning based on where they occur in a sentence and on their use within a specific context. Children frequently use approximations of pronouns as they develop oral language skills, and teachers can't easily "correct" these errors through modeled responses. For instance, if a child says, "Me and my friend went to the mall," it's not accurate to respond, "Oh, my friend and I went to mall?" since the teacher did not actually go to the mall. If a child writes this sentence, you will need to decide whether to leave the sentence in the child's own language or make editorial suggestions in an editing conference.

Fletcher (2007) suggests that by the time children are in Grade 3, teachers might support some language changes during editing, but even then he calls the decision about what to correct "a delicate balance." For instance, he would change the subject-verb agreement in "My cousin don't like girls" but not pronoun and noun reversals, calling "Me and my brother" a display of "authentic child-like voice." Not all agree with these decisions, though, and if you do decide to make children's writing sound like standard conventional English, you can do so sensitively during an editing conference.

First, you can introduce the conventional use of the pronoun by focusing on the order of a compound subject: "Claire, in our language there are rules that are somewhat like manners we use at the dinner table. One of those rules is that when you talk about doing something with another person, it is more polite to mention the other person first. So in this sentence, you would say, 'My friend and I went to mall.'" This introduces the child to a new language learning point, "Name the other person first." Later, as Claire develops more sophisticated control of pronouns, she will learn that there are "subject pronouns" and "object pronouns." But in the meantime, she will begin to internalize the more concrete rule about naming the other person first. It is important to teach one skill at a time, carefully correlating the objective to the child's developmental range and cognitive reach. Relative pronouns such as *each* and *everyone* and the correct usage of *there is* and *there are* present other subject-verb decisions writers must make, and you can also teach this usage at a developmentally appropriate time through the context of one-to-one editing conferences or small-group lessons.

Finally, pronoun choice can present a spelling issue as well. One example is the use of "its" and "it's." You can teach children how to consciously use decision making when they proofread for these two words: "Can I say 'it is' or can I substitute 'his'?" Although many rules guide accurate pronoun use, you can help children gradually build a framework to support the decision-making process regarding proper and conventional use through a combination of whole-class mini-lessons and individual and small-group editing conferences.

***Choosing Correct Homophones Based on Usage.*** Many times even adults confuse common homophones, or words that sound the same but have different meanings and spellings. See Figure 10.1 for a list of some common homophone errors. It is important to recognize that teachers often don't need to teach the correct spelling; rather, they need to teach a set of guiding questions that a child can use whenever the particular word arises, similar to the "its" and "it's" decision making we discussed in the previous section.

After introducing and teaching various homophone pairs (often during spelling lessons), you will have the opportunity to follow up with children during the proofreading stage, helping them apply their developing skills to their own writing. You can add a reminder to check for a specific pair on the child's individualized proofreading checklist. "I will use 'two' whenever it is the number 2." "I will use 'too' if I can say 'also' or ask, 'How many?' and answer 'too many.'" The end goal is for children to internalize the decision-making process. You'll know they have done so when children use homophones accurately during the drafting stage and need to make fewer changes during the later writing stages.

## Understanding How the Mechanics of Writing Impacts Writing Development

Mechanics refers to punctuation and capitalization. Writers use these conventions to express their ideas and leave cues for the intended audience. Sandra Wilde (1992) reminds us that punctuation and capitalization have bigger roles than simply signaling when a reader should pause; their use also carries meaning and provides important grammatical information, as in "mom" versus "Mom" and "its" versus "it's." The reciprocal processes of reading and writing play a particularly important role in helping children fully integrate the deliberate use of writing mechanics as they read with intonation based on the flow of the language and the punctuation. Conversely, they learn to write with the reader in mind, leaving clues for accurate transfer of the ideas through language and punctuation (Smith, 1982).

FIGURE 10.1  **Examples of Homophones That May Present Usage Errors**

| to | too | two |
|---|---|---|
| it's | its | |
| there | their | they're |
| heard | herd | |
| piece | peace | |
| meat | meet | |
| write | right | |
| hair | hare | |

*Punctuation.*   Let's review the various types and purposes of punctuation.

- *End punctuation:* Punctuation can signal sentence boundaries. These marks tell a reader to stop briefly, and at the same time, end punctuation can distinguish sentence types. Examples of end punctuation include periods, question marks, and exclamation points. (You will also need to teach children that they can use periods when writing abbreviations.)
- *Within sentences:* Punctuation within sentences can suggest a pause or identify specific phrases or clauses. These marks include commas, semi-colons, and colons. Commas can also function as useful markings in a variety of situations including dates, addresses, lists, direct addresses, greetings and closings of letters, introductory phrases such as "yes" and "no," direct addresses, and appositives.
- *Dialogue markings:* Quotation marks in combination with various "within" and "ending" punctuation marks identify changes in speakers when writers use direct speech, or they can be used to identify special wording.
- *Apostrophes:* Writers use apostrophes in both contractions and possessive pronouns and nouns.
- *Other markings:* Punctuation also includes more sophisticated signals such as hyphens, parentheses, dashes, ellipses, and bullets, to name a few. You might notice some elementary children trying out some of these markings in their own writing as they expand their awareness of these symbols (Wilde, 1992).

*Capitalization.*   Now let's turn our attention to the use of uppercase letters. As we mentioned in the opening section, children need to be able to recognize the difference between upper- and lowercase letters before they can begin intentionally using capital letters in their writing. Some uses of capital letters include:

- Sentence beginnings
- Proper nouns
- Titles (just the important words)
- The beginning of a direct quote
- Acronyms (Wilde, 1992)

Children will more easily learn to manage these decisions if you begin with concrete and easily grasped concepts such as how to correctly write names of family members and friends, days of the week, and beginnings of sentences. For punctuation, begin by teaching end punctuation using simple sentence structures. As with other skill instruction, start slowly and teach one skill at a time. Once again, we remind you to refer to your state and district guidelines so that your expectations are consistent with the suggested sequence for teaching these skills in your school system.

### Understanding How Handwriting Development and Writing Development Interact

Donald Graves describes handwriting as the "vehicle carrying information on its way to its destination" (2003, p. 171). He reminds teachers to look beyond the surface for the underlying meaning of a writer's work. Unfortunately, people often judge a writer's work based on surface features such as handwriting and neatness. We take the position that handwriting is important to the degree that it provides a legible output, something that the intended audience can read, and we also believe that children must learn to write fluidly so that they can record their ideas efficiently.

It is important to allow emergent writers to use any form of expression they can control, including invented letters and random markings. This does not mean that we shouldn't explicitly teach and reinforce handwriting skills, though; we just want to remind you that not all children will be ready to apply the same level of skills at the same point in time. Let's review the emergent processes in handwriting development.

***Early Handwriting Development.*** In the preschool years, children's drawing and writing can reveal their early thinking about written symbols (Clay, 1991). When children eventually write messages, you may notice left-to-right scribbles or lines moving across pages, and later, lines that look more like manuscript letters than cursive (Brittain, 1973). Children eventually begin to use the same hand each time they pick up a writing instrument. Handwriting requires small muscle development and coordination, eye-hand coordination, and the ability to hold a writing instrument appropriately (Donoghue, 1985). It is thus important for teachers to provide frequent opportunities for young children to develop these skills without overemphasizing children's precision (Schickedanz, 1989). Kindergarten and first-grade teachers will especially want to provide a variety of media so that children can experiment with crayons, pencils, markers, and other tools as they develop the manual dexterity they need to manage the fine motor skills of letter formation.

Many kindergarten teachers teach geometric shapes such as circles, squares, and triangles during children's structured handwriting practice, understanding that in order to create letters, children must first be able to distinguish among and understand the vocabulary of designs, such as *round, circle,* and *line.* Other important skills children need to develop include orienting their papers correctly and identifying top and bottom. The notion of white space becomes significant as emergent writers begin to experiment with spaces between letters, words, and lines, and eventually with margins (Hennings, 2002).

***Manuscript Writing.*** Many different handwriting programs for young children are available. Most children have already begun learning the preferred handwriting style of their families or preschools by the time they get to kindergarten. Often this writing is primarily uppercase letters. The early handwriting requirements of manuscript printing are lines, circles, and partial circles. One form of writing, D'Nealian (Thurber, 1988), varies from the more traditional early programs in that it incorporates letter slant and continuous strokes. A principal/teacher developed this model to facilitate the transition between printing and cursive writing (Machado, 2003). Other frequently used programs are Palmer, Handwriting without Tears, and Zaner-Bloser.

It is important to study the handwriting guides your school system provides so that you can use a consistent form of writing in your classroom. Also be sure to always model the appropriate use of upper- and lowercase letters on all of your own handwritten materials in your classroom such as charts, posters, and other teaching aids.

As young children gain control of uppercase letters, you may eventually notice them using a mixture of upper- and lowercase letters. You can support this gradual shift to writing with lowercase letters through explicit handwriting lessons for those children who have difficulties. Some teachers blend handwriting lessons with letter identification, sound-to-letter relationships, or spelling practice because these areas focus on individual letters and don't interfere with creating meaning during writing sessions. Handwriting cards, which are often arranged alphabetically with lowercase letters and picture supports, serve two purposes: They support young writers as they move from sounds to letters and simultaneously scaffold handwriting skills.

Each handwriting program usually targets letter formation, consistent letter size and proportion, spacing between letters and words, slant, and alignment (Tompkins, 2008). Be sure not to overemphasize perfection; rather, encourage children to strive for legibility as they gain competence and fluency. Most children already have a preferred handwriting grip by the time they enter school, and because they have already had multiple experiences using this grip, it may be very hard to change their habits, although early primary teachers are more likely than other teachers to be able to influence a child's grip. However, some children may resist the new muscle development that these changes require. Consult your handwriting program for ways to support children's development of grip and page orientation, also paying close attention to the specific directions for helping orient left-handed writers.

***Cursive Writing.***    Cursive writing is often introduced at the end of second grade or the beginning of third grade. Similar to manuscript writing, children will differ in their ability to transition to this form of writing. Some children may find cursive easier since the continuous flow eliminates some of the issues with spacing between letters and words. If you teach at the grade level where this form of writing is introduced, be sure to read your district's handwriting program manuals and provide explicit instruction to all children during the initial stages. When you have exposed all children to proper cursive letter formation, you can support learners in small groups as needed, for specific "reteaching" or general support.

Handwriting practice works best when children can focus on the art of handwriting. Some teachers put on relaxing music and allow children to choose their writing instruments such as colored pencils and a variety of paper to experiment with as they learn. Remember, too, the many "novel combinations" of letters that will require some explicit instruction. For instance, joining "o" and "r" or "o" and "t" in sequence requires special considerations and skills. Similar to manuscript, when teaching cursive, teachers need to consider shape, size and proportion, slant, spacing, steadiness of line, and styling (Hennings, 2002).

### Summary of Underlying Principles of Writing Conventions, Including Handwriting

Writing conventions, including handwriting, can be viewed as a type of audience courtesy. Teachers need to deliberately and thoughtfully teach the skills that children need to apply these "rules" so that developing writers are not overwhelmed by the task's complexities. If you teach children to consider the meaning behind grammar, usage, and mechanics during authentic writing and editing experiences, they will view these skills as valuable tools to use as needed to strengthen their messages. In turn, children will better appreciate the ways authors use these skills to provide meaningful opportunities for their readers.

## ASSESSING WRITING CONVENTIONS, INCLUDING HANDWRITING

Writing samples from children's daily work provide an ideal opportunity to monitor their developing control over writing conventions. You will also want to occasionally give children practice with "on-demand" writing prompts that they complete in one sitting, on an independent basis. That way, you can monitor how well a child is managing writing conventions without support. In this section we will describe various ways for teachers to measure children's use of writing conventions. We will address handwriting assessment only when it is related to writing conventions. For example, the slant of a letter does not necessarily affect legibility; however, the inability to fluently recall and form lowercase letters interferes with the appropriate placement of capital letters, thus affecting the legibility of a child's message.

### Formal or Published Measures for Assessing Writing Conventions

Similar to writing effectiveness, writing conventions are often assessed during large-scale testing, using either a holistic scoring rubric or an analytic scoring rubric. Many of the formal measures developed for use at national, state, district, and schoolwide levels are similar to those we've already described, although descriptors vary across assessments. Formal standardized tests have also been developed to measure and diagnose strengths and areas of need when a teacher is concerned about a child's overall writing skills. These assessments are usually administered individually, on an as-needed basis.

*Holistic Scoring Rubrics.* Tests used to assess writing effectiveness often include a separate numerical score of how well standard English conventions are developing in a child's writing. Interestingly, these tests often do not itemize specific grammar, usage, and mechanics; rather, they "lump" these factors into one category and determine whether the number of errors has affected meaning. As an example, let's take a look at the Massachusetts English Language Arts Composition Scoring Guide, which is a sample four-point scale for standard English conventions. See Figure 10.2. Be sure to research your state's scoring system in order to help your students become familiar with the scoring expectations.

*Analytic Scoring Rubrics.* Rubrics designed to evaluate children's writing are often analytic, which may be thought of as "combination" rubrics because they provide separate categories and descriptors for each aspect of the product or performance so that the person evaluating the writing can judge the different aspects of each. The Six-Trait Rubric (also mentioned in chapter 8) is an example of an analytic rubric and includes one category specifically for conventions. This rubric describes conventions with broad

### FIGURE 10.2  Holistic Scoring Guide for Massachusetts Curriculum Frameworks

| Standard English Conventions | | | |
|---|---|---|---|
| **1** | **2** | **3** | **4** |
| • Errors seriously interfere with communication and<br>• Little control of sentence structure, grammar and usage, and mechanics | • Errors interfere somewhat with communication and/or<br>• Too many errors relative to the length of the essay or complexity of sentence structure, grammar and usage, and mechanics | • Errors do not interfere with communication and/or<br>• Few errors relative to the length of essay or complexity of sentence structure, grammar and usage, and mechanics | • Control of sentence structure, grammar and usage, and mechanics (length and complexity of essay provide opportunity for student to show control of standard English conventions) |

Massachusetts English Language Arts Composition Scoring Guide. Used by permission from the Massachusetts Department of Elementary and Secondary Education.

strokes and scores them as a 5, 3, or 1. A "5" describes the writing of a child who uses punctuation, spelling, grammar and usage, capitalization, and paragraphing with few errors and whose writing requires "only light touch-ups" for publishing. A "1," on the other hand, describes the writing of a child who has many writing errors and limited control over writing conventions (Spandel, 2004).

Teams of specialists and teachers sometimes develop district and schoolwide analytic rubrics in order to measure children's development of conventions. In doing so, they frequently separate mechanics, handwriting, and spelling in order to provide more specific information about children's developing control in each of these areas.

***Formal Specialized Tests for Writing Conventions.***  Formal and commercial tests are available to measure children's writing, but teachers generally use these only when there is some question of why a child is not making adequate progress. Two tests, the Test of Early Written Language-TEWL-2 and the Test of Written Language-TOWL-3, are standardized tools that can help teachers identify specific areas of writing development in which a child needs specialized instruction (Hammill & Larsen, 1996; Hresko, Herron, & Peak, 2006). The TEWL-2 was specifically designed to extend the assessment range to younger children, and the Basic Writing Subtest portion of this assessment measures a child's spelling, capitalization, punctuation, sentence construction, and metacognitive language.

Language arts programs and basal reading programs often provide end-of-unit tests of various grammatical concepts that are taught throughout the program of study. Teachers should keep in mind that these contrived formats primarily measure a child's ability to choose what "looks right" or "sounds right" in the testing situations and do not necessarily indicate how a child carries the concepts tested over into her writing. For instance, a test segment may list four sentences, all with various placements of commas, and ask the child to identify the sentence that is punctuated correctly. Teachers can use these tools to supplement more authentic assessments such as student writing samples, however.

## Informal Measures for Assessing Writing Conventions, Including Handwriting

To informally assess writing conventions, you can use many of the same types of informal assessment strategies we described in previous chapters. The major difference is that your focus will be on the surface features of the writing rather than the process or content of the writing. Keep in mind that not every piece of writing requires the same level of analysis. The degree to which you evaluate a piece of writing depends on whether you're assessing the sample for summative purposes to evaluate and compare progress over time, or for formative purposes to select next instructional steps, or both. At times you will also want to include children's input in these assessments.

***Anecdotal Record Keeping.***  Children's confusions about writing conventions often appear while you are discussing other aspects of writing. By jotting down these confusions, you will be able to plan explicit teaching lessons for small groups or individual children at appropriate times. For instance, while discussing a child's plan for writing about his adventure in the park, you might notice that he is still confusing upper-and lowercase letters, particularly "j" and "f." Rather than interrupt the planning conference to discuss surface-level issues, a written note will remind you to address the confusion later in a small-group guided-writing lesson, which will allow you to include a few other children who also need that support. If you keep these notes organized in a monitoring notebook, they will also provide records of children's small progressive steps over time.

***Writing Samples with Accompanying Rubrics and Checklists.*** Benchmark writing samples such as the ones we described in chapter 8 can be useful for evaluating specific conventions that you are teaching and measuring at your grade level. Many teachers prefer to use checklists for mechanics because checklists give teachers a way to record evidence of a child's having mastered these skills as "yes" or "no." Teachers can also expand a checklist to describe evidence of a child's use of various features "Most of the time," "Some of the time," and "Not yet." Children, too, can be active participants in the evaluation process. Of course, it is always helpful when children have some input in developing the criteria. Figure 10.3 is an example of a checklist created with Grade 1 children in the area of punctuation.

Some rubrics combine specific identifiers in the form of a checklist within broader categories, similar to the Literacy Profile. This type of checklist may help you monitor specific skill development more closely, identifying which skills might need more attention and which skills children have mastered. For instance, Spandel (2004) offers a full-page primary rubric for conventions, identifying three items in the first stage (beginner) and expanding to eight items in the experienced-writer stage.

As you teach punctuation, capitalization, and usage skills, you may want to add each one to a classroom chart as proofreading reminders for children. For instance, if you teach a whole-class lesson on using capital letters to begin every sentence, put it onto the class proofreading chart using a shared writing approach. Each time you finish a piece of writing, you can then model the

FIGURE 10.3  **Sample Grade 1 Checklist for Writing Conventions**

| Convention | Most of the Time | Some of the Time | Not Yet |
|---|---|---|---|
| I use a period at the end of a sentence. | | | |
| I use an exclamation point at the end of a sentence to show excitement. | | | |
| I use a capital letter at the beginning of a sentence. | | | |
| I use a capital letter when I write someone's name. | | | |
| I use a capital letter when I name the day of the week. | | | |
| I use a capital letter when I name the month of the year. | | | |
| I use a comma in the date between the day and the year. | | | |
| I use spaces between words. | | | |
| I use lowercase letters unless I have a reason not to. | | | |

editing stage, using the posted chart and reviewing each item along the way. With repeated exposures, the language and process of editing will become natural and automatic to the children.

***Editing Sheets.*** Many teachers individualize children's proofreading checklists in order to target each child's specific needs and at the same time to closely monitor each child's growing independence in using these skills. The "I Am Learning/I Can" sheets described in chapter 8 work particularly well for proofreading (Ministry of Education, 1992). A teacher often keeps the proofreading checklist in a special editing folder, which a child uses as a last step before handing in the writing draft for teacher editing. See Figure 10.4 for an example of a Grade 3 "I Am Learning/I Can" sheet. Remember that children don't need to take every piece of writing to the final editing stage; the editing process, like all other processes, varies based on purpose and audience.

Children have probably internalized a specific skill when they are able to automatically use the convention during first draft writing and no longer need to attend to it while proofreading. The teacher then lists these skills in the "I Can" column because children no longer need external reminders to apply them. For example, after teaching a child the proper uses of "its" and "it's" and listing the skill as "I am learning how to use *it's* for *it is*, and *its* for *his*," from this point forward you expect the child to always proofread any "it's" or "its" in writing headed for publication. Eventually, you might notice that the child is accurately using these homophones without even needing to correct them during the proofreading process, indicating that the child has now internalized this skill and that you can move it to the "I Can" side of the form. Teachers can also encourage children to evaluate their growing control over conventions by referring to the "I Can" column during editing conferences.

**FIGURE 10.4  Sample Personalized Grade 3 "I Am Learning/I Can" Sheet**

| I am Learning | Chase's Proofreading Reminder List | I Can |
|---|---|---|
| 9/15 | Use a capital letter for naming specific places in the world like streets, cities, states. Example: 115 Oak Street, Westfield, Massachusetts | 10/8 |
| 9/20 | Use a comma when I list more than two things. Example: in a car, in a plane, and in a train | 10/21 |
| 9/30 | Indent to show a new paragraph to help the reader see how sentences are grouped together | |
| 10/8 | Use capital letters for acronyms like the names of states and specially created words. Example: MA and SCUBA (Self-Contained Underwater Breathing Apparatus) | |
| | | |
| | | |

### Summary of Assessing Writing Conventions, Including Handwriting

Teachers should manage and evaluate writing conventions separately from the other aspects of writing, keeping the emphasis on surface features in proper perspective. Most children eventually assimilate proofreading skills into their writing tasks naturally and meaningfully when they fully understand the purposes of the various conventions. Children will more readily embrace the final editing stage if they are able to feel successful in their process. Teachers can also monitor and address handwriting issues in much the same way they monitor and address any other language conventions. While some formal assessments of writing conventions are available, the most valid information for informing instruction will likely come from informal, ongoing assessments.

## INSTRUCTIONAL APPROACHES FOR WRITING CONVENTIONS, INCLUDING HANDWRITING

Writing conventions can be taught through meaningful writing experiences, but you will not be able to rely on proofreading conferences alone. For one thing, many children do not bring enough writing to the proofreading stage to have ample experiences with the wide variety of written conventions that they must learn (Calkins, 1994). Or, in the case of the "it's" and "its" decision-making process mentioned in the previous section, the child may not have enough opportunities to apply that specific skill if she does not use those words frequently in her writing. Also, in terms of efficiency, it makes a good deal of sense to teach grade-appropriate expectations for writing conventions to all children. Explicit instructional opportunities can enrich children's knowledge base, and with practice, children will develop the skills to apply this knowledge in their writing.

### Instructional Approaches for Writing Conventions, Including Handwriting, for All Students

Instruction in writing conventions can take place in both whole-group and small-group settings using mini-lessons or shared writing and employing the gradual release of responsibility model. You can use a variety of resources to make the lessons engaging and interactive while emphasizing the transfer of knowledge into real writing scenarios. In the following segments, we offer sample lesson suggestions from a variety of sources. Use these ideas as springboards for developing your own explorations into the world of writing conventions.

In addition to regular, planned mini-lessons that follow your curriculum, you will also want to target specific teaching concepts to individual children or small homogeneous groups as they enter the "zone of proximal development" in their personal writing pieces. You will be able to identify children's needs from your anecdotal note taking. Remember to keep your lesson objectives crystal clear and focus on only one new meaningful and manageable concept at a time so that you don't overwhelm your learners. Borrowing from the wise words of teacher-educator Jan Duncan, keep the lessons "short, sharp and snappy!"

***Teaching Grammar and Writing.*** Grammar and syntax can be thought of as an open-ended puzzle. By carefully selecting and putting words in a deliberate order, a writer can make the final product clear, effective, and pleasing to the audience. Teachers can replace repetitive skill-and-drill worksheets with interesting investigations that look at the deeper structures of syntax through natural language discussions.

*Parts of Speech.* If teachers use the vocabulary of grammar naturally during literacy discussions, the language will become familiar and controllable. For instance, when you use the word "adjective" as you read aloud and savor a descriptive word in a sentence, children will begin to associate the use of this type of language with that label, *adjective* (Ray, 1999). For example, after reading aloud Mem Fox's book *Tough Boris* (1994), you might comment on the word "scruffy" by saying, "Oh, I love that adjective 'scruffy' because it really describes how I think of pirates, with a stubbly beard, wrinkly clothes, and messy, unwashed hair." Although this approach to grammar lessons offers one necessary condition for learning, immersion, children will also benefit from explicit lessons.

Children love to play with language through the "cloze" technique. Have you ever used one of those fill-in-the-blank books to make silly stories? These books often prompt the writer to add a specific part of speech. When a child has finished filling in all the blanks, giggles abound because the resulting story is often so silly. You can use this technique to support children's practice by using parts of speech as prompts. For instance, take a short passage from a text at the independent level of your readers, and leave blanks for all the nouns. In partnerships, encourage children to supply the nouns they think might make sense within the passage. Next, supply the actual passage and let the children compare their ideas (Wiseman, Elish-Piper, & Wiseman, 2005).

Another technique allows children to construct their own definitions by using their inductive reasoning skills. List a group of words from the same part of speech, such as nouns, and then ask children to determine what the words have in common (Polette, 2008). For instance, "man, tree, boat, city, table" can be a list of common nouns. As a whole group, have the children record an agreed-upon definition for all to see and use as a resource. Following these introductory activities, you can ask children to continue listing other nouns that fit the agreed-upon definitions. You can also encourage children to highlight common nouns in their own writing, much like a scavenger hunt.

To introduce the vocabulary of grammar, you can also purchase children's books such as Ruth Heller's seven "eye-catching" and "lyrical" books that introduce and explore each part of speech (Heller, 1998a, 1998b, 1998c, 1998d, 1998e, 1999; Heller & Peskin, 2000). Children can also learn to identify and use the parts of speech through creative writing activities and examining poetry. Many poems provide rich examples of descriptive language (vivid verbs, sensory adjectives) and repetitive patterns. In whole-class settings, you can examine the construction of a chosen poem, create one together, and then encourage children to use the same pattern for their own creations.

*See Wishes, Lies, and Dreams: Teaching Children to Write Poetry* (Koch & Padgett, 2000) or *Rose, Where Did You Get That Red? Teaching Great Poetry to Children* (Koch, 1990) for excellent examples of patterned writing.

Besides poetry, many early children's books are designed around repetitive language structures, lending themselves beautifully to meaningful language discussions about usage. Returning to the Mem Fox book *Tough Boris*, the language structure using predicate adjectives is present throughout the book. As children begin to use and define describing words as adjectives, they can easily see the way they can use these adjectives after a state-of-being verb. "He was scruffy. All pirates are scruffy." As you discuss the richness and simplicity of this language use, children will become aware of how they, too, can use these constructions in their independent writing.

Another way students can examine the function of the parts of speech is to search for simple subjects and predicates. One method includes the phrasing, "Who?" "Did what?" By working together as a class, then in partnerships, and finally independently, children should eventually begin to identify the basic sentence structure, underlining the simple subject once and the verb twice. Later you can add more sophisticated structures such as prepositional phrases and direct objects. This early skill development can be fast-paced and short in duration but still provide children with a foundation for more sophisticated future language explorations.

*Sentence Structures.* Many instructional techniques support the development of varied sentence structures through published texts and children's own writing. Some of the specific techniques we highlight in this section are using sentence strips, expanding sentences, and combining sentences (Hennings, 2002; Routman, 2005; Tompkins, 2008).

Children can examine the structure of sentences by using cut-up sentences from their own writing. You can write a simple sentence on a sentence strip and then cut it apart. As children work to reassemble the words into a meaningful sentence, they begin to notice clues such as capital letters and end punctuation while developing an awareness of complete sentences.

You can also help children learn how to make sentences more varied and interesting through a technique called "expanding sentences." Take two words, a noun and a verb. Have children brainstorm ways to build the two-word sentence into a three-word sentence. Continue to add more and more words until the sentence becomes interesting and descriptive. For instance, "Children play" can be expanded (by adding one word at a time) into "The energetic children play many exhausting recess games."

Children can also learn to combine sentences and sentence parts by taking two simple sentences and "puzzling out" how they can combine the two sentences into one. For instance, children can combine the two sentences, "I went to the mall. My mother went to the mall too" into "My mother and I went to the mall." As children learn to comfortably combine subjects, you can move on to predicates and then entire sentences, using accurate punctuation and conjunctions.

**Teaching Language Usage.** Because teachers cannot assume that children will acquire formal and conventional language through their everyday oral language experiences, it is necessary for teachers to develop explicit lessons to support the development of these skills. Naturally, we hope that children would be immersed through reading and writing demonstrations in formal and written language structures on a daily basis, but that exposure might not be sufficient for children to include conventional usage in their own language repertoire.

First, don't hesitate to create quick mini-lessons to teach correct language use such as subject-verb agreement, verb tense agreement, proper pronoun use, and correct homophone choice. You can use any of the examples mentioned in this chapter or look in grade-level language arts texts for other suggestions. Use the same mini-lesson format in Appendix A-27 as a guide. Reinforce these skills through editing conferences and small-group lessons that use various interactive materials such as whiteboards, cut-up word sorts, and "T-charts" (two-column charts with headings).

Sometimes templates can also be useful for oral practice drills. When teaching verb tenses, for instance, the age-old template for past, present, future, and past participle tenses is still a great structure: "Yesterday I (played). Right now this moment I (play). Tomorrow I (will play). Many times I (<u>have played</u>)." Start with regular "-ed" words and eventually add irregular words such as *drink* and *burst*. You can incorporate many of these activities into spelling lessons and place them on anchor charts in full view of all children. (If fire code laws prohibit you from hanging charts in your classroom, place smaller charts on firm poster board, or use the inside surface of file folders and keep them readily accessible in the reference section of the classroom library.) Consult your curriculum guides to identify the degree of language usage skills to explicitly teach at your student's grade level.

The most effective teaching occurs, though, when you select specific teaching concepts from children's own writing samples. A child will likely be more invested in learning a language concept when it directly affects a personal piece of writing. Work side by side with the child or use a small-group setting to teach these lessons. Record the lessons on the "I Am Learning/I Can" sheet or add another list to the editing folder to support children in applying these skills. Most importantly, always incorporate the new knowledge and skill in real writing or real language usage activities.

***Teaching the Mechanics of Writing.***   One of the most effective ways to bring children's attention to the mechanics of writing is through oral activities. Use intonation during teacher read-alouds or shared reading to show children how you interpret the signals writers have given you. One excellent book for reinforcing the importance of punctuation is Chris Raschka's *Yo! Yes?* (1993). In this book, two boys hold a meaningful conversation through simple one-word phrases and varied punctuation such as, "Yo!" "Yes?" "Hey!" "Who?"

You can also model using these signals in your writing demonstrations and through the morning message. Again, use the actual vocabulary that describes the symbol, such as "period" instead of "stop mark." Even kindergarteners can use vocabulary such as "ellipses" naturally and effortlessly when their teachers use this type of language during reading and writing demonstrations.

Although demonstrations provide a great foundation, you will also need to give children guided practice so that they internalize and automatically apply a new type of punctuation mark. To do so, provide explicit teaching and then offer guided practice, allowing children to work collaboratively, first by reading sentences with the specific punctuation and then by creating some sentences together. When it makes sense to do so, you can easily blend lessons on applying punctuation with sentence structuring lessons. For instance, you might teach how to use commas in a series during a lesson on sentence combining.

Many teachers use a combination of personalized editing sheets and a supply of red pens that are prominently placed in the publishing center for children to use when they reach the editing process. By placing a colored pen into the hands of a child, you are reinforcing the importance of this aspect of the writing process and indicating that you want to know what the child is now able to edit independently. As children move into the proofreading phase of their personal writing, they can use their "I Am Learning/I Can" sheets in their editing folders to guide them as they consider the surface features of their writing. When children draw a line through the changes (rather than erasing them) and correct errors with a red pen, teachers can clearly identify which corrections the child made during this process. Children can also monitor their growing control of writing conventions when they look over their drafts in their portfolios, folders, or draft-writing notebooks.

***Teaching Handwriting.***   Three different types of instructional considerations impact how you organize handwriting instruction. First, you might be introducing letter formation for the first time, explicitly modeling and guiding the whole class. Or explicit instruction may already have taken place and you merely need to reteach or reinforce specific areas of instruction for children who need more guidance or are still confused. The third consideration is audience and purpose. You will want to help children determine the level of attention to place on various products based on who will be receiving and reading them.

When introducing letter formation for the first time, many teachers begin by having children practice writing in the air, using their whole arms and hands. As children "air-draw" the letters, the teacher and children together recite the steps for making the letter, reinforcing the movement and the language that will keep the shape consistent. Teachers of early primary children often combine letter-sound relationships with handwriting instruction. In that case, you can use alphabet cards with pictures and words for the individual letters to support your early reading program.

Children love selecting and experimenting with various media including multiple colors and different writing implements. Some primary teachers use shaving cream or finger paint in initial practice sessions. Another useful method is to pour small amounts of sand onto metal cookie trays and have children practice writing a letter in the sand, shaking the tray slightly after each letter to smooth out the surface.

When children are first learning to form letters, allow them to automatically transfer the shape from their mind to their hand and then to the page without limiting the space with lines. Specially designed handwriting papers can come later, as children learn to refine the shapes and work within designated spaces. Also, allow children to experiment without the stress of trying to write perfectly, and give them the chance to self-evaluate their letter formation by circling their favorites.

If children have already learned letter formation in a whole-group setting or in a previous grade, clear up any of their confusions or problem areas during small-group or individual instructional settings. You will need to go over only the letters that a child has trouble with or forms poorly. Give the child as much support as needed, until she habituates proper formation. Remember to be patient, since the child may have had many opportunities to practice the letter incorrectly. Add verbal guidance ("Start at the top and then go down and around") as needed.

There is no "correct" way to teach handwriting, but it is important to create consistency from grade to grade. Become familiar with the program your school district has chosen by reading the manuals carefully so that you can provide instructional sequences that are in line with those of other teachers in your school. The program will also guide you in purchasing the visual handwriting charts, handwriting paper, and letter strips that will support your handwriting lessons.

Whenever possible, incorporate real reading and writing into handwriting sessions. As children learn to appreciate the different audiences of their handwriting, they will understand that the purpose and audience of the writing will determine the appropriate level of neatness. For example, during draft writing, legibility is important, but not to the "artistic" level of the final piece. When making changes during drafting, teachers often recommend that children draw a line through mistakes and changes so that teachers can see the thinking behind the changes. However, appearance counts in final copies, so the child will want to erase or use correction tape to make changes. For instance, if a child is writing a thank you card during publishing, he can copy the final words from the completely edited rough draft.

If the final copy is meant to be mailed or delivered, it will need special attention at the publication stage, and children might need special support in preparing the envelope or figuring out the best delivery option. Children love to experiment with fancy fonts ("bubble letters" are a favorite) when they make book covers for their published work. Encourage children to search through the classroom library to compare various books, looking for ideas for their own covers. Handwriting instruction during the publishing phase is an ideal time to capture a child's interest. You will hear few complaints when children are initiating their own learning and producing material for a real audience.

## Instructional Approaches for Writing Conventions, Including Handwriting, for Students with Specific Needs

Students who need extra support to learn the writing conventions will especially benefit from specific proofreading lists that are tailored to each child's developmental level. The many layers of writing conventions can seem perplexing to children if the expectations and guidelines for success are vague or unstated. If children have a personalized sheet written with their input and clear examples, they will more likely be able to manage the process of proofreading.

An editing session might work best if you use a one-to-one approach, teaching a child how to read through a paper, looking first at sentences. Together you can ponder the completeness of each group of words, looking at the capital letters and end punctuation. Next, model how you return to the top of the paper, scanning each word for spelling errors. Be careful to identify only the words the child has already learned, and allow "temporary" spelling for the others during this initial proofreading stage.

Small, focused instructional settings also provide opportunities to address grammar, usage, and mechanics skills in ways that are tailored to the learners' needs. These smaller groups allow you to closely monitor the level of assistance that each child needs, thus ensuring the success of all learners.

***English Language Learners and Syntax.*** It is important for teachers to become aware of what makes various English expressions hard to learn. Freeman and Freeman (2004) agree that syntactic "acceptability" can be hard to define. They offer the example of "on" and "in." In English we might say, "I rode on the bus" and "I rode in the car," but it would sound odd to say, "I rode on the car." These situations are challenging for a nonnative English speaker, but an alert teacher can provide support and special attention when discussing the little nuances of our language during meaningful literacy activities. Small-group attention is very important for promoting low-risk language discussions.

When an English Language Learner begins to proofread her writing, be sure to keep supporting her application of the conventions of standard English, choosing only one skill or concept at a time that's within her zone of proximal development, a task that the child can accomplish with a little bit of support. Internalizing the use of conventions will be most successful if the writing is meaningful and the expectations are manageable for the learner. The individualized proofreading sheet offers this clarification by listing only those skills that are within a learner's reach.

***Using Technology to Support Grammar, Usage, Mechanics, and Handwriting.*** Software is available to support children in all aspects of using writing conventions, but "many of these programs are excellent for English Language Learners and children with Learning Disabilities because they have an audio component built into them" (Cohen & Cowen, 2008, p. 315). Word processing programs and desktop publishing programs can also benefit striving learners. Spell-check and grammar-check tools can highlight and support children's developing proofreading skills. Also, many children who struggle with handwriting and fine motor skills find relief in keyboarding programs. Technology offers many controlled and engaging ways for children to practice skill development and bring it to the level of automaticity, but it is important to incorporate pen-and-paper tasks as well. It is also important to discriminate between software that extends authentic writing opportunities and software that is merely worksheets on the computer.

As you look at each individual child's development, try to identify the next incremental step that will enable the young writer to become more independent in her or his use of the conventions of our written language.

## LOOKING CLOSELY AT ONE CHILD'S ASSESSMENTS FROM STRAND 10 OF THE LITERACY PROFILE

Willa is beginning to develop an awareness of many writing conventions in the areas of grammar, usage, mechanics, and handwriting. Refer to Figure 10.5 to see how Willa's developing skills are recorded in Strand 10 of the Literacy Profile. Based on three writing samples, two from March and one from June of her first-grade year, Willa demonstrates good control of sentence structure and word usage. Although she sometimes overuses the conjunction "and," this is typical of children at her stage of development, as early writers often overuse "and" when they attempt to use more complex sentence structures. In addition, Willa is beginning to use transition words such as "but" to include contrasting information.

Willa is also beginning to control verb tenses, telling her entire story about the duck and the fox (refer back to Figure 7.6 in chapter 7) in the past tense, matching the opening, "Once upon a time." She also used an auxiliary verb correctly when writing her penguin story, stating that the penguin "was saved." Pronoun use is appropriate as well, including correct choices for singular "I" and the plural "we" when including her sister. Willa also used "it" appropriately when referring back to a previously named common noun, "dynamite."

Willa is also beginning to internalize the use of some of the conventions of punctuation. In the story about penguins, there is little evidence of capitalization at the beginning of sentences (see Figure 8.9). Later, in the "duck and fox" story, Willa showed attention to mechanics while she was writing when she paused to proofread two sentences. She recognized that she needed to capitalize the beginning word in each sentence, as you can see in the sample. After she corrected those sentences, she applied this knowledge when she wrote the next two sentences using correct capitalization at their beginnings. In the final two sentences, however, she resumed writing in all lowercase letters. This independently written story provides strong evidence that Willa is becoming conscious of capitalization at the beginning of sentences, but this skill is still in the developing stage, and is not fully automatic. Willa usually uses ending punctuation in her sentences, even trying out exclamation points when there is excitement.

Willa is developing a legible and consistent handwriting style with spaces almost always marking word boundaries. She is able to print letters without using an alphabet card for support, automatically printing all lowercase letters except one, always using the capital letter *L* instead of the lowercase *l*. Willa is able to use lined paper and keep most of her letters within the lines, making the taller letters (*k*) approximately double the size of the smaller letters (*m*), and often making letters extend below the line when appropriate (*p*).

## FIGURE 10.5  Willa's Profile for Writing Conventions

Note: This figure has been excerpted from the full Literacy Profile chart for illustrative purposes. Please consult the full pull-out chart to identify the column headings and development phases.

| Strand *Question & Sample Assessment Tools* | Early–Mid Grade 1 | Late Grade 1–Early Grade 2 | Late Grade 2–Early Grade 3 | Late Grade 3–Early Grade 4 |
|---|---|---|---|---|
| **10. Writing Conventions and Handwriting** *To what degree does the child use acceptable conventions of grammar, usage, and mechanics in written language? How is handwriting developing?* **Sample Assessment Tools** · Writing samples and writing prompts, with scoring guides | Usually leaves spaces between words<br><br>Includes lowercase letters in writing<br><br>Attempts to use end punctuation *[even uses exclamations!] KI* | Uses capitals at beginning of sentences, lowercase within words *[mostly all lowercase, still a few confusions] KI*<br>Uses periods appropriately at the end of sentences *[some of the time, some run-ons, some overuse] KI*<br>Writes in complete sentences *[but not always punctuated correctly] KI*<br>Uses a consistent handwriting style, with spaces between words | Uses uppercase letters for proper nouns *[occasionally] KI*<br><br>Uses some expanded sentences in writing, such as compound sentences *[overusing periods but compound sentences are used effectvely] KI*<br><br>Uses a variety of end punctuation | Uses commas for lists<br><br>Uses a variety of sentences, including compound or complex sentences<br><br>Uses commas in a list<br><br>Writes contractions with apostrophes<br><br>Uses accurate end punctuation (. ? !)<br><br>Can write in cursive with some support |

Gray areas represent highlighting added by the teacher, preferably using a different color for each year (e.g., yellow highlights for Late K, orange highlights for Early–Mid Grade 1, etc.). Bracketed material represents teacher/examiner comments from June, Grade 1.

For a specific "I Am Learning" step, Willa could be taught to use the lowercase letter *l* instead of the uppercase *L*. As mentioned in chapter 9, Willa is ready to learn how to proofread by consciously going back to check for beginning capital letters and end punctuation after she has completed her writing. Willa is clearly beginning to understand the importance of writing conventions, and with support, she will continue to develop more consistency in her use of writing conventions.

If it were possible to see Willa's Literacy Profile in its entirety, you would notice linkages and patterns across the 10 strands. In Willa's case, she shows quite a bit of consistency across the strands, but please remember that not all children show consistency. Every child has a unique profile, and we hope that you have the opportunity to notice the fascinating varieties of children's literacy development and build from those strengths.

## REFERENCES

Beck, I. L., McKeon, M. G., & Kucan, L. (2002). *Bringing words to life.* New York: Guilford.

Bertrand, N. P., & Stice, C. F. (2002). *Good teaching: An integrated approach to language, literacy, and learning.* Portsmouth, NH: Heinemann.

Brittain, W. L. (1973). *Analysis of artistic behavior in young children* (Final Report). Ithaca, NY: Cornell University. (ERIC Document No. ED 128 091)

Calkins, L. M. (1986, 1994). *The art of teaching writing.* Portsmouth, NH: Heinemann.

Clay, M. M. (1991). *Becoming literate: The construction of inner control.* Portsmouth, NH: Heinemann.

Cohen, V. L., & Cowen, J. E. (2008). *Literacy for children in an information age: Teaching reading, writing, and thinking.* Belmont, CA: Thomson Higher Education.

Collier, L. (2007). Classroom choices that support English language learners. *The Council Chronicle.* Urbana, IL: National Council of Teachers of English.

Cotton, K. (2002). *Teaching composition: Research on effective practices, 1–18, School Improvement Research Series: Research you can use.* Portland, OR: Northwest Regional Educational Laboratory.

Donoghue, M. R. (1985). *The child and the English language arts*. Dubuque, IA: Brown.

Duncan, J. (1996). Quoted from personal conversation.

Fletcher, R. (2007). Stated during online TLN author conversations. Katonah, NY: Richard C. Owens. (tln@listserve.com)

Fox, M. (1994). *Tough Boris*. San Diego, CA: Voyager Books.

Freeman, D. E., & Freeman, Y. S. (2004). *Essential linguistics*. Portsmouth, NH: Heinemann.

Graves, D. (1994). *A fresh look at writing*. Portsmouth, NH: Heinemann.

Graves, D. (2003). *Writing: Teachers and children at work* (Twentieth-anniversary ed.). Portsmouth, NH: Heinemann.

Halliday, M. A. K. (1984). Three aspects of children's language development: Learning language, learning through language, and learning about language. In Y. Goodman, M. Haussler, & D. Strickland (Eds.), *Oral and written language development research: Impact on schools*. Urbana, IL: National Council of Teachers of English.

Hammill, D. D., & Larsen, S. C. (1996). *Test of written language examiner's manual* (3rd ed.). Austin, TX: Pro-Ed.

Heller, R. (1998a). *Behind the mask: A book about prepositions.* New York: Penguin Putnam.

Heller, R. (1998b). *Kites sail high: A book about verbs.* New York: Penguin Putnam.

Heller, R. (1998c). *Many luscious lollipops: A book about adjectives.* New York: Penguin Putnam.

Heller, R. (1998d). *Merry go round: A book about nouns.* New York: Penguin Putnam.

Heller, R. (1998e). *Up up and away: A book about adverbs.* New York: Penguin Putnam.

Heller, R. (1999). *Mine all mine: A book about pronouns.* New York: Penguin Putnam.

Heller, R., & Peskin, J. (2000). *Fantastic! Wow! And unreal! A book about interjections and conjunctions.* New York: Penguin Putnam.

Hennings, D. G. (2002). *Communication in action: Teaching literature-based language arts.* Boston: Houghton Mifflin.

Hillocks, G. (1986). *Research on written composition: New directions for teaching.* Urbana, IL: ERIC Clearinghouse on Reading and Communication Skills and the National Conference on Research in English.

Hresko, W., Herron, S., & Peak, P. (2006). *TEWL-2: Test of early written language.* Shoreview, MN: AGS Publishing.

Hunt, K., & O'Donnell, R. (1970). *An elementary school curriculum to develop better writing skills.* U.S. Office of Education Grant, Florida State University.

Koch, K. (1990). *Rose, where did you get that red? Teaching great poetry to children.* New York: Vintage/Anchor.

Koch, K., & Padgett, R. (2000). *Wishes, lies, and dreams: Teaching children to write poetry.* New York: Harper Paperbacks.

Machado, J. (2003). *Early childhood experiences in language arts: Emerging literacy* (7th ed.). Clifton Park, NY: Delmar Learning.

Ministry of Education. (1992). *Dancing with the pen.* Wellington, New Zealand: Author.

Neufeldt, V., & Guralnik, D. B. (Eds.). (1991). *Webster's new world dictionary of American English.* New York: Prentice Hall.

Polette, K. (2008). *Teaching grammar through writing.* Boston: Allyn & Bacon.

Raschka, C. (1993). *Yo! Yes?* New York: Scholastic.

Ray, K. W. (1999). *Wondrous words: Writers and writing in the elementary classroom.* Urbana, IL: National Council of Teachers of English.

Routman, R. (2005). *Writing essentials: Raising expectations and results while simplifying teaching.* Portsmouth, NH: Heinemann.

Schickedanz, J. A. (1989). What about preschoolers and academics? *Reading Today, 7*(1), 24.

Smith, F. (1982). *Writing and the writer.* New York: Holt, Rinehart, & Winston.

Spandel, V. (2004). *Creating young writers: Using the six traits to enrich writing process in primary classrooms*. Boston: Pearson/Allyn&Bacon.

Stahl, S., & Pagnucco, J. (1996). First graders' reading and writing instruction in traditional and process-oriented classes. *Journal of Educational Research, 89*(3), 131–144.

Strunk, W., Jr., & White, E. B. (2000). *Elements of style* (4th ed.) Upper Saddle River, NJ: Longman.

Thurber, D. N. (1988). *D'Nealian home/school activities: Manuscript practice for grades 1–3*. New York: Scott Foresman.

Tompkins, G. E. (2008). *Teaching writing: Balancing process and product.* Upper Saddle River, NJ: Pearson/Merrill Prentice Hall.

Warriner, J. (1988). *English composition and grammar: Complete course*. Orlando, FL: Harcourt Brace Jovanovich.

Weaver, C. (1996). *Teaching grammar in context.* Portsmouth, NH: Heinemann.

Wilde, S. (1992). *You kan red this! Spelling and punctuation for whole language classrooms, K–6.* Portsmouth, NH: Heinemann.

Wiseman, D. L., Elish-Piper, L., & Wiseman, A. M. (2005). *Learning to teach language arts in a field-based setting.* Scottsdale, AZ: Holcomb Hathaway.

# CONCLUSION

# Thinking Ahead

In the Introductory chapter, one of the first assumptions we discussed was the important relationship among three "ingredients": standards ("what"), instruction ("how"), and assessment ("how well"). It is critical that these ingredients work together for the benefit of learners. In this concluding chapter we will discuss some additional points to keep in mind, some questions to ask, and a few final thoughts.

## MORE TO KEEP IN MIND AND THINK ABOUT

The points listed below address some issues that are important to keep in mind while using the Literacy Profile. They involve considerations regarding teachers as learners, the importance of flexibility, building on students' strengths, and the importance of planning and communicating with others.

### Teachers as Learners

One of the most important points for teachers (as well as supervisors and administrators) to keep in mind is that teachers are learners too. Like our students, we have a "zone of proximal development," we need lots of support, and we need ample opportunities to practice new skills and new learning. Also, like the children whose progress we record on the Literacy Profile, we sometimes also have gaps and "fits and starts." It's important to acknowledge this and be patient with our own learning processes.

## Flexibility

Making standards, instruction, and assessment work together can sometimes be tricky, and often requires skillful decision making. For example, you may have found after using one assessment that the assessment did not really provide you with meaningful or valid information about a particular expectation (or standard) and thus decided to use an additional assessment to learn more about what the child can do in relation to that expectation and is ready to learn next. Or you may have tried an instructional technique and found that it wasn't challenging enough for the child; perhaps it wasn't appropriate for the child's "zone of proximal development." Flexibility is definitely called for.

As you continue to explore children's development using the Literacy Profile, you will discover that learning rarely occurs in a linear fashion (even though the left-to-right progression of the Literacy Profile might make you think so!). You'll probably notice that there are times when a child seems to have solid "control" over a skill, strategy, or concept, but then later in the year or the next year, the child seems to have forgotten the skill or concept. This might happen for a variety of reasons, given that learning to read (or write) is an interactive process that involves the child, the text, and the context. For instance, the text might be more complex than what the child is comfortable with, or maybe the classroom environment may have changed, with increased expectations for independent, silent reading or less opportunity for discussion of what was read. Perhaps a child's performance on a given assessment is surprising, and you suspect it may be because she did not get enough sleep the night before or because she is worried about how she will get home after school. For any of these reasons, you'll probably find that you need to use more than one assessment on more than one occasion.

## Building on Student Strengths

In addition, keep in mind that the Literacy Profile reveals both gaps and areas of strength in a child's learning, often in different strands. A child's strengths in one area can often "shore up" her development in another. So it will be especially helpful if you can use information about her weaknesses *and* her strengths to support her learning. For example, Tanya, a striving reader in second grade, loves writing and is quite fluent in creating her own stories. However, she struggles with both decoding and fluency in reading. Through some supported work during writer's workshop, where she is encouraged to frequently reread her stories both to herself and to an "audience," she is developing stronger skills in reading fluency, decoding, recognizing sight words, and also spelling.

## Planning

As you continue exploring the uses of the Literacy Profile and this Handbook, think about ways to systematically use the information in your planning. Every teacher has his or her own unique method of planning the next steps of instruction. Figure C.1 provides an example of a tool that many teachers have found useful in planning ahead (often for the next marking period) based on children's assessment patterns that teachers have observed. Appendix A-31 includes a blank copy of this planning sheet.

To use this tool along with the Literacy Profile, simply look at Literacy Profiles as well as actual assessments you've administered for children who have a similar pattern of need (e.g., using evidence from a text to support responses to reading). List their areas of need (skills, stragegies, or concepts) in the boxes at the top, and then list the children's names on the lines in the middle of the form. In the ovals at the bottom, identify a few instructional approaches or

FIGURE C.1 **Sample of Differentiation in Action Planning Sheet**

### Differentiation in Action
### Instructional Focus Planning Sheet

**Skills**
**Strategies**
**Concepts**

| | | |
|---|---|---|
| • *Phrasing + expression (oral reading)*<br><br>• *Attention to punctuation* | • *Identifying problem + solution in stories* | • *Expanding vocabulary* |

**Students**

| | | |
|---|---|---|
| *Lucy*<br>*Tim*<br>*Carla*<br>*Andrew* | *Andrew*<br>*Jodi*<br>*Kim T.*<br>*Kamil*<br>*T. J.* | *Carla*<br>*Kamil*<br>*T. J.* |

**Instructional**
**Methods/Moves**
**Strategies**

| | | |
|---|---|---|
| • *Phrased text lessons (during Guided Reading?)*<br><br>• *Readers' theater* | • *Somebody-Wanted- But-So (small-group lessons)*<br><br>• *Story maps* | • *Small-group lessons: previewing + reviewing teacher read-alouds (+ vocabulary)*<br><br>• *Personal vocabulary notebooks* |

**Date:** *January–February*

interventions that you want to use with those children over the next few weeks or months. This template allows you to use the results of ongoing assessment to inform instruction; we encourage you to use it on a regular basis.

## Communicating with Others

The Literacy Profile is a rich source of information for communicating with others about the literacy development of children. Who might benefit from this communication? Among others, we immediately think of:

- *Teachers at the next grade level.* At the end or the beginning of the school year, teachers at adjacent grade levels might meet to look at children's Literacy Profiles from the previous year and discuss children's strengths and needs.
- *Specialist teachers and classroom teachers who work together as a team.* Periodically, specialist teachers (i. e., Title 1, ELL, special education) and classroom teachers might meet to look closely at one or more children's Literacy Profile(s) and together plan the next steps.
- *Schools or teams implementing a "Response to Intervention" model.* The Literacy Profile and Handbook could be key resources for educators implementing a "Response to Intervention" (RTI) model. For more information about RTI and its implications for literacy instruction, visit the International Reading Association's Web site: http://www.reading.org/downloads/resources/IDEA_RTI_report.pdf
- *Parents.* Parents clearly care about their children's literacy development, and the Literacy Profile provides a valuable opportunity for teachers and parents to discuss the child's progress and future educational goals.
- *Students.* Students are curious about their own progress, and the Literacy Profile can provide a way for teachers and children to celebrate accomplishments and set goals together. This kind of conversation is most appropriate with children in Grades 2 and above.

## QUESTIONS, QUESTIONS, QUESTIONS

As you use the Literacy Profile, you will likely have some questions. That's a good thing! We have posed a few questions below, to add to the ones you may already be asking; discussing them in a group setting would be particularly beneficial.

- To what degree do the assessments currently in place in your classroom or school connect with the strands in the Literacy Profile?
- Are any strands not receiving sufficient instructional attention?
- Does using the Literacy Profile and Handbook help build your knowledge of literacy strands and expertise in using the results of assessment? What is clearer now, and what areas do you want to learn more about?
- Think about your professional development in regard to literacy development. Do you have enough support to implement the Literacy Profile? What other kinds of support might help?

## A FEW FINAL WORDS

In closing, we have three wishes, or hopes:

We hope that the time you have spent using the Literacy Profile and Handbook has helped you more fully understand at least one learner.

We hope that the Literacy Profile and Handbook help you see "the big picture" of children's literacy development.

And finally, we hope that as you follow your own learning path to build your knowledge and expertise in collaboration with others, you find helpful supports along the way.

# APPENDIX A  RESOURCES FOR ASSESSMENT AND INSTRUCTION

# Yopp-Singer Test of Phoneme Segmentation

Student's name _____     Date _____

**Score (number correct)** _____

**Directions:** Today we're going to play a word game. I'm going to say a word and I want you to break the word apart. You are going to tell me each sound in the word in order. For example, if I say "old," you should say /o/-/l/-/d/-." (*Administrator: Be sure to say the sounds, not the letters, in the word.*) Let's try a few together.

**Practice items:** (*Assist the child in segmenting these items as necessary.*)
ride, go, man

**Test items:** (*Circle those items that the student correctly segments; incorrect responses may be recorded on the blank line following the item.*)

| | |
|---|---|
| 1. dog _____ | 12. lay _____ |
| 2. keep _____ | 13. race _____ |
| 3. fine _____ | 14. zoo _____ |
| 4. no _____ | 15. three _____ |
| 5. she _____ | 16. job _____ |
| 6. wave _____ | 17. in _____ |
| 7. grew _____ | 18. ice _____ |
| 8. that _____ | 19. at _____ |
| 9. red _____ | 20. top _____ |
| 10. me _____ | 21. by _____ |
| 11. sat _____ | 22. do _____ |

Figure from Yopp, H. K. (1995, September). A test for assessing phonemic awareness in young children. *The Reading Teacher, 49*(1), 20–29. Reprinted with permission of the International Reading Association.

# Formative Assessment for Phonological Awareness (FAPA)

**Name of child:** _____     **Current grade:** _____     **Age:** _____

**Date:** _____     **Name of test administrator:** _____

**Directions for administering:**

This assessment is designed to determine a child's developmental level of phonological awareness along the continuum. It should be administered in short, relaxed sessions working one to one with the child, almost like playing a word game. Be sure to start with the practice questions before you begin recording the child's response. It is not necessary to complete the entire test; you are simply trying to identify an appropriate level of instruction for each individual child. Simply place a check mark on the corresponding line if the child scores a correct response. **If the child is required to name a word or tell a number, write the child's exact response for each of the six items on the blank line. When necessary, list each sound a child provides, separating with a dash or dot. Be sure to repeat the italicized prompt.**

## Section 1: Listening

- Practice: Are these words the same? cat-cat _____     **Score** _____ **of 6**     (Use a check mark for correct response.)
- Practice: Are these words the same? man-mat _____

*Are these words the same?*     1. dog-dog _____     2. pan-pin _____     3. show-show _____

4. top-top _____     5. please-sneeze _____     6. mink-monk _____

## Section 2: Recognizing Rhymes

- Practice: Do these words rhyme? man-pan _____     **Score** _____ **of 6**     (Use check mark for correct response.)
- Practice: Do these words rhyme? she-sheep _____

*Do these words rhyme?*     1. job-boy _____     2. dog-log _____     3. truck-luck _____

4. peach-plum _____     5. school-rule _____     6. yellow-jello _____

## Section 3: Producing Rhymes

- Practice: What word rhymes with hat? _____     **Score** _____ **of 6**     (Write the child's exact response such as mat for hat.)
- Practice: What word rhymes with book? _____

*What word rhymes with _____?*     1. play _____     2. feet _____     3. by _____

4. fun _____     5. blink _____     6. toy _____

# Formative Assessment for Phonological Awareness (FAPA)

## Section 4: Segmenting words

Score _____ of 6

- Practice: Tell me how many words are in the sentence I say. I like you. _____ (Write the number the child says such as 3.)
- Practice: Tell me how many words are in the sentence I say. We are at school. _____

*Tell me how many words are in the sentence I say.*

| | |
|---|---|
| 1. The sun is shining. _____ | 2. The girl ran home. _____ |
| 3. We read a good book. _____ | 4. I love to eat pizza. _____ |
| 5. He is funny. _____ | 6. The dog chased the cat. _____ |

## Section 5: Segmenting syllables

Score _____ of 6

- Practice: Tell me how many syllables are in the word: pencil. _____ (Write the number the child says such as 2.)
- Practice: Tell me how many syllables are in the word: top. _____

*Tell me how many syllables are in the word:*

| | | |
|---|---|---|
| 1. table _____ | 2. happy _____ | 3. remember _____ |
| 4. farm _____ | 5. shovel _____ | 6. tomorrow _____ |

## Section 6: Blending Onsets and Rimes

Score _____ of 6

- Practice: Listen and tell me the word I say: /p/ /at/. _____ (Write the child's exact response such as pat.)
- Practice: Listen and tell me the word I say: /t/ /op/. _____

*Listen and tell me the word I say:*

| | | |
|---|---|---|
| 1. /b/ /all/ _____ | 2. /f/ /un/ _____ | 3. /k/ /ite/ _____ |
| 4. /t/ /ack/ _____ | 5. /sh/ /ut/ _____ | 6. /fr/ /og/ _____ |

## Section 7: Hearing Onsets in One-Syllable Words

Score _____ of 6

- Practice: Tell me the first sound you hear in the word: mad. _____ (Write the SOUND the child says such as /m/ for mad.)
- Practice: Tell me the first sound you hear in the word: rock. _____

*Tell me the first sound you hear in the word:*

| | | |
|---|---|---|
| 1. feet _____ | 2. dig _____ | 3. cup _____ |
| 4. ban _____ | 5. pet _____ | 6. hot _____ |

# Formative Assessment for Phonological Awareness (FAPA)

## Section 8: Hearing Final Consonant Sounds in One-Syllable Words

Score _____ of 6

- Practice: Tell me the last sound you hear in the word: mad. _____ (Write the SOUND the child says such as /d/ for mad.)
- Practice: Tell me the last sound you hear in the word: rock. _____

*Tell me the last sound you hear in the word:*

1. feet _____
4. ban _____
2. dig _____
5. pet _____
3. cup _____
6. hot _____

## Section 9: Hearing Vowels in One-Syllable Words

Score _____ of 6

- Practice: Tell me the sound you hear in the middle of the word: mad. _____ (Write the SOUND the child says such as /a/ for mad.)
- Practice: Tell me the sound you hear in the middle of the word: rock. _____

*Tell me the sound you hear in the middle of the word:*

1. feet _____
4. ban _____
2. dig _____
5. pet _____
3. cup _____
6. hot _____

## Section 10: Blending Phonemes

Score _____ of 6

- Practice: Listen and tell me the word I say: /d/ /ay/. _____ (Write the child's exact response such as day for /d/ /ay/.)
- Practice: Listen and tell me the word I say: /m/ /o/ /p/. _____

*Listen and tell me the word I say:*

1. /h/ /ee/ _____
4. /m/ /ea/ /t/ _____
2. /s/ /u/ /n/ _____
5. /t/ /r/ /a/ /sh/ _____
3. /g/ /o/ /t/ _____
6. /f/ /l/ /a/ /t/ _____

## Section 11: Segmenting Phonemes

Score _____ of 6

- Practice: Tell me the sounds in sat. _____ (Write the SOUNDS the child says such as /s/ /a/ /t/ or s-a-t for sat.)
- Practice: Tell me the sounds in mom. _____

*Tell me the sounds in . . .*

1. home _____
4. move _____
2. pig _____
5. jump _____
3. went _____
6. box _____

# Formative Assessment for Phonological Awareness (FAPA)

## Section 12: Phoneme Deletion First Sound

Score _____ of 6

- Practice: Say the word tin, but leave off the /t/. _____ (Write the child's exact response such as in.)
- Practice: Say the word mat, but leave off the /m/. _____

Say the word _____, but leave off the /__/.

| | | |
|---|---|---|
| 1. fin . . . /f/ _____ | 2. love . . . /l/ _____ | 3. plate . . . /p/ _____ |
| 4. drum . . . /d/ _____ | 5. bike . . . /b/ _____ | 6. frog . . . /f/ _____ |

## Section 13: Phoneme Deletion Last Sound

Score _____ of 6

- Practice: Say the word tin, but leave off the /n/. _____ (Write the child's exact response such as ti.)
- Practice: Say the word mat, but leave off the /t/. _____

Say the word _____, but leave off the /__/.

| | | |
|---|---|---|
| 1. fin . . . /n/ _____ | 2. love . . . /v/ _____ | 3. plate . . . /t/ _____ |
| 4. drum . . . /m/ _____ | 5. bike . . . /k/ _____ | 6. frog . . . /g/ _____ |

## Section 14: Phoneme Substitution First Sound

Score _____ of 6

- Practice: Replace the first sound in pail with /t/. _____ (Write the child's exact response such as tail.)
- Practice: Replace the first sound in sad with /m/. _____

Replace the first sound in . . . .

| | | |
|---|---|---|
| 1. can with /m/ _____ | 2. mice with /d/ _____ | 3. hot with /n/ _____ |
| 4. tip with /fl/ _____ | 5. wish with /f/ _____ | 6. rip with /sh/ _____ |

## Section 15: Phoneme Substitution Last Sound

Score _____ of 6

- Practice: Replace the last sound in pail with /n/. _____ (Write the child's exact response such as pain.)
- Practice: Replace the last sound in sad with /m/. _____

Replace the last sound in . . . .

| | | |
|---|---|---|
| 1. can with /t/ _____ | 2. mice with /t/ _____ | 3. hot with /p/ _____ |
| 4. tip with /l/ _____ | 5. wish with /k/ _____ | 6. rip with /d/ _____ |

# Self-Assessment for Oral Presentations

Name:_____

Topic of presentation:_____

Date of self-evaluation:_____

| Goals for Presenting | My Progress | | |
|---|---|---|---|
| | Always | Occasionally | Not Yet |
| 1. I speak loudly enough for my audience to hear. | | | |
| 2. I speak clearly enough so that everyone can understand my words. | | | |
| 3. I make eye contact with my audience. | | | |
| 4. I speak slowly enough so that everyone can understand what I am saying. | | | |
| 5. I use gestures to liven up my words. | | | |
| 6. I use props to make my talk interesting. | | | |
| 7. I talk to my audience and use my paper only as a guide. | | | |

Something I was proud of about my presentation:

One goal I'd like to set for my next presentation:

Teacher comments:

Dorothy Grant Hennings, *Communication in Action: Teaching the Language Arts*, Eighth Edition, Copyright 2002 by Houghton Mifflin Company. Adapted with permission.

## Concepts of Print Checklist

Name of student:_____ Date: _____

| CONCEPT | TEACHER QUESTIONS | + or − |
|---|---|---|
| How to handle a book | Show me the front of the book. | |
| How to handle a book | Which page do we read first? | |
| Print contains the message *(focus on print, not the picture)* | I'll read this story. You help me. Show me where to start reading. | |
| Directional movement | Where do I begin? | |
| L - R | Which way do I go? | |
| Return sweeps | Where do I go when I get to the end of the line? | |
| One-to-one matching | Point as I read. *(Teacher reads text.)* | |
| Conventions of print | Next page . . . *(Teacher continues to read text.)* What is this? *(points to a period)* | |
| Conventions of print | Continue to read and when appropriate, What is this? *(points to a comma)* | |
| Conventions of print | Continue to read and when appropriate, What is this? *(points to a question mark)* | |
| Conventions of print | Continue to read and when appropriate, What is this? *(points to quotation marks)* | |
| Concept of letter | On a final page, read one sentence and show the child how to use the index card strips. *(Say, "I want you to push the cards across the story like this until all you can see is":)* <br> • Just one letter | |
| Letter concept | • Now show me two letters. | |
| Letter within word | • Show me the first letter of a word. | |
| Letter within word | • Show me the last letter of a word. | |
| Conventions of print | • Show me a capital letter. | |
| Word concept | • Show me just one word. | |
| Word concept | • Now show me two words. | |
| Word concept | • Show me the first word on this page. | |
| Word concept | • Show me the last word on this page. | |

## Untimed Letter Naming Test

| A | H | L | X | T | B |
|---|---|---|---|---|---|
| Y | S | V | C | N | R |
| D | G | E | K | J | M |
| P | W | U | F | O | Q |
| I | Z | h | l | x | t |
| b | y | s | v | c | n |
| a | d | g | e | f | o |
| q | i | k | j | m | p |
| w | u | z | r | g | a |

# Teacher Recording Form for Letter-Name Recognition

**Directions:** Make a check mark by those letters that a child can name accurately and independently. If necessary, suggest finger pointing as a strategy for tracking, or use a piece of blank paper to help the child track from left to right. Be sure to note these added teacher directions in the comments section. List any letter confusions or other notable behaviors that you observed during testing.

**Note:** Before using the test, fold down the title so children do not recoginze this as a "test."

Name: _____     Date: _____

| | | | | | | | | |
|---|---|---|---|---|---|---|---|---|
| ___A | ___Y | ___D | ___P | ___T | ___b | ___a | ___q | ___w |
| ___H | ___S | ___G | ___W | ___Z | ___y | ___d | ___i | ___u |
| ___L | ___V | ___E | ___U | ___h | ___s | ___g | ___k | ___z |
| ___X | ___C | ___K | ___F | ___l | ___v | ___e | ___j | ___r |
| ___I | ___N | ___J | ___O | ___x | ___c | ___f | ___m | ___g |
| ___B | ___R | ___M | ___Q | ___t | ___n | ___o | ___p | ___a |

Confusions:

Comments:

## Decoding Application Scale

| Name:_____  Text:_____  Date:_____ | 0  Not evident yet | 1  Just beginning | 2  Using this skill | 3  In place (or beyond) | Notes |
|---|---|---|---|---|---|
| Does the reader pay attention to the print? | | | | | |
| Does the reader look at all parts of the word? | | | | | |
| Does the reader use sound-symbol correspondences of consonants, blends, digraphs? | | | | | |
| Does the reader use successive blending? (not just b-a-g, but ba- bag)? | | | | | |
| Does the reader use a decoding-by-analogy strategy? | | | | | |
| Does the reader try different vowel patterns when needed? | | | | | |
| Does the reader use knowledge of syllable types to decode? | | | | | |

**Answer Key for Figure 4.5, Practice Exercise: Applying Oral Reading Miscues**

| Item | Answer | Explanation |
|------|--------|-------------|
| 1 | Circle S and V | Circle S because the substitution uses the same part of speech (verb).<br><br>Circle V because the student used some degree of graphophonic information (beginning and ending) in making the error.<br><br>Do not circle M, because the error does not make sense in the sentence. |
| 2 | Circle M, S, and V | Circle M because the error makes sense in the sentence.<br><br>Circle S because the substitution uses the same part of speech (adjective).<br><br>Circle V because the student used graphophonic information in making the error: the beginning letter and the ending "chunk." |
| 3 | Circle S and V | Circle M because the sentence as read makes sense.<br><br>Circle S because the substitution uses the same part of speech (verb).<br><br>Do not circle V, because no graphophonic information was used. |
| 4 | Circle M and S | Circle S because the substitution uses the same part of speech (verb).<br><br>Circle V because the student used some graphophonic information in making the error, although misused that information by reversing the order of letters (*was* for *saw*).<br><br>Do not circle M, because the sentence as read does not make sense. |

**Reading Strategies Self-Assessment: Early Processing Strategies**

| What do I try when I read? | No | Sometimes | Often | LOTS |
|---|---|---|---|---|
| Look closely at the word | | | | |
| Make the sounds for the letters | | | | |
| Think: does that make sense? | | | | |
| Think: does that sound right? | | | | |
| Use the picture | | | | |
| Try a different word | | | | |
| Go back and try reading it again | | | | |

## Reading Strategies Self-Assessment: Comprehension Strategies

| What strategies do I use when I read? | No | Sometimes | Often | LOTS |
|---|---|---|---|---|
| Check to see if I have understood what I just read | | | | |
| Think about what I already know, and how that connects with what I am reading | | | | |
| Predict what is coming next as I am reading | | | | |
| Summarize in my head as I am reading | | | | |
| Think about what the author is really trying to say | | | | |
| Make pictures in my head about what I am reading | | | | |
| Make notes on Post-its while I am reading | | | | |

# Reading Strategies and Dispositions Interview

**Name:** _____ **Grade:**_____

**Date:** _____ **Teacher:**_____

Ask only those questions that are logical to ask!

## 1. Early reading strategies

    a. What do you do when you come to a word you are not sure of, or when you come to a tricky part? Any other things you try?

    b. Does that work well for you? If not, what else do you think might work?

## 2. Use of comprehension strategies

    a. What strategies do you use to help you understand what you read? Any others?

    b. Does that work well for you? If not, what else do you think might work?

## 3. Reading dispositions and habits

    a. What kind of reader are you?

    b. What do you think you do well as a reader?

    c. What do you think is a next step for you as a reader? (something you'd like to work on)

## Book Log

_____

**Name:** _____    **Teacher:** _____

| Dates: when started, when finished | Title of Book Completed | Genre* | Easy (E), Just Right (JR), or Challenging (Ch)? | How I Rate This Book: (1–4 stars) |
|---|---|---|---|---|
| | | | | |
| | | | | |
| | | | | |
| | | | | |

\* Our Code for Genres:

F = Fiction

I = Informational (topic) book

P = Poetry

B = Biography

H = "How-to" book

M = Magazine

O = Other

## Individual Student Conference Form

**Name:** _____     **Date:** _____

○ Please bring me the book that you are reading for independent reading, and your reading log or reading notebook/folder.

Title of book/reading material: _____

Genre: _____

○ Why did you choose this?

○ What do you think about its difficulty for you?

_____ easy _____ just right or _____ hard

○ As you were reading this, did you do anything (use any strategies) to help yourself read or understand it better? Did they help?

○ Tell me what this is about, so far:

○ Read this part of the book for me . . . (Take notes as the student reads silently or orally.) If reading orally, you might take a running record or use the Quick Text-Level Check-In.

○ Tell me about what you just read.

○ How long do you think it will take you to complete this? What do you think you might read next?

○ Let's discuss your strengths as a reader, and what you need to work on next:

  ○ Strengths:

  ○ Needs/Goals:

## Reading Strategies

To do my best reading, I can . . . ★
★
★

_____ try it again, and think
about what would
make sense and sound right

_____ try it again, and look at all
the letters in the word

_____ think about another word
I know that is almost the same

_____ use the picture to help

_____ go back to reread
when something is
not quite right

# Text Structures and Signal Words

## Text Structures, Transition Words, Signal Words

| Classification, Label, List | Comparison-Contrast | Sequence, Explanation | Cause-Effect, Problem-Solution | Explanation |
|---|---|---|---|---|
| Several types, | Similarly, | To begin with, | Consequently, | For example, |
| Kinds, Ways, | On the one hand, | Initially, | Therefore, | For instance, |
| Characteristics, | On the other hand, | Following, | In conclusion, | In fact, |
| In addition, | However, Likewise, | Afterward, | As a result, | In other words, |
| Last, Lastly, | And yet, | Immediately, | Thus, | In short, |
| Likewise, | At the same time, | In the meantime, | Result, | In sum, |
| Moreover, | But, | Meanwhile, | Effect, | In brief, |
| Next, Secondly, | In contrast to this, | Soon, Next, | Problem, | Indeed, |
| Too, Further, | Nevertheless, | Then, | Solution | On the whole, |
| Finally, | Still, | First, Next, | | To be sure, |
| Equally important, | Yet | Eventually | | To sum up |
| Besides, | | | | |
| Another, | | | | |
| Still another, | | | | |
| Also | | | | |

## My Turn, Your Turn

(Predicting and questioning)
- ☐ I bet . . .
- ☐ I wonder . . .

(Making connections)
- ☐ This reminds me of . . .
- ☐ This connects with . . .

(Clarifying)
- ☐ I'm not sure about . . .
- ☐ I didn't get the part . . .

(Inferring, paraphrasing, or summarizing)
- ☐ I think they are saying that . . .
- ☐ This means . . .
- ☐ This part is mostly about . . .
- ☐ I think the author is telling us that . . .

## My Turn, Your Turn

 I wonder . . .

 I predict . . .

 This reminds me of . . .

 I'm not sure about . . .

 I think the author means . . .

This part is about . . .

**Three-Way Fluency Rubric**

**Directions:** Circle the phrases that describe how the text was read.

| | 1 | 2 | 3 |
|---|---|---|---|
| Phrasing and expression | Word-by-word reading with little attention to expression or punctuation | Used some pauses and expression and attention to punctuation | Used pauses, expression, and attention to punctuation—so it sounded like talking |
| Accuracy | Many errors | Some errors | No errors or very few errors |
| Rate | Very slow | Too fast or too slow | Just right |

**Keeping Track of Fluency During Rereading**

**Name of Reader:**_____

**Partner:**_____

**Date:**_____

**Directions:** Use Three-Way Fluency Rubric to note 1, 2, 3 in boxes below.

| | 1st read | 2nd read | 3rd read |
|---|---|---|---|
| Phrasing and expression | | | |
| Accuracy | | | |
| Rate | | | |

# Quick Text-Level Check-In

## Directions

1. The teacher selects a short piece of text to be read, counts 100 words, and marks that point lightly with a pencil.

2. The student reads aloud and the teacher records errors only with a tally mark for each one, jotting down the substitutions that the student has made, for later analysis.

3. As the student reads, the teacher notices the degree of fluency the student shows.

4. Following the 100-word passage, the teacher asks the student to read the next section of text silently, saying, "*When you are finished, I will ask you to tell me about the part you read.*"

5. After the child has finished reading, the teacher says: *"Now tell me about the part you just read."* The teacher then jots down what the student says. If the student volunteers very little, it will be necessary to probe with some general questions (as appropriate to the segment of text read) such as:

### *Narrative text*
- Where/when is this happening?
- What's going on in this part? Who was the author talking about?
- Tell me more about that.

### *Expository text*
- What's the main thing the author wanted you to learn in this part?
- Tell me more about that.
- Any other important details?
- Anything particularly interesting?

6. Summarize the student's comprehension by checking one of the boxes for "limited," "some," "acceptable," or "strong" comprehension of *this particular text*. Then, taking all three aspects of reading (accuracy, fluency, and comprehension) into account, mark the student's reading performance of this particular text: "too hard," "marginal," "okay," or "easy."

# Quick Text-Level Check-In

**Student:**_____

**Text:** _____

**Date:**_____ **Teacher:** _____ **Grade:**_____

**Level of text:**_____

**Part 1: Oral Reading Accuracy:** 100 words sampled: from Page #:_____
Tally errors:

(Note: Self-corrections do not count as errors.) Note cues used,
patterns observed.
**Check accuracy level below:**

| ☐ 11 or more (<90%) (frustration) | ☐ 8–10 (90–92%) (marginal instructional) | ☐ 6–7 (93–94%) (instructional) | ☐ 0–5 (95–100%) (independent) |
|---|---|---|---|
| **Check fluency level:** ☐ **A. Very little fluency;** all word-by-word reading with some long pauses between words; almost no recognition of syntax or phrasing (expressive interpretation); very little evidence of awareness of punctuation; perhaps a couple of two-word phrases but generally not fluent; some word groupings awkward. | ☐**B. Mostly** word-by-word reading but with some two-word phrasing and even a couple of three- or four-word phrases (expressive interpretation); some evidence of awareness of syntax and punctuation, although not consistently so; rereading for problem solving may not be present. | ☐ **C. A mixture** of word-by-word reading and fluent, phrased reading (expressive interpretation); there is evidence of attention to punctuation and syntax; rereading for problem solving may be present. (*Note: If fluency levels A, B, or C are marked, the teacher should check the student's rate of reading as well—perhaps at a later time.*) | ☐ **D.** Reads **primarily** in larger meaningful phrases; fluent, phrased reading with few word-by-word slow-downs for problem solving; expressive interpretation is evident at places throughout the reading; attention to punctuation and syntax; rereading for problem solving may be present but is generally fluent. |

(Adapted from NAEP Fluency Rubric for grade 4) © Biggam/Thompson 2003, Ms. T. Inc. Used with permission.

| **Part 2: Evidence of Surface Comprehension:** Ask the student to read the next section of text *silently*, saying, "When you are finished, I will ask you to tell me about the part you read . . ." (After reading, say, "Now, tell me about the part you just read.") | Gist: |
|---|---|
| ☐ Limited Comprehension | ☐ Some Comprehension |

| ☐ Limited Comprehension | ☐ Some Comprehension | ☐ Acceptable Comprehension | ☐ Strong Comprehension |
|---|---|---|---|

| **Summary Comments:** | **Overall Evaluation:** ☐ Easy  ☐ Okay  ☐ Marginal  ☐ Too hard  Level: _____ |
|---|---|

# Sample Checklist: Comprehension of Informational Text

**Directions:** Insert date or +, −, or ?

| Student | Listens to book read aloud | Begins to retell what was learned | Uses text features to locate important details | Answers literal questions | Identifies key ideas and details from informational text | Answers inferential questions; tells what author was trying to say |
|---------|---------|---------|---------|---------|---------|---------|
| | | | | | | |
| | | | | | | |
| | | | | | | |
| | | | | | | |
| | | | | | | |
| | | | | | | |
| | | | | | | |
| | | | | | | |
| | | | | | | |
| | | | | | | |
| | | | | | | |
| | | | | | | |
| | | | | | | |
| | | | | | | |
| | | | | | | |
| | | | | | | |
| | | | | | | |

## Checklist for Self-Assessment: My Summary of Informational Text

**Name:** _____ **Date:** _____

**What I read:** _____

_____ I included a **main-idea sentence** that tells what this
was mostly about.

_____ I included **only important details** that connect to
the main idea.

_____ I included **ENOUGH** important **details**.

_____ I used **mostly my own words**.

_____ You **can understand what I wrote**.

## QuEEC: A Tool for Self-Monitoring Our Answers to Text-Based Questions

| | 1<br>Getting started | 2<br>Almost there | 3<br>YES | 4<br>Really well done |
|---|---|---|---|---|
| **Qu (Question)**<br>Did I understand and answer the question, and include part of the question stem in my answer? | | | | |
| **E (Enough)**<br>Did I include enough to answer all of the parts of the question? | | | | |
| **E (Evidence)**<br>Did I include evidence (or my own experience) from the text—mostly in my own words? | | | | |
| **C (Correct and clear)**<br>Did I reread my answer to see whether it is correct and clear? | | | | |

© Susan Biggam

**Writing Interview**

_____

**Name:** _____ **Date:** _____ **Grade:** _____

1. Do you like to write?  Why or why not?

2. What kinds of stories or other pieces of writing do you like to write?

3. What is your favorite piece of writing that you have ever created?

4. Who is your favorite writer?

5. Where do you get your ideas for writing?

6. When you get an idea, how do you start?

7. Do you ever get stuck when you are writing? What do you do to get yourself "unstuck"?

8. What makes writing easy for you?

9. What makes writing hard for you?

10. What do you do once you finish your writing?

# Self-Assessment for Writing Process and Strategies

**Name:**_____

**Topic of writing:**_____

**Date of self-evaluation:** _____

| Goals for Writing | My Progress | | |
|---|---|---|---|
| | By myself | With help | Not yet |
| 1. I can think of a topic to write about. | | | |
| 2. I can name my audience. | | | |
| 3. I can plan for writing. | | | |
| 4. I can talk to others to explain my plan. | | | |
| 5. I can get my ideas down on paper. | | | |
| 6. I can reread my writing to add ideas, delete ideas, or make my writing clearer. | | | |
| 7. I can ask others for feedback to help me make my writing stronger. | | | |
| 8. I am willing to listen careflilly to others' responses and then change my writing to make it stronger. | | | |
| 9. I can reread my writing to check for spelling. | | | |
| 10. I can reread my writing to check for punctuation. | | | |
| 11. I can publish my writing by adding illustrations or other interesting graphics. | | | |
| 12. I can share my writing with the audience I chose. | | | |

Something about my writing I was proud of:

One goal I'd like to set for my next writing project:

Teacher Comments:

---

**Checklist for Writing Process**

---

1. _____ think of a topic and record T: _____
2. _____ name an audience and record A: _____
3. _____ identify a purpose for writing and record P: _____
4. _____ make a written plan
5. _____ sign up for a planning conference
6. _____ planning conference
7. _____ begin writing
8. _____ reread writing out loud to self, make changes if needed
9. _____ sign up for revision conference
10. _____ revision conference
11. _____ revise writing and reread
12. _____ use proofreading check sheet and colored pen to edit for capital letters, punctuation
13. _____ use spelling resources to check for spelling
14. _____ turn in completed draft and editing folder to teacher
15. _____ plan finished piece and begin publishing

## Analytic Writing Assessment Guide for Primary Grades

| | Level 4<br>Exceeds the standard | Level 3<br>Meets the standard | Level 2<br>Approaching the standard | Level 1<br>Beginning |
|---|---|---|---|---|
| **Purpose** | Establishes and maintains a clear purpose and focus. Piece makes sense and sticks to the topic. | Establishes a purpose and a focus. Sticks to the topic and makes sense most of the time. | Attempts to establish the purpose. Attempts to stick to the topic and makes sense, but the writing is not fully clear. | Purpose or focus not clear. Does not stick to the topic or make sense. |
| **Organization** | Organized from beginning and middle to the end. One part flows smoothly into the next part. All the parts fit together. | Writing flows but has a few problems in organization. | Parts that don't fit disrupt the flow of writing. Lack of a smooth flow from beginning to middle to end. | Serious errors in organization. The parts of the writing do not fit well together. |
| **Details** | Details are pertinent, vivid, and specific. They make the ideas very clear. | Details are specific and make ideas clear. | Details are not specific enough to add to the clarity of ideas. They may simply be listed or repeated. | Details are lacking, inappropriate, or random. |
| **Voice/Tone** | Distinctive personal expression or tone. Written in own words. Words and expressions fit the kind of piece well. Energy in the piece makes it interesting throughout. | Personal expression or effective tone exists throughout most of the piece. Most words and expressions fit the kind of piece. Energy in the piece makes it interesting. | Attempts personal expression or appropriate tone. Some energy exists in the piece. Words and expressions sometimes do not fit or enhance the kind of piece. | Flat. Lack of energy in the piece. Words and expressions may not fit the kind of piece. |

Adapted by Biggam, Herman, & Trubisz, from Vermont Analytic Assessment Guide, 1996

## Teacher Portfolio Slips

**Piece:** _____

I think this piece should be saved because

_____

_____

It shows . . .

_____

_____

_____

**Name:** _____

**Date:** _____

## Student Portfolio Slips

**Piece:** _____

I think this piece should be saved because

_____

_____

It shows . . .

_____

_____

_____

**Name:** _____

**Date:** _____

Developed by Biggam, Herman, & Trubisz, 1996

# What We Noticed about My Writing—Together

**Name:** _____

Title of piece of writing I chose:

_____

_____

What my teacher and I noticed I did well:

_____

_____

_____

_____

_____

My writing goals for next time:

_____

_____

_____

_____

_____

My family's response to this piece of writing:

_____

_____

_____

_____

**Date:** _____

Developed by Biggam, Herman, & Trubisz, 1996

# Mini-Lesson Template

**Mini-lesson for:** _____

**Step I.**   *Setting an objective:* Students will


   *Materials:*


**Step II.**   *Opening demonstration:*


**Step III.**   *Shared experience:*


**Step IV.**   *Supported practice with peers:*


**Step V.**   *Closure:*

## Spelling Application Grid: Reviewing Spelling in independent Writing

Student:_____    Grade:_____    Date:_____

Writing samples:_____    _____

Percentage of words spelled correctly:_____

Comments:

| Word | Correct spelling | Emergent | Letter-Name | Within-Word | Syllables and Affixes | Deriva-tional Relations | Features to Be Worked on (or used but confused) |
|------|------|------|------|------|------|------|------|
|  |  |  |  |  |  |  |  |
|  |  |  |  |  |  |  |  |
|  |  |  |  |  |  |  |  |
|  |  |  |  |  |  |  |  |
|  |  |  |  |  |  |  |  |

Notes for Next Steps:

## Spelling Conference Form

**Name:** _____ **Grade:** _____

**Date:** _____

| How I spelled the word | Correct spelling | What OTHER strategy might be good to use that would help me spell that word conventionally/correctly? |
|---|---|---|
|  |  |  |
|  |  |  |
|  |  |  |
|  |  |  |
|  |  |  |
|  |  |  |
|  |  |  |
|  |  |  |
|  |  |  |
|  |  |  |

### "I Am Learning/I Can" Sheet

| I Am Learning | _____'s Proofreading Reminder List | I Can |
|---|---|---|
| | | |
| | | |
| | | |
| | | |
| | | |
| | | |
| | | |
| | | |
| | | |
| | | |
| | | |
| | | |

Adapted from "I Am Learning/I Can . . ." and reproduced by permission of the publishers Learning Media Limited, PO Box 3293, Wellington, New Zealand. Copyright © Crown, 1996.

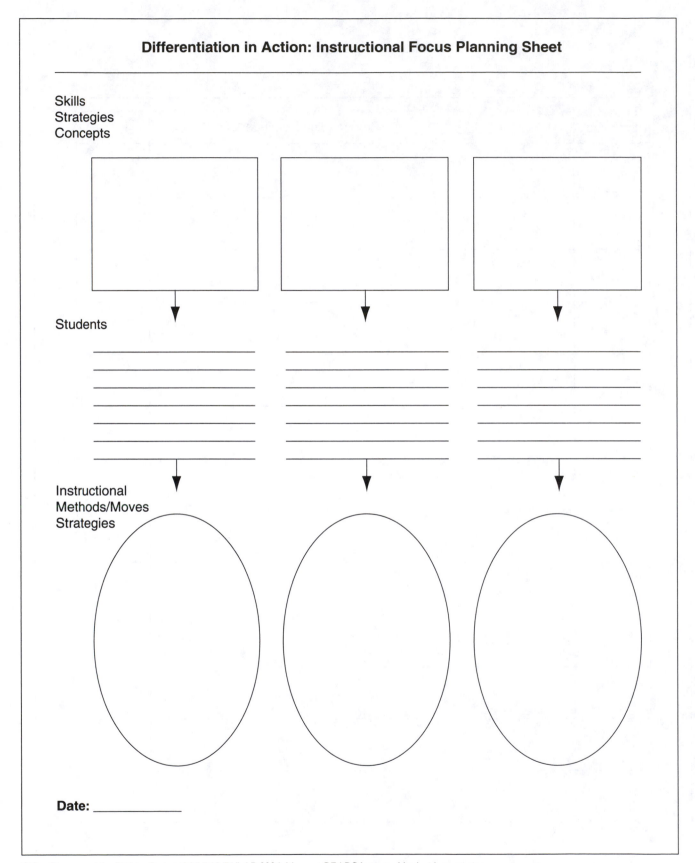

**Differentiation in Action: Instructional Focus Planning Sheet**

Skills
Strategies
Concepts

Students

Instructional
Methods/Moves
Strategies

**Date:** _____

# APPENDIX B

# FORMAL OR PUBLISHED ASSESSMENTS AND THEIR AREAS OF FOCUS

| Assessment (Formal and/or Published) | Source | Area(s) of Focus |
| --- | --- | --- |
| Analytical Reading Inventory | Merrill Prentice-Hall | Reading accuracy<br>Comprehension |
| Basic Reading Inventory, 9th Edition | Kendall-Hunt | Reading accuracy<br>Fluency<br>Letter knowledge |
| Comprehensive Receptive and Expressive Vocabulary Test | Harcourt Assessment Inc. | Expressive and receptive vocabulary |
| Comprehensive Test of Phonological Processing | Pro-Ed Publishing Co. | Phoneme awareness<br>Phonological awareness |
| Concepts of Comprehension Assessment | www.msularc.org | Informational text feature knowledge<br>Comprehension strategy use |
| Degrees of Reading Power | TASA (Touchstone Applied Science Associates) | Reading comprehension (informational text) |
| Developmental Reading Assessment (K–3) | Pearson Learning | Reading accuracy<br>Reading comprehension<br>Reading strategies |
| Developmental Reading Assessment (4–8) | Pearson Learning | Reading accuracy<br>Reading strategies<br>Reading comprehension<br>Reading fluency<br>Metacognitive awareness |
| Developmental Spelling Analysis | The Guilford Press | Spelling stage and features of spelling |

| Assessment (Formal and/or Published) | Source | Area(s) of Focus |
| --- | --- | --- |
| Dynamic Indicators of Basic Early Literacy Skills | University of Oregon | Reading comprehension<br>Decoding<br>Cipher knowledge<br>Phoneme awareness<br>Letter knowledge<br>Phonological awareness |
| Ekwall-Skanker Reading Inventory | Pearson—Allyn and Bacon | Word identification<br>Oral reading<br>Accuracy listening<br>Comprehension<br>Phonemic awareness<br>Concepts of print<br>Phonics<br>Letter knowledge<br>Reading comprehension |
| Elementary Reading Attitude Survey | International Reading Association (*The Reading Teacher*) | Reading attitude (recreational and academic) |
| Elementary Spelling Inventory—also Primary Spelling Inventory | Pearson Merrill Prentice Hall | Spelling stages |
| Gates-McGinitie | Riverside Publishing | Reading comprehension<br>Vocabulary |
| Gray Oral Reading Test | Pro-Ed Publishing Co. | Reading accuracy<br>Reading fluency<br>Reading comprehesion |
| Group Reading Assessment and Diagnostic Evaluation | American Guidance Service | Phonics/decoding<br>Comprehension<br>Vocabulary<br>Phonological awareness |

| Assessment (Formal and/or Published) | Source | Area(s) of Focus |
| --- | --- | --- |
| Iowa Tests of Basic Skills | Riverside Publishing | Vocabulary<br>Word analysis<br>Reading comprehension<br>Listening<br>Language<br>Mathematics |
| Monster Test | Heinemann | Spelling phase/ level for beginning spellers |
| Motivation to Read Profile | International Reading Association | Reading attitude, motivation |
| Names Test | International Reading Association | Phonics |
| Observation Survey of Early Literacy Achievement, Revised 2nd Edition | Heinemann | Decoding<br>Letter knowledge<br>Concepts about print |
| PALS: Phonological Awareness Literacy Screening | University of Virginia | Phonological awareness<br>Fluency comprehension |
| Peabody Picture Vocabulary Test | Pearson Assessments | Receptive vocabulary |
| Qualitative Reading Inventory IV | Allyn and Bacon | Reading accuracy<br>Background knowledge<br>Reading comprehension |
| Rigby Benchmark Assessment Kit | Rigby Publishing | Reading accuracy<br>Strategy use<br>Comprehension |

| Assessment (Formal and/or Published) | Source | Area(s) of Focus |
|---|---|---|
| Roswell-Chall Screening Tests | Educators Publishing Service | Auditory blending<br>Word analysis<br>Word recognition |
| Stanford Diagnostic Reading Test: 4th Edition | Harcourt Assessment | Phonemic awareness<br>Phonics<br>Vocabulary<br>Fluency comprehension |
| Strategic Cloze Assessment | www.msularc.org | Comprehension<br>Use of comprehension strategies |
| Teacher Rating of Oral Language and Literacy (TROLL): A Research-Based Tool | University of Michigan, Center for the Improvement of Early Reading Achievement | Rating scale for early literacy skills in language, reading, and writing |
| Test of Reading Comprehension (TORC) | Pro-Ed Publishing Co. | Vocabulary<br>Syntactic similarities<br>Paragraph reading<br>Sentence sequencing<br>Reading the directions of schoolwork |
| Test of Written Language—TOWL-3 | Pro-Ed Publishing Co. | Spelling<br>Capitalization<br>Punctuation<br>Sentence construction<br>Metacognitive knowledge<br>Contextual writing quotient |
| Test of Written Spelling | Pro-Ed | Spelling skill level in relation to peers |

| Assessment (Formal and/or Published) | Source | Area(s) of Focus |
|---|---|---|
| The Test of Early Written Language—TEWL-2 | Pearson Assessment Group | Spelling<br>Capitalization<br>Punctuation<br>Sentence construction<br>Metacognitive knowledge<br>Contextual writing quotient |
| The Test of Phonological Awareness | Pro-Ed Publishing Co. | Segmentation of phonemes |
| Title Recognition Test | International Reading Association | Breadth of reading |
| The Writer Self-Perception Scale | *Reading Teacher*, International Reading Association | Writer's self-efficacy of fourth- to sixth-grade students |
| The Writing Attitude Survey | *Reading Teacher*, International Reading Association | Writing attitudes of elementary-age children |
| Woodcock-Johnson Diagnostic Reading Battery | Riverside Publishing | Phonemic awareness<br>Phonics<br>Oral language comprehension<br>Fluency<br>Comprehension |
| Yopp-Singer Test of Phoneme Segmentation | *Reading Teacher*, International Reading Association | Segmentation of phonemes |

# NAME INDEX

# SUBJECT INDEX